Charters of Freedom

CHARTERS OF FREEDOM

DEMOCRACY'S FOUNDING DOCUMENTS

KONECKY&KONECKY

Konecky & Konecky
72 Ayers Point Rd.
Old Saybrook, CT 06475

ISBN: 978-1-56852-782-6

Manufactured in the U.S.A.

Table of Contents

Common Sense by Thomas Paine

Introduction To The Third Edition

PERHAPS the sentiments contained in the following pages, are not YET sufficiently fashionable to procure them general favour; a long habit of not thinking a thing WRONG, gives it a superficial appearance of being RIGHT, and raises at first a formidable outcry in defense of custom. But the tumult soon subsides. Time makes more converts than reason. As a long and violent abuse of power, is generally the Means of calling the right of it in question (and in Matters too which might never have been thought of, had not the Sufferers been aggravated into the inquiry) and as the King of England hath undertaken in his OWN RIGHT, to support the Parliament in what he calls THEIRS, and as the good people of this country are grievously oppressed by the combination, they have an undoubted privilege to inquire into the pretensions of both, and equally to reject the usurpation of either. In the following sheets, the author hath studiously avoided every thing which is personal among ourselves. Compliments as well as censure to individuals make no part thereof. The wise, and the worthy, need not the triumph of a pamphlet; and those whose sentiments are injudicious, or unfriendly, will cease of themselves unless too much pains are bestowed upon their conversion. The cause of America is in a great measure the cause of all mankind. Many circumstances hath, and will arise, which are not local, but universal, and through which the principles of all Lovers of Mankind are affected, and in the Event of which, their Affections are interested. The laying a Country desolate with Fire and Sword, declaring War against the natural rights of all Mankind, and extirpating the Defenders thereof from the Face of the Earth, is the Concern of every Man to whom Nature hath given the Power of feeling; of which Class, regardless of Party Censure, is the AUTHOR.

P. S. The Publication of this new Edition hath been delayed, with a View of taking notice (had it been necessary) of any Attempt to refute the Doctrine of Independence: As no Answer hath yet appeared, it is now presumed that none will, the Time needful for getting such a Performance ready for the Public being considerably past. Who the Author of this Production is, is wholly unnecessary to the Public, as the Object for Attention is the DOCTRINE ITSELF, not the MAN. Yet it may not be unnecessary to say, That he is unconnected with any Party, and under no sort of Influence public or private, but the influence of reason and principle.

Philadelphia, February 14, 1776

Of the Origin and Design of Government in General, with Concise Remarks on the English Constitution

SOME writers have so confounded society with government, as to leave little or no distinction between them; whereas they are not only different, but have different origins. Society is produced by our wants, and government by our wickedness; the former promotes our happiness POSITIVELY by uniting our affections, the latter NEGATIVELY by restraining our vices. The one encourages intercourse, the other creates distinctions. The first is a patron, the last a punisher.

Society in every state is a blessing, but Government, even in its best state, is but a necessary evil; in its worst state an intolerable one: for when we suffer, or are exposed to the same miseries BY A GOVERNMENT, which we might expect in a country WITHOUT GOVERNMENT, our calamity is heightened by reflecting that we furnish the means by which we suffer. Government, like dress, is the badge of lost innocence; the palaces of kings are built upon the ruins of the bowers of paradise. For were the impulses of conscience clear, uniform and irresistibly obeyed, man would need no other lawgiver; but that not being the case, he finds it necessary to surrender up a part of his property to furnish means for the protection of the rest; and this he is induced to do by the same prudence which in every other case advises him, out of two evils to choose the least. Wherefore, security being the true design and end of government, it unanswerably follows that whatever form thereof appears most likely to ensure it to us, with the least expense and greatest benefit, is preferable to all others.

In order to gain a clear and just idea of the design and end of government, let us suppose a small number of persons settled in some sequestered part of the earth, unconnected with the rest; they will then represent the first peopling of any country, or of the world. In this state of natural liberty, society will be their first thought. A thousand motives will excite them thereto; the strength of one man is so unequal to his wants, and his mind so unfitted for perpetual solitude, that he is soon obliged to seek assistance and relief of another, who in his turn requires the same. Four or five united would be able to raise a tolerable dwelling in the midst of a wilderness, but one man might labour out the common period of life without accomplishing any thing; when he had felled his timber he could not remove it, nor erect it after it was removed; hunger in the mean time would urge him to quit his work, and every different want would call him a different way. Disease, nay even misfortune, would be death; for, though neither might be mortal, yet either would disable him from living, and reduce him to a state in which he might rather be said to perish than to die.

Thus necessity, like a gravitating power, would soon form our newly arrived emigrants into society, the reciprocal blessings of which would supersede, and render the obligations of law and government unnecessary while they remained perfectly just to each other; but as nothing but Heaven is impregnable to vice, it will unavoidably happen that in proportion as they surmount the first difficulties of emigration, which bound them together in a common cause, they will begin to relax in their duty and attachment to each other: and this remissness will point out the necessity of establishing some form of government to supply the defect of moral virtue.

Some convenient tree will afford them a State House, under the branches of which the whole Colony may assemble to deliberate on public matters. It is more than probable that their first laws will have the title only of Regulations and be enforced by no other penalty than public disesteem. In this first parliament every man by natural right will have a seat.

But as the Colony encreases, the public concerns will encrease likewise, and the distance at which the members may be separated, will render it too inconvenient for all of them to meet on every occasion as at first, when their number was small, their habitations near, and the public concerns few and trifling. This will point out the convenience of their consenting to leave the legislative part to be managed by a select number chosen from the whole body, who are supposed to have the same concerns at stake which those have who appointed them, and who will act in the same manner as the whole body would act were they present. If the colony continue encreasing, it will become necessary to augment the number of representatives, and that the interest of every part of the colony may be attended to, it will be found best to divide the whole into convenient parts, each part sending its proper number: and that the ELECTED might never form to themselves an interest separate from the ELECTORS, prudence will point out the propriety of having elections often: because as the ELECTED might by that means return and mix again with the general body of the ELECTORS in a few months, their fidelity to the public will be secured by the prudent reflection of not making a rod for themselves. And as this frequent interchange will establish a common interest with every part of the community, they will mutually and naturally support each other, and on this, (not on the unmeaning name of king,) depends the STRENGTH OF GOVERNMENT, AND THE HAPPINESS OF THE GOVERNED.

Here then is the origin and rise of government; namely, a mode rendered necessary by the inability of moral virtue to govern the world; here too is the design and end of government, viz. Freedom and security. And however our eyes may be dazzled with show, or our ears deceived by sound; however prejudice may warp our wills, or interest darken our understanding, the simple voice of nature and reason will say, 'tis right.

I draw my idea of the form of government from a principle in nature which no art can overturn, viz. that the more simple any thing is, the less liable it is to be disordered, and the easier repaired when disordered; and with this maxim in view I offer a few remarks on the so much boasted constitution of England. That it was noble for the dark and slavish times in which it was erected, is granted. When the world was overrun with tyranny the least remove therefrom was a glorious rescue. But that it is imperfect, subject to convulsions, and incapable of producing what it seems to promise is easily demonstrated.

Absolute governments, (tho' the disgrace of human nature) have this advantage with them, they are simple; if the people suffer, they know the head from which their suffering springs; know likewise the remedy; and are not bewildered by a variety of causes and cures. But the constitution of England is so exceedingly complex, that the nation may suffer for years together without being able to discover in which part the fault lies; some will say in one and some in another, and every political physician will advise a different medicine.

I know it is difficult to get over local or long standing prejudices, yet if we will suffer ourselves to examine the component parts of the English Constitution, we shall find them to be the base remains of two ancient tyrannies, compounded with some new Republican materials.

First. — The remains of Monarchical tyranny in the person of the King.

Secondly. — The remains of Aristocratical tyranny in the persons of the Peers.

Thirdly. — The new Republican materials, in the persons of the Commons, on whose virtue depends the freedom of England.

The two first, by being hereditary, are independent of the People; wherefore in a CONSTITUTIONAL SENSE they contribute nothing towards the freedom of the State.

To say that the constitution of England is an UNION of three powers, reciprocally CHECKING each other, is farcical; either the words have no meaning, or they are flat contradictions.

First. — That the King it not to be trusted without being looked after; or in other words, that a thirst for absolute power is the natural disease of monarchy.

Secondly. — That the Commons, by being appointed for that purpose, are either wiser or more worthy of confidence than the Crown.

But as the same constitution which gives the Commons a power to check the King by withholding the supplies, gives afterwards the King a power to check the Commons, by empowering him to reject their other bills; it again supposes that the King is wiser than those whom it has already supposed to be wiser than him. A mere absurdity!

There is something exceedingly ridiculous in the composition of Monarchy; it first excludes a man from the means of information, yet empowers him to act in cases where the highest judgment is required. The state of a king shuts him from the World, yet the business of a king requires him to know it thoroughly; wherefore the different parts, by unnaturally opposing and destroying each other, prove the whole character to be absurd and useless.

Some writers have explained the English constitution thus: the King, say they, is one, the people another; the Peers are a house in behalf of the King, the commons in behalf of the people; but this hath all the distinctions of a house divided against itself; and though the expressions be pleasantly arranged, yet when examined they appear idle and ambiguous; and it will always happen, that the nicest construction that words are capable of, when applied to the description of something which either cannot exist, or is too incomprehensible to be within the compass of description, will be words of sound only, and though they may amuse the ear, they cannot inform the mind: for this explanation includes a previous question, viz. HOW CAME THE KING BY A POWER WHICH THE PEOPLE ARE AFRAID TO TRUST, AND ALWAYS OBLIGED TO CHECK? Such a power could not be the gift of a wise people, neither can any power, WHICH NEEDS CHECKING, be from God; yet the provision which the constitution makes supposes such a power to exist.

But the provision is unequal to the task; the means either cannot or will not accomplish the end, and the whole affair is a Felo de se: for as the greater weight will always carry up the less, and as all the wheels of a machine are put in motion by one, it only remains to know which power in the constitution has the most weight, for that will govern: and tho' the others, or a part of them, may clog, or, as the phrase is, check the rapidity of its motion, yet so long as they cannot stop it, their endeavours will be ineffectual: The first moving power will at last have its way, and what it wants in speed is supplied by time.

That the crown is this overbearing part in the English constitution needs not be mentioned, and that it derives its whole consequence merely from being the giver of places and pensions is self-evident; wherefore, though we have been wise enough to shut and lock a door against absolute Monarchy, we at the same time have been foolish enough to put the Crown in possession of the key.

The prejudice of Englishmen, in favour of their own government, by King, Lords and Commons, arises as much or more from national pride than reason. Individuals are undoubtedly safer in England than in some other countries: but the will of the king is as much the law of the land in Britain as in France, with this difference, that instead of proceeding directly from his mouth, it is handed to the people under the formidable shape of an act of parliament. For the fate of Charles the First hath only made kings more subtle — not more just.

Wherefore, laying aside all national pride and prejudice in favour of modes and forms, the plain truth is that IT IS WHOLLY OWING TO THE CONSTITUTION OF THE PEOPLE, AND NOT TO THE CONSTITUTION OF THE GOVERNMENT that the crown is not as oppressive in England as in Turkey.

An inquiry into the CONSTITUTIONAL ERRORS in the English form of government, is at this time highly necessary; for as we are never in a proper condition of doing justice to others, while we continue under the influence of some leading partiality, so neither are we capable of doing it to ourselves while we remain fettered by any obstinate prejudice. And as a man who is attached to a prostitute is unfitted to choose or judge of a wife, so any prepossession in favour of a rotten constitution of government will disable us from discerning a good one.

MANKIND being originally equals in the order of creation, the equality could only be destroyed by some subsequent circumstance: the distinctions of rich and poor may in a great measure be accounted for, and that without having recourse to the harsh ill-sounding names of oppression and avarice. Oppression is often the CONSEQUENCE, but seldom or never the MEANS of riches; and tho' avarice will preserve a man from being necessitously poor, it generally makes him too timorous to be wealthy.

But there is another and great distinction for which no truly natural or religious reason can be assigned, and that is the distinction of men into KINGS and SUBJECTS. Male and female are the distinctions of nature, good and bad the distinctions of Heaven; but how a race of men came into the world so exalted above the rest, and distinguished like some new species, is worth inquiring into, and whether they are the means of happiness or of misery to mankind.

In the early ages of the world, according to the scripture chronology there were no kings; the consequence of which was, there were no wars; it is the pride of kings which throws mankind into confusion. Holland, without a king hath enjoyed more peace for this last century than any of the monarchical governments in Europe. Antiquity favours the same remark; for the quiet and rural lives of the first Patriarchs have a snappy something in them, which vanishes when we come to the history of Jewish royalty.

Government by kings was first introduced into the world by the Heathens, from whom the children of Israel copied the custom. It was the most prosperous invention the Devil ever set on foot for the promotion of idolatry. The Heathens paid divine honours to their deceased kings, and the Christian World hath improved on the plan by doing the same to their living ones. How impious is the title of sacred Majesty applied to a worm, who in the midst of his splendor is crumbling into dust!

As the exalting one man so greatly above the rest cannot be justified on the equal rights of nature, so neither can it be defended on the authority of scripture; for the will of the Almighty as declared by Gideon, and the prophet Samuel, expressly disapproves of government by Kings.

All anti-monarchical parts of scripture have been very smoothly glossed over in monarchical governments, but they undoubtedly merit the attention of countries which have their governments yet to form. "Render unto Cesar the things which are Cesar's" is the scripture doctrine of courts, yet it is no support of monarchical government, for the Jews at that time were without a king, and in a state of vassalage to the Romans.

Near three thousand years passed away, from the Mosaic account of the creation, till the Jews under a national delusion requested a king. Till then their form of government (except in extraordinary cases where the Almighty interposed) was a kind of Republic, administered by a judge and the elders of the tribes. Kings they had none, and it was held sinful to acknowledge any being under that title but the Lord of Hosts. And when a man seriously reflects on the idolatrous homage which is paid to the persons of kings, he need not wonder that the Almighty, ever jealous of his honour, should disapprove a form of government which so impiously invades the prerogative of Heaven.

Monarchy is ranked in scripture as one of the sins of the Jews, for which a curse in reserve is denounced against them. The history of that transaction is worth attending to.

The children of Israel being oppressed by the Midianites, Gideon marched against them with a small army, and victory thro' the divine interposition decided in his favour. The Jews, elate with success, and attributing it to the generalship of Gideon, proposed making him a king, saying, "Rule thou over us, thou and thy son, and thy son's son." Here was temptation in its fullest extent; not a kingdom only, but an hereditary one; but Gideon in the piety of his soul replied, "I will not rule over you, neither shall my son rule over you. THE LORD SHALL RULE OVER YOU." Words need not be more explicit: Gideon doth not decline the honour, but denieth their right to give it; neither doth he compliment them with invented declarations of his thanks, but in the positive style of a prophet charges them with disaffection to their proper Sovereign, the King of Heaven.

About one hundred and thirty years after this, they fell again into the same error. The hankering which the Jews had for the idolatrous customs of the Heathens, is something exceedingly unaccountable; but so it was, that laying hold of the misconduct of Samuel's two sons, who were intrusted with some secular concerns, they came in an abrupt and clamorous manner to Samuel, saying, "Behold thou art old, and they sons walk not in thy ways, now make us a king to judge us like all the other nations." And here we cannot observe but that their motives were bad, viz. that they might be LIKE unto other nations, i. e. the Heathens, whereas their true glory lay in being as much UNLIKE them as possible. "But the thing displeased Samuel when they said, give us a King to judge us; and Samuel prayed unto the Lord, and the Lord said unto Samuel, hearken unto the voice of the people in all that they say unto thee, for they have not rejected thee, but they have rejected me, THAT I SHOULD NOT REIGN OVER THEM. According to all the works which they have done since the day that I brought them up out of Egypt even unto this day, wherewith they have forsaken me, and served other Gods: so do they also unto thee. Now therefore hearken unto their voice, howbeit, protest solemnly unto them and show them the manner of the King that shall reign over them," i.e. not of any particular King, but the general manner of the Kings of the earth whom Israel was so eagerly copying after. And notwithstanding the great distance of time and difference of manners, the character is still in fashion. "And Samuel told all the words of the Lord unto the people, that asked of him a King. And he said, This shall be the manner of the King that shall reign over you. He will take your sons and appoint them for himself for his chariots and to be his horsemen, and some shall run before his chariots" (this description agrees with the present mode of impressing men) "and he will appoint him captains over thousands and captains over fifties, will set them to clear his ground and to reap his harvest, and to make his instruments of war, and instruments of his chariots, And he will take your daughters to be confectionaries, and to be cooks, and to be bakers" (this describes the expense and luxury as well as the oppression of Kings) "and he will take your fields and your vineyards, and your olive yards, even the best of them, and give them to his servants. And he will take the tenth of your seed, and of your vineyards, and give them to his officers and to his servants" (by which we see that bribery, corruption, and favouritism, are the standing vices of Kings) "and he will take the tenth of your men servants, and your maid servants, and your goodliest young men, and your asses, and put them to his work: and he will take the tenth of your sheep, and ye shall be his servants, and ye shall cry out in that day because of your king which ye shell have chosen, AND THE LORD WILL NOT HEAR YOU IN THAT DAY." This accounts for the continuation of Monarchy; neither do the characters of the few good kings which have lived since, either sanctify the title, or blot out the sinfulness of the origin; the high encomium of David takes no notice of him OFFICIALLY AS A KING, but only as a MAN after God's own heart. "Nevertheless the people refused to obey the voice of Samuel, and they said, Nay, but we will have a king over us, that we may be like all the nations, and that our king may judge us, and go out before us and fight our battles." Samuel continued to reason with them but to no purpose; he set before them their ingratitude, but all would not avail; and seeing them fully bent on their folly, he cried out, "I will call unto the Lord, and he shall send thunder and rain" (which was then a punishment, being in the time of wheat harvest) "that ye may perceive and see that your wickedness is great which ye have done in the sight of the Lord, IN ASKING YOU A KING. So Samuel called unto the Lord, and the Lord sent thunder and rain that day, and all the people greatly feared the Lord and Samuel. And all the people said unto Samuel, Pray for thy servants unto the Lord thy God that we die not, for WE HAVE ADDED UNTO OUR SINS THIS EVIL, TO ASK A KING." These portions of scripture are direct and positive. They admit of no equivocal construction. That the Almighty hath here entered his protest against monarchical government is true, or the scripture is false. And a man hath good reason to believe that there is as much of kingcraft as priestcraft in withholding the scripture from the public in popish countries. For monarchy in every instance is the popery of government.

To the evil of monarchy we have added that of hereditary succession; and as the first is a degradation and lessening of ourselves, so the second, claimed as a matter of right, is an insult and imposition on posterity. For all men being originally equals, no one by birth could have a right to set up his own family in perpetual preference to all others for ever, and tho' himself might deserve some decent degree of honours of his contemporaries, yet his descendants might be far too unworthy to inherit them. One of the strongest natural proofs of the folly of hereditary right in Kings, is that nature disapproves it, otherwise she would not so frequently turn it into ridicule, by giving mankind an ASS FOR A LION.

Secondly, as no man at first could possess any other public honors than were bestowed upon him, so the givers of those honors could have no power to give away the right of posterity, and though they might say "We choose you for our head," they could not without manifest injustice to their children say "that your children and your children's children shall reign over ours forever." Because such an unwise, unjust, unnatural compact might (perhaps) in the next succession put them under the government of a rogue or a fool. Most wise men in their private sentiments have ever treated hereditary right with contempt; yet it is one of those evils which when once established is not easily removed: many submit from fear, others from superstition, and the more powerful part shares with the king the plunder of the rest.

This is supposing the present race of kings in the world to have had an honorable origin: whereas it is more than probable, that, could we take off the dark covering of antiquity and trace them to their first rise, we should find the first of them nothing better than the principal ruffian of some restless gang, whose savage manners of pre-eminence in subtilty obtained him the title of chief among plunderers; and who by increasing in power and extending his depredations, overawed the quiet and defenseless to purchase their safety by frequent contributions. Yet his electors could have no idea of giving hereditary right to his descendants, because such a perpetual exclusion of themselves was incompatible with the free and restrained principles they professed to live by. Wherefore, hereditary succession in the early ages of monarchy could not take place as a matter of claim, but as something casual or complemental; but as few or no records were extant in those days, the traditionary history stuff'd with fables, it was very easy, after the lapse of a few generations, to trump up some superstitious tale conveniently timed, Mahomet-like, to cram hereditary right down the throats of the vulgar. Perhaps the disorders which threatened, or seemed to threaten, on the decease of a leader and the choice of a new one (for elections among ruffians could not be very orderly) induced many at first to favour hereditary pretensions; by which means it happened, as it hath happened since, that what at first was submitted to as a convenience was afterwards claimed as a right.

England since the conquest hath known some few good monarchs, but groaned beneath a much larger number of bad ones: yet no man in his senses can say that their claim under William the Conqueror is a very honourable one. A French bastard landing with an armed Banditti and establishing himself king of England against the consent of the natives, is in plain terms a very paltry rascally original. It certainly hath no divinity in it. However it is needless to spend much time in exposing the folly of hereditary right; if there are any so weak as to believe it, let them promiscuously worship the Ass and the Lion, and welcome. I shall neither copy their humility, nor disturb their devotion.

Yet I should be glad to ask how they suppose kings came at first? The question admits but of three answers, viz. either by lot, by election, or by usurpation. If the first king was taken by lot, it establishes a precedent for the next, which excludes hereditary succession. Saul was by lot, yet the succession was not hereditary, neither does it appear from that transaction that there was any intention it ever should. If the first king of any country was by election, that likewise establishes a precedent for the next; for to say, that the right of all future generations is taken away, by the act of the first electors, in their choice not only of a king but of a family of kings for ever, hath no parallel in or out of scripture but the doctrine of original sin, which supposes the free will of all men lost in Adam; and from such comparison, and it will admit of no other, hereditary succession can derive no glory. for as in Adam all sinned, and as in the first electors all men obeyed; as in the one all mankind were subjected to Satan, and in the other to sovereignty; as our innocence was lost in the first, and our authority in the last; and as both disable us from reassuming some former state and privilege, it unanswerably follows that original sin and hereditary succession are parallels. Dishonourable rank! inglorious connection! yet the most subtle sophist cannot produce a juster simile.

As to usurpation, no man will be so hardy as to defend it; and that William the Conqueror was an usurper is a fact not to be contradicted. The plain truth is, that the antiquity of English monarchy will not bear looking into.

But it is not so much the absurdity as the evil of hereditary succession which concerns mankind. Did it ensure a race of good and wise men it would have the seal of divine authority, but as it opens a door to the FOOLISH, the WICKED, and the IMPROPER, it hath in it the nature of oppression. Men who look upon themselves born to reign, and others to obey, soon grow insolent. Selected from the rest of mankind, their minds are early poisoned by importance; and the world they act in differs so materially from the world at large, that they have but little opportunity of knowing its true interests, and when they succeed in the government are frequently the most ignorant and unfit of any throughout the dominions.

Another evil which attends hereditary succession is, that the throne is subject to be possessed by a minor at any age; all which time the regency acting under the cover of a king have every opportunity and inducement to betray their trust. The same national misfortune happens when a king worn out with age and infirmity enters the last stage of human weakness. In both these cases the public becomes a prey to every miscreant who can tamper successfully with the follies either of age or infancy.

The most plausible plea which hath ever been offered in favor of hereditary succession is, that it preserves a nation from civil wars; and were this true, it would be weighty; whereas it is the most bare-faced falsity ever imposed upon mankind. The whole history of England disowns the fact. Thirty kings and two minors have reigned in that distracted kingdom since the conquest, in which time there has been (including the revolution) no less than eight civil wars and nineteen Rebellions. Wherefore instead of making for peace, it makes against it, and destroys the very foundation it seems to stand upon.

The contest for monarchy and succession, between the houses of York and Lancaster, laid England in a scene of blood for many years. Twelve pitched battles besides skirmishes and sieges were fought between Henry and Edward. Twice was Henry prisoner to Edward, who in his turn was prisoner to Henry. And so uncertain is the fate of war and the temper of a nation, when nothing but personal matters are the ground of a quarrel, that Henry was taken in triumph from a prison to a palace, and Edward obliged to fly from a palace to a foreign land; yet, as sudden transitions of temper are seldom lasting, Henry in his turn was driven from the throne, and Edward re-called to succeed him. The parliament always following the strongest side.

This contest began in the reign of Henry the Sixth, and was not entirely extinguished till Henry the Seventh, in whom the families were united. Including a period of 67 years, viz. from 1422 to 1489.

In short, monarchy and succession have laid (not this or that kingdom only) but the world in blood and ashes. 'Tis a form of government which the word of God bears testimony against, and blood will attend it.

If we enquire into the business of a King, we shall find that in some countries they may have none; and after sauntering away their lives without pleasure to themselves or advantage to the nation, withdraw from the scene, and leave their successors to tread the same idle round. In absolute monarchies the whole weight of business civil and military lies on the King; the children of Israel in their request for a king urged this plea, "that he may judge us, and go out before us and fight our battles." But in countries where he is neither a Judge nor a General, as in England, a man would be puzzled to know what IS his business.

The nearer any government approaches to a Republic, the less business there is for a King. It is somewhat difficult to find a proper name for the government of England. Sir William Meredith calls it a Republic; but in its present state it is unworthy of the name, because the corrupt influence of the Crown, by having all the places in its disposal, hath so effectually swallowed up the power, and eaten out the virtue of the House of Commons (the Republican part in the constitution) that the government of England is nearly as monarchical as that of France or Spain. Men fall out with names without understanding them. For 'tis the Republican and not the Monarchical part of the Constitution of England which Englishmen glory in, viz. the liberty of choosing an House of Commons from out of their own body — and it is easy to see that when Republican virtues fail, slavery ensues. Why is the constitution of England sickly, but because monarchy hath poisoned the Republic; the Crown hath engrossed the Commons.

In England a King hath little more to do than to make war and give away places; which, in plain terms, is to empoverish the nation and set it together by the ears. A pretty business indeed for a man to be allowed eight hundred thousand sterling a year for, and worshipped into the bargain! Of more worth is one honest man to society, and in the sight of God, than all the crowned ruffians that ever lived.

IN the following pages I offer nothing more than simple facts, plain arguments, and common sense: and have no other preliminaries to settle with the reader, than that he will divest himself of prejudice and prepossession, and suffer his reason and his feelings to determine for themselves that he will put on, or rather that he will not put off, the true character of a man, and generously enlarge his views beyond the present day.

Volumes have been written on the subject of the struggle between England and America. Men of all ranks have embarked in the controversy, from different motives, and with various designs; but all have been ineffectual, and the period of debate is closed. Arms as the last resource decide the contest; the appeal was the choice of the King, and the Continent has accepted the challenge.

It hath been reported of the late Mr. Pelham (who tho' an able minister was not without his faults) that on his being attacked in the House of Commons on the score that his measures were only of a temporary kind, replied, "THEY WILL LAST MY TIME." Should a thought so fatal and unmanly possess the Colonies in the present contest, the name of ancestors will be remembered by future generations with detestation.

The Sun never shined on a cause of greater worth. 'Tis not the affair of a City, a County, a Province, or a Kingdom; but of a Continent — of at least one-eighth part of the habitable Globe. 'Tis not the concern of a day, a year, or an age; posterity are virtually involved in the contest, and will be more or less affected even to the end of time, by the proceedings now. Now is the seed-time of Continental union, faith and honour. The least fracture now will be like a name engraved with the point of a pin on the tender rind of a young oak; the wound would enlarge with the tree, and posterity read in it full grown characters.

By referring the matter from argument to arms, a new era for politics is struck — a new method of thinking hath arisen. All plans, proposals, &c. prior to the nineteenth of April, i.e. to the commencement of hostilities, are like the almanacks of the last year; which tho' proper then, are superseded and useless now. Whatever was advanced by the advocates on either side of the question then, terminated in one and the same point, viz. a union with Great Britain; the only difference between the parties was the method of effecting it; the one proposing force, the other friendship; but it hath so far happened that the first hath failed, and the second hath withdrawn her influence.

As much hath been said of the advantages of reconciliation, which, like an agreeable dream, hath passed away and left us as we were, it is but right that we should examine the contrary side of the argument, and enquire into some of the many material injuries which these Colonies sustain, and always will sustain, by being connected with and dependent on Great Britain. To examine that connection and dependence, on the principles of nature and common sense, to see what we have to trust to, if separated, and what we are to expect, if dependent.

I have heard it asserted by some, that as America has flourished under her former connection with Great Britain, the same connection is necessary towards her future happiness, and will always have the same effect. Nothing can be more fallacious than this kind of argument. We may as well assert that because a child has thrived upon milk, that it is never to have meat, or that the first twenty years of our lives is to become a precedent for the next twenty. But even this is admitting more than is true; for I answer roundly that America would have flourished as much, and probably much more, had no European power taken any notice of her. The commerce by which she hath enriched herself are the necessaries of life, and will always have a market while eating is the custom of Europe.

But she has protected us, say some. That she hath engrossed us is true, and defended the Continent at our expense as well as her own, is admitted; and she would have defended Turkey from the same motive, viz. — for the sake of trade and dominion.

Alas! we have been long led away by ancient prejudices and made large sacrifices to superstition. We have boasted the protection of Great Britain, without considering, that her motive was INTEREST not ATTACHMENT; and that she did not protect us from OUR ENEMIES on OUR ACCOUNT; but from HER ENEMIES on HER OWN ACCOUNT, from those who had no quarrel with us on any OTHER ACCOUNT, and who will always be our enemies on the SAME ACCOUNT. Let Britain waive her pretensions to the Continent, or the Continent throw off the dependence, and we should be at peace with France and Spain, were they at war with Britain. The miseries of Hanover last war ought to warn us against connections.

It hath lately been asserted in parliament, that the Colonies have no relation to each other but through the Parent Country, i.e. that Pennsylvania and the Jerseys and so on for the rest, are sister Colonies by the way of England; this is certainly a very roundabout way of proving relationship, but it is the nearest and only true way of proving enmity (or enemyship, if I may so call it.) France and Spain never were, nor perhaps ever will be, our enemies as AMERICANS, but as our being the SUBJECTS OF GREAT BRITAIN.

But Britain is the parent country, say some. Then the more shame upon her conduct. Even brutes do not devour their young, nor savages make war upon their families. Wherefore, the assertion, if true, turns to her reproach; but it happens not to be true, or only partly so, and the phrase PARENT OR MOTHER COUNTRY hath been jesuitically adopted by the King and his parasites, with a low papistical design of gaining an unfair bias on the credulous weakness of our minds. Europe, and not England, is the parent country of America. This new World hath been the asylum for the persecuted lovers of civil and religious liberty from EVERY PART of Europe. Hither have they fled, not from the tender embraces of the mother, but from the cruelty of the monster; and it is so far true of England, that the same tyranny which drove the first emigrants from home, pursues their descendants still.

In this extensive quarter of the globe, we forget the narrow limits of three hundred and sixty miles (the extent of England) and carry our friendship on a larger scale; we claim brotherhood with every European Christian, and triumph in the generosity of the sentiment.

It is pleasant to observe by what regular gradations we surmount the force of local prejudices, as we enlarge our acquaintance with the World. A man born in any town in England divided into parishes, will naturally associate most with his fellow parishioners (because their interests in many cases will be common) and distinguish him by the name of NEIGHBOR; if he meet him but a few miles from home, he drops the narrow idea of a street, and salutes him by the name of TOWNSMAN; if he travel out of the county and meet him in any other, he forgets the minor divisions of street and town, and calls him COUNTRYMAN, i.e. COUNTYMAN; but if in their foreign excursions they should associate in France, or any other part of EUROPE, their local remembrance would be enlarged into that of ENGLISHMEN. And by a just parity of reasoning, all Europeans meeting in America, or any other quarter of the globe, are COUNTRYMEN; for England, Holland, Germany, or Sweden, when compared with the whole, stand in the same places on the larger scale, which the divisions of street, town, and county do on the smaller ones; Distinctions too limited for Continental minds. Not one third of the inhabitants, even of this province, [Pennsylvania], are of English descent. Wherefore, I reprobate the phrase of Parent or Mother Country applied to England only, as being false, selfish, narrow and ungenerous.

But, admitting that we were all of English descent, what does it amount to? Nothing. Britain, being now an open enemy, extinguishes every other name and title: and to say that reconciliation is our duty, is truly farcical. The first king of England, of the present line (William the Conqueror) was a Frenchman, and half the peers of England are descendants from the same country; wherefore, by the same method of reasoning, England ought to be governed by France.

Much hath been said of the united strength of Britain and the Colonies, that in conjunction they might bid defiance to the world. But this is mere presumption; the fate of war is uncertain, neither do the expressions mean anything; for this continent would never suffer itself to be drained of inhabitants, to support the British arms in either Asia, Africa, or Europe.

Besides, what have we to do with setting the world at defiance? Our plan is commerce, and that, well attended to, will secure us the peace and friendship of all Europe; because it is the interest of all Europe to have America a free port. Her trade will always be a protection, and her barrenness of gold and silver secure her from invaders.

I challenge the warmest advocate for reconciliation to show a single advantage that this continent can reap by being connected with Great Britain. I repeat the challenge; not a single advantage is derived. Our corn will fetch its price in any market in Europe, and our imported goods must be paid for buy them where we will.

But the injuries and disadvantages which we sustain by that connection, are without number; and our duty to mankind at large, as well as to ourselves, instruct us to renounce the alliance: because, any submission to, or dependence on, Great Britain, tends directly to involve this Continent in European wars and quarrels, and set us at variance with nations who would otherwise seek our friendship, and against whom we have neither anger nor complaint. As Europe is our market for trade, we ought to form no partial connection with any part of it. It is the true interest of America to steer clear of European contentions, which she never can do, while, by her dependence on Britain, she is made the makeweight in the scale of British politics.

Europe is too thickly planted with Kingdoms to be long at peace, and whenever a war breaks out between England and any foreign power, the trade of America goes to ruin, BECAUSE OF HER CONNECTION WITH BRITAIN. The next war may not turn out like the last, and should it not, the advocates for reconciliation now will be wishing for separation then, because neutrality in that case would be a safer convoy than a man of war. Every thing that is right or reasonable pleads for separation. The blood of the slain, the weeping voice of nature cries, 'TIS TIME TO PART. Even the distance at which the Almighty hath placed England and America is a strong and natural proof that the authority of the one over the other, was never the design of Heaven. The time likewise at which the Continent was discovered, adds weight to the argument, and the manner in which it was peopled, encreases the force of it. The Reformation was preceded by the discovery of America: As if the Almighty graciously meant to open a sanctuary to the persecuted in future years, when home should afford neither friendship nor safety.

The authority of Great Britain over this continent, is a form of government, which sooner or later must have an end: And a serious mind can draw no true pleasure by looking forward, under the painful and positive conviction that what he calls "the present constitution" is merely temporary. As parents, we can have no joy, knowing that this government is not sufficiently lasting to ensure any thing which we may bequeath to posterity: And by a plain method of argument, as we are running the next generation into debt, we ought to do the work of it, otherwise we use them meanly and pitifully. In order to discover the line of our duty rightly, we should take our children in our hand, and fix our station a few years farther into life; that eminence will present a prospect which a few present fears and prejudices conceal from our sight.

Though I would carefully avoid giving unnecessary offence, yet I am inclined to believe, that all those who espouse the doctrine of reconciliation, may be included within the following descriptions. Interested men, who are not to be trusted, weak men who CANNOT see, prejudiced men who will not see, and a certain set of moderate men who think better of the European world than it deserves; and this last class, by an ill-judged deliberation, will be the cause of more calamities to this Continent than all the other three.

It is the good fortune of many to live distant from the scene of present sorrow; the evil is not sufficiently brought to their doors to make them feel the precariousness with which all American property is possessed. But let our imaginations transport us a few moments to Boston; that seat of wretchedness will teach us wisdom, and instruct us for ever to renounce a power in whom we can have no trust. The inhabitants of that unfortunate city who but a few months ago were in ease and affluence, have now no other alternative than to stay and starve, or turn out to beg. Endangered by the fire of their friends if they continue within the city and plundered by the soldiery if they leave it, in their present situation they are prisoners without the hope of redemption, and in a general attack for their relief they would be exposed to the fury of both armies.

Men of passive tempers look somewhat lightly over the offences of Great Britain, and, still hoping for the best, are apt to call out, "Come, come, we shall be friends again for all this." But examine the passions and feelings of mankind: bring the doctrine of reconciliation to the touchstone of nature, and then tell me whether you can hereafter love, honour, and faithfully serve the power that hath carried fire and sword into your land? If you cannot do all these, then are you only deceiving yourselves, and by your delay bringing ruin upon posterity. Your future connection with Britain, whom you can neither love nor honour, will be forced and unnatural, and being formed only on the plan of present convenience, will in a little time fall into a relapse more wretched than the first. But if you say, you can still pass the violations over, then I ask, hath your house been burnt? Hath your property been destroyed before your face? Are your wife and children destitute of a bed to lie on, or bread to live on? Have you lost a parent or a child by their hands, and yourself the ruined and wretched survivor? If you have not, then are you not a judge of those who have. But if you have, and can still shake hands with the murderers, then are you unworthy the name of husband, father, friend or lover, and whatever may be your rank or title in life, you have the heart of a coward, and the spirit of a sycophant.

This is not inflaming or exaggerating matters, but trying them by those feelings and affections which nature justifies, and without which, we should be incapable of discharging the social duties of life, or enjoying the felicities of it. I mean not to exhibit horror for the purpose of provoking revenge, but to awaken us from fatal and unmanly slumbers, that we may pursue determinately some fixed object. It is not in the power of Britain or of Europe to conquer America, if she do not conquer herself by delay and timidity. The present winter is worth an age if rightly employed, but if lost or neglected, the whole continent will partake of the misfortune; and there is no punishment which that man will not deserve, be he who, or what, or where he will, that may be the means of sacrificing a season so precious and useful.

It is repugnant to reason, to the universal order of things to all examples from former ages, to suppose, that this continent can longer remain subject to any external power. The most sanguine in Britain does not think so. The utmost stretch of human wisdom cannot, at this time, compass a plan short of separation, which can promise the continent even a year's security. Reconciliation is now a falacious dream. Nature hath deserted the connexion, and Art cannot supply her place. For, as Milton wisely expresses, "never can true reconcilement grow where wounds of deadly hate have pierced so deep."

Every quiet method for peace hath been ineffectual. Our prayers have been rejected with disdain; and only tended to convince us, that nothing flatters vanity, or confirms obstinacy in Kings more than repeated petitioning — and nothing hath contributed more than that very measure to make the Kings of Europe absolute: Witness Denmark and Sweden. Wherefore, since nothing but blows will do, for God's sake, let us come to a final separation, and not leave the next generation to be cutting throats, under the violated unmeaning names of parent and child.

To say, they will never attempt it again is idle and visionary, we thought so at the repeal of the stamp act, yet a year or two undeceived us; as well may we suppose that nations, which have been once defeated, will never renew the quarrel.

As to government matters, it is not in the power of Britain to do this continent justice: The business of it will soon be too weighty, and intricate, to be managed with any tolerable degree of convenience, by a power, so distant from us, and so very ignorant of us; for if they cannot conquer us, they cannot govern us. To be always running three or four thousand miles with a tale or a petition, waiting four or five months for an answer, which when obtained requires five or six more to explain it in, will in a few years be looked upon as folly and childishness — There was a time when it was proper, and there is a proper time for it to cease.

Small islands not capable of protecting themselves, are the proper objects for kingdoms to take under their care; but there is something very absurd, in supposing a continent to be perpetually governed by an island. In no instance hath nature made the satellite larger than its primary planet, and as England and America, with respect to each other, reverses the common order of nature, it is evident they belong to different systems: England to Europe, America to itself.

I am not induced by motives of pride, party, or resentment to espouse the doctrine of separation and independence; I am clearly, positively, and conscientiously persuaded that it is the true interest of this continent to be so; that every thing short of that is mere patchwork, that it can afford no lasting felicity, — that it is leaving the sword to our children, and shrinking back at a time, when, a little more, a little farther, would have rendered this continent the glory of the earth.

As Britain hath not manifested the least inclination towards a compromise, we may be assured that no terms can be obtained worthy the acceptance of the continent, or any ways equal to the expense of blood and treasure we have been already put to.

The object, contended for, ought always to bear some just proportion to the expense. The removal of North, or the whole detestable junto, is a matter unworthy the millions we have expended. A temporary stoppage of trade, was an inconvenience, which would have sufficiently balanced the repeal of all the acts complained of, had such repeals been obtained; but if the whole continent must take up arms, if every man must be a soldier, it is scarcely worth our while to fight against a contemptible ministry only. Dearly, dearly, do we pay for the repeal of the acts, if that is all we fight for; for in a just estimation, it is as great a folly to pay a Bunker-hill price for law, as for land. As I have always considered the independency of this continent, as an event, which sooner or later must arrive, so from the late rapid progress of the continent to maturity, the event could not be far off. Wherefore, on the breaking out of hostilities, it was not worth the while to have disputed a matter, which time would have finally redressed, unless we meant to be in earnest; otherwise, it is like wasting an estate on a suit at law, to regulate the trespasses of a tenant, whose lease is just expiring. No man was a warmer wisher for reconciliation than myself, before the fatal nineteenth of April 1775, but the moment the event of that day was made known, I rejected the hardened, sullen tempered Pharaoh of England for ever; and disdain the wretch, that with the pretended title of FATHER OF HIS PEOPLE, can unfeelingly hear of their slaughter, and composedly sleep with their blood upon his soul.

But admitting that matters were now made up, what would be the event? I answer, the ruin of the continent. And that for several reasons.

First. The powers of governing still remaining in the hands of the king, he will have a negative over the whole legislation of this continent. And as he hath shewn himself such an inveterate enemy to liberty, and discovered such a thirst for arbitrary power; is he, or is he not, a proper man to say to these colonies, "You shall make no laws but what I please." And is there any inhabitant in America so ignorant, as not to know, that according to what is called the present constitution, that this continent can make no laws but what the king gives it leave to; and is there any man so unwise, as not to see, that (considering what has happened) he will suffer no law to be made here, but such as suit his purpose. We may be as effectually enslaved by the want of laws in America, as by submitting to laws made for us in England. After matters are made up (as it is called) can there be any doubt, but the whole power of the crown will be exerted, to keep this continent as low and humble as possible? Instead of going forward we shall go backward, or be perpetually quarrelling or ridiculously petitioning. — We are already greater than the king wishes us to be, and will he not hereafter endeavour to make us less? To bring the matter to one point. Is the power who is jealous of our prosperity, a proper power to govern us? Whoever says No to this question is an independent, for independency means no more, than, whether we shall make our own laws, or, whether the king, the greatest enemy this continent hath, or can have, shall tell us, "there shall be no laws but such as I like."

But the king you will say has a negative in England; the people there can make no laws without his consent. In point of right and good order, there is something very ridiculous, that a youth of twenty-one (which hath often happened) shall say to several millions of people, older and wiser than himself, I forbid this or that act of yours to be law. But in this place I decline this sort of reply, though I will never cease to expose the absurdity of it, and only answer, that England being the King's residence, and America not so, make quite another case. The king's negative here is ten times more dangerous and fatal than it can be in England, for there he will scarcely refuse his consent to a bill for putting England into as strong a state of defence as possible, and in America he would never suffer such a bill to be passed.

America is only a secondary object in the system of British politics, England consults the good of this country, no farther than it answers her own purpose. Wherefore, her own interest leads her to suppress the growth of ours in every case which doth not promote her advantage, or in the least interferes with it. A pretty state we should soon be in under such a second-hand government, considering what has happened! Men do not change from enemies to friends by the alteration of a name: And in order to shew that reconciliation now is a dangerous doctrine, I affirm, that it would be policy in the king at this time, to repeal the acts for the sake of reinstating himself in the government of the provinces; in order that HE MAY ACCOMPLISH BY CRAFT AND SUBTILITY, IN THE LONG RUN, WHAT HE CANNOT DO BY FORCE AND VIOLENCE IN THE SHORT ONE. Reconciliation and ruin are nearly related.

Secondly. That as even the best terms, which we can expect to obtain, can amount to no more than a temporary expedient, or a kind of government by guardianship, which can last no longer than till the colonies come of age, so the general face and state of things, in the interim, will be unsettled and unpromising. Emigrants of property will not choose to come to a country whose form of government hangs but by a thread, and who is every day tottering on the brink of commotion and disturbance; and numbers of the present inhabitants would lay hold of the interval, to dispose of their effects, and quit the continent.

But the most powerful of all arguments, is, that nothing but independence, i. e. a continental form of government, can keep the peace of the continent and preserve it inviolate from civil wars. I dread the event of a reconciliation with Britain now, as it is more than probable, that it will followed by a revolt somewhere or other, the consequences of which may be far more fatal than all the malice of Britain.

Thousands are already ruined by British barbarity; (thousands more will probably suffer the same fate.) Those men have other feelings than us who have nothing suffered. All they now possess is liberty, what they before enjoyed is sacrificed to its service, and having nothing more to lose, they disdain submission. Besides, the general temper of the colonies, towards a British government, will be like that of a youth, who is nearly out of his time; they will care very little about her. And a government which cannot preserve the peace, is no government at all, and in that case we pay our money for nothing; and pray what is it that Britain can do, whose power will be wholly on paper, should a civil tumult break out the very day after reconciliation? I have heard some men say, many of whom I believe spoke without thinking, that they dreaded an independence, fearing that it would produce civil wars. It is but seldom that our first thoughts are truly correct, and that is the case here; for there are ten times more to dread from a patched up connexion than from independence. I make the sufferers case my own, and I protest, that were I driven from house and home, my property destroyed, and my circumstances ruined, that as a man, sensible of injuries, I could never relish the doctrine of reconciliation, or consider myself bound thereby.

The colonies have manifested such a spirit of good order and obedience to continental government, as is sufficient to make every reasonable person easy and happy on that head. No man can assign the least pretence for his fears, on any other grounds, that such as are truly childish and ridiculous, viz. that one colony will be striving for superiority over another.

Where there are no distinctions there can be no superiority, perfect equality affords no temptation. The republics of Europe are all (and we may say always) in peace. Holland and Swisserland are without wars, foreign or domestic: Monarchical governments, it is true, are never long at rest; the crown itself is a temptation to enterprizing ruffians at home; and that degree of pride and insolence ever attendant on regal authority, swells into a rupture with foreign powers, in instances, where a republican government, by being formed on more natural principles, would negotiate the mistake.

If there is any true cause of fear respecting independence, it is because no plan is yet laid down. Men do not see their way out — Wherefore, as an opening into that business, I offer the following hints; at the same time modestly affirming, that I have no other opinion of them myself, than that they may be the means of giving rise to something better. Could the straggling thoughts of individuals be collected, they would frequently form materials for wise and able men to improve into useful matter.

Let the assemblies be annual, with a President only. The representation more equal. Their business wholly domestic, and subject to the authority of a Continental Congress.

Let each colony be divided into six, eight, or ten, convenient districts, each district to send a proper number of delegates to Congress, so that each colony send at least thirty. The whole number in Congress will be least 390. Each Congress to sit and to choose a president by the following method. When the delegates are met, let a colony be taken from the whole thirteen colonies by lot, after which, let the whole Congress choose (by ballot) a president from out of the delegates of that province. In the next Congress, let a colony be taken by lot from twelve only, omitting that colony from which the president was taken in the former Congress, and so proceeding on till the whole thirteen shall have had their proper rotation. And in order that nothing may pass into a law but what is satisfactorily just, not less than three fifths of the Congress to be called a majority. — He that will promote discord, under a government so equally formed as this, would have joined Lucifer in his revolt.

But as there is a peculiar delicacy, from whom, or in what manner, this business must first arise, and as it seems most agreeable and consistent that it should come from some intermediate body between the governed and the governors, that is, between the Congress and the people, let a CONTINENTAL CONFERENCE be held, in the following manner, and for the following purpose.

A committee of twenty-six members of Congress, viz. two for each colony. Two members for each House of Assembly, or Provincial Convention; and five representatives of the people at large, to be chosen in the capital city or town of each province, for, and in behalf of the whole province, by as many qualified voters as shall think proper to attend from all parts of the province for that purpose; or, if more convenient, the representatives may be chosen in two or three of the most populous parts thereof. In this conference, thus assembled, will be united, the two grand principles of business, knowledge and power. The members of Congress, Assemblies, or Conventions, by having had experience in national concerns, will be able and useful counsellors, and the whole, being impowered by the people, will have a truly legal authority.

The conferring members being met, let their business be to frame a CONTINENTAL CHARTER, or Charter of the United Colonies; (answering to what is called the Magna Charta of England) fixing the number and manner of choosing members of Congress, members of Assembly, with their date of sitting, and drawing the line of business and jurisdiction between them: (Always remembering, that our strength is continental, not provincial:) Securing freedom and property to all men, and above all things, the free exercise of religion, according to the dictates of conscience; with such other matter as is necessary for a charter to contain. Immediately after which, the said Conference to dissolve, and the bodies which shall be chosen comformable to the said charter, to be the legislators and governors of this continent for the time being: Whose peace and happiness, may God preserve, Amen.

Should any body of men be hereafter delegated for this or some similar purpose, I offer them the following extracts from that wise observer on governments Dragonetti. "The science" says he "of the politician consists in fixing the true point of happiness and freedom. Those men would deserve the gratitude of ages, who should discover a mode of government that contained the greatest sum of individual happiness, with the least national expense."

"Dragonetti on virtue and rewards."

But where says some is the King of America? I'll tell you Friend, he reigns above, and doth not make havoc of mankind like the Royal Brute of Britain. Yet that we may not appear to be defective even in earthly honors, let a day be solemnly set apart for proclaiming the charter; let it be brought forth placed on the divine law, the word of God; let a crown be placed thereon, by which the world may know, that so far as we approve as monarchy, that in America THE LAW IS KING. For as in absolute governments the King is law, so in free countries the law ought to be King; and there ought to be no other. But lest any ill use should afterwards arise, let the crown at the conclusion of the ceremony be demolished, and scattered among the people whose right it is.

A government of our own is our natural right: And when a man seriously reflects on the precariousness of human affairs, he will become convinced, that it is infinitely wiser and safer, to form a constitution of our own in a cool deliberate manner, while we have it in our power, than to trust such an interesting event to time and chance. If we omit it now, some, Massanello may hereafter arise, who laying hold of popular disquietudes, may collect together the desperate and discontented, and by assuming to themselves the powers of government, may sweep away the liberties of the continent like a deluge. Should the government of America return again into the hands of Britain, the tottering situation of things, will be a temptation for some desperate adventurer to try his fortune; and in such a case, what relief can Britain give? Ere she could hear the news, the fatal business might be done; and ourselves suffering like the wretched Britons under the oppression of the Conqueror. Ye that oppose independence now, ye know not what ye do; ye are opening a door to eternal tyranny, by keeping vacant the seat of government. There are thousands, and tens of thousands, who would think it glorious to expel from the continent, that barbarous and hellish power, which hath stirred up the Indians and Negroes to destroy us, the cruelty hath a double guilt, it is dealing brutally by us, and treacherously by them.

To talk of friendship with those in whom our reason forbids us to have faith, and our affections wounded through a thousand pores instruct us to detest, is madness and folly. Every day wears out the little remains of kindred between us and them, and can there be any reason to hope, that as the relationship expires, the affection will increase, or that we shall agree better, when we have ten times more and greater concerns to quarrel over than ever?

Ye that tell us of harmony and reconciliation, can ye restore to us the time that is past? Can ye give to prostitution its former innocence? Neither can ye reconcile Britain and America. The last cord now is broken, the people of England are presenting addresses against us. There are injuries which nature cannot forgive; she would cease to be nature if she did. As well can the lover forgive the ravisher of his mistress, as the continent forgive the murders of Britain. The Almighty hath implanted in us these unextinguishable feelings for good and wise purposes. They are the guardians of his image in our hearts. They distinguish us from the herd of common animals. The social compact would dissolve, and justice be extirpated from the earth, or have only a casual existence were we callous to the touches of affection. The robber, and the murderer, would often escape unpunished, did not the injuries which our tempers sustain, provoke us into justice.

O ye that love mankind! Ye that dare oppose, not only the tyranny, but the tyrant, stand forth! Every spot of the old world is overrun with oppression. Freedom hath been hunted round the globe. Asia, and Africa, have long expelled her. — Europe regards her like a stranger, and England hath given her warning to depart. O! receive the fugitive, and prepare in time an asylum for mankind.

Of the Present Ability of America: with some Miscellaneous Reflections

I HAVE never met with a man, either in England or America, who hath not confessed his opinion, that a separation between the countries would take place one time or other: And there is no instance in which we have shown less judgment, than in endeavoring to describe, what we call, the ripeness or fitness of the continent for independence.

As all men allow the measure, and vary only in their opinion of the time, let us, in order to remove mistakes, take a general survey of things, and endeavor if possible to find out the VERY time. But I need not go far, the inquiry ceases at once, for the TIME HATH FOUND US. The general concurrence, the glorious union of all things, proves the fact.

'Tis not in numbers but in unity that our great strength lies: yet our present numbers are sufficient to repel the force of all the world. The Continent hath at this time the largest body of armed and disciplined men of any power under Heaven: and is just arrived at that pitch of strength, in which no single colony is able to support itself, and the whole, when united, is able to do any thing. Our land force is more than sufficient, and as to Naval affairs, we cannot be insensible that Britain would never suffer an American man of war to be built, while the Continent remained in her hands. Wherefore, we should be no forwarder an hundred years hence in that branch than we are now; but the truth is, we should be less so, because the timber of the Country is every day diminishing, and that which will remain at last, will be far off or difficult to procure.

Were the Continent crowded with inhabitants, her sufferings under the present circumstances would be intolerable. The more seaport-towns we had, the more should we have both to defend and to lose. Our present numbers are so happily proportioned to our wants, that no man need be idle. The diminution of trade affords an army, and the necessities of an army create a new trade.

Debts we have none: and whatever we may contract on this account will serve as a glorious memento of our virtue. Can we but leave posterity with a settled form of government, an independent constitution of its own, the purchase at any price will be cheap. But to expend millions for the sake of getting a few vile acts repealed, and routing the present ministry only, is unworthy the charge, and is using posterity with the utmost cruelty; because it is leaving them the great work to do, and a debt upon their backs from which they derive no advantage. Such a thought's unworthy a man of honour, and is the true characteristic of a narrow heart and a piddling politician.

The debt we may contract doth not deserve our regard if the work be but accomplished. No nation ought to be without a debt. A national debt is a national bond; and when it bears no interest, is in no case a grievance. Britain is oppressed with a debt of upwards of one hundred and forty millions sterling, for which she pays upwards of four millions interest. And as a compensation for her debt, she has a large navy; America is without a debt, and without a navy; yet for the twentieth part of the English national debt, could have a navy as large again. The navy of England is not worth at this time more than three millions and a half sterling.

The first and second editions of this pamphlet were published without the following calculations, which are now given as a proof that the above estimation of the navy is a just one. See Entic's "Naval History," Intro., p. 56.

The charge of building a ship of each rate, and furnishing her with masts, yards, sails, and rigging, together with a proportion of eight months boatswain's and carpenter's sea-stores, as calculated by Mr. Burchett, Secretary to the navy.

For a ship of 100 guns,	...... 35,553 £
90 "	 29,886
80 "	 23,638
70 "	 17,785
60 "	 14,197
50 "	 10,606
40 "	 7,558
30 "	 5,846
20 "	 3,710

And hence it is easy to sum up the value, or cost, rather, of the whole British navy, which, in the year 1757, when it was at its greatest glory, consisted of the following ships and guns.

Ships	Guns	Cost of One	Cost of All
6 ...	100	35,553 £	213,318 £
12 ...	90	29,886	358,632
12 ...	80	23,638	283,656
43 ...	70	17,785	764,755
35 ...	60	14,197	496,895
40 ...	50	10,605	424,240
45 ...	40	7,558	340,110
58 ...	20	3,710	215,180

85 sloops, bombs, and fireships,
one with another at 2,000 ... 170,000
Cost, ... 3,266,786 £
Remains for guns, ... 233,214
Total, ... 3,500,000 £

No country on the globe is so happily situated, or so internally capable of raising a fleet as America. Tar, timber, iron, and cordage are her natural produce. We need go abroad for nothing. Whereas the Dutch, who make large profits by hiring out their ships of war to the Spaniards and Portuguese, are obliged to import most of the materials they use. We ought to view the building a fleet as an article of commerce, it being the natural manufactory of this country. 'Tis the best money we can lay out. A navy when finished is worth more than it cost: And is that nice point in national policy, in which commerce and protection are united. Let us build; if we want them not, we can sell; and by that means replace our paper currency with ready gold and silver.

In point of manning a fleet, people in general run into great errors; it is not necessary that one-fourth part should be sailors. The Terrible privateer, captain Death, stood the hottest engagement of any ship last war, yet had not twenty sailors on board, though her complement of men was upwards of two hundred. A few able and social sailors will soon instruct a sufficient number of active landsmen in the common work of a ship. Wherefore we never can be more capable of beginning on maritime matters than now, while our timber is standing, our fisheries blocked up, and our sailors and shipwrights out of employ. Men of war, of seventy and eighty guns, were built forty years ago in New England, and why not the same now? Ship building is America's greatest pride, and in which she will, in time, excel the whole world. The great empires of the east are mainly inland, and consequently excluded from the possibility of rivalling her. Africa is in a state of barbarism; and no power in Europe hath either such an extent of coast, or such an internal supply of materials. Where nature hath given the one, she hath withheld the other; to America only hath she been liberal to both. The vast empire of Russia is almost shut out from the sea; wherefore her boundless forests, her tar, iron and cordage are only articles of commerce.

In point of safety, ought we to be without a fleet? We are not the little people now which we were sixty years ago; at that time we might have trusted our property in the streets, or fields rather, and slept securely without locks or bolts to our doors and windows. The case is now altered, and our methods of defence ought to improve with our increase of property. A common pirate, twelve months ago, might have come up the Delaware, and laid the city of Philadelphia under contribution for what sum he pleased; and the same might have happened to other places. Nay, any daring fellow, in a brig of fourteen or sixteen guns, might have robbed the whole Continent, and carried off half a million of money. These are circumstances which demand our attention, and point out the necessity of naval protection.

Some perhaps will say, that after we have made it up with Britain, she will protect us. Can they be so unwise as to mean that she will keep a navy in our harbors for that purpose? Common sense will tell us that the power which hath endeavoured to subdue us, is of all others the most improper to defend us. Conquest may be effected under the pretence of friendship; and ourselves, after a long and brave resistance, be at last cheated into slavery. And if her ships are not to be admitted into our harbours, I would ask, how is she going to protect us? A navy three or four thousand miles off can be of little use, and on sudden emergencies, none at all. Wherefore if we must hereafter protect ourselves, why not do it for ourselves? Why do it for another?

The English list of ships of war is long and formidable, but not a tenth part of them are at any time fit for service, numbers of them are not in being; yet their names are pompously continued in the list; if only a plank be left of the ship; and not a fifth part of such as are fit for service can be spared on any one station at one time. The East and West Indies, Mediterranean, Africa, and other parts, over which Britain extends her claim, make large demands upon her navy. From a mixture of prejudice and inattention we have contracted a false notion respecting the navy of England, and have talked as if we should have the whole of it to encounter at once, and for that reason supposed that we must have one as large; which not being instantly practicable, has been made use of by a set of disguised Tories to discourage our beginning thereon. Nothing can be further from truth than this; for if America had only a twentieth part of the naval force of Britain, she would be by far an over-match for her; because, as we neither have, nor claim any foreign dominion, our whole force would be employed on our own coast, where we should, in the long run, have two to one the advantage of those who had three or four thousand miles to sail over before they could attack us, and the same distance to return in order to refit and recruit. And although Britain, by her fleet, hath a check over our trade to Europe, we have as large a one over her trade to the West Indies, which, by laying in the neighborhood of the Continent, lies entirely at its mercy.

Some method might be fallen on to keep up a naval force in time of peace, if we should judge it necessary to support a constant navy. If premiums were to be given to merchants to build and employ in their service ships mounted with twenty, thirty, forty, or fifty guns (the premiums to be in proportion to the loss of bulk to the merchant), fifty or sixty of those ships, with a few guardships on constant duty, would keep up a sufficient navy, and that without burdening ourselves with the evil so loudly complained of in England, of suffering their fleet in time of peace to lie rotting in the docks. To unite the sinews of commerce and defence is sound policy; for when our strength and our riches play into each other's hand, we need fear no external enemy.

In almost every article of defence we abound. Hemp flourishes even to rankness so that we need not want cordage. Our iron is superior to that of other countries. Our small arms equal to any in the world. Cannon we can cast at pleasure. Saltpetre and gunpowder we are every day producing. Our knowledge is hourly improving. Resolution is our inherent character, and courage hath never yet forsaken us. Wherefore, what is it that we want? Why is it that we hesitate? From Britain we can expect nothing but ruin. If she is once admitted to the government of America again, this Continent will not be worth living in. Jealousies will be always arising; insurrections will be constantly happening; and who will go forth to quell them? Who will venture his life to reduce his own countrymen to a foreign obedience? The difference between Pennsylvania and Connecticut, respecting some unlocated lands, shows the insignificance of a British government, and fully proves that nothing but Continental authority can regulate Continental matters.

Another reason why the present time is preferable to all others is, that the fewer our numbers are, the more land there is yet unoccupied, which, instead of being lavished by the king on his worthless dependents, may be hereafter applied, not only to the discharge of the present debt, but to the constant support of government. No nation under Heaven hath such an advantage as this.

The infant state of the Colonies, as it is called, so far from being against, is an argument in favour of independence. We are sufficiently numerous, and were we more so we might be less united. 'Tis a matter worthy of observation that the more a country is peopled, the smaller their armies are. In military numbers, the ancients far exceeded the moderns; and the reason is evident, for trade being the consequence of population, men became too much absorbed thereby to attend to anything else. Commerce diminishes the spirit both of patriotism and military defence. And history sufficiently informs us that the bravest achievements were always accomplished in the non-age of a nation. With the increase of commerce England hath lost its spirit. The city of London, notwithstanding its numbers, submits to continued insults with the patience of a coward. The more men have to lose, the less willing are they to venture. The rich are in general slaves to fear, and submit to courtly power with the trembling duplicity of a spaniel.

Youth is the seed-time of good habits as well in nations as in individuals. It might be difficult, if not impossible, to form the Continent into one government half a century hence. The vast variety of interests, occasioned by an increase of trade and population, would create confusion. Colony would be against colony. Each being able would scorn each other's assistance; and while the proud and foolish gloried in their little distinctions the wise would lament that the union had not been formed before. Wherefore the present time is the true time for establishing it. The intimacy which is contracted in infancy, and the friendship which is formed in misfortune, are of all others the most lasting and unalterable. Our present union is marked with both these characters; we are young, and we have been distressed; but our concord hath withstood our troubles, and fixes a memorable era for posterity to glory in.

The present time, likewise, is that peculiar time which never happens to a nation but once, viz., the time of forming itself into a government. Most nations have let slip the opportunity, and by that means have been compelled to receive laws from their conquerors, instead of making laws for themselves. First, they had a king, and then a form of government; whereas the articles or charter of government should be formed first, and men delegated to execute them afterwards; but from the errors of other nations let us learn wisdom, and lay hold of the present opportunity — TO BEGIN GOVERNMENT AT THE RIGHT END.

When William the Conqueror subdued England, he gave them law at the point of the sword; and, until we consent that the seat of government in America be legally and authoritatively occupied, we shall be in danger of having it filled by some fortunate ruffian, who may treat us in the same manner, and then, where will be our freedom? Where our property?

As to religion, I hold it to be the indispensable duty of government to protect all conscientious professors thereof, and I know of no other business which government hath to do therewith. Let a man throw aside that narrowness of soul, that selfishness of principle, which the niggards of all professions are so unwilling to part with, and he will be at once delivered of his fears on that head. Suspicion is the companion of mean souls, and the bane of all good society. For myself, I fully and conscientiously believe that it is the will of the Almighty that there should be a diversity of religious opinions among us. It affords a larger field for our Christian kindness; were we all of one way of thinking, our religious dispositions would want matter for probation; and on this liberal principle I look on the various denominations among us to be like children of the same family, differing only in what is called their Christian names.

In page [97] I threw out a few thoughts on the propriety of a Continental Charter (for I only presume to offer hints, not plans) and in this place I take the liberty of re-mentioning the subject, by observing that a charter is to be understood as a bond of solemn obligation, which the whole enters into, to support the right of every separate part, whether of religion, professional freedom, or property. A firm bargain and a right reckoning make long friends.

I have heretofore likewise mentioned the necessity of a large and equal representation; and there is no political matter which more deserves our attention. A small number of electors, or a small number of representatives, are equally dangerous. But if the number of the representatives be not only small, but unequal, the danger is increased. As an instance of this, I mention the following: when the petition of the associators was before the House of Assembly of Pennsylvania, twenty-eight members only were present; all the Bucks county members, being eight, voted against it, and had seven of the Chester members done the same, this whole province had been governed by two counties only; and this danger it is always exposed to. The unwarrantable stretch likewise, which that house made in their last sitting, to gain an undue authority over the delegates of that province, ought to warn the people at large how they trust power out of their own hands. A set of instructions for their delegates were put together, which in point of sense and business would have dishonoured a school-boy, and after being approved by a few, a very few, without doors, were carried into the house, and there passed IN BEHALF OF THE WHOLE COLONY; whereas, did the whole colony know with what ill will that house had entered on some necessary public measures, they would not hesitate a moment to think them unworthy of such a trust.

Immediate necessity makes many things convenient, which if continued would grow into oppressions. Expedience and right are different things. When the calamities of America required a consultation, there was no method so ready, or at that time so proper, as to appoint persons from the several houses of assembly for that purpose; and the wisdom with which they have proceeded hath preserved this Continent from ruin. But as it is more than probable that we shall never be without a CONGRESS, every well wisher to good order must own that the mode for choosing members of that body deserves consideration. And I put it as a question to those who make a study of mankind, whether representation and election is not too great a power for one and the same body of men to possess? When we are planning for posterity, we ought to remember that virtue is not hereditary.

It is from our enemies that we often gain excellent maxims, and are frequently surprised into reason by their mistakes. Mr. Cornwall (one of the Lords of the Treasury) treated the petition of the New York Assembly with contempt, because THAT house, he said, consisted but of twenty-six members, which trifling number, he argued, could not with decency be put for the whole. We thank him for his involuntary honesty.

To CONCLUDE, however strange it may appear to some, or however unwilling they may be to think so, matters not, but many strong and striking reasons may be given to show that nothing can settle our affairs so expeditiously as an open and determined declaration for independence. Some of which are,

First. — It is the custom of Nations, when any two are at war, for some other powers, not engaged in the quarrel, to step in as mediators, and bring about the preliminaries of a peace; But while America calls herself the subject of Great Britain, no power, however well disposed she may be, can offer her mediation. Wherefore, in our present state we may quarrel on for ever.

Secondly. — It is unreasonable to suppose that France or Spain will give us any kind of assistance, if we mean only to make use of that assistance for the purpose of repairing the breach, and strengthening the connection between Britain and America; because, those powers would be sufferers by the consequences.

Thirdly. — While we profess ourselves the subjects of Britain, we must, in the eyes of foreign nations, be considered as Rebels. The precedent is somewhat dangerous to their peace, for men to be in arms under the name of subjects; we, on the spot, can solve the paradox; but to unite resistance and subjection requires an idea much too refined for common understanding.

Fourthly. — Were a manifesto to be published, and despatched to foreign Courts, setting forth the miseries we have endured, and the peaceful methods which we have ineffectually used for redress; declaring at the same time that not being able longer to live happily or safely under the cruel disposition of the British Court, we had been driven to the necessity of breaking off all connections with her; at the same time, assuring all such Courts of our peaceable disposition towards them, and of our desire of entering into trade with them; such a memorial would produce more good effects to this Continent than if a ship were freighted with petitions to Britain.

Under our present denomination of British subjects, we can neither be received nor heard abroad; the custom of all Courts is against us, and will be so, until by an independence we take rank with other nations.

These proceedings may at first seem strange and difficult, but like all other steps which we have already passed over, will in a little time become familiar and agreeable; and until an independence is declared, the Continent will feel itself like a man who continues putting off some unpleasant business from day to day, yet knows it must be done, hates to set about it, wishes it over, and is continually haunted with the thoughts of its necessity.

SINCE the publication of the first edition of this pamphlet, or rather, on the same day on which it came out, the king's speech made its appearance in this city. Had the spirit of prophecy directed the birth of this production, it could not have brought it forth at a more seasonable juncture, or at a more necessary time. The bloody-mindedness of the one, shows the necessity of pursuing the doctrine of the other. Men read by way of revenge. And the speech, instead of terrifying, prepared a way for the manly principles of independence.

Ceremony, and even silence, from whatever motives they may arise, have a hurtful tendency when they give the least degree of countenance to base and wicked performances, wherefore, if this maxim be admitted, it naturally follows, that the king's speech, IS being a piece of finished villany, deserved and still deserves, a general execration, both by the Congress and the people.

Yet, as the domestic tranquillity of a nation, depends greatly on the chastity of what might properly be called NATIONAL MANNERS, it is often better to pass some things over in silent disdain, than to make use of such new methods of dislike, as might introduce the least innovation on that guardian of our peace and safety. And, perhaps, it is chiefly owing to this prudent delicacy, that the king's speech hath not before now suffered a public execution. The speech, if it may be called one, is nothing better than a wilful audacious libel against the truth, the common good, and the existence of mankind; and is a formal and pompous method of offering up human sacrifices to the pride of tyrants.

But this general massacre of mankind, is one of the privileges and the certain consequences of kings, for as nature knows them not, they know not her, and although they are beings of our own creating, they know not us, and are become the gods of their creators. The speech hath one good quality, which is, that it is not calculated to deceive, neither can we, even if we would, be deceived by it. Brutality and tyranny appear on the face of it. It leaves us at no loss: And every line convinces, even in the moment of reading, that he who hunts the woods for prey, the naked and untutored Indian, is less savage than the king of Britain. Sir John Dalrymple, the putative father of a whining jesuitical piece, fallaciously called, "The address of the people of

England to the inhabitants of America," hath perhaps from a vain supposition that the people here were to be frightened at the pomp and description of a king, given (though very unwisely on his part) the real character of the present one: "But," says this writer, "if you are inclined to pay compliments to an administration, which we do not complain of (meaning the Marquis of Rockingham's at the repeal of the Stamp Act) it is very unfair in you to withhold them from that prince, by whose NOD ALONE they were permitted to do any thing." This is toryism with a witness! Here is idolatry even without a mask: And he who can calmly hear and digest such doctrine, hath forfeited his claim to rationality an apostate from the order of manhood and ought to be considered as one who hath not only given up the proper dignity of man, but sunk himself beneath the rank of animals, and contemptibly crawls through the world like a worm.

However, it matters very little now what the king of England either says or does; he hath wickedly broken through every moral and human obligation, trampled nature and conscience beneath his feet, and by a steady and constitutional spirit of insolence and cruelty procured for himself an universal hatred. It is now the interest of America to provide for herself. She hath already a large and young family, whom it is more her duty to take care of, than to be granting away her property to support a power who is become a reproach to the names of men and christians, whose office it is to watch the morals of a nation, of whatsoever sect or denomination ye are of, as well as ye who are more immediately the guardians of the public liberty, if ye wish to preserve your native country uncontaminated by European corruption, ye must in secret wish a separation. But leaving the moral part to private reflection, I shall chiefly confine my further remarks to the following heads:

First, That it is the interest of America to be separated from Britain.

Secondly, Which is the easiest and most practicable plan, RECONCILIATION or INDEPENDENCE? with some occasional remarks.

In support of the first, I could, if I judged it proper, produce the opinion of some of the ablest and most experienced men on this continent: and whose sentiments on that head, are not yet publicly known. It is in reality a self-evident position: for no nation in a state of foreign dependence, limited in its commerce, and cramped and fettered in its legislative powers, can ever arrive at any material eminence. America doth not yet know what opulence is; and although the progress which she hath made stands unparalleled in the history of other nations, it is but childhood compared with what she would be capable of arriving at, had she, as she ought to have, the legislative powers in her own hands. England is at this time proudly coveting what would do her no good were she to accomplish it; and the continent hesitating on a matter which will be her final ruin if neglected. It is the commerce and not the conquest of America by which England is to be benefited, and that would in a great measure continue, were the countries as independent of each other as France and Spain; because the specious errors of those who speak without reflecting. And among the many which I have heard, the following seems the most general, viz. that had this rupture happened forty or fifty years hence, instead of now, the continent would have been more able to have shaken off the dependence. To which I reply, that our military ability, at this time, arises from the experience gained in the last war, and which in forty or fifty years' time, would be totally extinct. The continent would not, by that time, have a quitrent reserved thereon will always lessen, and in time will wholly support, the yearly expense of government. It matters not how long the debt is in paying, so that the lands when sold be applied to the discharge of it, and for the execution of which the Congress for the time being will be the continental trustees.

I proceed now to the second head, viz. Which is the easiest and most practicable plan, reconciliation or independence; with some occasional remarks.

He who takes nature for his guide, is not easily beaten out of his argument, and on that ground, I answer generally that independence being a single simple line, contained within ourselves; and reconciliation, a matter exceedingly perplexed and complicated, and in which a treacherous capricious court is to interfere, gives the answer without a doubt.

The present state of America is truly alarming to every man who is capable of reflection. Without law, without government, without any other mode of power than what is founded on, and granted by, courtesy. Held together by an unexampled occurrence of sentiment, which is nevertheless subject to change, and which every secret enemy is endeavoring to dissolve. Our present condition is, Legislation without law; wisdom without a plan; a constitution without a name; and, what is strangely astonishing, perfect independence contending for dependence. The instance is without a precedent, the case never existed before, and who can tell what may be the event? The property of no man is secure in the present un-braced system of things. The mind of the multitude is left at random, and seeing no fixed object before them, they pursue such as fancy or opinion presents. Nothing is criminal; there is no such thing as treason, wherefore, every one thinks himself at liberty to act as he pleases. The Tories would not have dared to assemble offensively, had they known that their lives, by that act, were forfeited to the laws of the state. A line of distinction should be drawn between English soldiers taken in battle, and inhabitants of America taken in arms. The first are prisoners, but the latter traitors. The one forfeits his liberty, the other his head.

Notwithstanding our wisdom, there is a visible feebleness in some of our proceedings which gives encouragement to dissensions. The continental belt is too loosely buckled: And if something is not done in time, it will be too late to do any thing, and we shall fall into a state, in which neither reconciliation nor independence will be practicable. The king and his worthless adherents are got at their old game of dividing the continent, and there are not wanting among us printers who will be busy in spreading specious falsehoods. The artful and hypocritical letter which appeared a few months ago in two of the New York papers, and likewise in two others, is an evidence that there are men who want both judgment and honesty.

It is easy getting into holes and corners, and talking of reconciliation: But do such men seriously consider how difficult the task is, and how dangerous it may prove, should the continent divide thereon? Do they take within their view all the various orders of men whose situation and circumstances, as well as their own, are to be considered therein? Do they put themselves in the place of the sufferer whose all is already gone, and of the soldier, who hath quitted all for the defence of his country? If their ill-judged moderation be suited to their own private situations only, regardless of others, the event will convince them that "they are reckoning without their host."

Put us, say some, on the footing we were in the year 1763: To which I answer, the request is not now in the power of Britain to comply with, neither will she propose it; but if it were, and even should be granted, I ask, as a reasonable question, By what means is such a corrupt and faithless court to be kept to its engagements? Another parliament, nay, even the present, may hereafter repeal the obligation, on the pretence of its being violently obtained, or not wisely granted; and, in that case, Where is our redress? No going to law with nations; cannon are the barristers of crowns; and the sword, not of justice, but of war, decides the suit. To be on the footing of 1763, it is not sufficient, that the laws only be put in the same state, but, that our circumstances likewise be put in the same state; our burnt and destroyed towns repaired or built up, our private losses made good, our public debts (contracted for defence) discharged; otherwise we shall be millions worse than we were at that enviable period. Such a request, had it been complied with a year ago, would have won the heart and soul of the continent, but now it is too late. "The Rubicon is passed." Besides, the taking up arms, merely to enforce the repeal of a pecuniary law, seems as unwarrantable by the divine law, and as repugnant to human feelings, as the taking up arms to enforce obedience thereto. The object, on either side, doth not justify the means; for the lives of men are too valuable to be cast away on such trifles. It is the violence which is done and threatened to our persons; the destruction of our property by an armed force; the invasion of our country by fire and sword, which conscientiously qualifies the use of arms: and the instant in which such mode of defence became necessary, all subjection to Britain ought to have ceased; and the independence of America should have been considered as dating its era from, and published by, the first musket that was fired against her. This line is a line of consistency; neither drawn by caprice, nor extended by ambition; but produced by a chain of events, of which the colonies were not the authors.

I shall conclude these remarks, with the following timely and well-intended hints. We ought to reflect, that there are three different ways by which an independency may hereafter be effected, and that one of those three, will, one day or other, be the fate of America, viz. By the legal voice of the people in Congress; by a military power, or by a mob: It may not always happen that our soldiers are citizens, and the multitude a body of reasonable men; virtue, as I have already remarked, is not hereditary, neither is it perpetual. Should an independency be brought about by the first of those means, we have every opportunity and every encouragement before us, to form the noblest, purest constitution on the face of the earth. We have it in our power to begin the world over again. A situation, similar to the present, hath not happened since the days of Noah until now.

The birthday of a new world is at hand, and a race of men, perhaps as numerous as all Europe contains, are to receive their portion of freedom from the events of a few months. The reflection is awful, and in this point of view, how trifling, how ridiculous, do the little paltry cavilings of a few weak or interested men appear, when weighed against the business of a world.

Should we neglect the present favorable and inviting period, and independence be hereafter effected by any other means, we must charge the consequence to ourselves, or to those rather whose narrow and prejudiced souls are habitually opposing the measure, without either inquiring or reflecting. There are reasons to be given in support of independence which men should rather privately think of, than be publicly told of. We ought not now to be debating whether we shall be independent or not, but anxious to accomplish it on a firm, secure, and honorable basis, and uneasy rather that it is not yet began upon. Every day convinces us of its necessity. Even the Tories (if such beings yet remain among us) should, of all men, be the most solicitous to promote it; for as the appointment of committees at first protected them from popular rage, so, a wise and well established form of government will be the only certain means of continuing it securely to them. Wherefore, if they have not virtue enough to be WHIGS, they ought to have prudence enough to wish for independence.

In short, independence is the only bond that tie and keep us together. We shall then see our object, and our ears will be legally shut against the schemes of an intriguing, as well as cruel, enemy. We shall then, too, be on a proper footing to treat with Britain; for there is reason to conclude, that the pride of that court will be less hurt by treating with the American States for terms of peace, than with those, whom she denominates "rebellious subjects," for terms of accommodation. It is our delaying in that, encourages her to hope for conquest, and our backwardness tends only to prolong the war. As we have, without any good effect therefrom, withheld our trade to obtain a redress of our grievances, let us now try the alternative, by independently redressing them ourselves, and then offering to open the trade. The mercantile and reasonable part of England, will be still with us; because, peace, with trade, is preferable to war without it. And if this offer be not accepted, other courts may be applied to.

On these grounds I rest the matter. And as no offer hath yet been made to refute the doctrine contained in the former editions of this pamphlet, it is a negative proof, that either the doctrine cannot be refuted, or, that the party in favor of it are too numerous to be opposed. WHEREFORE, instead of gazing at each other with suspicious or doubtful curiosity, let each of us hold out to his neighbor the hearty hand of friendship, and unite in drawing a line, which, like an act of oblivion, shall bury in forgetfulness every former dissension. Let the names of Whig and Tory be extinct; and let none other be heard among us, than those of a good citizen, an open and resolute friend, and a virtuous supporter of the RIGHTS of MANKIND, and of the FREE AND INDEPENDENT STATES OF AMERICA.

The Declaration of Independence

IN CONGRESS, JULY 4, 1776

The unanimous Declaration of the thirteen united States of America

When in the Course of human events it becomes necessary for one people to dissolve the political bands which have connected them with another and to assume among the powers of the earth, the separate and equal station to which the Laws of Nature and of Nature's God entitle them, a decent respect to the opinions of mankind requires that they should declare the causes which impel them to the separation.

We hold these truths to be self-evident, that all men are created equal, that they are endowed by their Creator with certain unalienable Rights, that among these are Life, Liberty and the pursuit of Happiness. — That to secure these rights, Governments are instituted among Men, deriving their just powers from the consent of the governed, — That whenever any Form of Government becomes destructive of these ends, it is the Right of the People to alter or to abolish it, and to institute new Government, laying its foundation on such principles and organizing its powers in such form, as to them shall seem most likely to effect their Safety and Happiness. Prudence, indeed, will dictate that Governments long established should not be changed for light and transient causes; and accordingly all experience hath shewn that mankind are more disposed to suffer, while evils are sufferable than to right themselves by abolishing the forms to which they are accustomed. But when a long train of abuses and usurpations, pursuing invariably the same Object evinces a design to reduce them under absolute Despotism, it is their right, it is their duty, to throw off such Government, and to provide new Guards for their future security. — Such has been the patient sufferance of these Colonies; and such is now the necessity which constrains them to alter their former Systems of Government. The history of the present King of Great Britain is a history of repeated injuries and usurpations, all having in direct object the establishment of an absolute Tyranny over these States. To prove this, let Facts be submitted to a candid world.

He has refused his Assent to Laws, the most wholesome and necessary for the public good.

He has forbidden his Governors to pass Laws of immediate and pressing importance, unless suspended in their operation till his Assent should be obtained; and when so suspended, he has utterly neglected to attend to them.

He has refused to pass other Laws for the accommodation of large districts of people, unless those people would relinquish the right of Representation in the Legislature, a right inestimable to them and formidable to tyrants only.

He has called together legislative bodies at places unusual, uncomfortable, and distant from the depository of their Public Records, for the sole purpose of fatiguing them into compliance with his measures.

He has dissolved Representative Houses repeatedly, for opposing with manly firmness his invasions on the rights of the people.

He has refused for a long time, after such dissolutions, to cause others to be elected, whereby the Legislative Powers, incapable of Annihilation, have returned to the People at large for their exercise; the State remaining in the mean time exposed to all the dangers of invasion from without, and convulsions within.

He has endeavoured to prevent the population of these States; for that purpose obstructing the Laws for Naturalization of Foreigners; refusing to pass others to encourage their migrations hither, and raising the conditions of new Appropriations of Lands.

He has obstructed the Administration of Justice by refusing his Assent to Laws for establishing Judiciary Powers.

He has made Judges dependent on his Will alone for the tenure of their offices, and the amount and payment of their salaries.

He has erected a multitude of New Offices, and sent hither swarms of Officers to harass our people and eat out their substance.

He has kept among us, in times of peace, Standing Armies without the Consent of our legislatures.

He has affected to render the Military independent of and superior to the Civil Power.

He has combined with others to subject us to a jurisdiction foreign to our constitution, and unacknowledged by our laws; giving his Assent to their Acts of pretended Legislation:

For quartering large bodies of armed troops among us:

For protecting them, by a mock Trial from punishment for any Murders which they should commit on the Inhabitants of these States:

For cutting off our Trade with all parts of the world:

For imposing Taxes on us without our Consent:

For depriving us in many cases, of the benefit of Trial by Jury:

For transporting us beyond Seas to be tried for pretended offences:

For abolishing the free System of English Laws in a neighbouring Province, establishing therein an Arbitrary government, and enlarging its Boundaries so as to render it at once an example and fit instrument for introducing the same absolute rule into these Colonies

For taking away our Charters, abolishing our most valuable Laws and altering fundamentally the Forms of our Governments:

For suspending our own Legislatures, and declaring themselves invested with power to legislate for us in all cases whatsoever.

He has abdicated Government here, by declaring us out of his Protection and waging War against us.

He has plundered our seas, ravaged our coasts, burnt our towns, and destroyed the lives of our people.

He is at this time transporting large Armies of foreign Mercenaries to compleat the works of death, desolation, and tyranny, already begun with circumstances of Cruelty & Perfidy scarcely paralleled in the most barbarous ages, and totally unworthy the Head of a civilized nation.

He has constrained our fellow Citizens taken Captive on the high Seas to bear Arms against their Country, to become the executioners of their friends and Brethren, or to fall themselves by their Hands.

He has excited domestic insurrections amongst us, and has endeavoured to bring on the inhabitants of our frontiers, the merciless Indian Savages whose known rule of warfare, is an undistinguished destruction of all ages, sexes and conditions.

In every stage of these Oppressions We have Petitioned for Redress in the most humble terms: Our repeated Petitions have been answered only by repeated injury. A Prince, whose character is thus marked by every act which may define a Tyrant, is unfit to be the ruler of a free people.

Nor have We been wanting in attentions to our British brethren. We have warned them from time to time of attempts by their legislature to extend an unwarrantable jurisdiction over us. We have reminded them of the circumstances of our emigration and settlement here. We have appealed to their native justice and magnanimity, and we have conjured them by the ties of our common kindred to disavow these usurpations, which would inevitably interrupt our connections and correspondence. They too have been deaf to the voice of justice and of consanguinity. We must, therefore, acquiesce in the necessity, which denounces our Separation, and hold them, as we hold the rest of mankind, Enemies in War, in Peace Friends.

We, therefore, the Representatives of the united States of America, in General Congress, Assembled, appealing to the Supreme Judge of the world for the rectitude of our intentions, do, in the Name, and by Authority of the good People of these Colonies, solemnly publish and declare, That these united Colonies are, and of Right ought to be Free and Independent States, that they are Absolved from all Allegiance to the British Crown, and that all political connection between them and the State of Great Britain, is and ought to be totally dissolved; and that as Free and Independent States, they have full Power to levy War, conclude Peace, contract Alliances, establish Commerce, and to do all other Acts and Things which Independent States may of right do. — And for the support of this Declaration, with a firm reliance on the protection of Divine Providence, we mutually pledge to each other our Lives, our Fortunes, and our sacred Honor.

New Hampshire: *Josiah Bartlett, William Whipple, Matthew Thornton*

Massachusetts: *John Hancock, Samuel Adams, John Adams, Robert Treat Paine, Elbridge Gerry*

Rhode Island: *Stephen Hopkins, William Ellery*

Connecticut: *Roger Sherman, Samuel Huntington, William Williams, Oliver Wolcott*

New York: *William Floyd, Philip Livingston, Francis Lewis, Lewis Morris*

New Jersey: *Richard Stockton, John Witherspoon, Francis Hopkinson, John Hart, Abraham Clark*

Pennsylvania: *Robert Morris, Benjamin Rush, Benjamin Franklin, John Morton, George Clymer, James Smith, George Taylor, James Wilson, George Ross*

Delaware: *Caesar Rodney, George Read, Thomas McKean*

Maryland: *Samuel Chase, William Paca, Thomas Stone, Charles Carroll of Carrollton*

Virginia: *George Wythe, Richard Henry Lee, Thomas Jefferson, Benjamin Harrison, Thomas Nelson, Jr., Francis Lightfoot Lee, Carter Braxton*

North Carolina: *William Hooper, Joseph Hewes, John Penn*

South Carolina: *Edward Rutledge, Thomas Heyward, Jr., Thomas Lynch, Jr., Arthur Middleton*

Georgia: *Button Gwinnett, Lyman Hall, George Walton*

The Articles of Confederation (1777)

To all to whom these Presents shall come, we, the undersigned Delegates of the States affixed to our Names send greeting. Whereas the Delegates of the United States of America in Congress assembled did on the fifteenth day of November in the year of our Lord One Thousand Seven Hundred and Seventy seven, and in the Second Year of the Independence of America agree to certain articles of Confederation and perpetual Union between the States of Newhampshire, Massachusetts-bay, Rhodeisland and Providence Plantations, Connecticut, New York, New Jersey, Pennsylvania, Delaware, Maryland, Virginia, North Carolina, South Carolina, and Georgia in the Words following, viz. "Articles of Confederation and perpetual Union between the States of Newhampshire, Massachusetts-bay, Rhodeisland and Providence Plantations, Connecticut, New York, New Jersey, Pennsylvania, Delaware, Maryland, Virginia, North Carolina, South Carolina, and Georgia.

Article I. The Stile of this confederacy shall be, "The United States of America."

Article II. Each state retains its sovereignty, freedom and independence, and every Power, Jurisdiction and right, which is not by this confederation expressly delegated to the United States, in Congress assembled.

Article III. The said states hereby severally enter into a firm league of friendship with each other, for their common defence, the security of their Liberties, and their mutual and general welfare, binding themselves to assist each other, against all force offered to, or attacks made upon them, or any of them, on account of religion, sovereignty, trade, or any other pretence whatever.

Article IV. The better to secure and perpetuate mutual friendship and intercourse among the people of the different states in this union, the free inhabitants of each of these states, paupers, vagabonds and fugitives from Justice excepted, shall be entitled to all privileges and immunities of free citizens in the several states; and the people of each state shall have free ingress and regress to and from any other state, and shall enjoy therein all the privileges of trade and commerce, subject to the same duties, impositions and restrictions as the inhabitants thereof respectively, provided that such restrictions shall not extend so far as to prevent the removal of property imported into any state, to any other State of which the Owner is an inhabitant; provided also that no imposition, duties or restriction shall be laid by any state, on the property of the united states, or either of them.

If any Person guilty of, or charged with, treason, felony, or other high misdemeanor in any state, shall flee from Justice, and be found in any of the united states, he shall upon demand of the Governor or executive power of the state from which he fled, be delivered up, and removed to the state having jurisdiction of his offence.

Full faith and credit shall be given in each of these states to the records, acts and judicial proceedings of the courts and magistrates of every other state.

Article V. For the more convenient management of the general interests of the united states, delegates shall be annually appointed in such manner as the legislature of each state shall direct, to meet in Congress on the first Monday in November, in every year, with a power reserved to each state to recall its delegates, or any of them, at any time within the year, and to send others in their stead, for the remainder of the Year.

No State shall be represented in Congress by less than two, nor by more than seven Members; and no person shall be capable of being delegate for more than three years, in any term of six years; nor shall any person, being a delegate, be capable of holding any office under the united states, for which he, or another for his benefit receives any salary, fees or emolument of any kind.

Each State shall maintain its own delegates in a meeting of the states, and while they act as members of the committee of the states.

In determining questions in the united states, in Congress assembled, each state shall have one vote.

Freedom of speech and debate in Congress shall not be impeached or questioned in any Court, or place out of Congress, and the members of congress shall be protected in their persons from arrests and imprisonments, during the time of their going to and from, and attendance on congress, except for treason, felony, or breach of the peace.

Article VI. No State, without the Consent of the united States, in congress assembled, shall send any embassy to, or receive any embassy from, or enter into any conferrence, agreement, alliance, or treaty, with any King prince or state; nor shall any person holding any office of profit or trust under the united states, or any of them, accept of any present, emolument, office, or title of any kind whatever, from any king, prince, or foreign state; nor shall the united states, in congress assembled, or any of them, grant any title of nobility.

No two or more states shall enter into any treaty, confederation, or alliance whatever between them, without the consent of the united states, in congress assembled, specifying accurately the purposes for which the same is to be entered into, and how long it shall continue.

No State shall lay any imposts or duties, which may interfere with any stipulations in treaties, entered into by the united States in congress assembled, with any king, prince, or State, in pursuance of any treaties already proposed by congress, to the courts of France and Spain.

No vessels of war shall be kept up in time of peace, by any state, except such number only, as shall be deemed necessary by the united states, in congress assembled, for the defence of such state, or its trade; nor shall any body of forces be kept up, by any state, in time of peace, except such number only as, in the judgment of the united states, in congress assembled, shall be deemed requisite to garrison the forts necessary for the defence of such state; but every state shall always keep up a well regulated and disciplined militia, sufficiently armed and accounted, and shall provide and constantly have ready for use, in public stores, a due number of field pieces and tents, and a proper quantity of arms, ammunition, and camp equipage.

No State shall engage in any war without the consent of the united States in congress assembled, unless such State be actually invaded by enemies, or shall have received certain advice of a resolution being formed by some nation of Indians to invade such State, and the danger is so imminent as not to admit of a delay till the united states in congress assembled, can be consulted: nor shall any state grant commissions to any ships or vessels of war, nor letters of marque or reprisal, except it be after a declaration of war by the united states in congress assembled, and then only against the kingdom or State, and the subjects thereof, against which war has been so declared, and under such regulations as shall be established by the united states in congress assembled, unless such state be infested by pirates, in which case vessels of war may be fitted out for that occasion, and kept so long as the danger shall continue, or until the united states in congress assembled shall determine otherwise.

Article VII. When land forces are raised by any state, for the common defence, all officers of or under the rank of colonel, shall be appointed by the legislature of each state respectively by whom such forces shall be raised, or in such manner as such state shall direct, and all vacancies shall be filled up by the state which first made appointment.

Article VIII. All charges of war, and all other expenses that shall be incurred for the common defence or general welfare, and allowed by the united states in congress assembled, shall be defrayed out of a common treasury, which shall be supplied by the several states, in proportion to the value of all land within each state, granted to or surveyed for any Person, as such land and the buildings and improvements thereon shall be estimated, according to such mode as the united states, in congress assembled, shall, from time to time, direct and appoint. The taxes for paying that proportion shall be laid and levied by the authority and direction of the legislatures of the several states within the time agreed upon by the united states in congress assembled.

Article IX. The united states, in congress assembled, shall have the sole and exclusive right and power of determining on peace and war, except in the cases mentioned in the sixth article — of sending and receiving ambassadors — entering into treaties and alliances, provided that no treaty of commerce shall be made, whereby the legislative power of the respective states shall be restrained from imposing such imposts and duties on foreigners, as their own people are subjected to, or from prohibiting the exportation or importation of any species of goods or commodities whatsoever — of establishing rules for deciding, in all cases, what captures on land or water shall be legal, and in what manner prizes taken by land or naval forces in the service of the united Sates, shall be divided or appropriated — of granting letters of marque and reprisal in times of peace — appointing courts for the trial of piracies and felonies committed on the high seas; and establishing courts; for receiving and determining finally appeals in all cases of captures; provided that no member of congress shall be appointed a judge of any of the said courts.

The united states, in congress assembled, shall also be the last resort on appeal, in all disputes and differences now subsisting, or that hereafter may arise between two or more states concerning boundary, jurisdiction, or any other cause whatever; which authority shall always be exercised in the manner following. Whenever the legislative or executive authority, or lawful agent of any state in controversy with another, shall present a petition to congress, stating the matter in question, and praying for a hearing, notice thereof shall be given, by order of congress, to the legislative or executive authority of the other state in controversy, and a day assigned for the appearance of the parties by their lawful agents, who shall then be directed to appoint, by joint consent, commissioners or judges to constitute a court for hearing and determining the matter in question: but if they cannot agree, congress shall name three persons out of each of the united states, and from the list of such persons each party shall alternately strike out one, the petitioners beginning, until the number shall be reduced to thirteen; and from that number not less than seven, nor more than nine names, as congress shall direct, shall, in the presence of congress, be drawn out by lot, and the persons whose names shall be so drawn, or any five of them, shall be commissioners or judges, to hear and finally determine the controversy, so always as a major part of the judges, who shall hear the cause, shall agree in the determination: and if either party shall neglect to attend at the day appointed, without showing reasons which congress shall judge sufficient, or being present, shall refuse to strike, the congress shall proceed to nominate three persons out of each State, and the secretary of congress shall strike in behalf of such party absent or refusing; and the judgment and sentence of the court, to be appointed in the manner before prescribed, shall be final and conclusive; and if any of the parties shall refuse to submit to the authority of such court, or to appear or defend their claim or cause, the court shall nevertheless proceed to pronounce sentence, or judgment, which shall in like manner be final and decisive; the judgment or sentence and other proceedings being in either case transmitted to congress, and lodged among the acts of congress, for the security of the parties concerned: provided that every commissioner, before he sits in judgment, shall take an oath to be administered by one of the judges of the supreme or superior court of the State where the cause shall be tried, "well and truly to hear and determine the matter in question, according to the best of his judgment, without favour, affection, or hope of reward: "provided, also, that no State shall be deprived of territory for the benefit of the united states.

All controversies concerning the private right of soil claimed under different grants of two or more states, whose jurisdictions as they may respect such lands, and the states which passed such grants are adjusted, the said grants or either of them being at the same time claimed to have originated antecedent to such settlement of jurisdiction, shall, on the petition of either party to the congress of the united states, be finally determined, as near as may be, in the same manner as is before prescribed for deciding disputes respecting territorial jurisdiction between different states.

The united states, in congress assembled, shall also have the sole and exclusive right and power of regulating the alloy and value of coin struck by their own authority, or by that of the respective states — fixing the standard of weights and measures throughout the united states — regulating the trade and managing all affairs with the Indians, not members of any of the states; provided that the legislative right of any state, within its own limits, be not infringed or violated — establishing and regulating post-offices from one state to another, throughout all the united states, and exacting such postage on the papers passing through the same, as may be requisite to defray the expenses of the said office — appointing all officers of the land forces in the service of the united States, excepting regimental officers — appointing all the officers of the naval forces, and commissioning all officers whatever in the service of the united states; making rules for the government and regulation of the said land and naval forces, and directing their operations.

The united States, in congress assembled, shall have authority to appoint a committee, to sit in the recess of congress, to be denominated, "A Committee of the States," and to consist of one delegate from each State; and to appoint such other committees and civil officers as may be necessary for managing the general affairs of the united states under their direction — to appoint one of their number to preside; provided that no person be allowed to serve in the office of president more than one year in any term of three years; to ascertain the necessary sums of money to be raised for the service of the united states, and to appropriate and apply the same for defraying the public expenses; to borrow money or emit bills on the credit of the united states, transmitting every half year to the respective states an account of the sums of money so borrowed or emitted, — to build and equip a navy — to agree upon the number of land forces, and to make requisitions from each state for its quota, in proportion to the number of white inhabitants in such state, which requisition shall be binding; and thereupon the legislature of each state shall appoint the regimental officers, raise the men, and clothe, arm, and equip them, in a soldier-like manner, at the expense of the united states; and the officers and men so clothed, armed, and equipped, shall march to the place appointed, and within the time agreed on by the united states, in congress assembled; but if the united states, in congress assembled, shall, on consideration of circumstances, judge proper that any state should not raise men, or should raise a smaller number than its quota, and that any other state should raise a greater number of men than the quota thereof, such extra number shall be raised, officered, clothed, armed, and equipped in the same manner as the quota of such state, unless the legislature of such state shall judge that such extra number cannot be safely spared out of the same, in which case they shall raise, officer, clothe, arm, and equip, as many of such extra number as they judge can be safely spared. And the officers and men so clothed, armed, and equipped, shall march to the place appointed, and within the time agreed on by the united states in congress assembled.

The united states, in congress assembled, shall never engage in a war, nor grant letters of marque and reprisal in time of peace, nor enter into any treaties or alliances, nor coin money, nor regulate the value thereof nor ascertain the sums and expenses necessary for the defence and welfare of the united states, or any of them, nor emit bills, nor borrow money on the credit of the united states, nor appropriate money, nor agree upon the number of vessels of war to be built or purchased, or the number of land or sea forces to be raised, nor appoint a commander in chief of the army or navy, unless nine states assent to the same, nor shall a question on any other point, except for adjourning from day to day, be determined, unless by the votes of a majority of the united states in congress assembled.

The congress of the united states shall have power to adjourn to any time within the year, and to any place within the united states, so that no period of adjournment be for a longer duration than the space of six Months, and shall publish the Journal of their proceedings monthly, except such parts thereof relating to treaties, alliances, or military operations, as in their judgment require secrecy; and the yeas and nays of the delegates of each State, on any question, shall be entered on the Journal, when it is desired by any delegate; and the delegates of a State, or any of them, at his or their request, shall be furnished with a transcript of the said Journal, except such parts as are above excepted, to lay before the legislatures of the several states.

Article X. The committee of the states, or any nine of them, shall be authorized to execute, in the recess of congress, such of the powers of congress as the united states, in congress assembled, by the consent of nine states, shall, from time to time, think expedient to vest them with; provided that no power be delegated to the said committee, for the exercise of which, by the articles of confederation, the voice of nine states, in the congress of the united states assembled, is requisite.

Article XI. Canada acceding to this confederation, and joining in the measures of the united states, shall be admitted into, and entitled to all the advantages of this union: but no other colony shall be admitted into the same, unless such admission be agreed to by nine states.

Article XII. All bills of credit emitted, monies borrowed, and debts contracted by or under the authority of congress, before the assembling of the united states, in pursuance of the present confederation, shall be deemed and considered as a charge against the united States, for payment and satisfaction whereof the said united states and the public faith are hereby solemnly pledged.

Article XIII. Every State shall abide by the determinations of the united states, in congress assembled, on all questions which by this confederation are submitted to them. And the Articles of this confederation shall be inviolably observed by every state, and the union shall be perpetual; nor shall any alteration at any time hereafter be made in any of them, unless such alteration be agreed to in a congress of the united states, and be afterwards con-firmed by the legislatures of every state.

And Whereas it hath pleased the Great Governor of the World to incline the hearts of the legislatures we respectively represent in congress, to approve of, and to authorize us to ratify the said articles of confederation and perpetual union, Know Ye, that we, the undersigned delegates, by virtue of the power and authority to us given for that purpose, do, by these presents, in the name and in behalf of our respective constituents, fully and entirely ratify and confirm each and every of the said articles of confederation and perpetual union, and all and singular the matters and things therein contained. And we do further solemnly plight and engage the faith of our respective constituents, that they shall abide by the determinations of the united states in congress assembled, on all questions, which by the said confederation are submitted to them. And that the articles thereof shall be inviolably observed by the states we respectively represent, and that the union shall be perpetual. In Witness whereof, we have hereunto set our hands, in Congress. Done at Philadelphia, in the State of Pennsylvania, the ninth Day of July, in the Year of our Lord one Thousand seven Hundred and Seventy eight, and in the third year of the Independence of America.

The Constitution of the United States

We the People of the United States, in Order to form a more perfect Union, establish Justice, insure domestic Tranquility, provide for the common defence, promote the general Welfare, and secure the Blessings of Liberty to ourselves and our Posterity, do ordain and establish this Constitution for the United States of America.

Article. I.

Section. 1. All legislative Powers herein granted shall be vested in a Congress of the United States, which shall consist of a Senate and House of Representatives.

Section. 2. The House of Representatives shall be composed of Members chosen every second Year by the People of the several States, and the Electors in each State shall have the Qualifications requisite for Electors of the most numerous Branch of the State Legislature.

No Person shall be a Representative who shall not have attained to the Age of twenty five Years, and been seven Years a Citizen of the United States, and who shall not, when elected, be an Inhabitant of that State in which he shall be chosen.

Representatives and direct Taxes shall be apportioned among the several States which may be included within this Union, according to their respective Numbers, which shall be determined by adding to the whole Number of free Persons, including those bound to Service for a Term of Years, and excluding Indians not taxed, three fifths of all other Persons [Modified by Amendment XIV]. The actual Enumeration shall be made within three Years after the first Meeting of the Congress of the United States, and within every subsequent Term of ten Years, in such Manner as they shall by Law direct. The Number of Representatives shall not exceed one for every thirty Thousand, but each State shall have at Least one Representative; and until such enumeration shall be made, the State of New Hampshire shall be entitled to chuse three, Massachusetts eight, Rhode-Island and Providence Plantations one, Connecticut five, New-York six, New Jersey four, Pennsylvania eight, Delaware one, Maryland six, Virginia ten, North Carolina five, South Carolina five, and Georgia three.

When vacancies happen in the Representation from any State, the Executive Authority thereof shall issue Writs of Election to fill such Vacancies.

The House of Representatives shall chuse their Speaker and other Officers; and shall have the sole Power of Impeachment.

Section. 3. The Senate of the United States shall be composed of two Senators from each State, chosen by the Legislature thereof [Modified by Amendment XVII], for six Years; and each Senator shall have one Vote.

Immediately after they shall be assembled in Consequence of the first Election, they shall be divided as equally as may be into three Classes. The Seats of the Senators of the first Class shall be vacated at the Expiration of the second Year, of the second Class at the Expiration of the fourth Year, and of the third Class at the Expiration of the sixth Year, so that one third may be chosen every second Year; and if Vacancies happen by Resignation, or otherwise, during the Recess of the Legislature of any State, the Executive thereof may make temporary Appointments until the next Meeting of the Legislature, which shall then fill such Vacancies [Modified by Amendment XVII].

No Person shall be a Senator who shall not have attained to the Age of thirty Years, and been nine Years a Citizen of the United States, and who shall not, when elected, be an Inhabitant of that State for which he shall be chosen.

The Vice President of the United States shall be President of the Senate, but shall have no Vote, unless they be equally divided.

The Senate shall chuse their other Officers, and also a President pro tempore, in the Absence of the Vice President, or when he shall exercise the Office of President of the United States.

The Senate shall have the sole Power to try all Impeachments. When sitting for that Purpose, they shall be on Oath or Affirmation. When the President of the United States is tried, the Chief Justice shall preside: And no Person shall be convicted without the Concurrence of two thirds of the Members present.

Judgment in Cases of Impeachment shall not extend further than to removal from Office, and disqualification to hold and enjoy any Office of honor, Trust or Profit under the United States: but the Party convicted shall nevertheless be liable and subject to Indictment, Trial, Judgment and Punishment, according to Law.

Section. 4. The Times, Places and Manner of holding Elections for Senators and Representatives, shall be prescribed in each State by the Legislature thereof; but the Congress may at any time by Law make or alter such Regulations, except as to the Places of chusing Senators.

The Congress shall assemble at least once in every Year, and such Meeting shall be on the first Monday in December [Modified by Amendment XX], unless they shall by Law appoint a different Day.

Section. 5. Each House shall be the Judge of the Elections, Returns and Qualifications of its own Members, and a Majority of each shall constitute a Quorum to do Business; but a smaller Number may adjourn from day to day, and may be authorized to compel the Attendance of absent Members, in such Manner, and under such Penalties as each House may provide.

Each House may determine the Rules of its Proceedings, punish its Members for disorderly Behaviour, and, with the Concurrence of two thirds, expel a Member.

Each House shall keep a Journal of its Proceedings, and from time to time publish the same, excepting such Parts as may in their Judgment require Secrecy; and the Yeas and Nays of the Members of either House on any question shall, at the Desire of one fifth of those Present, be entered on the Journal.

Neither House, during the Session of Congress, shall, without the Consent of the other, adjourn for more than three days, nor to any other Place than that in which the two Houses shall be sitting.

Section. 6. The Senators and Representatives shall receive a Compensation for their Services, to be ascertained by Law, and paid out of the Treasury of the United States. They shall in all Cases, except Treason, Felony and Breach of the Peace, be privileged from Arrest during their Attendance at the Session of their respective Houses, and in going to and returning from the same; and for any Speech or Debate in either House, they shall not be questioned in any other Place.

No Senator or Representative shall, during the Time for which he was elected, be appointed to any civil Office under the Authority of the United States, which shall have been created, or the Emoluments whereof shall have been encreased during such time; and no Person holding any Office under the United States, shall be a Member of either House during his Continuance in Office.

Section. 7. All Bills for raising Revenue shall originate in the House of Representatives; but the Senate may propose or concur with Amendments as on other Bills.

Every Bill which shall have passed the House of Representatives and the Senate, shall, before it become a Law, be presented to the President of the United States;[2] If he approve he shall sign it, but if not he shall return it, with his Objections to that House in which it shall have originated, who shall enter the Objections at large on their Journal, and proceed to reconsider it. If after such Reconsideration two thirds of that House shall agree to pass the Bill, it shall be sent, together with the Objections, to the other House, by which it shall likewise be reconsidered, and if approved by two thirds of that House, it shall become a Law. But in all such Cases the Votes of both Houses shall be determined by yeas and Nays, and the Names of the Persons voting for and against the Bill shall be entered on the Journal of each House respectively. If any Bill shall not be returned by the President within ten Days (Sundays excepted) after it shall have been presented to him, the Same shall be a Law, in like Manner as if he had signed it, unless the Congress by their Adjournment prevent its Return, in which Case it shall not be a Law.

Every Order, Resolution, or Vote to which the Concurrence of the Senate and House of Representatives may be necessary (except on a question of Adjournment) shall be presented to the President of the United States; and before the Same shall take Effect, shall be approved by him, or being disapproved by him, shall be repassed by two thirds of the Senate and House of Representatives, according to the Rules and Limitations prescribed in the Case of a Bill.

Section. 8. The Congress shall have Power To lay and collect Taxes, Duties, Imposts and Excises, to pay the Debts and provide for the common Defence and general Welfare of the United States; but all Duties, Imposts and Excises shall be uniform throughout the United States;

To borrow Money on the credit of the United States;

To regulate Commerce with foreign Nations, and among the several States, and with the Indian Tribes;

To establish an uniform Rule of Naturalization, and uniform Laws on the subject of Bankruptcies throughout the United States;

To coin Money, regulate the Value thereof, and of foreign Coin, and fix the Standard of Weights and Measures;

To provide for the Punishment of counterfeiting the Securities and current Coin of the United States;

To establish Post Offices and post Roads;

To promote the Progress of Science and useful Arts, by securing for limited Times to Authors and Inventors the exclusive Right to their respective Writings and Discoveries;

To constitute Tribunals inferior to the supreme Court;

To define and punish Piracies and Felonies committed on the high Seas, and Offences against the Law of Nations;

To declare War, grant Letters of Marque and Reprisal, and make Rules concerning Captures on Land and Water;

To raise and support Armies, but no Appropriation of Money to that Use shall be for a longer Term than two Years;

To provide and maintain a Navy;

To make Rules for the Government and Regulation of the land and naval Forces;

To provide for calling forth the Militia to execute the Laws of the Union, suppress Insurrections and repel Invasions;

To provide for organizing, arming, and disciplining, the Militia, and for governing such Part of them as may be employed in the Service of the United States, reserving to the States respectively, the Appointment of the Officers, and the Authority of training the Militia according to the discipline prescribed by Congress;

To exercise exclusive Legislation in all Cases whatsoever, over such District (not exceeding ten Miles square) as may, by Cession of particular States, and the Acceptance of Congress, become the Seat of the Government of the United States, and to exercise like Authority over all Places purchased by the Consent of the Legislature of the State in which the Same shall be, for the Erection of Forts, Magazines, Arsenals, dock-Yards, and other needful Buildings; — And

To make all Laws which shall be necessary and proper for carrying into Execution the foregoing Powers, and all other Powers vested by this Constitution in the Government of the United States, or in any Department or Officer thereof.

Section. 9. The Migration or Importation of such Persons as any of the States now existing shall think proper to admit, shall not be prohibited by the Congress prior to the Year one thousand eight hundred and eight, but a Tax or duty may be imposed on such Importation, not exceeding ten dollars for each Person.

The Privilege of the Writ of Habeas Corpus shall not be suspended, unless when in Cases of Rebellion or Invasion the public Safety may require it.

No Bill of Attainder or ex post facto Law shall be passed.

No Capitation, or other direct, Tax shall be laid, unless in Proportion to the Census or Enumeration herein before directed to be taken.

No Tax or Duty shall be laid on Articles exported from any State.

No Preference shall be given by any Regulation of Commerce or Revenue to the Ports of one State over those of another; nor shall Vessels bound to, or from, one State, be obliged to enter, clear, or pay Duties in another.

No Money shall be drawn from the Treasury, but in Consequence of Appropriations made by Law; and a regular Statement and Account of the Receipts and Expenditures of all public Money shall be published from time to time.

No Title of Nobility shall be granted by the United States: And no Person holding any Office of Profit or Trust under them, shall, without the Consent of the Congress, accept of any present, Emolument, Office, or Title, of any kind whatever, from any King, Prince, or foreign State.

Section. 10. No State shall enter into any Treaty, Alliance, or Confederation; grant Letters of Marque and Reprisal; coin Money; emit Bills of Credit; make any Thing but gold and silver Coin a Tender in Payment of Debts; pass any Bill of Attainder, ex post facto Law, or Law impairing the Obligation of Contracts, or grant any Title of Nobility.

No State shall, without the Consent of the Congress, lay any Imposts or Duties on Imports or Exports, except what may be absolutely necessary for executing it's inspection Laws; and the net Produce of all Duties and Imposts, laid by any State on Imports or Exports, shall be for the Use of the Treasury of the United States; and all such Laws shall be subject to the Revision and Controul of the Congress.

No State shall, without the Consent of Congress, lay any Duty of Tonnage, keep Troops, or Ships of War in time of Peace, enter into any Agreement or Compact with another State, or with a foreign Power, or engage in War, unless actually invaded, or in such imminent Danger as will not admit of delay.

Article. II.

Section. 1. The executive Power shall be vested in a President of the United States of America. He shall hold his Office during the Term of four Years, and, together with the Vice President, chosen for the same Term, be elected, as follows:

Each State shall appoint, in such Manner as the Legislature thereof may direct, a Number of Electors, equal to the whole Number of Senators and Representatives to which the State may be entitled in the Congress: but no Senator or Representative, or Person holding an Office of Trust or Profit under the United States, shall be appointed an Elector.

The Electors shall meet in their respective States, and vote by Ballot for two Persons, of whom one at least shall not be an Inhabitant of the same State with themselves. And they shall make a List of all the Persons voted for, and of the Number of Votes for each; which List they shall sign and certify, and transmit sealed to the Seat of the Government of the United States, directed to the President of the Senate. The President of the Senate shall, in the Presence of the Senate and House of Representatives, open all the Certificates, and the Votes shall then be counted. The Person having the greatest Number of Votes shall be the President, if such Number be a Majority of the whole Number of Electors appointed; and if there be more than one who have such Majority, and have an equal Number of Votes, then the House of Representatives shall immediately chuse by Ballot one of them for President; and if no Person have a Majority, then from the five highest on the List the said House shall in like Manner chuse the President. But in chusing the President, the Votes shall be taken by States, the Representation from each State having one Vote;

a quorum for this Purpose shall consist of a Member or Members from two thirds of the States, and a Majority of all the States shall be necessary to a Choice. In every Case, after the Choice of the President, the Person having the greatest Number of Votes of the Electors shall be the Vice President. But if there should remain two or more who have equal Votes, the Senate shall chuse from them by Ballot the Vice President [Modified by Amendment XII].

The Congress may determine the Time of chusing the Electors, and the Day on which they shall give their Votes; which Day shall be the same throughout the United States.

No Person except a natural born Citizen, or a Citizen of the United States, at the time of the Adoption of this Constitution, shall be eligible to the Office of President; neither shall any Person be eligible to that Office who shall not have attained to the Age of thirty five Years, and been fourteen Years a Resident within the United States.

In Case of the Removal of the President from Office, or of his Death, Resignation, or Inability to discharge the Powers and Duties of the said Office, the Same shall devolve on the Vice President, and the Congress may by Law provide for the Case of Removal, Death, Resignation or Inability, both of the President and Vice President, declaring what Officer shall then act as President, and such Officer shall act accordingly, until the Disability be removed, or a President shall be elected [Modified by Amendment XXV].

The President shall, at stated Times, receive for his Services, a Compensation, which shall neither be increased nor diminished during the Period for which he shall have been elected, and he shall not receive within that Period any other Emolument from the United States, or any of them.

Before he enter on the Execution of his Office, he shall take the following Oath or Affirmation: — "I do solemnly swear (or affirm) that I will faithfully execute the Office of President of the United States, and will to the best of my Ability, preserve, protect and defend the Constitution of the United States."

Section. 2. The President shall be Commander in Chief of the Army and Navy of the United States, and of the Militia of the several States, when called into the actual Service of the United States; he may require the Opinion, in writing, of the principal Officer in each of the executive Departments, upon any Subject relating to the

Duties of their respective Offices, and he shall have Power to grant Reprieves and Pardons for Offences against the United States, except in Cases of Impeachment.

He shall have Power, by and with the Advice and Consent of the Senate, to make Treaties, provided two thirds of the Senators present concur; and he shall nominate, and by and with the Advice and Consent of the Senate, shall appoint Ambassadors, other public Ministers and Consuls, Judges of the supreme Court, and all other Officers of the United States, whose Appointments are not herein otherwise provided for, and which shall be established by Law: but the Congress may by Law vest the Appointment of such inferior Officers, as they think proper, in the President alone, in the Courts of Law, or in the Heads of Departments.

The President shall have Power to fill up all Vacancies that may happen during the Recess of the Senate, by granting Commissions which shall expire at the End of their next Session.

Section. 3. He shall from time to time give to the Congress Information of the State of the Union, and recommend to their Consideration such Measures as he shall judge necessary and expedient; he may, on extraordinary Occasions, convene both Houses, or either of them, and in Case of Disagreement between them, with Respect to the Time of Adjournment, he may adjourn them to such Time as he shall think proper; he shall receive Ambassadors and other public Ministers; he shall take Care that the Laws be faithfully executed, and shall Commission all the Officers of the United States.

Section. 4. The President, Vice President and all civil Officers of the United States, shall be removed from Office on Impeachment for, and Conviction of, Treason, Bribery, or other high Crimes and Misdemeanors.

Article. III.

Section. 1. The judicial Power of the United States shall be vested in one supreme Court, and in such inferior Courts as the Congress may from time to time ordain and establish. The Judges, both of the supreme and inferior Courts, shall hold their Offices during good Behaviour, and shall, at stated Times, receive for their Services a Compensation, which shall not be diminished during their Continuance

in Office.

Section. 2. The judicial Power shall extend to all Cases, in Law and Equity, arising under this Constitution, the Laws of the United States, and Treaties made, or which shall be made, under their Authority; — to all Cases affecting Ambassadors, other public Ministers and Consuls; — to all Cases of admiralty and maritime Jurisdiction; — to Controversies to which the United States shall be a Party; — to Controversies between two or more States; — between a State and Citizens of another State [Modified by Amendment XI]; — between Citizens of different States; — between Citizens of the same State claiming Lands under Grants of different States, and between a State, or the Citizens thereof, and foreign States, Citizens or Subjects.

In all Cases affecting Ambassadors, other public Ministers and Consuls, and those in which a State shall be Party, the supreme Court shall have original Jurisdiction. In all the other Cases before mentioned, the supreme Court shall have appellate Jurisdiction, both as to Law and Fact, with such Exceptions, and under such Regulations as the Congress shall make.

The Trial of all Crimes, except in Cases of Impeachment, shall be by Jury; and such Trial shall be held in the State where the said Crimes shall have been committed; but when not committed within any State, the Trial shall be at such Place or Places as the Congress may by Law have directed.

Section. 3. Treason against the United States shall consist only in levying War against them, or in adhering to their Enemies, giving them Aid and Comfort. No Person shall be convicted of Treason unless on the Testimony of two Witnesses to the same overt Act, or on Confession in open Court.

The Congress shall have Power to declare the Punishment of Treason, but no Attainder of Treason shall work Corruption of Blood, or Forfeiture except during the Life of the Person attainted.

Article. IV.

Section. 1. Full Faith and Credit shall be given in each State to the public Acts, Records, and judicial Proceedings of every other State. And the Congress may by general Laws prescribe the Manner in which such Acts, Records and Proceedings shall be proved, and the

Effect thereof.

Section. 2. The Citizens of each State shall be entitled to all Privileges and Immunities of Citizens in the several States.

A Person charged in any State with Treason, Felony, or other Crime, who shall flee from Justice, and be found in another State, shall on Demand of the executive Authority of the State from which he fled, be delivered up, to be removed to the State having Jurisdiction of the Crime.

No Person held to Service or Labour in one State, under the Laws thereof, escaping into another, shall, in Consequence of any Law or Regulation therein, be discharged from such Service or Labour, but shall be delivered up on Claim of the Party to whom such Service or Labour may be due [Modified by Amendment XIII].

Section. 3. New States may be admitted by the Congress into this Union; but no new State shall be formed or erected within the Jurisdiction of any other State; nor any State be formed by the Junction of two or more States, or Parts of States, without the Consent of the Legislatures of the States concerned as well as of the Congress.

The Congress shall have Power to dispose of and make all needful Rules and Regulations respecting the Territory or other Property belonging to the United States; and nothing in this Constitution shall be so construed as to Prejudice any Claims of the United States, or of any particular State.

Section. 4. The United States shall guarantee to every State in this Union a Republican Form of Government, and shall protect each of them against Invasion; and on Application of the Legislature, or of the Executive (when the Legislature cannot be convened), against domestic Violence.

Article. V.

The Congress, whenever two thirds of both Houses shall deem it necessary, shall propose Amendments to this Constitution, or, on the Application of the Legislatures of two thirds of the several States, shall call a Convention for proposing Amendments, which, in either Case, shall be valid to all Intents and Purposes, as Part of this Constitution, when ratified by the Legislatures of three fourths of the several States, or by Conventions in three fourths thereof, as the one or the other Mode of Ratification may be proposed by the Congress; Provided that no Amendment which may be made prior to the Year One thousand eight hundred and eight shall in any Manner affect the first and fourth Clauses in the Ninth Section of the first Article; and that no State, without its Consent, shall be deprived of its equal Suffrage in the Senate.

Article. VI.

All Debts contracted and Engagements entered into, before the Adoption of this Constitution, shall be as valid against the United States under this Constitution, as under the Confederation.

This Constitution, and the Laws of the United States which shall be made in Pursuance thereof; and all Treaties made, or which shall be made, under the Authority of the United States, shall be the supreme Law of the Land; and the Judges in every State shall be bound thereby, any Thing in the Constitution or Laws of any State to the Contrary notwithstanding.

The Senators and Representatives before mentioned, and the Members of the several State Legislatures, and all executive and judicial Officers, both of the United States and of the several States, shall be bound by Oath or Affirmation, to support this Constitution; but no religious Test shall ever be required as a Qualification to any Office or public Trust under the United States.

Article. VII.

The Ratification of the Conventions of nine States, shall be sufficient for the Establishment of this Constitution between the States so ratifying the Same.

The Word, "the," being interlined between the seventh and eighth Lines of the first Page, The Word "Thirty" being partly written on an Erazure in the fifteenth Line of the first Page, The Words "is tried" being interlined between the thirty second and thirty third Lines of the first Page and the Word "the" being interlined between the forty third and forty fourth Lines of the second Page.

Attest William Jackson Secretary

done in Convention by the Unanimous Consent of the States present the Seventeenth Day of September in the Year of our Lord one thousand seven hundred and Eighty seven and of the Independence of the United States of America the Twelfth In witness whereof We have hereunto subscribed our Names,

Go. Washington
Presidt. and deputy from Virginia

New Hampshire
John Langdon
Nicholas Gilman

Massachusetts
Nathaniel Gorham
Rufus King

Connecticut
Wm. Saml. Johnson
Roger Sherman

New York
Alexander Hamilton

New Jersey
Wil: Livingston
David Brearley.
Wm. Paterson.
Jona: Dayton

Pennsylvania
B Franklin
Thomas Mifflin
Robt Morris
Geo. Clymer
Thos. Fitz Simons
Jared Ingersoll
James Wilson
Gouv Morris

Delaware
Geo: Read
Gunning Bedford Jun
John Dickinson
Richard Bassett
Jaco: Broom

Maryland
James Mchenry
Dan of St Thos. Jenifer
Danl Carroll

Virginia
John Blair
James Madison Jr

North Carolina
Wm. Blount
Richd. Dobbs Spaight
Hu Williamson

South Carolina
J. Rutledge
Charles Cotesworth Pinckney
Charles Pinckney
Pierce Butler

Georgia
William Few
Abr Baldwin

The Bill of Rights

The Preamble to The Bill of Rights

Congress of the United States begun and held at the City of New-York, on Wednesday the fourth of March, one thousand seven hundred and eighty nine.

THE Conventions of a number of the States, having at the time of their adopting the Constitution, expressed a desire, in order to prevent misconstruction or abuse of its powers, that further declaratory and restrictive clauses should be added: And as extending the ground of public confidence in the Government, will best ensure the beneficent ends of its institution.

RESOLVED by the Senate and House of Representatives of the United States of America, in Congress assembled, two thirds of both Houses concurring, that the following Articles be proposed to the Legislatures of the several States, as amendments to the Constitution of the United States, all, or any of which Articles, when ratified by three fourths of the said Legislatures, to be valid to all intents and purposes, as part of the said Constitution; viz.

ARTICLES in addition to, and Amendment of the Constitution of the United States of America, proposed by Congress, and ratified by the Legislatures of the several States, pursuant to the fifth Article of the original Constitution.

Amendment I

Congress shall make no law respecting an establishment of religion, or prohibiting the free exercise thereof; or abridging the freedom of speech, or of the press; or the right of the people peaceably to assemble, and to petition the Government for a redress of grievances.

Amendment II

A well regulated Militia, being necessary to the security of a free

State, the right of the people to keep and bear Arms, shall not be infringed.

Amendment III

No Soldier shall, in time of peace be quartered in any house, without the consent of the Owner, nor in time of war, but in a manner to be prescribed by law.

Amendment IV

The right of the people to be secure in their persons, houses, papers, and effects, against unreasonable searches and seizures, shall not be violated, and no Warrants shall issue, but upon probable cause, supported by Oath or affirmation, and particularly describing the place to be searched, and the persons or things to be seized.

Amendment V

No person shall be held to answer for a capital, or otherwise infamous crime, unless on a presentment or indictment of a Grand Jury, except in cases arising in the land or naval forces, or in the Militia, when in actual service in time of War or public danger; nor shall any person be subject for the same offence to be twice put in jeopardy of life or limb; nor shall be compelled in any criminal case to be a witness against himself, nor be deprived of life, liberty, or property, without due process of law; nor shall private property be taken for public use, without just compensation.

Amendment VI

In all criminal prosecutions, the accused shall enjoy the right to a speedy and public trial, by an impartial jury of the State and district wherein the crime shall have been committed, which district shall have been previously ascertained by law, and to be informed of the nature and cause of the accusation; to be confronted with the witnesses against him; to have compulsory process for obtaining witnesses in his favor, and to have the Assistance of Counsel for his defence.

Amendment VII

In Suits at common law, where the value in controversy shall exceed twenty dollars, the right of trial by jury shall be preserved, and no fact tried by a jury, shall be otherwise re-examined in any Court of the United States, than according to the rules of the common law.

Amendment VIII

Excessive bail shall not be required, nor excessive fines imposed, nor cruel and unusual punishments inflicted.

Amendment IX

The enumeration in the Constitution, of certain rights, shall not be construed to deny or disparage others retained by the people.

Amendment X

The powers not delegated to the United States by the Constitution, nor prohibited by it to the States, are reserved to the States respectively, or to the people.

Amendments 11–27 to the Constitution

Amendment XI

The Judicial power of the United States shall not be construed to extend to any suit in law or equity, commenced or prosecuted against one of the United States by Citizens of another State, or by Citizens or Subjects of any Foreign State.

Passed by Congress March 4, 1794. Ratified February 7, 1795.
Note: Article III, section 2, of the Constitution was modified by amendment 11.

Amendment XII

The Electors shall meet in their respective states and vote by ballot for President and Vice-President, one of whom, at least, shall not be an inhabitant of the same state with themselves; they shall name in their ballots the person voted for as President, and in distinct ballots the person voted for as Vice-President, and they shall make distinct lists of all persons voted for as President, and of all persons voted for as Vice-President, and of the number of votes for each, which lists they shall sign and certify, and transmit sealed to the seat of the government of the United States, directed to the President of the Senate; — the President of the Senate shall, in the presence of the Senate and House of Representatives, open all the certificates and the votes shall then be counted; — The person having the greatest number of votes for President, shall be the President, if such number be a majority of the whole number of Electors appointed; and if no person have such majority, then from the persons having the highest numbers not exceeding three on the list of those voted for as President, the House of Representatives shall choose immediately, by ballot, the President. But in choosing the President, the votes shall be taken by states, the representation from each state having one vote; a quorum for this purpose shall consist of a member or members from two-thirds

of the states, and a majority of all the states shall be necessary to a choice. [And if the House of Representatives shall not choose a President whenever the right of choice shall devolve upon them, before the fourth day of March next following, then the Vice-President shall act as President, as in case of the death or other constitutional disability of the President. —]* The person having the greatest number of votes as Vice-President, shall be the Vice-President, if such number be a majority of the whole number of Electors appointed, and if no person have a majority, then from the two highest numbers on the list, the Senate shall choose the Vice-President; a quorum for the purpose shall consist of two-thirds of the whole number of Senators, and a majority of the whole number shall be necessary to a choice. But no person constitutionally ineligible to the office of President shall be eligible to that of Vice-President of the United States.
**Superseded by section 3 of the 20th amendment.*

Passed by Congress December 9, 1803. Ratified June 15, 1804.
Note: A portion of Article II, section 1 of the Constitution was superseded by the 12th amendment.

Amendment XIII

Section 1.

Neither slavery nor involuntary servitude, except as a punishment for crime whereof the party shall have been duly convicted, shall exist within the United States, or any place subject to their jurisdiction.

Section 2.

Congress shall have power to enforce this article by appropriate legislation.

Passed by Congress January 31, 1865. Ratified December 6, 1865.
Note: A portion of Article IV, section 2, of the Constitution was superseded by the 13th amendment.

Amendment XIV

Section 1.

All persons born or naturalized in the United States, and subject to the jurisdiction thereof, are citizens of the United States and of the State wherein they reside. No State shall make or enforce any law which shall abridge the privileges or immunities of citizens of the United States; nor shall any State deprive any person of life, liberty, or property, without due process of law; nor deny to any person within its jurisdiction the equal protection of the laws.

Section 2.

Representatives shall be apportioned among the several States according to their respective numbers, counting the whole number of persons in each State, excluding Indians not taxed. But when the right to vote at any election for the choice of electors for President and Vice-President of the United States, Representatives in Congress, the Executive and Judicial officers of a State, or the members of the Legislature thereof, is denied to any of the male inhabitants of such State, being twenty-one years of age,* and citizens of the United States, or in any way abridged, except for participation in rebellion, or other crime, the basis of representation therein shall be reduced in the proportion which the number of such male citizens shall bear to the whole number of male citizens twenty-one years of age in such State.

Section 3.

No person shall be a Senator or Representative in Congress, or elector of President and Vice-President, or hold any office, civil or military, under the United States, or under any State, who, having previously taken an oath, as a member of Congress, or as an officer of the United States, or as a member of any State legislature, or as an executive or judicial officer of any State, to support the Constitution of the United States, shall have engaged in insurrection or rebellion against the same, or given aid or comfort to the enemies thereof. But Congress may by a vote of two-thirds of each House, remove such disability.

Section 4.

The validity of the public debt of the United States, authorized by law, including debts incurred for payment of pensions and bounties for services in suppressing insurrection or rebellion, shall not be questioned. But neither the United States nor any State shall assume or pay any debt or obligation incurred in aid of insurrection or rebellion against the United States, or any claim for the loss or emancipation of any slave; but all such debts, obligations and claims shall be held illegal and void.

Section 5.

The Congress shall have the power to enforce, by appropriate legislation, the provisions of this article.

**Changed by section 1 of the 26th amendment.*

Passed by Congress June 13, 1866. Ratified July 9, 1868.

Note: Article I, section 2, of the Constitution was modified by section 2 of the 14th amendment.

Amendment XV

Section 1.

The right of citizens of the United States to vote shall not be denied or abridged by the United States or by any State on account of race, color, or previous condition of servitude —

Section 2.

The Congress shall have the power to enforce this article by appropriate legislation.

Passed by Congress February 26, 1869. Ratified February 3, 1870.

Amendment XVI

The Congress shall have power to lay and collect taxes on incomes, from whatever source derived, without apportionment among the several States, and without regard to any census or enumeration.

Passed by Congress July 2, 1909. Ratified February 3, 1913.

Note: Article I, section 9, of the Constitution was modified by amendment 16.

Amendment XVII

The Senate of the United States shall be composed of two Senators from each State, elected by the people thereof, for six years; and each Senator shall have one vote. The electors in each State shall have the qualifications requisite for electors of the most numerous branch of the State legislatures.

When vacancies happen in the representation of any State in the Senate, the executive authority of such State shall issue writs of election to fill such vacancies: Provided, That the legislature of any State may empower the executive thereof to make temporary appointments until the people fill the vacancies by election as the legislature may direct.

This amendment shall not be so construed as to affect the election or term of any Senator chosen before it becomes valid as part of the Constitution.

Passed by Congress May 13, 1912. Ratified April 8, 1913.
Note: Article I, section 3, of the Constitution was modified by the 17th amendment.

Amendment XVIII

Section 1.

After one year from the ratification of this article the manufacture, sale, or transportation of intoxicating liquors within, the importation thereof into, or the exportation thereof from the United States and all territory subject to the jurisdiction thereof for beverage purposes is hereby prohibited.

Section 2.

The Congress and the several States shall have concurrent power to enforce this article by appropriate legislation.

Section 3.

This article shall be inoperative unless it shall have been ratified as an amendment to the Constitution by the legislatures of the several States, as provided in the Constitution, within seven years from the date of the submission hereof to the States by the Congress.

Passed by Congress December 18, 1917. Ratified January 16, 1919. Repealed by amendment 21.

Amendment XIX

The right of citizens of the United States to vote shall not be denied or abridged by the United States or by any State on account of sex.

Congress shall have power to enforce this article by appropriate legislation.

Passed by Congress June 4, 1919. Ratified August 18, 1920.

Amendment XX

Section 1.

The terms of the President and the Vice President shall end at noon on the 20th day of January, and the terms of Senators and Representatives at noon on the 3d day of January, of the years in which such terms would have ended if this article had not been ratified; and the terms of their successors shall then begin.

Section 2.

The Congress shall assemble at least once in every year, and such meeting shall begin at noon on the 3d day of January, unless they shall by law appoint a different day.

Section 3.

If, at the time fixed for the beginning of the term of the President, the President elect shall have died, the Vice President elect shall become President. If a President shall not have been chosen before the time fixed for the beginning of his term, or if the President elect shall have failed to qualify, then the Vice President elect shall act as President until a President shall have qualified; and the Congress may by law provide for the case wherein neither a President elect nor a Vice President shall have qualified, declaring who shall then act as President, or the manner in which one who is to act shall be selected, and such person shall act accordingly until a President or Vice President shall have qualified.

Section 4.

The Congress may by law provide for the case of the death of any of the persons from whom the House of Representatives may choose a President whenever the right of choice shall have devolved upon them, and for the case of the death of any of the persons from whom the Senate may choose a Vice President whenever the right of choice shall have devolved upon them.

Section 5.

Sections 1 and 2 shall take effect on the 15th day of October following the ratification of this article.

Section 6.

This article shall be inoperative unless it shall have been ratified as an amendment to the Constitution by the legislatures of three-fourths of the several States within seven years from the date of its submission.

Passed by Congress March 2, 1932. Ratified January 23, 1933.

Note: Article I, section 4, of the Constitution was modified by section 2 of this amendment. In addition, a portion of the 12th amendment was superseded by section 3.

Amendment XXI

Section 1.

The eighteenth article of amendment to the Constitution of the United States is hereby repealed.

Section 2.

The transportation or importation into any State, Territory, or Possession of the United States for delivery or use therein of intoxicating liquors, in violation of the laws thereof, is hereby prohibited.

Section 3.

This article shall be inoperative unless it shall have been ratified as an amendment to the Constitution by conventions in the several States, as provided in the Constitution, within seven years from the date of the submission hereof to the States by the Congress.

Passed by Congress February 20, 1933. Ratified December 5, 1933.

Amendment XXII

Section 1.

No person shall be elected to the office of the President more than twice, and no person who has held the office of President, or acted as President, for more than two years of a term to which some other person was elected President shall be elected to the office of President more than once. But this Article shall not apply to any person holding the office of President when this Article was proposed by Congress, and shall not prevent any person who may be holding the office of President, or acting as President, during the term within which this Article becomes operative from holding the office of President or acting as President during the remainder of such term.

Section 2.

This article shall be inoperative unless it shall have been ratified as an amendment to the Constitution by the legislatures of three-fourths of the several States within seven years from the date of its submission to the States by the Congress.

Passed by Congress March 21, 1947. Ratified February 27, 1951.

Amendment XXIII

Section 1.

The District constituting the seat of Government of the United States shall appoint in such manner as Congress may direct:

A number of electors of President and Vice President equal to the whole number of Senators and Representatives in Congress to which the District would be entitled if it were a State, but in no event more than the least populous State; they shall be in addition to those appointed by the States, but they shall be considered, for the purposes of the election of President and Vice President, to be electors appointed by a State; and they shall meet in the District and perform such duties as provided by the twelfth article of amendment.

Section 2.

The Congress shall have power to enforce this article by appropriate legislation.

Passed by Congress June 16, 1960. Ratified March 29, 1961.

Amendment XXIV

Section 1.

The right of citizens of the United States to vote in any primary or other election for President or Vice President, for electors for President or Vice President, or for Senator or Representative in Congress, shall not be denied or abridged by the United States or any State by reason of failure to pay poll tax or other tax.

Section 2.

The Congress shall have power to enforce this article by appropriate legislation.

Passed by Congress August 27, 1962. Ratified January 23, 1964.

Amendment XXV

Section 1.

In case of the removal of the President from office or of his death or resignation, the Vice President shall become President.

Section 2.

Whenever there is a vacancy in the office of the Vice President, the President shall nominate a Vice President who shall take office upon confirmation by a majority vote of both Houses of Congress.

Section 3.

Whenever the President transmits to the President pro tempore of the Senate and the Speaker of the House of Representatives his written declaration that he is unable to discharge the powers and duties of his office, and until he transmits to them a written declaration to the contrary, such powers and duties shall be discharged by the Vice President as Acting President.

Section 4.

Whenever the Vice President and a majority of either the principal officers of the executive departments or of such other body as Congress may by law provide, transmit to the President pro tempore of the Senate and the Speaker of the House of Representatives their written declaration that the President is unable to discharge the powers and duties of his office, the Vice President shall immediately assume the powers and duties of the office as Acting President.

Thereafter, when the President transmits to the President pro tempore of the Senate and the Speaker of the House of Representatives his written declaration that no inability exists, he shall resume the powers and duties of his office unless the Vice President and a majority of either the principal officers of the executive department or of such other body as Congress may by law provide, transmit within four days to the President pro tempore of the Senate and the Speaker of the House of Representatives their written declaration that the President is unable to discharge the powers and duties of his office. Thereupon Congress shall decide the issue, assembling within forty-eight hours for that purpose if not in session. If the Congress, within twenty-one days after receipt of the latter written declaration, or, if Congress is not in session, within twenty-one days after Congress is required to assemble, determines by two-thirds vote of both Houses that the President is unable to discharge the powers and duties of his office, the Vice President shall continue to discharge the same as Acting President; otherwise, the President shall resume the powers and duties of his office.

Passed by Congress July 6, 1965. Ratified February 10, 1967.

Note: Article II, section 1, of the Constitution was affected by the 25th amendment.

Amendment XXVI

Section 1.

The right of citizens of the United States, who are eighteen years of age or older, to vote shall not be denied or abridged by the United States or by any State on account of age.

Section 2.

The Congress shall have power to enforce this article by appropriate legislation.

Passed by Congress March 23, 1971. Ratified July 1, 1971.
Note: Amendment 14, section 2, of the Constitution was modified by section 1 of the 26th amendment.

Amendment XXVII

No law, varying the compensation for the services of the Senators and Representatives, shall take effect, until an election of representatives shall have intervened.

Originally proposed Sept. 25, 1789. Ratified May 7, 1992.

The Federalist Papers (A Selection)

Federalist No. 1

General Introduction

For the Independent Journal.

HAMILTON

To the People of the State of New York:

AFTER an unequivocal experience of the inefficacy of the subsisting federal government, you are called upon to deliberate on a new Constitution for the United States of America. The subject speaks its own importance; comprehending in its consequences nothing less than the existence of the UNION, the safety and welfare of the parts of which it is composed, the fate of an empire in many respects the most interesting in the world. It has been frequently remarked that it seems to have been reserved to the people of this country, by their conduct and example, to decide the important question, whether societies of men are really capable or not of establishing good government from reflection and choice, or whether they are forever destined to depend for their political constitutions on accident and force. If there be any truth in the remark, the crisis at which we are arrived may with propriety be regarded as the era in which that decision is to be made; and a wrong election of the part we shall act may, in this view, deserve to be considered as the general misfortune of mankind.

This idea will add the inducements of philanthropy to those of patriotism, to heighten the solicitude which all considerate and good men must feel for the event. Happy will it be if our choice should be directed by a judicious estimate of our true interests, unperplexed and unbiased by considerations not connected with the public good. But this is a thing more ardently to be wished than seriously to be expected. The plan offered to our deliberations affects too many particular interests, innovates upon too many local institutions, not to involve in its discussion a variety of objects foreign to its merits, and of views, passions and prejudices little favorable to the discovery of truth.

Among the most formidable of the obstacles which the new Constitution will have to encounter may readily be distinguished the obvious interest of a certain class of men in every State to resist all changes which may hazard a diminution of the power, emolument, and consequence of the offices they hold under the State establishments; and the perverted ambition of another class of men, who will either hope to aggrandize themselves by the confusions of their country, or will flatter themselves with fairer prospects of elevation from the subdivision of the empire into several partial confederacies than from its union under one government.

It is not, however, my design to dwell upon observations of this nature. I am well aware that it would be disingenuous to resolve indiscriminately the opposition of any set of men (merely because their situations might subject them to suspicion) into interested or ambitious views. Candor will oblige us to admit that even such men may be actuated by upright intentions; and it cannot be doubted that much of the opposition which has made its appearance, or may hereafter make its appearance, will spring from sources, blameless at least, if not respectable—the honest errors of minds led astray by preconceived jealousies and fears. So numerous indeed and so powerful are the causes which serve to give a false bias to the judgment, that we, upon many occasions, see wise and good men on the wrong as well as on the right side of questions of the first magnitude to society. This circumstance, if duly attended to, would furnish a lesson of moderation to those who are ever so much persuaded of their being in the right in any controversy. And a further reason for caution, in this respect, might be drawn from the reflection that we are not always sure that those who advocate the truth are influenced by purer principles than their antagonists. Ambition, avarice, personal animosity, party opposition, and many other motives not more laudable than these, are apt to operate as well upon those who support as those who oppose the right side of a question. Were there not even these inducements to moderation, nothing could be more ill-judged than that intolerant spirit which has, at all times, characterized political parties. For in politics, as in religion, it is equally absurd to aim at making proselytes by fire and sword. Heresies in either can rarely be cured by persecution.

And yet, however just these sentiments will be allowed to be, we have already sufficient indications that it will happen in this as in all former cases of great national discussion. A torrent of angry and malignant passions will be let loose. To judge from the conduct of the opposite parties, we shall be led to conclude that they will mutually hope to evince the justness of their opinions, and to increase the number of their converts by the loudness of their declamations and the bitterness of their invectives. An enlightened zeal for the energy and efficiency of government will be stigmatized as the offspring of a temper fond of despotic power and hostile to the principles of liberty. An over-scrupulous jealousy of danger to the rights of the people, which is more commonly the fault of the head than of the heart, will be represented as mere pretense and artifice, the stale bait for popularity at the expense of the public good. It will be forgotten, on the one hand, that jealousy is the usual concomitant of love, and that the noble enthusiasm of liberty is apt to be infected with a spirit of narrow and illiberal distrust. On the other hand, it will be equally forgotten that the vigor of government is essential to the security of liberty; that, in the contemplation of a sound and well-informed judgment, their interest can never be separated; and that a dangerous ambition more often lurks behind the specious mask of zeal for the rights of the people than under the forbidden appearance of zeal for the firmness and efficiency of government. History will teach us that the former has been found a much more certain road to the introduction of despotism than the latter, and that of those men who have overturned the liberties of republics, the greatest number have begun their career by paying an obsequious court to the people; commencing demagogues, and ending tyrants.

In the course of the preceding observations, I have had an eye, my fellow-citizens, to putting you upon your guard against all attempts, from whatever quarter, to influence your decision in a matter of the utmost moment to your welfare, by any impressions other than those which may result from the evidence of truth. You will, no doubt, at the same time, have collected from the general scope of them, that they proceed from a source not unfriendly to the new Constitution. Yes, my countrymen, I own to you that, after having given it an attentive consideration, I am clearly of opinion it is your interest to adopt it. I am convinced that this is the safest course for your liberty, your dignity, and your happiness. I affect not reserves which I do not feel. I will not amuse you with an appearance of deliberation when I have decided. I frankly acknowledge to you my convictions, and I will freely lay before you the reasons on which they are founded. The consciousness of good intentions disdains ambiguity. I shall not, however, multiply professions on this head. My motives must remain in the depository of my own breast. My arguments will be open to all, and may be judged of by all. They shall at least be offered in a spirit which will not disgrace the cause of truth.

I propose, in a series of papers, to discuss the following interesting particulars:

THE UTILITY OF THE UNION TO YOUR POLITICAL PROSPERITY

THE INSUFFICIENCY OF THE PRESENT CONFEDERATION TO PRESERVE THAT UNION THE NECESSITY OF A GOVERNMENT AT LEAST EQUALLY ENERGETIC WITH THE ONE PROPOSED, TO THE ATTAINMENT OF THIS OBJECT THE CONFORMITY OF THE PROPOSED CONSTITUTION TO THE TRUE PRINCIPLES OF REPUBLICAN GOVERNMENT ITS ANALOGY TO YOUR OWN STATE CONSTITUTION and lastly, THE ADDITIONAL SECURITY WHICH ITS ADOPTION WILL AFFORD TO THE PRESERVATION OF THAT SPECIES OF GOVERNMENT, TO LIBERTY, AND TO PROPERTY.

In the progress of this discussion I shall endeavor to give a satisfactory answer to all the objections which shall have made their appearance, that may seem to have any claim to your attention.

It may perhaps be thought superfluous to offer arguments to prove the utility of the UNION, a point, no doubt, deeply engraved on the hearts of the great body of the people in every State, and one, which it may be imagined, has no adversaries. But the fact is, that we already hear it whispered in the private circles of those who oppose the new Constitution, that the thirteen States are of too great extent for any general system, and that we must of necessity resort to separate confederacies of distinct portions of the whole. [1] This doctrine will, in all probability, be gradually propagated, till it has votaries enough to countenance an open avowal of it. For nothing can be more evident, to those who are able to take an enlarged view of the subject, than the alternative of an adoption of the new Constitution or a dismemberment of the Union. It will therefore be of use to begin by examining the advantages of that Union, the certain evils, and the probable dangers, to which every State will be exposed from its dissolution. This shall accordingly constitute the subject of my next address.

PUBLIUS.

[1] The same idea, tracing the arguments to their consequences, is held out in several of the late publications against the new Constitution.

Federalist No. 4

Concerning Dangers From Foreign Force and Influence

For the Independent Journal.

JAY

To the People of the State of New York:

MY LAST paper assigned several reasons why the safety of the people would be best secured by union against the danger it may be exposed to by JUST causes of war given to other nations; and those reasons show that such causes would not only be more rarely given, but would also be more easily accommodated, by a national government than either by the State governments or the proposed little confederacies.

But the safety of the people of America against dangers from FOREIGN force depends not only on their forbearing to give JUST causes of war to other nations, but also on their placing and continuing themselves in such a situation as not to INVITE hostility or insult; for it need not be observed that there are PRETENDED as well as just causes of war.

It is too true, however disgraceful it may be to human nature, that nations in general will make war whenever they have a prospect of getting anything by it; nay, absolute monarchs will often make war when their nations are to get nothing by it, but for the purposes and objects merely personal, such as thirst for military glory, revenge for personal affronts, ambition, or private compacts to aggrandize or support their particular families or partisans. These and a variety of other motives, which affect only the mind of the sovereign, often lead him to engage in wars not sanctified by justice or the voice and interests of his people. But, independent of these inducements to war, which are more prevalent in absolute monarchies, but which well deserve our attention, there are others which affect nations as often as kings; and some of them will on examination be found to grow out of our relative situation and circumstances.

With France and with Britain we are rivals in the fisheries, and can supply their markets cheaper than they can themselves, notwithstanding any efforts to prevent it by bounties on their own or duties on foreign fish.

With them and with most other European nations we are rivals in navigation and the carrying trade; and we shall deceive ourselves if we suppose that any of them will rejoice to see it flourish; for, as our carrying trade cannot increase without in some degree diminishing theirs, it is more their interest, and will be more their policy, to restrain than to promote it.

In the trade to China and India, we interfere with more than one nation, inasmuch as it enables us to partake in advantages which they had in a manner monopolized, and as we thereby supply ourselves with commodities which we used to purchase from them.

The extension of our own commerce in our own vessels cannot give pleasure to any nations who possess territories on or near this continent, because the cheapness and excellence of our productions, added to the circumstance of vicinity, and the enterprise and address of our merchants and navigators, will give us a greater share in the advantages which those territories afford, than consists with the wishes or policy of their respective sovereigns.

Spain thinks it convenient to shut the Mississippi against us on the one side, and Britain excludes us from the Saint Lawrence on the other; nor will either of them permit the other waters which are between them and us to become the means of mutual intercourse and traffic.

From these and such like considerations, which might, if consistent with prudence, be more amplified and detailed, it is easy to see that jealousies and uneasinesses may gradually slide into the minds and cabinets of other nations, and that we are not to expect that they should regard our advancement in union, in power and consequence by land and by sea, with an eye of indifference and composure.

The people of America are aware that inducements to war may arise out of these circumstances, as well as from others not so obvious at present, and that whenever such inducements may find fit time and opportunity for operation, pretenses to color and justify them will not be wanting. Wisely, therefore, do they consider union and a good national government as necessary to put and keep them in SUCH A SITUATION as, instead of INVITING war, will tend to repress and discourage it. That situation consists in the best possible state of defense, and necessarily depends on the government, the arms, and the resources of the country.

As the safety of the whole is the interest of the whole, and cannot be provided for without government, either one or more or many, let us inquire whether one good government is not, relative to the object in question, more competent than any other given number whatever.

One government can collect and avail itself of the talents and experience of the ablest men, in whatever part of the Union they may be found. It can move on uniform principles of policy. It can harmonize, assimilate, and protect the several parts and members, and extend the benefit of its foresight and precautions to each. In the formation of treaties, it will regard the interest of the whole, and the particular interests of the parts as connected with that of the whole. It can apply the resources and power of the whole to the defense of any particular part, and that more easily and expeditiously than State governments or separate confederacies can possibly do, for want of concert and unity of system. It can place the militia under one plan of discipline, and, by putting their officers in a proper line of subordination to the Chief Magistrate, will, as it were, consolidate them into one corps, and thereby render them more efficient than if divided into thirteen or into three or four distinct independent companies.

What would the militia of Britain be if the English militia obeyed the government of England, if the Scotch militia obeyed the government of Scotland, and if the Welsh militia obeyed the government of Wales? Suppose an invasion; would those three governments (if they agreed at all) be able, with all their respective forces, to operate against the enemy so effectually as the single government of Great Britain would?

We have heard much of the fleets of Britain, and the time may come, if we are wise, when the fleets of America may engage attention. But if one national government, had not so regulated the navigation of Britain as to make it a nursery for seamen—if one national government had not called forth all the national means and materials for forming fleets, their prowess and their thunder would never have been celebrated. Let England have its navigation and fleet—let Scotland have its navigation and fleet—let Wales have its navigation and fleet—let Ireland have its navigation and fleet—let those four of the constituent parts of the British empire be under four independent governments, and it is easy to perceive how soon they would each dwindle into comparative insignificance.

Apply these facts to our own case. Leave America divided into thirteen or, if you please, into three or four independent governments—what armies could they raise and pay—what fleets could they ever hope to have? If one was attacked, would the others fly to its succor, and spend their blood and money in its defense? Would there be no danger of their being flattered into neutrality by its specious promises, or seduced by a too great fondness for peace to decline hazarding their tranquillity and present safety for the sake of neighbors, of whom perhaps they have been jealous, and whose importance they are content to see diminished? Although such conduct would not be wise, it would, nevertheless, be natural. The history of the states of Greece, and of other countries, abounds with such instances, and it is not improbable that what has so often happened would, under similar circumstances, happen again.

But admit that they might be willing to help the invaded State or confederacy. How, and when, and in what proportion shall aids of men and money be afforded? Who shall command the allied armies, and from which of them shall he receive his orders? Who shall settle the terms of peace, and in case of disputes what umpire shall decide between them and compel acquiescence? Various difficulties and inconveniences would be inseparable from such a situation; whereas one government, watching over the general and common interests, and combining and directing the powers and resources of the whole, would be free from all these embarrassments, and conduce far more to the safety of the people.

But whatever may be our situation, whether firmly united under one national government, or split into a number of confederacies, certain it is, that foreign nations will know and view it exactly as it is; and they will act toward us accordingly. If they see that our national government is efficient and well administered, our trade prudently regulated, our militia properly organized and disciplined, our resources and finances discreetly managed, our credit re-established, our people free, contented, and united, they will be much more disposed to cultivate our friendship than provoke our resentment. If, on the other hand, they find us either destitute of an effectual government (each State doing right or wrong, as to its rulers may seem convenient), or split into three or four independent and probably discordant republics or confederacies, one inclining to Britain, another to France, and a third to Spain, and perhaps played off against each other by the three, what a poor, pitiful figure will America make in their eyes! How liable would she become not only to their contempt but to their outrage, and how soon would dear-bought experience proclaim that when a people or family so divide, it never fails to be against themselves.

PUBLIUS.

Federalist No. 5

The Same Subject Continued
(Concerning Dangers From Foreign Force and Influence)
For the Independent Journal.

JAY

To the People of the State of New York:

QUEEN ANNE, in her letter of the 1st July, 1706, to the Scotch Parliament, makes some observations on the importance of the UNION then forming between England and Scotland, which merit our attention. I shall present the public with one or two extracts from it: "An entire and perfect union will be the solid foundation of lasting peace: It will secure your religion, liberty, and property; remove the animosities amongst yourselves, and the jealousies and differences betwixt our two kingdoms. It must increase your strength, riches, and trade; and by this union the whole island, being joined in affection and free from all apprehensions of different interest, will be ENABLED TO RESIST ALL ITS ENEMIES." "We most earnestly recommend to you calmness and unanimity in this great and weighty affair, that the union may be brought to a happy conclusion, being the only EFFECTUAL way to secure our present and future happiness, and disappoint the designs of our and your enemies, who will doubtless, on this occasion, USE THEIR UTMOST ENDEAVORS TO PREVENT OR DELAY THIS UNION."

It was remarked in the preceding paper, that weakness and divisions at home would invite dangers from abroad; and that nothing would tend more to secure us from them than union, strength, and good government within ourselves. This subject is copious and cannot easily be exhausted.

The history of Great Britain is the one with which we are in general the best acquainted, and it gives us many useful lessons. We may profit by their experience without paying the price which it cost them. Although it seems obvious to common sense that the people of such an island should be but one nation, yet we find that they were for ages divided into three, and that those three were almost constantly embroiled in quarrels and wars with one another. Notwithstanding their true interest with respect to the continental nations was really the same, yet by the arts and policy and practices of those nations, their mutual jealousies were perpetually kept inflamed, and for a long series of years they were far more inconvenient and troublesome than they were useful and assisting to each other.

Should the people of America divide themselves into three or four nations, would not the same thing happen? Would not similar jealousies arise, and be in like manner cherished? Instead of their being "joined in affection" and free from all apprehension of different "interests," envy and jealousy would soon extinguish confidence and affection, and the partial interests of each confederacy, instead of the general interests of all America, would be the only objects of their policy and pursuits. Hence, like most other BORDERING nations, they would always be either involved in disputes and war, or live in the constant apprehension of them.

The most sanguine advocates for three or four confederacies cannot reasonably suppose that they would long remain exactly on an equal footing in point of strength, even if it was possible to form them so at first; but, admitting that to be practicable, yet what human contrivance can secure the continuance of such equality? Independent of those local circumstances which tend to beget and increase power in one part and to impede its progress in another, we must advert to the effects of that superior policy and good management which would probably distinguish the government of one above the rest, and by which their relative equality in strength and consideration would be destroyed. For it cannot be presumed that the same degree of sound policy, prudence, and foresight would uniformly be observed by each of these confederacies for a long succession of years.

Whenever, and from whatever causes, it might happen, and happen it would, that any one of these nations or confederacies should rise on the scale of political importance much above the degree of her neighbors, that moment would those neighbors behold her with envy and with fear. Both those passions would lead them to countenance, if not to promote, whatever might promise to diminish her importance; and would also restrain them from measures calculated to advance or even to secure her prosperity. Much time would not be necessary to enable her to discern these unfriendly dispositions. She would soon begin, not only to lose confidence in her neighbors, but also to feel a disposition equally unfavorable to them. Distrust naturally creates distrust, and by nothing is good-will and kind conduct more speedily changed than by invidious jealousies and uncandid imputations, whether expressed or implied.

The North is generally the region of strength, and many local circumstances render it probable that the most Northern of the proposed confederacies would, at a period not very distant, be unquestionably more formidable than any of the others. No sooner would this become evident than the NORTHERN HIVE would excite the same ideas and sensations in the more southern parts of America which it formerly did in the southern parts of Europe. Nor does it appear to be a rash conjecture that its young swarms might often be tempted to gather honey in the more blooming fields and milder air of their luxurious and more delicate neighbors.

They who well consider the history of similar divisions and confederacies will find abundant reason to apprehend that those in contemplation would in no other sense be neighbors than as they would be borderers; that they would neither love nor trust one another, but on the contrary would be a prey to discord, jealousy, and mutual injuries; in short, that they would place us exactly in the situations in which some nations doubtless wish to see us, viz., FORMIDABLE ONLY TO EACH OTHER.

From these considerations it appears that those gentlemen are greatly mistaken who suppose that alliances offensive and defensive might be formed between these confederacies, and would produce that combination and union of wills of arms and of resources, which would be necessary to put and keep them in a formidable state of defense against foreign enemies.

When did the independent states, into which Britain and Spain were formerly divided, combine in such alliance, or unite their forces against a foreign enemy? The proposed confederacies will be DISTINCT NATIONS. Each of them would have its commerce with foreigners to regulate by distinct treaties; and as their productions and commodities are different and proper for different markets, so would those treaties be essentially different. Different commercial concerns must create different interests, and of course different degrees of political attachment to and connection with different foreign nations. Hence it might and probably would happen that the foreign nation with whom the SOUTHERN confederacy might be at war would be the one with whom the NORTHERN confederacy would be the most desirous of preserving peace and friendship. An alliance so contrary to their immediate interest would not therefore be easy to form, nor, if formed, would it be observed and fulfilled with perfect good faith.

Nay, it is far more probable that in America, as in Europe, neighboring nations, acting under the impulse of opposite interests and unfriendly passions, would frequently be found taking different sides. Considering our distance from Europe, it would be more natural for these confederacies to apprehend danger from one another than from distant nations, and therefore that each of them should be more desirous to guard against the others by the aid of foreign alliances, than to guard against foreign dangers by alliances between themselves. And here let us not forget how much more easy it is to receive foreign fleets into our ports, and foreign armies into our country, than it is to persuade or compel them to depart. How many conquests did the Romans and others make in the characters of allies, and what innovations did they under the same character introduce into the governments of those whom they pretended to protect.

Let candid men judge, then, whether the division of America into any given number of independent sovereignties would tend to secure us against the hostilities and improper interference of foreign nations.

PUBLIUS.

Federalist No. 6

Concerning Dangers from Dissensions between the States

For the Independent Journal.

HAMILTON

To the People of the State of New York:

THE three last numbers of this paper have been dedicated to an enumeration of the dangers to which we should be exposed, in a state of disunion, from the arms and arts of foreign nations. I shall now proceed to delineate dangers of a different and, perhaps, still more alarming kind—those which will in all probability flow from dissensions between the States themselves, and from domestic factions and convulsions. These have been already in some instances slightly anticipated; but they deserve a more particular and more full investigation.

A man must be far gone in Utopian speculations who can seriously doubt that, if these States should either be wholly disunited, or only united in partial confederacies, the subdivisions into which they might be thrown would have frequent and violent contests with each other. To presume a want of motives for such contests as an argument against their existence, would be to forget that men are ambitious, vindictive, and rapacious. To look for a continuation of harmony between a number of independent, unconnected sovereignties in the same neighborhood, would be to disregard the uniform course of human events, and to set at defiance the accumulated experience of ages.

The causes of hostility among nations are innumerable. There are some which have a general and almost constant operation upon the collective bodies of society. Of this description are the love of power or the desire of pre-eminence and dominion—the jealousy of power, or the desire of equality and safety. There are others which have a more circumscribed though an equally operative influence within their spheres. Such are the rivalships and competitions of commerce between commercial nations. And there are others, not less numerous than either of the former, which take their origin entirely in private passions; in the attachments, enmities, interests, hopes, and fears of leading individuals in the communities of which they are members. Men of this class, whether the favorites of a king or of a people, have in too many instances abused the confidence they possessed; and assuming the pretext of some public motive, have not scrupled to sacrifice the national tranquillity to personal advantage or personal gratification.

The celebrated Pericles, in compliance with the resentment of a prostitute, [1] at the expense of much of the blood and treasure of his countrymen, attacked, vanquished, and destroyed the city of the SAMNIANS. The same man, stimulated by private pique against the MEGARENSIANS, [2] another nation of Greece, or to avoid a prosecution with which he was threatened as an accomplice of a supposed theft of the statuary Phidias, [3] or to get rid of the accusations prepared to be brought against him for dissipating the funds of the state in the purchase of popularity, [4] or from a combination of all these causes, was the primitive author of that famous and fatal war, distinguished in the Grecian annals by the name of the PELOPONNESIAN war; which, after various vicissitudes, intermissions, and renewals, terminated in the ruin of the Athenian commonwealth.

The ambitious cardinal, who was prime minister to Henry VIII., permitting his vanity to aspire to the triple crown, [5] entertained hopes of succeeding in the acquisition of that splendid prize by the influence of the Emperor Charles V. To secure the favor and interest of this enterprising and powerful monarch, he precipitated England into a war with France, contrary to the plainest dictates of policy, and at the hazard of the safety and independence, as well of the kingdom over which he presided by his counsels, as of Europe in general. For if there ever was a sovereign who bid fair to realize the project of universal monarchy, it was the Emperor Charles V., of whose intrigues Wolsey was at once the instrument and the dupe.

The influence which the bigotry of one female, [6] the petulance of another, [7] and the cabals of a third, [8] had in the contemporary policy, ferments, and pacifications, of a considerable part of Europe, are topics that have been too often descanted upon not to be generally known.

To multiply examples of the agency of personal considerations in the production of great national events, either foreign or domestic, according to their direction, would be an unnecessary waste of time. Those who have but a superficial acquaintance with the sources from which they are to be drawn, will themselves recollect a variety of instances; and those who have a tolerable knowledge of human nature will not stand in need of such lights to form their opinion either of the reality or extent of that agency. Perhaps, however, a reference, tending to illustrate the general principle, may with propriety be made to a case which has lately happened among ourselves. If Shays had not been a DESPERATE DEBTOR, it is much to be doubted whether Massachusetts would have been plunged into a civil war.

But notwithstanding the concurring testimony of experience, in this particular, there are still to be found visionary or designing men, who stand ready to advocate the paradox of perpetual peace between the States, though dismembered and alienated from each other. The genius of republics (say they) is pacific; the spirit of commerce has a tendency to soften the manners of men, and to extinguish those inflammable humors which have so often kindled into wars. Commercial republics, like ours, will never be disposed to waste themselves in ruinous contentions with each other. They will be governed by mutual interest, and will cultivate a spirit of mutual amity and concord.

Is it not (we may ask these projectors in politics) the true interest of all nations to cultivate the same benevolent and philosophic spirit? If this be their true interest, have they in fact pursued it? Has it not, on the contrary, invariably been found that momentary passions, and immediate interest, have a more active and imperious control over human conduct than general or remote considerations of policy, utility or justice? Have republics in practice been less addicted to war than monarchies? Are not the former administered by MEN as well as the latter? Are there not aversions, predilections, rivalships, and desires of unjust acquisitions, that affect nations as well as kings? Are not popular assemblies frequently subject to the impulses of rage, resentment, jealousy, avarice, and of other irregular and violent propensities? Is it not well known that their determinations are often governed by a few individuals in whom they place confidence, and are, of course, liable to be tinctured by the passions and views of those individuals? Has commerce hitherto done anything more than change the objects of war? Is not the love of wealth as domineering and enterprising a passion as that of power or glory? Have there not been as many wars founded upon commercial motives since that has become the prevailing system of nations, as were before occasioned by the cupidity of territory or dominion? Has not the spirit of commerce, in many instances, administered new incentives to the appetite, both for the one and for the other? Let experience, the least fallible guide of human opinions, be appealed to for an answer to these inquiries.

Sparta, Athens, Rome, and Carthage were all republics; two of them, Athens and Carthage, of the commercial kind. Yet were they as often engaged in wars, offensive and defensive, as the neighboring monarchies of the same times. Sparta was little better than a well-regulated camp; and Rome was never sated of carnage and conquest.

Carthage, though a commercial republic, was the aggressor in the very war that ended in her destruction. Hannibal had carried her arms into the heart of Italy and to the gates of Rome, before Scipio, in turn, gave him an overthrow in the territories of Carthage, and made a conquest of the commonwealth.

Venice, in later times, figured more than once in wars of ambition, till, becoming an object to the other Italian states, Pope Julius II. found means to accomplish that formidable league, [9] which gave a deadly blow to the power and pride of this haughty republic.

The provinces of Holland, till they were overwhelmed in debts and taxes, took a leading and conspicuous part in the wars of Europe. They had furious contests with England for the dominion of the sea, and were among the most persevering and most implacable of the opponents of Louis XIV.

In the government of Britain the representatives of the people compose one branch of the national legislature. Commerce has been for ages the predominant pursuit of that country. Few nations, nevertheless, have been more frequently engaged in war; and the wars in which that kingdom has been engaged have, in numerous instances, proceeded from the people.

There have been, if I may so express it, almost as many popular as royal wars. The cries of the nation and the importunities of their representatives have, upon various occasions, dragged their monarchs into war, or continued them in it, contrary to their inclinations, and sometimes contrary to the real interests of the State. In that memorable struggle for superiority between the rival houses of AUSTRIA and BOURBON, which so long kept Europe in a flame, it is well known that the antipathies of the English against the French, seconding the ambition, or rather the avarice, of a favorite leader, [10] protracted the war beyond the limits marked out by sound policy, and for a considerable time in opposition to the views of the court.

The wars of these two last-mentioned nations have in a great measure grown out of commercial considerations,—the desire of supplanting and the fear of being supplanted, either in particular branches of traffic or in the general advantages of trade and navigation.

From this summary of what has taken place in other countries, whose situations have borne the nearest resemblance to our own, what reason can we have to confide in those reveries which would seduce us into an expectation of peace and cordiality between the members of the present confederacy, in a state of separation? Have we not already seen enough of the fallacy and extravagance of those idle theories which have amused us with promises of an exemption from the imperfections, weaknesses and evils incident to society in every shape? Is it not time to awake from the deceitful dream of a golden age, and to adopt as a practical maxim for the direction of our political conduct that we, as well as the other inhabitants of the globe, are yet remote from the happy empire of perfect wisdom and perfect virtue?

Let the point of extreme depression to which our national dignity and credit have sunk, let the inconveniences felt everywhere from a lax and ill administration of government, let the revolt of a part of the State of North Carolina, the late menacing disturbances in Pennsylvania, and the actual insurrections and rebellions in Massachusetts, declare—!

So far is the general sense of mankind from corresponding with the tenets of those who endeavor to lull asleep our apprehensions of discord and hostility between the States, in the event of disunion, that it has from long observation of the progress of society become a sort of axiom in politics, that vicinity or nearness of situation, constitutes nations natural enemies. An intelligent writer expresses himself on this subject to this effect: "NEIGHBORING NATIONS (says he) are naturally enemies of each other unless their common weakness forces them to league in a CONFEDERATE REPUBLIC, and their constitution prevents the differences that neighborhood occasions, extinguishing that secret jealousy which disposes all states to aggrandize themselves at the expense of their neighbors." [11] This passage, at the same time, points out the EVIL and suggests the REMEDY.

PUBLIUS.

[1] Aspasia, vide "Plutarch's Life of Pericles."

[2] Ibid.

[3] Ibid.

[4] Ibid. Phidias was supposed to have stolen some public gold, with the connivance of Pericles, for the embellishment of the statue of Minerva.

[5] Worn by the popes.

[6] Madame de Maintenon.

[7] Duchess of Marlborough.

[8] Madame de Pompadour.

[9] The League of Cambray, comprehending the Emperor, the King of France, the King of Aragon, and most of the Italian princes and states.

[10] The Duke of Marlborough.

[11] Vide "Principes des Negociations" par l'Abbé de Mably.

Federalist No. 7

The Same Subject Continued
(Concerning Dangers from Dissensions Between the States)
For the Independent Journal.
HAMILTON
To the People of the State of New York:

IT IS sometimes asked, with an air of seeming triumph, what inducements could the States have, if disunited, to make war upon each other? It would be a full answer to this question to say—precisely the same inducements which have, at different times, deluged in blood all the nations in the world. But, unfortunately for us, the question admits of a more particular answer. There are causes of differences within our immediate contemplation, of the tendency of which, even under the restraints of a federal constitution, we have had sufficient experience to enable us to form a judgment of what might be expected if those restraints were removed.

Territorial disputes have at all times been found one of the most fertile sources of hostility among nations. Perhaps the greatest proportion of wars that have desolated the earth have sprung from this origin. This cause would exist among us in full force. We have a vast tract of unsettled territory within the boundaries of the United States. There still are discordant and undecided claims between several of them, and the dissolution of the Union would lay a foundation for similar claims between them all. It is well known that they have heretofore had serious and animated discussion concerning the rights to the lands which were ungranted at the time of the Revolution, and which usually went under the name of crown lands. The States within the limits of whose colonial governments they were comprised have claimed them as their property, the others have contended that the rights of the crown in this article devolved upon the Union; especially as to all that part of the Western territory which, either by actual possession, or through the submission of the Indian proprietors, was subjected to the jurisdiction of the king of Great Britain, till it was relinquished in the treaty of peace. This, it has been said, was at all events an acquisition to the Confederacy by compact with a foreign power. It has been the prudent policy of Congress to appease this controversy, by prevailing upon the States to make cessions to the United States for the benefit of the whole. This has been so far accomplished as, under a continuation of the Union, to afford a decided prospect of an amicable termination of the dispute. A dismemberment of the Confederacy, however, would revive this dispute, and would create others on the same subject. At present, a large part of the vacant Western territory is, by cession at least, if not by any anterior right, the common property of the Union. If that were at an end, the States which made the cession, on a principle of federal compromise, would be apt when the motive of the grant had ceased, to reclaim the lands as a reversion. The other States would no doubt insist on a proportion, by right of representation. Their argument would be, that a grant, once made, could not be revoked; and that the justice of participating in territory acquired or secured by the joint efforts of the Confederacy, remained undiminished. If, contrary to probability, it should be admitted by all the States, that each had a right to a share of this common stock, there would still be a difficulty to be surmounted, as to a proper rule of apportionment. Different principles would be set up by different States for this purpose; and as they would affect the opposite interests of the parties, they might not easily be susceptible of a pacific adjustment.

In the wide field of Western territory, therefore, we perceive an ample theatre for hostile pretensions, without any umpire or common judge to interpose between the contending parties. To reason from the past to the future, we shall have good ground to apprehend, that the sword would sometimes be appealed to as the arbiter of their differences. The circumstances of the dispute between Connecticut and Pennsylvania, respecting the land at Wyoming, admonish us not to be sanguine in expecting an easy accommodation of such differences. The articles of confederation obliged the parties to submit the matter to the decision of a federal court. The submission was made, and the court decided in favor of Pennsylvania. But Connecticut gave strong indications of dissatisfaction with that determination; nor did she appear to be entirely resigned to it, till, by negotiation and management, something like an equivalent was found for the loss she supposed herself to have sustained. Nothing here said is intended to convey the slightest censure on the conduct of that State. She no doubt sincerely believed herself to have been injured by the decision; and States, like individuals, acquiesce with great reluctance in determinations to their disadvantage.

Those who had an opportunity of seeing the inside of the transactions which attended the progress of the controversy between this State and the district of Vermont, can vouch the opposition we experienced, as well from States not interested as from those which were interested in the claim; and can attest the danger to which the peace of the Confederacy might have been exposed, had this State attempted to assert its rights by force. Two motives preponderated in that opposition: one, a jealousy entertained of our future power; and the other, the interest of certain individuals of influence in the neighboring States, who had obtained grants of lands under the actual government of that district. Even the States which brought forward claims, in contradiction to ours, seemed more solicitous to dismember this State, than to establish their own pretensions. These were New Hampshire, Massachusetts, and Connecticut. New Jersey and Rhode Island, upon all occasions, discovered a warm zeal for the independence of Vermont; and Maryland, till alarmed by the appearance of a connection between Canada and that State, entered deeply into the same views. These being small States, saw with an unfriendly eye the perspective of our growing greatness. In a review of these transactions we may trace some of the causes which would be likely to embroil the States with each other, if it should be their unpropitious destiny to become disunited.

The competitions of commerce would be another fruitful source of contention. The States less favorably circumstanced would be desirous of escaping from the disadvantages of local situation, and of sharing in the advantages of their more fortunate neighbors. Each State, or separate confederacy, would pursue a system of commercial policy peculiar to itself. This would occasion distinctions, preferences, and exclusions, which would beget discontent. The habits of intercourse, on the basis of equal privileges, to which we have been accustomed since the earliest settlement of the country, would give a keener edge to those causes of discontent than they would naturally have independent of this circumstance. WE SHOULD BE READY TO DENOMINATE INJURIES THOSE THINGS WHICH WERE IN REALITY THE JUSTIFIABLE ACTS OF INDEPENDENT SOVEREIGNTIES CONSULTING A DISTINCT INTEREST. The spirit of enterprise, which characterizes the commercial part of America, has left no occasion of displaying itself unimproved. It is not at all probable that this unbridled spirit would pay much respect to those regulations of trade by which particular States might endeavor to secure exclusive benefits to their own citizens. The infractions of these regulations, on one side, the efforts to prevent and repel them, on the other, would naturally lead to outrages, and these to reprisals and wars.

The opportunities which some States would have of rendering others tributary to them by commercial regulations would be impatiently submitted to by the tributary States. The relative situation of New York, Connecticut, and New Jersey would afford an example of this kind. New York, from the necessities of revenue, must lay duties on her importations. A great part of these duties must be paid by the inhabitants of the two other States in the capacity of consumers of what we import. New York would neither be willing nor able to forego this advantage. Her citizens would not consent that a duty paid by them should be remitted in favor of the citizens of her neighbors; nor would it be practicable, if there were not this impediment in the way, to distinguish the customers in our own markets. Would Connecticut and New Jersey long submit to be taxed by New York for her exclusive benefit? Should we be long permitted to remain in the quiet and undisturbed enjoyment of a metropolis, from the possession of which we derived an advantage so odious to our neighbors, and, in their opinion, so oppressive? Should we be able to preserve it against the incumbent weight of Connecticut on the one side, and the co-operating pressure of New Jersey on the other? These are questions that temerity alone will answer in the affirmative.

The public debt of the Union would be a further cause of collision between the separate States or confederacies. The apportionment, in the first instance, and the progressive extinguishment afterward, would be alike productive of ill-humor and animosity. How would it be possible to agree upon a rule of apportionment satisfactory to all? There is scarcely any that can be proposed which is entirely free from real objections. These, as usual, would be exaggerated by the adverse interest of the parties. There are even dissimilar views among the States as to the general principle of discharging the public debt. Some of them, either less impressed with the importance of national credit, or because their citizens have little, if any, immediate interest in the question, feel an indifference, if not a repugnance, to the payment of the domestic debt at any rate. These would be inclined to magnify the difficulties of a distribution. Others of them, a numerous body of whose citizens are creditors to the public beyond proportion of the State in the total amount of the national debt, would be strenuous for some equitable and effective provision. The procrastinations of the former would excite the resentments of the latter. The settlement of a rule would, in the meantime, be postponed by real differences of opinion and affected delays. The citizens of the States interested would clamour; foreign powers would urge for the satisfaction of their just demands, and the peace of the States would be hazarded to the double contingency of external invasion and internal contention.

Suppose the difficulties of agreeing upon a rule surmounted, and the apportionment made. Still there is great room to suppose that the rule agreed upon would, upon experiment, be found to bear harder upon some States than upon others. Those which were sufferers by it would naturally seek for a mitigation of the burden. The others would as naturally be disinclined to a revision, which was likely to end in an increase of their own incumbrances. Their refusal would be too plausible a pretext to the complaining States to withhold their contributions, not to be embraced with avidity; and the non-compliance of these States with their engagements would be a ground of bitter discussion and altercation. If even the rule adopted should in practice justify the equality of its principle, still delinquencies in payments on the part of some of the States would result from a diversity of other causes—the real deficiency of resources; the mismanagement of their finances; accidental disorders in the management of the government; and, in addition to the rest, the reluctance with which men commonly part with money for purposes that have outlived the exigencies which produced them, and interfere with the supply of immediate wants. Delinquencies, from whatever causes, would be productive of complaints, recriminations, and quarrels. There is, perhaps, nothing more likely to disturb the tranquillity of nations than their being bound to mutual contributions for any common object that does not yield an equal and coincident benefit. For it is an observation, as true as it is trite, that there is nothing men differ so readily about as the payment of money.

Laws in violation of private contracts, as they amount to aggressions on the rights of those States whose citizens are injured by them, may be considered as another probable source of hostility. We are not authorized to expect that a more liberal or more equitable spirit would preside over the legislations of the individual States hereafter, if unrestrained by any additional checks, than we have heretofore seen in too many instances disgracing their several codes. We have observed the disposition to retaliation excited in Connecticut in consequence of the enormities perpetrated by the Legislature of Rhode Island; and we reasonably infer that, in similar cases, under other circumstances, a war, not of PARCHMENT, but of the sword, would chastise such atrocious breaches of moral obligation and social justice.

The probability of incompatible alliances between the different States or confederacies and different foreign nations, and the effects of this situation upon the peace of the whole, have been sufficiently unfolded in some preceding papers. From the view they have exhibited of this part of the subject, this conclusion is to be drawn, that America, if not connected at all, or only by the feeble tie of a simple league, offensive and defensive, would, by the operation of such jarring alliances, be gradually entangled in all the pernicious labyrinths of European politics and wars; and by the destructive contentions of the parts into which she was divided, would be likely to become a prey to the artifices and machinations of powers equally the enemies of them all. Divide et impera [1] must be the motto of every nation that either hates or fears us. [2]

PUBLIUS.

[1] Divide and command.

[2] In order that the whole subject of these papers may as soon as possible be laid before the public, it is proposed to publish them four times a week—on Tuesday in the New York Packet and on Thursday in the Daily Advertiser.

Federalist No. 8

The Consequences of Hostilities Between the States

From the New York Packet.
Tuesday, November 20, 1787.
HAMILTON

To the People of the State of New York:

ASSUMING it therefore as an established truth that the several States, in case of disunion, or such combinations of them as might happen to be formed out of the wreck of the general Confederacy, would be subject to those vicissitudes of peace and war, of friendship and enmity, with each other, which have fallen to the lot of all neighboring nations not united under one government, let us enter into a concise detail of some of the consequences that would attend such a situation.

War between the States, in the first period of their separate existence, would be accompanied with much greater distresses than it commonly is in those countries where regular military establishments have long obtained. The disciplined armies always kept on foot on the continent of Europe, though they bear a malignant aspect to liberty and economy, have, notwithstanding, been productive of the signal advantage of rendering sudden conquests impracticable, and of preventing that rapid desolation which used to mark the progress of war prior to their introduction. The art of fortification has contributed to the same ends. The nations of Europe are encircled with chains of fortified places, which mutually obstruct invasion. Campaigns are wasted in reducing two or three frontier garrisons, to gain admittance into an enemy's country. Similar impediments occur at every step, to exhaust the strength and delay the progress of an invader. Formerly, an invading army would penetrate into the heart of a neighboring country almost as soon as intelligence of its approach could be received; but now a comparatively small force of disciplined troops, acting on the defensive, with the aid of posts, is able to impede, and finally to frustrate, the enterprises of one much more considerable. The history of war, in that quarter of the globe, is no longer a history of nations subdued and empires overturned, but of towns taken and retaken; of battles that decide nothing; of retreats more beneficial than victories; of much effort and little acquisition.

In this country the scene would be altogether reversed. The jealousy of military establishments would postpone them as long as possible. The want of fortifications, leaving the frontiers of one state open to another, would facilitate inroads. The populous States would, with little difficulty, overrun their less populous neighbors. Conquests would be as easy to be made as difficult to be retained. War, therefore, would be desultory and predatory. PLUNDER and devastation ever march in the train of irregulars. The calamities of individuals would make the principal figure in the events which would characterize our military exploits.

This picture is not too highly wrought; though, I confess, it would not long remain a just one. Safety from external danger is the most powerful director of national conduct. Even the ardent love of liberty will, after a time, give way to its dictates. The violent destruction of life and property incident to war, the continual effort and alarm attendant on a state of continual danger, will compel nations the most attached to liberty to resort for repose and security to institutions which have a tendency to destroy their civil and political rights. To be more safe, they at length become willing to run the risk of being less free.

The institutions chiefly alluded to are STANDING ARMIES and the correspondent appendages of military establishments. Standing armies, it is said, are not provided against in the new Constitution; and it is therefore inferred that they may exist under it. [1] Their existence, however, from the very terms of the proposition, is, at most, problematical and uncertain. But standing armies, it may be replied, must inevitably result from a dissolution of the Confederacy. Frequent war and constant apprehension, which require a state of as constant preparation, will infallibly produce them. The weaker States or confederacies would first have recourse to them, to put themselves upon an equality with their more potent neighbors. They would endeavor to supply the inferiority of population and resources by a more regular and effective system of defense, by disciplined troops, and by fortifications. They would, at the same time, be necessitated to strengthen the executive arm of government, in doing which their constitutions would acquire a progressive direction toward monarchy. It is of the nature of war to increase the executive at the expense of the legislative authority.

The expedients which have been mentioned would soon give the States or confederacies that made use of them a superiority over their neighbors. Small states, or states of less natural strength, under vigorous governments, and with the assistance of disciplined armies, have often triumphed over large states, or states of greater natural strength, which have been destitute of these advantages. Neither the pride nor the safety of the more important States or confederacies would permit them long to submit to this mortifying and adventitious superiority. They would quickly resort to means similar to those by which it had been effected, to reinstate themselves in their lost pre-eminence. Thus, we should, in a little time, see established in every part of this country the same engines of despotism which have been the scourge of the Old World. This, at least, would be the natural course of things; and our reasonings will be the more likely to be just, in proportion as they are accommodated to this standard.

These are not vague inferences drawn from supposed or speculative defects in a Constitution, the whole power of which is lodged in the hands of a people, or their representatives and delegates, but they are solid conclusions, drawn from the natural and necessary progress of human affairs.

It may, perhaps, be asked, by way of objection to this, why did not standing armies spring up out of the contentions which so often distracted the ancient republics of Greece? Different answers, equally satisfactory, may be given to this question. The industrious habits of the people of the present day, absorbed in the pursuits of gain, and devoted to the improvements of agriculture and commerce, are incompatible with the condition of a nation of soldiers, which was the true condition of the people of those republics. The means of revenue, which have been so greatly multiplied by the increase of gold and silver and of the arts of industry, and the science of finance, which is the offspring of modern times, concurring with the habits of nations, have produced an entire revolution in the system of war, and have rendered disciplined armies, distinct from the body of the citizens, the inseparable companions of frequent hostility.

There is a wide difference, also, between military establishments in a country seldom exposed by its situation to internal invasions, and in one which is often subject to them, and always apprehensive of them. The rulers of the former can have a good pretext, if they are even so inclined, to keep on foot armies so numerous as must of necessity be maintained in the latter. These armies being, in the first case, rarely, if at all, called into activity for interior defense, the people are in no danger of being broken to military subordination. The laws are not accustomed to relaxations, in favor of military exigencies; the civil state remains in full vigor, neither corrupted, nor confounded with the principles or propensities of the other state. The smallness of the army renders the natural strength of the community an over-match for it; and the citizens, not habituated to look up to the military power for protection, or to submit to its oppressions, neither love nor fear the soldiery; they view them with a spirit of jealous acquiescence in a necessary evil, and stand ready to resist a power which they suppose may be exerted to the prejudice of their rights. The army under such circumstances may usefully aid the magistrate to suppress a small faction, or an occasional mob, or insurrection; but it will be unable to enforce encroachments against the united efforts of the great body of the people.

In a country in the predicament last described, the contrary of all this happens. The perpetual menacings of danger oblige the government to be always prepared to repel it; its armies must be numerous enough for instant defense. The continual necessity for their services enhances the importance of the soldier, and proportionably degrades the condition of the citizen. The military state becomes elevated above the civil. The inhabitants of territories, often the theatre of war, are unavoidably subjected to frequent infringements on their rights, which serve to weaken their sense of those rights; and by degrees the people are brought to consider the soldiery not only as their protectors, but as their superiors. The transition from this disposition to that of considering them masters, is neither remote nor difficult; but it is very difficult to prevail upon a people under such impressions, to make a bold or effectual resistance to usurpations supported by the military power.

The kingdom of Great Britain falls within the first description. An insular situation, and a powerful marine, guarding it in a great measure against the possibility of foreign invasion, supersede the necessity of a numerous army within the kingdom. A sufficient force to make head against a sudden descent, till the militia could have time to rally and embody, is all that has been deemed requisite. No motive of national policy has demanded, nor would public opinion have tolerated, a larger number of troops upon its domestic establishment. There has been, for a long time past, little room for the operation of the other causes, which have been enumerated as the consequences of internal war. This peculiar felicity of situation has, in a great degree, contributed to preserve the liberty which that country to this day enjoys, in spite of the prevalent venality and corruption. If, on the contrary, Britain had been situated on the continent, and had been compelled, as she would have been, by that situation, to make her military establishments at home coextensive with those of the other great powers of Europe, she, like them, would in all probability be, at this day, a victim to the absolute power of a single man. 'Tis possible, though not easy, that the people of that island may be enslaved from other causes; but it cannot be by the prowess of an army so inconsiderable as that which has been usually kept up within the kingdom.

If we are wise enough to preserve the Union we may for ages enjoy an advantage similar to that of an insulated situation. Europe is at a great distance from us. Her colonies in our vicinity will be likely to continue too much disproportioned in strength to be able to give us any dangerous annoyance. Extensive military establishments cannot, in this position, be necessary to our security. But if we should be disunited, and the integral parts should either remain separated, or, which is most probable, should be thrown together into two or three confederacies, we should be, in a short course of time, in the predicament of the continental powers of Europe —our liberties would be a prey to the means of defending ourselves against the ambition and jealousy of each other.

This is an idea not superficial or futile, but solid and weighty. It deserves the most serious and mature consideration of every prudent and honest man of whatever party. If such men will make a firm and solemn pause, and meditate dispassionately on the importance of this interesting idea; if they will contemplate it in all its attitudes, and trace it to all its consequences, they will not hesitate to part with trivial objections to a Constitution, the rejection of which would in all probability put a final period to the Union. The airy phantoms that flit before the distempered imaginations of some of its adversaries would quickly give place to the more substantial forms of dangers, real, certain, and formidable.

PUBLIUS.

[1] This objection will be fully examined in its proper place, and it will be shown that the only natural precaution which could have been taken on this subject has been taken; and a much better one than is to be found in any constitution that has been heretofore framed in America, most of which contain no guard at all on this subject.

Federalist No. 9

The Union as a Safeguard Against Domestic Faction and Insurrection

For the Independent Journal.

HAMILTON

To the People of the State of New York:

A FIRM Union will be of the utmost moment to the peace and liberty of the States, as a barrier against domestic faction and insurrection. It is impossible to read the history of the petty republics of Greece and Italy without feeling sensations of horror and disgust at the distractions with which they were continually agitated, and at the rapid succession of revolutions by which they were kept in a state of perpetual vibration between the extremes of tyranny and anarchy. If they exhibit occasional calms, these only serve as short-lived contrast to the furious storms that are to succeed. If now and then intervals of felicity open to view, we behold them with a mixture of regret, arising from the reflection that the pleasing scenes before us are soon to be overwhelmed by the tempestuous waves of sedition and party rage. If momentary rays of glory break forth from the gloom, while they dazzle us with a transient and fleeting brilliancy, they at the same time admonish us to lament that the vices of government should pervert the direction and tarnish the lustre of those bright talents and exalted endowments for which the favored soils that produced them have been so justly celebrated.

From the disorders that disfigure the annals of those republics the advocates of despotism have drawn arguments, not only against the forms of republican government, but against the very principles of civil liberty. They have decried all free government as inconsistent with the order of society, and have indulged themselves in malicious exultation over its friends and partisans. Happily for mankind, stupendous fabrics reared on the basis of liberty, which have flourished for ages, have, in a few glorious instances, refuted their gloomy sophisms. And, I trust, America will be the broad and solid foundation of other edifices, not less magnificent, which will be equally permanent monuments of their errors.

But it is not to be denied that the portraits they have sketched of republican government were too just copies of the originals from which they were taken. If it had been found impracticable to have devised models of a more perfect structure, the enlightened friends to liberty would have been obliged to abandon the cause of that species of government as indefensible. The science of politics, however, like most other sciences, has received great improvement. The efficacy of various principles is now well understood, which were either not known at all, or imperfectly known to the ancients. The regular distribution of power into distinct departments; the introduction of legislative balances and checks; the institution of courts composed of judges holding their offices during good behavior; the representation of the people in the legislature by deputies of their own election: these are wholly new discoveries, or have made their principal progress towards perfection in modern times. They are means, and powerful means, by which the excellences of republican government may be retained and its imperfections lessened or avoided. To this catalogue of circumstances that tend to the amelioration of popular systems of civil government, I shall venture, however novel it may appear to some, to add one more, on a principle which has been made the foundation of an objection to the new Constitution; I mean the ENLARGEMENT of the ORBIT within which such systems are to revolve, either in respect to the dimensions of a single State or to the consolidation of several smaller States into one great Confederacy. The latter is that which immediately concerns the object under consideration. It will, however, be of use to examine the principle in its application to a single State, which shall be attended to in another place.

The utility of a Confederacy, as well to suppress faction and to guard the internal tranquillity of States, as to increase their external force and security, is in reality not a new idea. It has been practiced upon in different countries and ages, and has received the sanction of the most approved writers on the subject of politics. The opponents of the plan proposed have, with great assiduity, cited and circulated the observations of Montesquieu on the necessity of a contracted territory for a republican government. But they seem not to have been apprised of the sentiments of that great man expressed in another part of his work, nor to have adverted to the consequences of the principle to which they subscribe with such ready acquiescence.

When Montesquieu recommends a small extent for republics, the standards he had in view were of dimensions far short of the limits of almost every one of these States. Neither Virginia, Massachusetts, Pennsylvania, New York, North Carolina, nor Georgia can by any means be compared with the models from which he reasoned and to which the terms of his description apply. If we therefore take his ideas on this point as the criterion of truth, we shall be driven to the alternative either of taking refuge at once in the arms of monarchy, or of splitting ourselves into an infinity of little, jealous, clashing, tumultuous commonwealths, the wretched nurseries of unceasing discord, and the miserable objects of universal pity or contempt. Some of the writers who have come forward on the other side of the question seem to have been aware of the dilemma; and have even been bold enough to hint at the division of the larger States as a desirable thing. Such an infatuated policy, such a desperate expedient, might, by the multiplication of petty offices, answer the views of men who possess not qualifications to extend their influence beyond the narrow circles of personal intrigue, but it could never promote the greatness or happiness of the people of America.

Referring the examination of the principle itself to another place, as has been already mentioned, it will be sufficient to remark here that, in the sense of the author who has been most emphatically quoted upon the occasion, it would only dictate a reduction of the SIZE of the more considerable MEMBERS of the Union, but would not militate against their being all comprehended in one confederate government. And this is the true question, in the discussion of which we are at present interested.

So far are the suggestions of Montesquieu from standing in opposition to a general Union of the States, that he explicitly treats of a CONFEDERATE REPUBLIC as the expedient for extending the sphere of popular government, and reconciling the advantages of monarchy with those of republicanism.

"It is very probable," (says he [1]) "that mankind would have been obliged at length to live constantly under the government of a single person, had they not contrived a kind of constitution that has all the internal advantages of a republican, together with the external force of a monarchical government. I mean a CONFEDERATE REPUBLIC.

"This form of government is a convention by which several smaller

STATES agree to become members of a larger ONE, which they intend to form. It is a kind of assemblage of societies that constitute a new one, capable of increasing, by means of new associations, till they arrive to such a degree of power as to be able to provide for the security of the united body.

"A republic of this kind, able to withstand an external force, may support itself without any internal corruptions. The form of this society prevents all manner of inconveniences.

"If a single member should attempt to usurp the supreme authority, he could not be supposed to have an equal authority and credit in all the confederate states. Were he to have too great influence over one, this would alarm the rest. Were he to subdue a part, that which would still remain free might oppose him with forces independent of those which he had usurped and overpower him before he could be settled in his usurpation.

"Should a popular insurrection happen in one of the confederate states the others are able to quell it. Should abuses creep into one part, they are reformed by those that remain sound. The state may be destroyed on one side, and not on the other; the confederacy may be dissolved, and the confederates preserve their sovereignty.

"As this government is composed of small republics, it enjoys the internal happiness of each; and with respect to its external situation, it is possessed, by means of the association, of all the advantages of large monarchies."

I have thought it proper to quote at length these interesting passages, because they contain a luminous abridgment of the principal arguments in favor of the Union, and must effectually remove the false impressions which a misapplication of other parts of the work was calculated to make. They have, at the same time, an intimate connection with the more immediate design of this paper; which is, to illustrate the tendency of the Union to repress domestic faction and insurrection.

A distinction, more subtle than accurate, has been raised between a CONFEDERACY and a CONSOLIDATION of the States. The essential characteristic of the first is said to be, the restriction of its authority to the members in their collective capacities, without reaching to the individuals of whom they are composed. It is contended that the national council ought to have no concern with any object of internal administration. An exact equality of suffrage between the members has also been insisted upon as a leading feature of a confederate government. These positions are, in the main, arbitrary; they are supported neither by principle nor precedent. It has indeed happened, that governments of this kind have generally operated in the manner which the distinction taken notice of, supposes to be inherent in their nature; but there have been in most of them extensive exceptions to the practice, which serve to prove, as far as example will go, that there is no absolute rule on the subject. And it will be clearly shown in the course of this investigation that as far as the principle contended for has prevailed, it has been the cause of incurable disorder and imbecility in the government.

The definition of a CONFEDERATE REPUBLIC seems simply to be "an assemblage of societies," or an association of two or more states into one state. The extent, modifications, and objects of the federal authority are mere matters of discretion. So long as the separate organization of the members be not abolished; so long as it exists, by a constitutional necessity, for local purposes; though it should be in perfect subordination to the general authority of the union, it would still be, in fact and in theory, an association of states, or a confederacy. The proposed Constitution, so far from implying an abolition of the State governments, makes them constituent parts of the national sovereignty, by allowing them a direct representation in the Senate, and leaves in their possession certain exclusive and very important portions of sovereign power. This fully corresponds, in every rational import of the terms, with the idea of a federal government.

In the Lycian confederacy, which consisted of twenty-three CITIES or republics, the largest were entitled to THREE votes in the COMMON COUNCIL, those of the middle class to TWO, and the smallest to ONE. The COMMON COUNCIL had the appointment of all the judges and magistrates of the respective CITIES. This was certainly the most, delicate species of interference in their internal administration; for if there be any thing that seems exclusively appropriated to the local jurisdictions, it is the appointment of their own officers. Yet Montesquieu, speaking of this association, says: "Were I to give a model of an excellent Confederate Republic, it would be that of Lycia." Thus we perceive that the distinctions insisted upon were not within the contemplation of this enlightened civilian; and we shall be led to conclude, that they are the novel refinements of an erroneous theory.

PUBLIUS.

[1] "Spirit of Laws," vol. i., book ix., chap. i.

Federalist No. 10

The Same Subject Continued

(The Union as a Safeguard Against Domestic Faction and Insurrection)

From the New York Packet.

Friday, November 23, 1787.

MADISON

To the People of the State of New York:

AMONG the numerous advantages promised by a well-constructed Union, none deserves to be more accurately developed than its tendency to break and control the violence of faction. The friend of popular governments never finds himself so much alarmed for their character and fate, as when he contemplates their propensity to this dangerous vice. He will not fail, therefore, to set a due value on any plan which, without violating the principles to which he is attached, provides a proper cure for it. The instability, injustice, and confusion introduced into the public councils, have, in truth, been the mortal diseases under which popular governments have everywhere perished; as they continue to be the favorite and fruitful topics from which the adversaries to liberty derive their most specious declamations. The valuable improvements made by the American constitutions on the popular models, both ancient and modern, cannot certainly be too much admired; but it would be an unwarrantable partiality, to contend that they have as effectually obviated the danger on this side, as was wished and expected. Complaints are everywhere heard from our most considerate and virtuous citizens, equally the friends of public and private faith, and of public and personal liberty, that our governments are too unstable, that the public good is disregarded in the conflicts of rival parties, and that measures are too often decided, not according to the rules of justice and the rights of the minor party, but by the superior force of an interested and overbearing majority. However anxiously we may wish that these complaints had no foundation, the evidence, of known facts will not permit us to deny that they are in some degree true. It will be found, indeed, on a candid review of our situation, that some of the distresses under which we labor have been erroneously charged on the operation of our governments; but it will be found, at the same time, that other causes will not alone account for many of our heaviest misfortunes; and, particularly, for that prevailing and increasing distrust of public engagements, and alarm for private rights, which are echoed from one end of the continent to the other. These must be chiefly, if not wholly, effects of the unsteadiness and injustice with which a factious spirit has tainted our public administrations.

By a faction, I understand a number of citizens, whether amounting to a majority or a minority of the whole, who are united and actuated by some common impulse of passion, or of interest, adversed to the rights of other citizens, or to the permanent and aggregate interests of the community.

There are two methods of curing the mischiefs of faction: the one, by removing its causes; the other, by controlling its effects.

There are again two methods of removing the causes of faction: the one, by destroying the liberty which is essential to its existence; the other, by giving to every citizen the same opinions, the same passions, and the same interests.

It could never be more truly said than of the first remedy, that it was worse than the disease. Liberty is to faction what air is to fire, an aliment without which it instantly expires. But it could not be less folly to abolish liberty, which is essential to political life, because it nourishes faction, than it would be to wish the annihilation of air, which is essential to animal life, because it imparts to fire its destructive agency.

The second expedient is as impracticable as the first would be unwise. As long as the reason of man continues fallible, and he is at liberty to exercise it, different opinions will be formed. As long as the connection subsists between his reason and his self-love, his opinions and his passions will have a reciprocal influence on each other; and the former will be objects to which the latter will attach themselves. The diversity in the faculties of men, from which the rights of property originate, is not less an insuperable obstacle to a uniformity of interests. The protection of these faculties is the first object of government. From the protection of different and unequal faculties of acquiring property, the possession of different degrees and kinds of property immediately results; and from the influence of these on the sentiments and views of the respective proprietors, ensues a division of the society into different interests and parties.

The latent causes of faction are thus sown in the nature of man; and we see them everywhere brought into different degrees of activity, according to the different circumstances of civil society. A zeal for different opinions concerning religion, concerning government, and many other points, as well of speculation as of practice; an attachment to different leaders ambitiously contending for pre-eminence and power; or to persons of other descriptions whose fortunes have been interesting to the human passions, have, in turn, divided mankind into parties, inflamed them with mutual animosity, and rendered them much more disposed to vex and oppress each other than to co-operate for their common good. So strong is this propensity of mankind to fall into mutual animosities, that where no substantial occasion presents itself, the most frivolous and fanciful distinctions have been sufficient to kindle their unfriendly passions and excite their most violent conflicts. But the most common and durable source of factions has been the various and unequal distribution of property. Those who hold and those who are without property have ever formed distinct interests in society. Those who are creditors, and those who are debtors, fall under a like discrimination. A landed interest, a manufacturing interest, a mercantile interest, a moneyed interest, with many lesser interests, grow up of necessity in civilized nations, and divide them into different classes, actuated by different sentiments and views. The regulation of these various and interfering interests forms the principal task of modern legislation, and involves the spirit of party and faction in the necessary and ordinary operations of the government.

No man is allowed to be a judge in his own cause, because his interest would certainly bias his judgment, and, not improbably, corrupt his integrity. With equal, nay with greater reason, a body of men are unfit to be both judges and parties at the same time; yet what are many of the most important acts of legislation, but so many judicial determinations, not indeed concerning the rights of single persons, but concerning the rights of large bodies of citizens? And what are the different classes of legislators but advocates and parties to the causes which they determine? Is a law proposed concerning private debts? It is a question to which the creditors are parties on one side and the debtors on the other. Justice ought to hold the balance between them. Yet the parties are, and must be, themselves the judges;

and the most numerous party, or, in other words, the most powerful faction must be expected to prevail. Shall domestic manufactures be encouraged, and in what degree, by restrictions on foreign manufactures? are questions which would be differently decided by the landed and the manufacturing classes, and probably by neither with a sole regard to justice and the public good. The apportionment of taxes on the various descriptions of property is an act which seems to require the most exact impartiality; yet there is, perhaps, no legislative act in which greater opportunity and temptation are given to a predominant party to trample on the rules of justice. Every shilling with which they overburden the inferior number, is a shilling saved to their own pockets.

It is in vain to say that enlightened statesmen will be able to adjust these clashing interests, and render them all subservient to the public good. Enlightened statesmen will not always be at the helm. Nor, in many cases, can such an adjustment be made at all without taking into view indirect and remote considerations, which will rarely prevail over the immediate interest which one party may find in disregarding the rights of another or the good of the whole.

The inference to which we are brought is, that the CAUSES of faction cannot be removed, and that relief is only to be sought in the means of controlling its EFFECTS.

If a faction consists of less than a majority, relief is supplied by the republican principle, which enables the majority to defeat its sinister views by regular vote. It may clog the administration, it may convulse the society; but it will be unable to execute and mask its violence under the forms of the Constitution. When a majority is included in a faction, the form of popular government, on the other hand, enables it to sacrifice to its ruling passion or interest both the public good and the rights of other citizens. To secure the public good and private rights against the danger of such a faction, and at the same time to preserve the spirit and the form of popular government, is then the great object to which our inquiries are directed. Let me add that it is the great desideratum by which this form of government can be rescued from the opprobrium under which it has so long labored, and be recommended to the esteem and adoption of mankind.

By what means is this object attainable? Evidently by one of two only. Either the existence of the same passion or interest in a majority at the same time must be prevented, or the majority, having such coexistent passion or interest, must be rendered, by their number and local situation, unable to concert and carry into effect schemes of oppression. If the impulse and the opportunity be suffered to coincide, we well know that neither moral nor religious motives can be relied on as an adequate control. They are not found to be such on the injustice and violence of individuals, and lose their efficacy in proportion to the number combined together, that is, in proportion as their efficacy becomes needful.

From this view of the subject it may be concluded that a pure democracy, by which I mean a society consisting of a small number of citizens, who assemble and administer the government in person, can admit of no cure for the mischiefs of faction. A common passion or interest will, in almost every case, be felt by a majority of the whole; a communication and concert result from the form of government itself; and there is nothing to check the inducements to sacrifice the weaker party or an obnoxious individual. Hence it is that such democracies have ever been spectacles of turbulence and contention; have ever been found incompatible with personal security or the rights of property; and have in general been as short in their lives as they have been violent in their deaths. Theoretic politicians, who have patronized this species of government, have erroneously supposed that by reducing mankind to a perfect equality in their political rights, they would, at the same time, be perfectly equalized and assimilated in their possessions, their opinions, and their passions.

A republic, by which I mean a government in which the scheme of representation takes place, opens a different prospect, and promises the cure for which we are seeking. Let us examine the points in which it varies from pure democracy, and we shall comprehend both the nature of the cure and the efficacy which it must derive from the Union.

The two great points of difference between a democracy and a republic are: first, the delegation of the government, in the latter, to a small number of citizens elected by the rest; secondly, the greater number of citizens, and greater sphere of country, over which the latter may be extended.

The effect of the first difference is, on the one hand, to refine and enlarge the public views, by passing them through the medium of a chosen body of citizens, whose wisdom may best discern the true interest of their country, and whose patriotism and love of justice will be least likely to sacrifice it to temporary or partial considerations. Under such a regulation, it may well happen that the public voice, pronounced by the representatives of the people, will be more consonant to the public good than if pronounced by the people themselves, convened for the purpose. On the other hand, the effect may be inverted. Men of factious tempers, of local prejudices, or of sinister designs, may, by intrigue, by corruption, or by other means, first obtain the suffrages, and then betray the interests, of the people. The question resulting is, whether small or extensive republics are more favorable to the election of proper guardians of the public weal; and it is clearly decided in favor of the latter by two obvious considerations:

In the first place, it is to be remarked that, however small the republic may be, the representatives must be raised to a certain number, in order to guard against the cabals of a few; and that, however large it may be, they must be limited to a certain number, in order to guard against the confusion of a multitude. Hence, the number of representatives in the two cases not being in proportion to that of the two constituents, and being proportionally greater in the small republic, it follows that, if the proportion of fit characters be not less in the large than in the small republic, the former will present a greater option, and consequently a greater probability of a fit choice.

In the next place, as each representative will be chosen by a greater number of citizens in the large than in the small republic, it will be more difficult for unworthy candidates to practice with success the vicious arts by which elections are too often carried; and the suffrages of the people being more free, will be more likely to centre in men who possess the most attractive merit and the most diffusive and established characters.

It must be confessed that in this, as in most other cases, there is a mean, on both sides of which inconveniences will be found to lie. By enlarging too much the number of electors, you render the representatives too little acquainted with all their local circumstances and lesser interests; as by reducing it too much, you render him unduly attached to these, and too little fit to comprehend and pursue great and national objects. The federal Constitution forms a happy combination in this respect; the great and aggregate interests being referred to the national, the local and particular to the State legislatures.

The other point of difference is, the greater number of citizens and extent of territory which may be brought within the compass of republican than of democratic government; and it is this circumstance principally which renders factious combinations less to be dreaded in the former than in the latter. The smaller the society, the fewer probably will be the distinct parties and interests composing it; the fewer the distinct parties and interests, the more frequently will a majority be found of the same party; and the smaller the number of individuals composing a majority, and the smaller the compass within which they are placed, the more easily will they concert and execute their plans of oppression. Extend the sphere, and you take in a greater variety of parties and interests; you make it less probable that a majority of the whole will have a common motive to invade the rights of other citizens; or if such a common motive exists, it will be more difficult for all who feel it to discover their own strength, and to act in unison with each other. Besides other impediments, it may be remarked that, where there is a consciousness of unjust or dishonorable purposes, communication is always checked by distrust in proportion to the number whose concurrence is necessary.

Hence, it clearly appears, that the same advantage which a republic has over a democracy, in controlling the effects of faction, is enjoyed by a large over a small republic,—is enjoyed by the Union over the States composing it. Does the advantage consist in the substitution of representatives whose enlightened views and virtuous sentiments render them superior to local prejudices and schemes of injustice? It will not be denied that the representation of the Union will be most likely to possess these requisite endowments. Does it consist in the greater security afforded by a greater variety of parties, against the event of any one party being able to outnumber and oppress the rest? In an equal degree does the increased variety of parties comprised within the Union, increase this security. Does it, in fine, consist in the greater obstacles opposed to the concert and accomplishment of the secret wishes of an unjust and interested majority? Here, again, the extent of the Union gives it the most palpable advantage.

The influence of factious leaders may kindle a flame within their particular States, but will be unable to spread a general conflagration through the other States. A religious sect may degenerate into a political faction in a part of the Confederacy; but the variety of sects dispersed over the entire face of it must secure the national councils against any danger from that source. A rage for paper money, for an abolition of debts, for an equal division of property, or for any other improper or wicked project, will be less apt to pervade the whole body of the Union than a particular member of it; in the same proportion as such a malady is more likely to taint a particular county or district, than an entire State.

In the extent and proper structure of the Union, therefore, we behold a republican remedy for the diseases most incident to republican government. And according to the degree of pleasure and pride we feel in being republicans, ought to be our zeal in cherishing the spirit and supporting the character of Federalists.

PUBLIUS.

Federalist No. 12

The Utility of the Union In Respect to Revenue

From the New York Packet.
Tuesday, November 27, 1787.

HAMILTON

To the People of the State of New York:

THE effects of Union upon the commercial prosperity of the States have been sufficiently delineated. Its tendency to promote the interests of revenue will be the subject of our present inquiry.

The prosperity of commerce is now perceived and acknowledged by all enlightened statesmen to be the most useful as well as the most productive source of national wealth, and has accordingly become a primary object of their political cares. By multiplying the means of gratification, by promoting the introduction and circulation of the precious metals, those darling objects of human avarice and enterprise, it serves to vivify and invigorate the channels of industry, and to make them flow with greater activity and copiousness. The assiduous merchant, the laborious husbandman, the active mechanic, and the industrious manufacturer,—all orders of men, look forward with eager expectation and growing alacrity to this pleasing reward of their toils. The often-agitated question between agriculture and commerce has, from indubitable experience, received a decision which has silenced the rivalship that once subsisted between them, and has proved, to the satisfaction of their friends, that their interests are intimately blended and interwoven. It has been found in various countries that, in proportion as commerce has flourished, land has risen in value. And how could it have happened otherwise? Could that which procures a freer vent for the products of the earth, which furnishes new incitements to the cultivation of land, which is the most powerful instrument in increasing the quantity of money in a state—could that, in fine, which is the faithful handmaid of labor and industry, in every shape, fail to augment that article, which is the prolific parent of far the greatest part of the objects upon which they are exerted? It is astonishing that so simple a truth should ever have had an adversary; and it is one, among a multitude of proofs, how apt a spirit of ill-informed jealousy, or of too great abstraction and refinement, is to lead men astray from the plainest truths of reason and conviction.

The ability of a country to pay taxes must always be proportioned, in a great degree, to the quantity of money in circulation, and to the celerity with which it circulates. Commerce, contributing to both these objects, must of necessity render the payment of taxes easier, and facilitate the requisite supplies to the treasury. The hereditary dominions of the Emperor of Germany contain a great extent of fertile, cultivated, and populous territory, a large proportion of which is situated in mild and luxuriant climates. In some parts of this territory are to be found the best gold and silver mines in Europe. And yet, from the want of the fostering influence of commerce, that monarch can boast but slender revenues. He has several times been compelled to owe obligations to the pecuniary succors of other nations for the preservation of his essential interests, and is unable, upon the strength of his own resources, to sustain a long or continued war.

But it is not in this aspect of the subject alone that Union will be seen to conduce to the purpose of revenue. There are other points of view, in which its influence will appear more immediate and decisive. It is evident from the state of the country, from the habits of the people, from the experience we have had on the point itself, that it is impracticable to raise any very considerable sums by direct taxation. Tax laws have in vain been multiplied; new methods to enforce the collection have in vain been tried; the public expectation has been uniformly disappointed, and the treasuries of the States have remained empty. The popular system of administration inherent in the nature of popular government, coinciding with the real scarcity of money incident to a languid and mutilated state of trade, has hitherto defeated every experiment for extensive collections, and has at length taught the different legislatures the folly of attempting them.

No person acquainted with what happens in other countries will be surprised at this circumstance. In so opulent a nation as that of Britain, where direct taxes from superior wealth must be much more tolerable, and, from the vigor of the government, much more practicable, than in America, far the greatest part of the national revenue is derived from taxes of the indirect kind, from imposts, and from excises. Duties on imported articles form a large branch of this latter description.

In America, it is evident that we must a long time depend for the means of revenue chiefly on such duties. In most parts of it, excises must be confined within a narrow compass. The genius of the people will ill brook the inquisitive and peremptory spirit of excise laws. The pockets of the farmers, on the other hand, will reluctantly yield but scanty supplies, in the unwelcome shape of impositions on their houses and lands; and personal property is too precarious and invisible a fund to be laid hold of in any other way than by the inperceptible agency of taxes on consumption.

If these remarks have any foundation, that state of things which will best enable us to improve and extend so valuable a resource must be best adapted to our political welfare. And it cannot admit of a serious doubt, that this state of things must rest on the basis of a general Union. As far as this would be conducive to the interests of commerce, so far it must tend to the extension of the revenue to be drawn from that source. As far as it would contribute to rendering regulations for the collection of the duties more simple and efficacious, so far it must serve to answer the purposes of making the same rate of duties more productive, and of putting it into the power of the government to increase the rate without prejudice to trade.

The relative situation of these States; the number of rivers with which they are intersected, and of bays that wash there shores; the facility of communication in every direction; the affinity of language and manners; the familiar habits of intercourse; —all these are circumstances that would conspire to render an illicit trade between them a matter of little difficulty, and would insure frequent evasions of the commercial regulations of each other. The separate States or confederacies would be necessitated by mutual jealousy to avoid the temptations to that kind of trade by the lowness of their duties. The temper of our governments, for a long time to come, would not permit those rigorous precautions by which the European nations guard the avenues into their respective countries, as well by land as by water; and which, even there, are found insufficient obstacles to the adventurous stratagems of avarice.

In France, there is an army of patrols (as they are called) constantly employed to secure their fiscal regulations against the inroads of the dealers in contraband trade. Mr. Neckar computes the number of these patrols at upwards of twenty thousand. This shows the immense difficulty in preventing that species of traffic, where there is an inland communication, and places in a strong light the disadvantages with which the collection of duties in this country would be encumbered, if by disunion the States should be placed in a situation, with respect to each other, resembling that of France with respect to her neighbors. The arbitrary and vexatious powers with which the patrols are necessarily armed, would be intolerable in a free country.

If, on the contrary, there be but one government pervading all the States, there will be, as to the principal part of our commerce, but ONE SIDE to guard—the ATLANTIC COAST. Vessels arriving directly from foreign countries, laden with valuable cargoes, would rarely choose to hazard themselves to the complicated and critical perils which would attend attempts to unlade prior to their coming into port. They would have to dread both the dangers of the coast, and of detection, as well after as before their arrival at the places of their final destination. An ordinary degree of vigilance would be competent to the prevention of any material infractions upon the rights of the revenue. A few armed vessels, judiciously stationed at the entrances of our ports, might at a small expense be made useful sentinels of the laws. And the government having the same interest to provide against violations everywhere, the co-operation of its measures in each State would have a powerful tendency to render them effectual. Here also we should preserve by Union, an advantage which nature holds out to us, and which would be relinquished by separation. The United States lie at a great distance from Europe, and at a considerable distance from all other places with which they would have extensive connections of foreign trade. The passage from them to us, in a few hours, or in a single night, as between the coasts of France and Britain, and of other neighboring nations, would be impracticable. This is a prodigious security against a direct contraband with foreign countries; but a circuitous contraband to one State, through the medium of another, would be both easy and safe. The difference between a direct importation from abroad, and an indirect importation through the channel of a neighboring State, in small parcels, according to time and opportunity, with the additional facilities of inland communication, must be palpable to every man of discernment.

It is therefore evident, that one national government would be able, at much less expense, to extend the duties on imports, beyond comparison, further than would be practicable to the States separately, or to any partial confederacies. Hitherto, I believe, it may safely be asserted, that these duties have not upon an average exceeded in any State three per cent. In France they are estimated to be about fifteen per cent., and in Britain they exceed this proportion. [1] There seems to be nothing to hinder their being increased in this country to at least treble their present amount. The single article of ardent spirits, under federal regulation, might be made to furnish a considerable revenue. Upon a ratio to the importation into this State, the whole quantity imported into the United States may be estimated at four millions of gallons; which, at a shilling per gallon, would produce two hundred thousand pounds. That article would well bear this rate of duty; and if it should tend to diminish the consumption of it, such an effect would be equally favorable to the agriculture, to the economy, to the morals, and to the health of the society. There is, perhaps, nothing so much a subject of national extravagance as these spirits.

What will be the consequence, if we are not able to avail ourselves of the resource in question in its full extent? A nation cannot long exist without revenues. Destitute of this essential support, it must resign its independence, and sink into the degraded condition of a province. This is an extremity to which no government will of choice accede. Revenue, therefore, must be had at all events. In this country, if the principal part be not drawn from commerce, it must fall with oppressive weight upon land. It has been already intimated that excises, in their true signification, are too little in unison with the feelings of the people, to admit of great use being made of that mode of taxation; nor, indeed, in the States where almost the sole employment is agriculture, are the objects proper for excise sufficiently numerous to permit very ample collections in that way. Personal estate (as has been before remarked), from the difficulty in tracing it, cannot be subjected to large contributions, by any other means than by taxes on consumption. In populous cities, it may be enough the subject of conjecture, to occasion the oppression of individuals, without much aggregate benefit to the State; but beyond these circles, it must, in a great measure, escape the eye and the hand of the tax-gatherer. As the necessities of the State, nevertheless, must be satisfied in some mode or other, the defect of other resources must throw the principal weight of public burdens on the possessors of land. And as, on the other hand, the wants of the government can never obtain an adequate supply, unless all the sources of revenue are open to its demands, the finances of the community, under such embarrassments, cannot be put into a situation consistent with its respectability or its security. Thus we shall not even have the consolations of a full treasury, to atone for the oppression of that valuable class of the citizens who are employed in the cultivation of the soil. But public and private distress will keep pace with each other in gloomy concert; and unite in deploring the infatuation of those counsels which led to disunion.

PUBLIUS.

[1] If my memory be right they amount to twenty per cent.

Federalist No. 14

Objections to the Proposed Constitution From Extent of Territory Answered

From the New York Packet.

Friday, November 30, 1787.

MADISON

To the People of the State of New York:

WE HAVE seen the necessity of the Union, as our bulwark against foreign danger, as the conservator of peace among ourselves, as the guardian of our commerce and other common interests, as the only substitute for those military establishments which have subverted the liberties of the Old World, and as the proper antidote for the diseases of faction, which have proved fatal to other popular governments, and of which alarming symptoms have been betrayed by our own. All that remains, within this branch of our inquiries, is to take notice of an objection that may be drawn from the great extent of country which the Union embraces. A few observations on this subject will be the more proper, as it is perceived that the adversaries of the new Constitution are availing themselves of the prevailing prejudice with regard to the practicable sphere of republican administration, in order to supply, by imaginary difficulties, the want of those solid objections which they endeavor in vain to find.

The error which limits republican government to a narrow district has been unfolded and refuted in preceding papers. I remark here only that it seems to owe its rise and prevalence chiefly to the confounding of a republic with a democracy, applying to the former reasonings drawn from the nature of the latter. The true distinction between these forms was also adverted to on a former occasion. It is, that in a democracy, the people meet and exercise the government in person; in a republic, they assemble and administer it by their representatives and agents. A democracy, consequently, will be confined to a small spot. A republic may be extended over a large region.

To this accidental source of the error may be added the artifice of some celebrated authors, whose writings have had a great share in forming the modern standard of political opinions. Being subjects either of an absolute or limited monarchy, they have endeavored to heighten the advantages, or palliate the evils of those forms, by placing in comparison the vices and defects of the republican, and by citing as specimens of the latter the turbulent democracies of ancient Greece and modern Italy. Under the confusion of names, it has been an easy task to transfer to a republic observations applicable to a democracy only; and among others, the observation that it can never be established but among a small number of people, living within a small compass of territory.

Such a fallacy may have been the less perceived, as most of the popular governments of antiquity were of the democratic species; and even in modern Europe, to which we owe the great principle of representation, no example is seen of a government wholly popular, and founded, at the same time, wholly on that principle. If Europe has the merit of discovering this great mechanical power in government, by the simple agency of which the will of the largest political body may be concentred, and its force directed to any object which the public good requires, America can claim the merit of making the discovery the basis of unmixed and extensive republics. It is only to be lamented that any of her citizens should wish to deprive her of the additional merit of displaying its full efficacy in the establishment of the comprehensive system now under her consideration.

As the natural limit of a democracy is that distance from the central point which will just permit the most remote citizens to assemble as often as their public functions demand, and will include no greater number than can join in those functions; so the natural limit of a republic is that distance from the centre which will barely allow the representatives to meet as often as may be necessary for the administration of public affairs. Can it be said that the limits of the United States exceed this distance? It will not be said by those who recollect that the Atlantic coast is the longest side of the Union, that during the term of thirteen years, the representatives of the States have been almost continually assembled, and that the members from the most distant States are not chargeable with greater intermissions of attendance than those from the States in the neighborhood of Congress.

That we may form a juster estimate with regard to this interesting subject, let us resort to the actual dimensions of the Union. The limits, as fixed by the treaty of peace, are: on the east the Atlantic, on the south the latitude of thirty-one degrees, on the west the Mississippi, and on the north an irregular line running in some instances beyond the forty-fifth degree, in others falling as low as the forty-second. The southern shore of Lake Erie lies below that latitude. Computing the distance between the thirty-first and forty-fifth degrees, it amounts to nine hundred and seventy-three common miles; computing it from thirty-one to forty-two degrees, to seven hundred and sixty-four miles and a half. Taking the mean for the distance, the amount will be eight hundred and sixty-eight miles and three-fourths. The mean distance from the Atlantic to the Mississippi does not probably exceed seven hundred and fifty miles. On a comparison of this extent with that of several countries in Europe, the practicability of rendering our system commensurate to it appears to be demonstrable. It is not a great deal larger than Germany, where a diet representing the whole empire is continually assembled; or than Poland before the late dismemberment, where another national diet was the depositary of the supreme power. Passing by France and Spain, we find that in Great Britain, inferior as it may be in size, the representatives of the northern extremity of the island have as far to travel to the national council as will be required of those of the most remote parts of the Union.

Favorable as this view of the subject may be, some observations remain which will place it in a light still more satisfactory.

In the first place it is to be remembered that the general government is not to be charged with the whole power of making and administering laws. Its jurisdiction is limited to certain enumerated objects, which concern all the members of the republic, but which are not to be attained by the separate provisions of any. The subordinate governments, which can extend their care to all those other subjects which can be separately provided for, will retain their due authority and activity. Were it proposed by the plan of the convention to abolish the governments of the particular States, its adversaries would have some ground for their objection; though it would not be difficult to show that if they were abolished the general government would be compelled, by the principle of self-preservation, to reinstate them in their proper jurisdiction.

A second observation to be made is that the immediate object of the federal Constitution is to secure the union of the thirteen primitive States, which we know to be practicable; and to add to them such other States as may arise in their own bosoms, or in their neighborhoods, which we cannot doubt to be equally practicable. The arrangements that may be necessary for those angles and fractions of our territory which lie on our northwestern frontier, must be left to those whom further discoveries and experience will render more equal to the task.

Let it be remarked, in the third place, that the intercourse throughout the Union will be facilitated by new improvements. Roads will everywhere be shortened, and kept in better order; accommodations for travelers will be multiplied and meliorated; an interior navigation on our eastern side will be opened throughout, or nearly throughout, the whole extent of the thirteen States. The communication between the Western and Atlantic districts, and between different parts of each, will be rendered more and more easy by those numerous canals with which the beneficence of nature has intersected our country, and which art finds it so little difficult to connect and complete.

A fourth and still more important consideration is, that as almost every State will, on one side or other, be a frontier, and will thus find, in regard to its safety, an inducement to make some sacrifices for the sake of the general protection; so the States which lie at the greatest distance from the heart of the Union, and which, of course, may partake least of the ordinary circulation of its benefits, will be at the same time immediately contiguous to foreign nations, and will consequently stand, on particular occasions, in greatest need of its strength and resources. It may be inconvenient for Georgia, or the States forming our western or northeastern borders, to send their representatives to the seat of government; but they would find it more so to struggle alone against an invading enemy, or even to support alone the whole expense of those precautions which may be dictated by the neighborhood of continual danger. If they should derive less benefit, therefore, from the Union in some respects than the less distant States, they will derive greater benefit from it in other respects, and thus the proper equilibrium will be maintained throughout.

I submit to you, my fellow-citizens, these considerations, in full confidence that the good sense which has so often marked your decisions will allow them their due weight and effect; and that you will never suffer difficulties, however formidable in appearance, or however fashionable the error on which they may be founded, to drive you into the gloomy and perilous scene into which the advocates for disunion would conduct you. Hearken not to the unnatural voice which tells you that the people of America, knit together as they are by so many cords of affection, can no longer live together as members of the same family; can no longer continue the mutual guardians of their mutual happiness; can no longer be fellow citizens of one great, respectable, and flourishing empire. Hearken not to the voice which petulantly tells you that the form of government recommended for your adoption is a novelty in the political world; that it has never yet had a place in the theories of the wildest projectors; that it rashly attempts what it is impossible to accomplish. No, my countrymen, shut your ears against this unhallowed language. Shut your hearts against the poison which it conveys; the kindred blood which flows in the veins of American citizens, the mingled blood which they have shed in defense of their sacred rights, consecrate their Union, and excite horror at the idea of their becoming aliens, rivals, enemies. And if novelties are to be shunned, believe me, the most alarming of all novelties, the most wild of all projects, the most rash of all attempts, is that of rendering us in pieces, in order to preserve our liberties and promote our happiness. But why is the experiment of an extended republic to be rejected, merely because it may comprise what is new? Is it not the glory of the people of America, that, whilst they have paid a decent regard to the opinions of former times and other nations, they have not suffered a blind veneration for antiquity, for custom, or for names, to overrule the suggestions of their own good sense, the knowledge of their own situation, and the lessons of their own experience? To this manly spirit, posterity will be indebted for the possession, and the world for the example, of the numerous innovations displayed on the American theatre, in favor of private rights and public happiness. Had no important step been taken by the leaders of the Revolution for which a precedent could not be discovered, no government established of which an exact model did not present itself, the people of the United States might, at this moment have been numbered among the melancholy victims of misguided councils, must at best have been laboring under the weight of some of those forms which have crushed the liberties of the rest of mankind. Happily for America, happily, we trust, for the whole human race, they pursued a new and more noble course. They accomplished a revolution which has no parallel in the annals of human society. They reared the fabrics of governments which have no model on the face of the globe. They formed the design of a great Confederacy, which it is incumbent on their successors to improve and perpetuate. If their works betray imperfections, we wonder at the fewness of them. If they erred most in the structure of the Union, this was the work most difficult to be executed; this is the work which has been new modelled by the act of your convention, and it is that act on which you are now to deliberate and to decide.

PUBLIUS.

Federalist No. 15

The Insufficiency of the Present Confederation to Preserve the Union

For the Independent Journal.

HAMILTON

To the People of the State of New York.

IN THE course of the preceding papers, I have endeavored, my fellow-citizens, to place before you, in a clear and convincing light, the importance of Union to your political safety and happiness. I have unfolded to you a complication of dangers to which you would be exposed, should you permit that sacred knot which binds the people of America together be severed or dissolved by ambition or by avarice, by jealousy or by misrepresentation. In the sequel of the inquiry through which I propose to accompany you, the truths intended to be inculcated will receive further confirmation from facts and arguments hitherto unnoticed. If the road over which you will still have to pass should in some places appear to you tedious or irksome, you will recollect that you are in quest of information on a subject the most momentous which can engage the attention of a free people, that the field through which you have to travel is in itself spacious, and that the difficulties of the journey have been unnecessarily increased by the mazes with which sophistry has beset the way. It will be my aim to remove the obstacles from your progress in as compendious a manner as it can be done, without sacrificing utility to despatch.

In pursuance of the plan which I have laid down for the discussion of the subject, the point next in order to be examined is the "insufficiency of the present Confederation to the preservation of the Union." It may perhaps be asked what need there is of reasoning or proof to illustrate a position which is not either controverted or doubted, to which the understandings and feelings of all classes of men assent, and which in substance is admitted by the opponents as well as by the friends of the new Constitution. It must in truth be acknowledged that, however these may differ in other respects, they in general appear to harmonize in this sentiment, at least, that there are material imperfections in our national system, and that something is necessary to be done to rescue us from impending anarchy. The facts that support this opinion are no longer objects of speculation. They have forced themselves upon the sensibility of the people at large, and have at length extorted from those, whose mistaken policy has had the principal share in precipitating the extremity at which we are arrived, a reluctant confession of the reality of those defects in the scheme of our federal government, which have been long pointed out and regretted by the intelligent friends of the Union.

We may indeed with propriety be said to have reached almost the last stage of national humiliation. There is scarcely anything that can wound the pride or degrade the character of an independent nation which we do not experience. Are there engagements to the performance of which we are held by every tie respectable among men? These are the subjects of constant and unblushing violation. Do we owe debts to foreigners and to our own citizens contracted in a time of imminent peril for the preservation of our political existence? These remain without any proper or satisfactory provision for their discharge. Have we valuable territories and important posts in the possession of a foreign power which, by express stipulations, ought long since to have been surrendered? These are still retained, to the prejudice of our interests, not less than of our rights. Are we in a condition to resent or to repel the aggression? We have neither troops, nor treasury, nor government. [1] Are we even in a condition to remonstrate with dignity? The just imputations on our own faith, in respect to the same treaty, ought first to be removed. Are we entitled by nature and compact to a free participation in the navigation of the Mississippi? Spain excludes us from it. Is public credit an indispensable resource in time of public danger? We seem to have abandoned its cause as desperate and irretrievable. Is commerce of importance to national wealth? Ours is at the lowest point of declension. Is respectability in the eyes of foreign powers a safeguard against foreign encroachments? The imbecility of our government even forbids them to treat with us. Our ambassadors abroad are the mere pageants of mimic sovereignty. Is a violent and unnatural decrease in the value of land a symptom of national distress? The price of improved land in most parts of the country is much lower than can be accounted for by the quantity of waste land at market, and can only be fully explained by that want of private and public confidence, which are so alarmingly prevalent among all ranks, and which have a direct tendency to depreciate property of every kind. Is private credit the friend and patron of industry? That most useful kind which relates to borrowing and lending is reduced within the narrowest limits, and this still more from an opinion of insecurity than from the scarcity of money. To shorten an enumeration of particulars which can afford neither pleasure nor instruction, it may in general be demanded, what indication is there of national disorder, poverty, and insignificance that could befall a community so peculiarly blessed with natural advantages as we are, which does not form a part of the dark catalogue of our public misfortunes?

This is the melancholy situation to which we have been brought by those very maxims and councils which would now deter us from adopting the proposed Constitution; and which, not content with having conducted us to the brink of a precipice, seem resolved to plunge us into the abyss that awaits us below. Here, my countrymen, impelled by every motive that ought to influence an enlightened people, let us make a firm stand for our safety, our tranquillity, our dignity, our reputation. Let us at last break the fatal charm which has too long seduced us from the paths of felicity and prosperity.

It is true, as has been before observed that facts, too stubborn to be resisted, have produced a species of general assent to the abstract proposition that there exist material defects in our national system; but the usefulness of the concession, on the part of the old adversaries of federal measures, is destroyed by a strenuous opposition to a remedy, upon the only principles that can give it a chance of success. While they admit that the government of the United States is destitute of energy, they contend against conferring upon it those powers which are requisite to supply that energy. They seem still to aim at things repugnant and irreconcilable; at an augmentation of federal authority, without a diminution of State authority; at sovereignty in the Union, and complete independence in the members. They still, in fine, seem to cherish with blind devotion the political monster of an imperium in imperio. This renders a full display of the principal defects of the Confederation necessary, in order to show that the evils we experience do not proceed from minute or partial imperfections, but from fundamental errors in the structure of the building, which cannot be amended otherwise than by an alteration in the first principles and main pillars of the fabric.

The great and radical vice in the construction of the existing Confederation is in the principle of LEGISLATION for STATES or GOVERNMENTS, in their CORPORATE or COLLECTIVE CAPACITIES, and as contradistinguished from the INDIVIDUALS of which they consist. Though this principle does not run through all the powers delegated to the Union, yet it pervades and governs those on which the efficacy of the rest depends. Except as to the rule of appointment, the United States has an indefinite discretion to make requisitions for men and money; but they have no authority to raise either, by regulations extending to the individual citizens of America. The consequence of this is, that though in theory their resolutions concerning those objects are laws, constitutionally binding on the members of the Union, yet in practice they are mere recommendations which the States observe or disregard at their option.

It is a singular instance of the capriciousness of the human mind, that after all the admonitions we have had from experience on this head, there should still be found men who object to the new Constitution, for deviating from a principle which has been found the bane of the old, and which is in itself evidently incompatible with the idea of GOVERNMENT; a principle, in short, which, if it is to be executed at all, must substitute the violent and sanguinary agency of the sword to the mild influence of the magistracy.

There is nothing absurd or impracticable in the idea of a league or alliance between independent nations for certain defined purposes precisely stated in a treaty regulating all the details of time, place, circumstance, and quantity; leaving nothing to future discretion; and depending for its execution on the good faith of the parties. Compacts of this kind exist among all civilized nations, subject to the usual vicissitudes of peace and war, of observance and non-observance, as the interests or passions of the contracting powers dictate. In the early part of the present century there was an epidemical rage in Europe for this species of compacts, from which the politicians of the times fondly hoped for benefits which were never realized. With a view to establishing the equilibrium of power and the peace of that part of the world, all the resources of negotiation were exhausted, and triple and quadruple alliances were formed; but they were scarcely formed before they were broken, giving an instructive but afflicting lesson to mankind, how little dependence is to be placed on treaties which have no other sanction than the obligations of good faith, and which oppose general considerations of peace and justice to the impulse of any immediate interest or passion.

If the particular States in this country are disposed to stand in a similar relation to each other, and to drop the project of a general DISCRETIONARY SUPERINTENDENCE, the scheme would indeed be pernicious, and would entail upon us all the mischiefs which have been enumerated under the first head; but it would have the merit of being, at least, consistent and practicable Abandoning all views towards a confederate government, this would bring us to a simple alliance offensive and defensive; and would place us in a situation to be alternate friends and enemies of each other, as our mutual jealousies and rivalships, nourished by the intrigues of foreign nations, should prescribe to us.

But if we are unwilling to be placed in this perilous situation; if we still will adhere to the design of a national government, or, which is the same thing, of a superintending power, under the direction of a common council, we must resolve to incorporate into our plan those ingredients which may be considered as forming the characteristic difference between a league and a government; we must extend the authority of the Union to the persons of the citizens, —the only proper objects of government.

Government implies the power of making laws. It is essential to the idea of a law, that it be attended with a sanction; or, in other words, a penalty or punishment for disobedience. If there be no penalty annexed to disobedience, the resolutions or commands which pretend to be laws will, in fact, amount to nothing more than advice or recommendation. This penalty, whatever it may be, can only be inflicted in two ways: by the agency of the courts and ministers of justice, or by military force; by the COERCION of the magistracy, or by the COERCION of arms. The first kind can evidently apply only to men; the last kind must of necessity, be employed against bodies politic, or communities, or States. It is evident that there is no process of a court by which the observance of the laws can, in the last resort, be enforced. Sentences may be denounced against them for violations of their duty; but these sentences can only be carried into execution by the sword. In an association where the general authority is confined to the collective bodies of the communities, that compose it, every breach of the laws must involve a state of war; and military execution must become the only instrument of civil obedience. Such a state of things can certainly not deserve the name of government, nor would any prudent man choose to commit his happiness to it.

There was a time when we were told that breaches, by the States, of the regulations of the federal authority were not to be expected; that a sense of common interest would preside over the conduct of the respective members, and would beget a full compliance with all the constitutional requisitions of the Union. This language, at the present day, would appear as wild as a great part of what we now hear from the same quarter will be thought, when we shall have received further lessons from that best oracle of wisdom, experience. It at all times betrayed an ignorance of the true springs by which human conduct is actuated, and belied the original inducements to the establishment of civil power. Why has government been instituted at all? Because the passions of men will not conform to the dictates of reason and justice, without constraint. Has it been found that bodies of men act with more rectitude or greater disinterestedness than individuals? The contrary of this has been inferred by all accurate observers of the conduct of mankind; and the inference is founded upon obvious reasons. Regard to reputation has a less active influence, when the infamy of a bad action is to be divided among a number than when it is to fall singly upon one. A spirit of faction, which is apt to mingle its poison in the deliberations of all bodies of men, will often hurry the persons of whom they are composed into improprieties and excesses, for which they would blush in a private capacity.

In addition to all this, there is, in the nature of sovereign power, an impatience of control, that disposes those who are invested with the exercise of it, to look with an evil eye upon all external attempts to restrain or direct its operations. From this spirit it happens, that in every political association which is formed upon the principle of uniting in a common interest a number of lesser sovereignties, there will be found a kind of eccentric tendency in the subordinate or inferior orbs, by the operation of which there will be a perpetual effort in each to fly off from the common centre. This tendency is not difficult to be accounted for. It has its origin in the love of power. Power controlled or abridged is almost always the rival and enemy of that power by which it is controlled or abridged. This simple proposition will teach us how little reason there is to expect, that the persons intrusted with the administration of the affairs of the particular members of a confederacy will at all times be ready, with perfect good-humor, and an unbiased regard to the public weal, to execute the resolutions or decrees of the general authority. The reverse of this results from the constitution of human nature.

If, therefore, the measures of the Confederacy cannot be executed without the intervention of the particular administrations, there will be little prospect of their being executed at all. The rulers of the respective members, whether they have a constitutional right to do it or not, will undertake to judge of the propriety of the measures themselves. They will consider the conformity of the thing proposed or required to their immediate interests or aims; the momentary conveniences or inconveniences that would attend its adoption. All this will be done; and in a spirit of interested and suspicious scrutiny, without that knowledge of national circumstances and reasons of state, which is essential to a right judgment, and with that strong predilection in favor of local objects, which can hardly fail to mislead the decision. The same process must be repeated in every member of which the body is constituted; and the execution of the plans, framed by the councils of the whole, will always fluctuate on the discretion of the ill-informed and prejudiced opinion of every part. Those who have been conversant in the proceedings of popular assemblies; who have seen how difficult it often is, where there is no exterior pressure of circumstances, to bring them to harmonious resolutions on important points, will readily conceive how impossible it must be to induce a number of such assemblies, deliberating at a distance from each other, at different times, and under different impressions, long to co-operate in the same views and pursuits.

In our case, the concurrence of thirteen distinct sovereign wills is requisite, under the Confederation, to the complete execution of every important measure that proceeds from the Union. It has happened as was to have been foreseen. The measures of the Union have not been executed; the delinquencies of the States have, step by step, matured themselves to an extreme, which has, at length, arrested all the wheels of the national government, and brought them to an awful stand. Congress at this time scarcely possess the means of keeping up the forms of administration, till the States can have time to agree upon a more substantial substitute for the present shadow of a federal government. Things did not come to this desperate extremity at once. The causes which have been specified produced at first only unequal and disproportionate degrees of compliance with the requisitions of the Union. The greater deficiencies of some States furnished the pretext of example and the temptation of interest to the complying, or to the least delinquent States. Why should we do more in proportion than those who are embarked with us in the same political voyage? Why should we consent to bear more than our proper share of the common burden? These were suggestions which human selfishness could not withstand, and which even speculative men, who looked forward to remote consequences, could not, without hesitation, combat. Each State, yielding to the persuasive voice of immediate interest or convenience, has successively withdrawn its support, till the frail and tottering edifice seems ready to fall upon our heads, and to crush us beneath its ruins.

PUBLIUS.

[1] "I mean for the Union."

Federalist No. 17

The Same Subject Continued
(The Insufficiency of the Present Confederation to Preserve the Union)
For the Independent Journal.
HAMILTON

To the People of the State of New York:

AN OBJECTION, of a nature different from that which has been stated and answered, in my last address, may perhaps be likewise urged against the principle of legislation for the individual citizens of America. It may be said that it would tend to render the government of the Union too powerful, and to enable it to absorb those residuary authorities, which it might be judged proper to leave with the States for local purposes. Allowing the utmost latitude to the love of power which any reasonable man can require, I confess I am at a loss to discover what temptation the persons intrusted with the administration of the general government could ever feel to divest the States of the authorities of that description. The regulation of the mere domestic police of a State appears to me to hold out slender allurements to ambition. Commerce, finance, negotiation, and war seem to comprehend all the objects which have charms for minds governed by that passion; and all the powers necessary to those objects ought, in the first instance, to be lodged in the national depository. The administration of private justice between the citizens of the same State, the supervision of agriculture and of other concerns of a similar nature, all those things, in short, which are proper to be provided for by local legislation, can never be desirable cares of a general jurisdiction. It is therefore improbable that there should exist a disposition in the federal councils to usurp the powers with which they are connected; because the attempt to exercise those powers would be as troublesome as it would be nugatory; and the possession of them, for that reason, would contribute nothing to the dignity, to the importance, or to the splendor of the national government.

But let it be admitted, for argument's sake, that mere wantonness and lust of domination would be sufficient to beget that disposition; still it may be safely affirmed, that the sense of the constituent body of the national representatives, or, in other words, the people of the several States, would control the indulgence of so extravagant an appetite. It will always be far more easy for the State governments to encroach upon the national authorities than for the national government to encroach upon the State authorities. The proof of this proposition turns upon the greater degree of influence which the State governments if they administer their affairs with uprightness and prudence, will generally possess over the people; a circumstance which at the same time teaches us that there is an inherent and intrinsic weakness in all federal constitutions; and that too much pains cannot be taken in their organization, to give them all the force which is compatible with the principles of liberty.

The superiority of influence in favor of the particular governments would result partly from the diffusive construction of the national government, but chiefly from the nature of the objects to which the attention of the State administrations would be directed.

It is a known fact in human nature, that its affections are commonly weak in proportion to the distance or diffusiveness of the object. Upon the same principle that a man is more attached to his family than to his neighborhood, to his neighborhood than to the community at large, the people of each State would be apt to feel a stronger bias towards their local governments than towards the government of the Union; unless the force of that principle should be destroyed by a much better administration of the latter.

This strong propensity of the human heart would find powerful auxiliaries in the objects of State regulation.

The variety of more minute interests, which will necessarily fall under the superintendence of the local administrations, and which will form so many rivulets of influence, running through every part of the society, cannot be particularized, without involving a detail too tedious and uninteresting to compensate for the instruction it might afford.

There is one transcendant advantage belonging to the province of the State governments, which alone suffices to place the matter in a clear and satisfactory light,—I mean the ordinary administration of criminal and civil justice. This, of all others, is the most powerful, most universal, and most attractive source of popular obedience and attachment. It is that which, being the immediate and visible guardian of life and property, having its benefits and its terrors in constant activity before the public eye, regulating all those personal interests and familiar concerns to which the sensibility of individuals is more immediately awake, contributes, more than any other circumstance, to impressing upon the minds of the people, affection, esteem, and reverence towards the government. This great cement of society, which will diffuse itself almost wholly through the channels of the particular governments, independent of all other causes of influence, would insure them so decided an empire over their respective citizens as to render them at all times a complete counterpoise, and, not unfrequently, dangerous rivals to the power of the Union.

The operations of the national government, on the other hand, falling less immediately under the observation of the mass of the citizens, the benefits derived from it will chiefly be perceived and attended to by speculative men. Relating to more general interests, they will be less apt to come home to the feelings of the people; and, in proportion, less likely to inspire an habitual sense of obligation, and an active sentiment of attachment.

The reasoning on this head has been abundantly exemplified by the experience of all federal constitutions with which we are acquainted, and of all others which have borne the least analogy to them.

Though the ancient feudal systems were not, strictly speaking, confederacies, yet they partook of the nature of that species of association. There was a common head, chieftain, or sovereign, whose authority extended over the whole nation; and a number of subordinate vassals, or feudatories, who had large portions of land allotted to them, and numerous trains of INFERIOR vassals or retainers, who occupied and cultivated that land upon the tenure of fealty or obedience, to the persons of whom they held it. Each principal vassal was a kind of sovereign, within his particular demesnes. The consequences of this situation were a continual opposition to authority of the sovereign, and frequent wars between the great barons or chief feudatories themselves. The power of the head of the nation was commonly too weak, either to preserve the public peace, or to protect the people against the oppressions of their immediate lords. This period of European affairs is emphatically styled by historians, the times of feudal anarchy.

When the sovereign happened to be a man of vigorous and warlike temper and of superior abilities, he would acquire a personal weight and influence, which answered, for the time, the purpose of a more regular authority. But in general, the power of the barons triumphed over that of the prince; and in many instances his dominion was entirely thrown off, and the great fiefs were erected into independent principalities or States. In those instances in which the monarch finally prevailed over his vassals, his success was chiefly owing to the tyranny of those vassals over their dependents. The barons, or nobles, equally the enemies of the sovereign and the oppressors of the common people, were dreaded and detested by both; till mutual danger and mutual interest effected a union between them fatal to the power of the aristocracy. Had the nobles, by a conduct of clemency and justice, preserved the fidelity and devotion of their retainers and followers, the contests between them and the prince must almost always have ended in their favor, and in the abridgment or subversion of the royal authority.

This is not an assertion founded merely in speculation or conjecture. Among other illustrations of its truth which might be cited, Scotland will furnish a cogent example. The spirit of clanship which was, at an early day, introduced into that kingdom, uniting the nobles and their dependants by ties equivalent to those of kindred, rendered the aristocracy a constant overmatch for the power of the monarch, till the incorporation with England subdued its fierce and ungovernable spirit, and reduced it within those rules of subordination which a more rational and more energetic system of civil polity had previously established in the latter kingdom.

The separate governments in a confederacy may aptly be compared with the feudal baronies; with this advantage in their favor, that from the reasons already explained, they will generally possess the confidence and good-will of the people, and with so important a support, will be able effectually to oppose all encroachments of the national government. It will be well if they are not able to counteract its legitimate and necessary authority. The points of similitude consist in the rivalship of power, applicable to both, and in the CONCENTRATION of large portions of the strength of the community into particular DEPOSITS, in one case at the disposal of individuals, in the other case at the disposal of political bodies.

A concise review of the events that have attended confederate governments will further illustrate this important doctrine; an inattention to which has been the great source of our political mistakes, and has given our jealousy a direction to the wrong side. This review shall form the subject of some ensuing papers.

PUBLIUS.

Federalist No. 20

The Same Subject Continued
(The Insufficiency of the Present Confederation to Preserve the Union)

From the New York Packet.

Tuesday, December 11, 1787.

HAMILTON AND MADISON

To the People of the State of New York:

THE United Netherlands are a confederacy of republics, or rather of aristocracies of a very remarkable texture, yet confirming all the lessons derived from those which we have already reviewed.

The union is composed of seven coequal and sovereign states, and each state or province is a composition of equal and independent cities. In all important cases, not only the provinces but the cities must be unanimous.

The sovereignty of the Union is represented by the States-General, consisting usually of about fifty deputies appointed by the provinces. They hold their seats, some for life, some for six, three, and one years; from two provinces they continue in appointment during pleasure.

The States-General have authority to enter into treaties and alliances; to make war and peace; to raise armies and equip fleets; to ascertain quotas and demand contributions. In all these cases, however, unanimity and the sanction of their constituents are requisite. They have authority to appoint and receive ambassadors; to execute treaties and alliances already formed; to provide for the collection of duties on imports and exports; to regulate the mint, with a saving to the provincial rights; to govern as sovereigns the dependent territories. The provinces are restrained, unless with the general consent, from entering into foreign treaties; from establishing imposts injurious to others, or charging their neighbors with higher duties than their own subjects. A council of state, a chamber of accounts, with five colleges of admiralty, aid and fortify the federal administration.

The executive magistrate of the union is the stadtholder, who is now an hereditary prince. His principal weight and influence in the republic are derived from this independent title; from his great patrimonial estates; from his family connections with some of the chief potentates of Europe; and, more than all, perhaps, from his being stadtholder in the several provinces, as well as for the union; in which provincial quality he has the appointment of town magistrates under certain regulations, executes provincial decrees, presides when he pleases in the provincial tribunals, and has throughout the power of pardon.

As stadtholder of the union, he has, however, considerable prerogatives.

In his political capacity he has authority to settle disputes between the provinces, when other methods fail; to assist at the deliberations of the States-General, and at their particular conferences; to give audiences to foreign ambassadors, and to keep agents for his particular affairs at foreign courts.

In his military capacity he commands the federal troops, provides for garrisons, and in general regulates military affairs; disposes of all appointments, from colonels to ensigns, and of the governments and posts of fortified towns.

In his marine capacity he is admiral-general, and superintends and directs every thing relative to naval forces and other naval affairs; presides in the admiralties in person or by proxy; appoints lieutenant-admirals and other officers; and establishes councils of war, whose sentences are not executed till he approves them.

His revenue, exclusive of his private income, amounts to three hundred thousand florins. The standing army which he commands consists of about forty thousand men.

Such is the nature of the celebrated Belgic confederacy, as delineated on parchment. What are the characters which practice has stamped upon it? Imbecility in the government; discord among the provinces; foreign influence and indignities; a precarious existence in peace, and peculiar calamities from war.

It was long ago remarked by Grotius, that nothing but the hatred of his countrymen to the house of Austria kept them from being ruined by the vices of their constitution.

The union of Utrecht, says another respectable writer, reposes an authority in the States-General, seemingly sufficient to secure harmony, but the jealousy in each province renders the practice very different from the theory.

The same instrument, says another, obliges each province to levy certain contributions; but this article never could, and probably never will, be executed; because the inland provinces, who have little commerce, cannot pay an equal quota.

In matters of contribution, it is the practice to waive the articles of the constitution. The danger of delay obliges the consenting provinces to furnish their quotas, without waiting for the others; and then to obtain reimbursement from the others, by deputations, which are frequent, or otherwise, as they can. The great wealth and influence of the province of Holland enable her to effect both these purposes.

It has more than once happened, that the deficiencies had to be ultimately collected at the point of the bayonet; a thing practicable, though dreadful, in a confederacy where one of the members exceeds in force all the rest, and where several of them are too small to meditate resistance; but utterly impracticable in one composed of members, several of which are equal to each other in strength and resources, and equal singly to a vigorous and persevering defense.

Foreign ministers, says Sir William Temple, who was himself a foreign minister, elude matters taken ad referendum, by tampering with the provinces and cities. In 1726, the treaty of Hanover was delayed by these means a whole year. Instances of a like nature are numerous and notorious.

In critical emergencies, the States-General are often compelled to overleap their constitutional bounds. In 1688, they concluded a treaty of themselves at the risk of their heads. The treaty of Westphalia, in 1648, by which their independence was formerly and finally recognized, was concluded without the consent of Zealand. Even as recently as the last treaty of peace with Great Britain, the constitutional principle of unanimity was departed from. A weak constitution must necessarily terminate in dissolution, for want of proper powers, or the usurpation of powers requisite for the public safety. Whether the usurpation, when once begun, will stop at the salutary point, or go forward to the dangerous extreme, must depend on the contingencies of the moment. Tyranny has perhaps oftener grown out of the assumptions of power, called for, on pressing exigencies, by a defective constitution, than out of the full exercise of the largest constitutional authorities.

Notwithstanding the calamities produced by the stadtholdership, it has been supposed that without his influence in the individual provinces, the causes of anarchy manifest in the confederacy would long ago have dissolved it. "Under such a government," says the Abbé Mably, "the Union could never have subsisted, if the provinces had not a spring within themselves, capable of quickening their tardiness, and compelling them to the same way of thinking. This spring is the stadtholder." It is remarked by Sir William Temple, "that in the intermissions of the stadtholdership, Holland, by her riches and her authority, which drew the others into a sort of dependence, supplied the place."

These are not the only circumstances which have controlled the tendency to anarchy and dissolution. The surrounding powers impose an absolute necessity of union to a certain degree, at the same time that they nourish by their intrigues the constitutional vices which keep the republic in some degree always at their mercy.

The true patriots have long bewailed the fatal tendency of these vices, and have made no less than four regular experiments by EXTRAORDINARY ASSEMBLIES, convened for the special purpose, to apply a remedy. As many times has their laudable zeal found it impossible to UNITE THE PUBLIC COUNCILS in reforming the known, the acknowledged, the fatal evils of the existing constitution. Let us pause, my fellow-citizens, for one moment, over this melancholy and monitory lesson of history; and with the tear that drops for the calamities brought on mankind by their adverse opinions and selfish passions, let our gratitude mingle an ejaculation to Heaven, for the propitious concord which has distinguished the consultations for our political happiness.

A design was also conceived of establishing a general tax to be administered by the federal authority. This also had its adversaries and failed.

This unhappy people seem to be now suffering from popular convulsions, from dissensions among the states, and from the actual invasion of foreign arms, the crisis of their destiny. All nations have their eyes fixed on the awful spectacle. The first wish prompted by humanity is, that this severe trial may issue in such a revolution of their government as will establish their union, and render it the parent of tranquillity, freedom and happiness: The next, that the asylum under which, we trust, the enjoyment of these blessings will speedily be secured in this country, may receive and console them for the catastrophe of their own.

I make no apology for having dwelt so long on the contemplation of these federal precedents. Experience is the oracle of truth; and where its responses are unequivocal, they ought to be conclusive and sacred. The important truth, which it unequivocally pronounces in the present case, is that a sovereignty over sovereigns, a government over governments, a legislation for communities, as contradistinguished from individuals, as it is a solecism in theory, so in practice it is subversive of the order and ends of civil polity, by substituting VIOLENCE in place of LAW, or the destructive COERCION of the SWORD in place of the mild and salutary COERCION of the MAGISTRACY.

PUBLIUS.

Federalist No. 21
Other Defects of the Present Confederation
For the Independent Journal.

HAMILTON

To the People of the State of New York:

HAVING in the three last numbers taken a summary review of the principal circumstances and events which have depicted the genius and fate of other confederate governments, I shall now proceed in the enumeration of the most important of those defects which have hitherto disappointed our hopes from the system established among ourselves. To form a safe and satisfactory judgment of the proper remedy, it is absolutely necessary that we should be well acquainted with the extent and malignity of the disease.

The next most palpable defect of the subsisting Confederation, is the total want of a SANCTION to its laws. The United States, as now composed, have no powers to exact obedience, or punish disobedience to their resolutions, either by pecuniary mulcts, by a suspension or divestiture of privileges, or by any other constitutional mode. There is no express delegation of authority to them to use force against delinquent members; and if such a right should be ascribed to the federal head, as resulting from the nature of the social compact between the States, it must be by inference and construction, in the face of that part of the second article, by which it is declared, "that each State shall retain every power, jurisdiction, and right, not EXPRESSLY delegated to the United States in Congress assembled." There is, doubtless, a striking absurdity in supposing that a right of this kind does not exist, but we are reduced to the dilemma either of embracing that supposition, preposterous as it may seem, or of contravening or explaining away a provision, which has been of late a repeated theme of the eulogies of those who oppose the new Constitution; and the want of which, in that plan, has been the subject of much plausible animadversion, and severe criticism. If we are unwilling to impair the force of this applauded provision, we shall be obliged to conclude, that the United States afford the extraordinary spectacle of a government destitute even of the shadow of constitutional power to enforce the execution of its own laws. It will appear, from the specimens which have been cited, that the American Confederacy, in this particular, stands discriminated from every other institution of a similar kind, and exhibits a new and unexampled phenomenon in the political world.

The want of a mutual guaranty of the State governments is another capital imperfection in the federal plan. There is nothing of this kind declared in the articles that compose it; and to imply a tacit guaranty from considerations of utility, would be a still more flagrant departure from the clause which has been mentioned, than to imply a tacit power of coercion from the like considerations. The want of a guaranty, though it might in its consequences endanger the Union, does not so immediately attack its existence as the want of a constitutional sanction to its laws.

Without a guaranty the assistance to be derived from the Union in repelling those domestic dangers which may sometimes threaten the existence of the State constitutions, must be renounced. Usurpation may rear its crest in each State, and trample upon the liberties of the people, while the national government could legally do nothing more than behold its encroachments with indignation and regret. A successful faction may erect a tyranny on the ruins of order and law, while no succor could constitutionally be afforded by the Union to the friends and supporters of the government. The tempestuous situation from which Massachusetts has scarcely emerged, evinces that dangers of this kind are not merely speculative. Who can determine what might have been the issue of her late convulsions, if the malcontents had been headed by a Caesar or by a Cromwell? Who can predict what effect a despotism, established in Massachusetts, would have upon the liberties of New Hampshire or Rhode Island, of Connecticut or New York?

The inordinate pride of State importance has suggested to some minds an objection to the principle of a guaranty in the federal government, as involving an officious interference in the domestic concerns of the members. A scruple of this kind would deprive us of one of the principal advantages to be expected from union, and can only flow from a misapprehension of the nature of the provision itself. It could be no impediment to reforms of the State constitution by a majority of the people in a legal and peaceable mode. This right would remain undiminished. The guaranty could only operate against changes to be effected by violence. Towards the preventions of calamities of this kind, too many checks cannot be provided. The peace of society and the stability of government depend absolutely on the efficacy of the precautions adopted on this head. Where the whole power of the government is in the hands of the people, there is the less pretense for the use of violent remedies in partial or occasional distempers of the State. The natural cure for an ill-administration, in a popular or representative constitution, is a change of men. A guaranty by the national authority would be as much levelled against the usurpations of rulers as against the ferments and outrages of faction and sedition in the community.

The principle of regulating the contributions of the States to the common treasury by QUOTAS is another fundamental error in the Confederation. Its repugnancy to an adequate supply of the national exigencies has been already pointed out, and has sufficiently appeared from the trial which has been made of it. I speak of it now solely with a view to equality among the States. Those who have been accustomed to contemplate the circumstances which produce and constitute national wealth, must be satisfied that there is no common standard or barometer by which the degrees of it can be ascertained. Neither the value of lands, nor the numbers of the people, which have been successively proposed as the rule of State contributions, has any pretension to being a just representative. If we compare the wealth of the United Netherlands with that of Russia or Germany, or even of France, and if we at the same time compare the total value of the lands and the aggregate population of that contracted district with the total value of the lands and the aggregate population of the immense regions of either of the three last-mentioned countries, we shall at once discover that there is no comparison between the proportion of either of these two objects and that of the relative wealth of those nations. If the like parallel were to be run between several of the American States, it would furnish a like result. Let Virginia be contrasted with North Carolina, Pennsylvania with Connecticut, or Maryland with New Jersey, and we shall be convinced that the respective abilities of those States, in relation to revenue, bear little or no analogy to their comparative stock in lands or to their comparative population. The position may be equally illustrated by a similar process between the counties of the same State. No man who is acquainted with the State of New York will doubt that the active wealth of King's County bears a much greater proportion to that of Montgomery than it would appear to be if we should take either the total value of the lands or the total number of the people as a criterion!

The wealth of nations depends upon an infinite variety of causes. Situation, soil, climate, the nature of the productions, the nature of the government, the genius of the citizens, the degree of information they possess, the state of commerce, of arts, of industry, these circumstances and many more, too complex, minute, or adventitious to admit of a particular specification, occasion differences hardly conceivable in the relative opulence and riches of different countries. The consequence clearly is that there can be no common measure of national wealth, and, of course, no general or stationary rule by which the ability of a state to pay taxes can be determined. The attempt, therefore, to regulate the contributions of the members of a confederacy by any such rule, cannot fail to be productive of glaring inequality and extreme oppression.

This inequality would of itself be sufficient in America to work the eventual destruction of the Union, if any mode of enforcing a compliance with its requisitions could be devised. The suffering States would not long consent to remain associated upon a principle which distributes the public burdens with so unequal a hand, and which was calculated to impoverish and oppress the citizens of some States, while those of others would scarcely be conscious of the small proportion of the weight they were required to sustain. This, however, is an evil inseparable from the principle of quotas and requisitions.

There is no method of steering clear of this inconvenience, but by authorizing the national government to raise its own revenues in its own way. Imposts, excises, and, in general, all duties upon articles of consumption, may be compared to a fluid, which will, in time, find its level with the means of paying them. The amount to be contributed by each citizen will in a degree be at his own option, and can be regulated by an attention to his resources. The rich may be extravagant, the poor can be frugal; and private oppression may always be avoided by a judicious selection of objects proper for such impositions. If inequalities should arise in some States from duties on particular objects, these will, in all probability, be counterbalanced by proportional inequalities in other States, from the duties on other objects. In the course of time and things, an equilibrium, as far as it is attainable in so complicated a subject, will be established everywhere. Or, if inequalities should still exist, they would neither be so great in their degree, so uniform in their operation, nor so odious in their appearance, as those which would necessarily spring from quotas, upon any scale that can possibly be devised.

It is a signal advantage of taxes on articles of consumption, that they contain in their own nature a security against excess. They prescribe their own limit; which cannot be exceeded without defeating the end proposed, that is, an extension of the revenue. When applied to this object, the saying is as just as it is witty, that, "in political arithmetic, two and two do not always make four."

If duties are too high, they lessen the consumption; the collection is eluded; and the product to the treasury is not so great as when they are confined within proper and moderate bounds. This forms a complete barrier against any material oppression of the citizens by taxes of this class, and is itself a natural limitation of the power of imposing them.

Impositions of this kind usually fall under the denomination of indirect taxes, and must for a long time constitute the chief part of the revenue raised in this country. Those of the direct kind, which principally relate to land and buildings, may admit of a rule of apportionment. Either the value of land, or the number of the people, may serve as a standard. The state of agriculture and the populousness of a country have been considered as nearly connected with each other. And, as a rule, for the purpose intended, numbers, in the view of simplicity and certainty, are entitled to a preference. In every country it is a herculean task to obtain a valuation of the land; in a country imperfectly settled and progressive in improvement, the difficulties are increased almost to impracticability. The expense of an accurate valuation is, in all situations, a formidable objection. In a branch of taxation where no limits to the discretion of the government are to be found in the nature of things, the establishment of a fixed rule, not incompatible with the end, may be attended with fewer inconveniences than to leave that discretion altogether at large.

PUBLIUS.

Federalist No. 22

The Same Subject Continued
(Other Defects of the Present Confederation)
From the New York Packet.
Friday, December 14, 1787.
HAMILTON
To the People of the State of New York:

IN ADDITION to the defects already enumerated in the existing federal system, there are others of not less importance, which concur in rendering it altogether unfit for the administration of the affairs of the Union.

The want of a power to regulate commerce is by all parties allowed to be of the number. The utility of such a power has been anticipated under the first head of our inquiries; and for this reason, as well as from the universal conviction entertained upon the subject, little need be added in this place. It is indeed evident, on the most superficial view, that there is no object, either as it respects the interests of trade or finance, that more strongly demands a federal superintendence. The want of it has already operated as a bar to the formation of beneficial treaties with foreign powers, and has given occasions of dissatisfaction between the States. No nation acquainted with the nature of our political association would be unwise enough to enter into stipulations with the United States, by which they conceded privileges of any importance to them, while they were apprised that the engagements on the part of the Union might at any moment be violated by its members, and while they found from experience that they might enjoy every advantage they desired in our markets, without granting us any return but such as their momentary convenience might suggest. It is not, therefore, to be wondered at that Mr. Jenkinson, in ushering into the House of Commons a bill for regulating the temporary intercourse between the two countries, should preface its introduction by a declaration that similar provisions in former bills had been found to answer every purpose to the commerce of Great Britain, and that it would be prudent to persist in the plan until it should appear whether the American government was likely or not to acquire greater consistency. [1]

Several States have endeavored, by separate prohibitions, restrictions, and exclusions, to influence the conduct of that kingdom in this particular, but the want of concert, arising from the want of a general authority and from clashing and dissimilar views in the State, has hitherto frustrated every experiment of the kind, and will continue to do so as long as the same obstacles to a uniformity of measures continue to exist.

The interfering and unneighborly regulations of some States, contrary to the true spirit of the Union, have, in different instances, given just cause of umbrage and complaint to others, and it is to be feared that examples of this nature, if not restrained by a national control, would be multiplied and extended till they became not less serious sources of animosity and discord than injurious impediments to the intercourse between the different parts of the Confederacy. "The commerce of the German empire [2] is in continual trammels from the multiplicity of the duties which the several princes and states exact upon the merchandises passing through their territories, by means of which the fine streams and navigable rivers with which Germany is so happily watered are rendered almost useless." Though the genius of the people of this country might never permit this description to be strictly applicable to us, yet we may reasonably expect, from the gradual conflicts of State regulations, that the citizens of each would at length come to be considered and treated by the others in no better light than that of foreigners and aliens.

The power of raising armies, by the most obvious construction of the articles of the Confederation, is merely a power of making requisitions upon the States for quotas of men. This practice in the course of the late war, was found replete with obstructions to a vigorous and to an economical system of defense. It gave birth to a competition between the States which created a kind of auction for men. In order to furnish the quotas required of them, they outbid each other till bounties grew to an enormous and insupportable size. The hope of a still further increase afforded an inducement to those who were disposed to serve to procrastinate their enlistment, and disinclined them from engaging for any considerable periods. Hence, slow and scanty levies of men, in the most critical emergencies of our affairs; short enlistments at an unparalleled expense; continual fluctuations in the troops, ruinous to their discipline and subjecting the public safety frequently to the perilous crisis of a disbanded army. Hence, also, those oppressive expedients for raising men which were upon several occasions practiced, and which nothing but the enthusiasm of liberty would have induced the people to endure.

This method of raising troops is not more unfriendly to economy and vigor than it is to an equal distribution of the burden. The States near the seat of war, influenced by motives of self-preservation, made efforts to furnish their quotas, which even exceeded their abilities; while those at a distance from danger were, for the most part, as remiss as the others were diligent, in their exertions. The immediate pressure of this inequality was not in this case, as in that of the contributions of money, alleviated by the hope of a final liquidation. The States which did not pay their proportions of money might at least be charged with their deficiencies; but no account could be formed of the deficiencies in the supplies of men. We shall not, however, see much reason to regret the want of this hope, when we consider how little prospect there is, that the most delinquent States will ever be able to make compensation for their pecuniary failures. The system of quotas and requisitions, whether it be applied to men or money, is, in every view, a system of imbecility in the Union, and of inequality and injustice among the members.

The right of equal suffrage among the States is another exceptionable part of the Confederation. Every idea of proportion and every rule of fair representation conspire to condemn a principle, which gives to Rhode Island an equal weight in the scale of power with Massachusetts, or Connecticut, or New York; and to Deleware an equal voice in the national deliberations with Pennsylvania, or Virginia, or North Carolina. Its operation contradicts the fundamental maxim of republican government, which requires that the sense of the majority should prevail. Sophistry may reply, that sovereigns are equal, and that a majority of the votes of the States will be a majority of confederated America. But this kind of logical legerdemain will never counteract the plain suggestions of justice and common-sense. It may happen that this majority of States is a small minority of the people of America [3]; and two thirds of the people of America could not long be persuaded, upon the credit of artificial distinctions and syllogistic subtleties, to submit their interests to the management and disposal of one third. The larger States would after a while revolt from the idea of receiving the law from the smaller. To acquiesce in such a privation of their due importance in the political scale, would be not merely to be insensible to the love of power, but even to sacrifice the desire of equality. It is neither rational to expect the first, nor just to require the last. The smaller States, considering how peculiarly their safety and welfare depend on union, ought readily to renounce a pretension which, if not relinquished, would prove fatal to its duration.

It may be objected to this, that not seven but nine States, or two thirds of the whole number, must consent to the most important resolutions; and it may be thence inferred that nine States would always comprehend a majority of the Union. But this does not obviate the impropriety of an equal vote between States of the most unequal dimensions and populousness; nor is the inference accurate in point of fact; for we can enumerate nine States which contain less than a majority of the people [4]; and it is constitutionally possible that these nine may give the vote. Besides, there are matters of considerable moment determinable by a bare majority; and there are others, concerning which doubts have been entertained, which, if interpreted in favor of the sufficiency of a vote of seven States, would extend its operation to interests of the first magnitude. In addition to this, it is to be observed that there is a probability of an increase in the number of States, and no provision for a proportional augmentation of the ratio of votes.

But this is not all: what at first sight may seem a remedy, is, in reality, a poison. To give a minority a negative upon the majority (which is always the case where more than a majority is requisite to a decision), is, in its tendency, to subject the sense of the greater number to that of the lesser. Congress, from the nonattendance of a few States, have been frequently in the situation of a Polish diet, where a single VOTE has been sufficient to put a stop to all their movements. A sixtieth part of the Union, which is about the proportion of Delaware and Rhode Island, has several times been able to oppose an entire bar to its operations. This is one of those refinements which, in practice, has an effect the reverse of what is expected from it in theory. The necessity of unanimity in public bodies, or of something approaching towards it, has been founded upon a supposition that it would contribute to security. But its real operation is to embarrass the administration, to destroy the energy of the government, and to substitute the pleasure, caprice, or artifices of an insignificant, turbulent, or corrupt junto, to the regular deliberations and decisions of a respectable majority. In those emergencies of a nation, in which the goodness or badness, the weakness or strength of its government, is of the greatest importance, there is commonly a necessity for action. The public business must, in some way or other, go forward. If a pertinacious minority can control the opinion of a majority, respecting the best mode of conducting it, the majority, in order that something may be done, must conform to the views of the minority; and thus the sense of the smaller number will overrule that of the greater, and give a tone to the national proceedings. Hence, tedious delays; continual negotiation and intrigue; contemptible compromises of the public good. And yet, in such a system, it is even happy when such compromises can take place: for upon some occasions things will not admit of accommodation; and then the measures of government must be injuriously suspended, or fatally defeated. It is often, by the impracticability of obtaining the concurrence of the necessary number of votes, kept in a state of inaction. Its situation must always savor of weakness, sometimes border upon anarchy.

It is not difficult to discover, that a principle of this kind gives greater scope to foreign corruption, as well as to domestic faction, than that which permits the sense of the majority to decide; though the contrary of this has been presumed. The mistake has proceeded from not attending with due care to the mischiefs that may be occasioned by obstructing the progress of government at certain critical seasons. When the concurrence of a large number is required by the Constitution to the doing of any national act, we are apt to rest satisfied that all is safe, because nothing improper will be likely TO BE DONE, but we forget how much good may be prevented, and how much ill may be produced, by the power of hindering the doing what may be necessary, and of keeping affairs in the same unfavorable posture in which they may happen to stand at particular periods.

Suppose, for instance, we were engaged in a war, in conjunction with one foreign nation, against another. Suppose the necessity of our situation demanded peace, and the interest or ambition of our ally led him to seek the prosecution of the war, with views that might justify us in making separate terms. In such a state of things, this ally of ours would evidently find it much easier, by his bribes and intrigues, to tie up the hands of government from making peace, where two thirds of all the votes were requisite to that object, than where a simple majority would suffice. In the first case, he would have to corrupt a smaller number; in the last, a greater number. Upon the same principle, it would be much easier for a foreign power with which we were at war to perplex our councils and embarrass our exertions. And, in a commercial view, we may be subjected to similar inconveniences. A nation, with which we might have a treaty of commerce, could with much greater facility prevent our forming a connection with her competitor in trade, though such a connection should be ever so beneficial to ourselves.

Evils of this description ought not to be regarded as imaginary. One of the weak sides of republics, among their numerous advantages, is that they afford too easy an inlet to foreign corruption. An hereditary monarch, though often disposed to sacrifice his subjects to his ambition, has so great a personal interest in the government and in the external glory of the nation, that it is not easy for a foreign power to give him an equivalent for what he would sacrifice by treachery to the state. The world has accordingly been witness to few examples of this species of royal prostitution, though there have been abundant specimens of every other kind.

In republics, persons elevated from the mass of the community, by the suffrages of their fellow-citizens, to stations of great pre-eminence and power, may find compensations for betraying their trust, which, to any but minds animated and guided by superior virtue, may appear to exceed the proportion of interest they have in the common stock, and to overbalance the obligations of duty. Hence it is that history furnishes us with so many mortifying examples of the prevalency of foreign corruption in republican governments. How much this contributed to the ruin of the ancient commonwealths has been already delineated. It is well known that the deputies of the United Provinces have, in various instances, been purchased by the emissaries of the neighboring kingdoms. The Earl of Chesterfield (if my memory serves me right), in a letter to his court, intimates that his success in an important negotiation must depend on his obtaining a major's commission for one of those deputies. And in Sweden the parties were alternately bought by France and England in so barefaced and notorious a manner that it excited universal disgust in the nation, and was a principal cause that the most limited monarch in Europe, in a single day, without tumult, violence, or opposition, became one of the most absolute and uncontrolled.

A circumstance which crowns the defects of the Confederation remains yet to be mentioned, the want of a judiciary power. Laws are a dead letter without courts to expound and define their true meaning and operation. The treaties of the United States, to have any force at all, must be considered as part of the law of the land. Their true import, as far as respects individuals, must, like all other laws, be ascertained by judicial determinations. To produce uniformity in these determinations, they ought to be submitted, in the last resort, to one SUPREME TRIBUNAL. And this tribunal ought to be instituted under the same authority which forms the treaties themselves. These ingredients are both indispensable. If there is in each State a court of final jurisdiction, there may be as many different final determinations on the same point as there are courts. There are endless diversities in the opinions of men. We often see not only different courts but the judges of the came court differing from each other. To avoid the confusion which would unavoidably result from the contradictory decisions of a number of independent judicatories, all nations have found it necessary to establish one court paramount to the rest, possessing a general superintendence, and authorized to settle and declare in the last resort a uniform rule of civil justice.

This is the more necessary where the frame of the government is so compounded that the laws of the whole are in danger of being contravened by the laws of the parts. In this case, if the particular tribunals are invested with a right of ultimate jurisdiction, besides the contradictions to be expected from difference of opinion, there will be much to fear from the bias of local views and prejudices, and from the interference of local regulations. As often as such an interference was to happen, there would be reason to apprehend that the provisions of the particular laws might be preferred to those of the general laws; for nothing is more natural to men in office than to look with peculiar deference towards that authority to which they owe their official existence. The treaties of the United States, under the present Constitution, are liable to the infractions of thirteen different legislatures, and as many different courts of final jurisdiction, acting under the authority of those legislatures. The faith, the reputation, the peace of the whole Union, are thus continually at the mercy of the prejudices, the passions, and the interests of every member of which it is composed. Is it possible that foreign nations can either respect or confide in such a government? Is it possible that the people of America will longer consent to trust their honor, their happiness, their safety, on so precarious a foundation?

In this review of the Confederation, I have confined myself to the exhibition of its most material defects; passing over those imperfections in its details by which even a great part of the power intended to be conferred upon it has been in a great measure rendered abortive. It must be by this time evident to all men of reflection, who can divest themselves of the prepossessions of preconceived opinions, that it is a system so radically vicious and unsound, as to admit not of amendment but by an entire change in its leading features and characters.

The organization of Congress is itself utterly improper for the exercise of those powers which are necessary to be deposited in the Union. A single assembly may be a proper receptacle of those slender, or rather fettered, authorities, which have been heretofore delegated to the federal head; but it would be inconsistent with all the principles of good government, to intrust it with those additional powers which, even the moderate and more rational adversaries of the proposed Constitution admit, ought to reside in the United States. If that plan should not be adopted, and if the necessity of the Union should be able to withstand the ambitious aims of those men who may indulge magnificent schemes of personal aggrandizement from its dissolution, the probability would be, that we should run into the project of conferring supplementary powers upon Congress, as they are now constituted; and either the machine, from the intrinsic feebleness of its structure, will moulder into pieces, in spite of our ill-judged efforts to prop it; or, by successive augmentations of its force an energy, as necessity might prompt, we shall finally accumulate, in a single body, all the most important prerogatives of sovereignty, and thus entail upon our posterity one of the most execrable forms of government that human infatuation ever contrived. Thus, we should create in reality that very tyranny which the adversaries of the new Constitution either are, or affect to be, solicitous to avert.

It has not a little contributed to the infirmities of the existing federal system, that it never had a ratification by the PEOPLE. Resting on no better foundation than the consent of the several legislatures, it has been exposed to frequent and intricate questions concerning the validity of its powers, and has, in some instances, given birth to the enormous doctrine of a right of legislative repeal. Owing its ratification to the law of a State, it has been contended that the same authority might repeal the law by which it was ratified. However gross a heresy it may be to maintain that a PARTY to a COMPACT has a right to revoke that COMPACT, the doctrine itself has had respectable advocates. The possibility of a question of this nature proves the necessity of laying the foundations of our national government deeper than in the mere sanction of delegated authority. The fabric of American empire ought to rest on the solid basis of THE CONSENT OF THE PEOPLE. The streams of national power ought to flow immediately from that pure, original fountain of all legitimate authority.

PUBLIUS.

[1] This, as nearly as I can recollect, was the sense of his speech on introducing the last bill.

[2] Encyclopedia, article "Empire."

[3] New Hampshire, Rhode Island, New Jersey, Delaware, Georgia, South Carolina, and Maryland are a majority of the whole number of the States, but they do not contain one third of the people.

[4] Add New York and Connecticut to the foregoing seven, and they will be less than a majority.

Federalist No. 23

The Necessity of a Government as Energetic as the One Proposed to the Preservation of the Union

From the New York Packet.
Tuesday, December 18, 1787.
HAMILTON

To the People of the State of New York:

THE necessity of a Constitution, at least equally energetic with the one proposed, to the preservation of the Union, is the point at the examination of which we are now arrived.

This inquiry will naturally divide itself into three branches the objects to be provided for by the federal government, the quantity of power necessary to the accomplishment of those objects, the persons upon whom that power ought to operate. Its distribution and organization will more properly claim our attention under the succeeding head.

The principal purposes to be answered by union are these: the common defense of the members; the preservation of the public peace as well against internal convulsions as external attacks; the regulation of commerce with other nations and between the States; the superintendence of our intercourse, political and commercial, with foreign countries.

The authorities essential to the common defense are these: to raise armies; to build and equip fleets; to prescribe rules for the government of both; to direct their operations; to provide for their support. These powers ought to exist without limitation, BECAUSE IT IS IMPOSSIBLE TO FORESEE OR DEFINE THE EXTENT AND VARIETY OF NATIONAL EXIGENCIES, OR THE CORRESPONDENT EXTENT AND VARIETY OF THE MEANS WHICH MAY BE NECESSARY TO SATISFY THEM. The circumstances that endanger the safety of nations are infinite, and for this reason no constitutional shackles can wisely be imposed on the power to which the care of it is committed. This power ought to be coextensive with all the possible combinations of such circumstances; and ought to be under the direction of the same councils which are appointed to preside over the common defense.

This is one of those truths which, to a correct and unprejudiced mind, carries its own evidence along with it; and may be obscured, but cannot be made plainer by argument or reasoning. It rests upon axioms as simple as they are universal; the MEANS ought to be proportioned to the END; the persons, from whose agency the attainment of any END is expected, ought to possess the MEANS by which it is to be attained.

Whether there ought to be a federal government intrusted with the care of the common defense, is a question in the first instance, open for discussion; but the moment it is decided in the affirmative, it will follow, that that government ought to be clothed with all the powers requisite to complete execution of its trust. And unless it can be shown that the circumstances which may affect the public safety are reducible within certain determinate limits; unless the contrary of this position can be fairly and rationally disputed, it must be admitted, as a necessary consequence, that there can be no limitation of that authority which is to provide for the defense and protection of the community, in any matter essential to its efficacy that is, in any matter essential to the FORMATION, DIRECTION, or SUPPORT of the NATIONAL FORCES.

Defective as the present Confederation has been proved to be, this principle appears to have been fully recognized by the framers of it; though they have not made proper or adequate provision for its exercise. Congress have an unlimited discretion to make requisitions of men and money; to govern the army and navy; to direct their operations. As their requisitions are made constitutionally binding upon the States, who are in fact under the most solemn obligations to furnish the supplies required of them, the intention evidently was that the United States should command whatever resources were by them judged requisite to the "common defense and general welfare." It was presumed that a sense of their true interests, and a regard to the dictates of good faith, would be found sufficient pledges for the punctual performance of the duty of the members to the federal head.

The experiment has, however, demonstrated that this expectation was ill-founded and illusory; and the observations, made under the last head, will, I imagine, have sufficed to convince the impartial and discerning, that there is an absolute necessity for an entire change in the first principles of the system; that if we are in earnest about giving the Union energy and duration, we must abandon the vain project of legislating upon the States in their collective capacities; we must extend the laws of the federal government to the individual citizens of America; we must discard the fallacious scheme of quotas and requisitions, as equally impracticable and unjust. The result from all this is that the Union ought to be invested with full power to levy troops; to build and equip fleets; and to raise the revenues which will be required for the formation and support of an army and navy, in the customary and ordinary modes practiced in other governments.

If the circumstances of our country are such as to demand a compound instead of a simple, a confederate instead of a sole, government, the essential point which will remain to be adjusted will be to discriminate the OBJECTS, as far as it can be done, which shall appertain to the different provinces or departments of power; allowing to each the most ample authority for fulfilling the objects committed to its charge. Shall the Union be constituted the guardian of the common safety? Are fleets and armies and revenues necessary to this purpose? The government of the Union must be empowered to pass all laws, and to make all regulations which have relation to them. The same must be the case in respect to commerce, and to every other matter to which its jurisdiction is permitted to extend. Is the administration of justice between the citizens of the same State the proper department of the local governments? These must possess all the authorities which are connected with this object, and with every other that may be allotted to their particular cognizance and direction. Not to confer in each case a degree of power commensurate to the end, would be to violate the most obvious rules of prudence and propriety, and improvidently to trust the great interests of the nation to hands which are disabled from managing them with vigor and success.

Who is likely to make suitable provisions for the public defense, as that body to which the guardianship of the public safety is confided; which, as the centre of information, will best understand the extent and urgency of the dangers that threaten; as the representative of the WHOLE, will feel itself most deeply interested in the preservation of every part; which, from the responsibility implied in the duty assigned to it, will be most sensibly impressed with the necessity of proper exertions; and which, by the extension of its authority throughout the States, can alone establish uniformity and concert in the plans and measures by which the common safety is to be secured? Is there not a manifest inconsistency in devolving upon the federal government the care of the general defense, and leaving in the State governments the EFFECTIVE powers by which it is to be provided for? Is not a want of co-operation the infallible consequence of such a system? And will not weakness, disorder, an undue distribution of the burdens and calamities of war, an unnecessary and intolerable increase of expense, be its natural and inevitable concomitants? Have we not had unequivocal experience of its effects in the course of the revolution which we have just accomplished?

Every view we may take of the subject, as candid inquirers after truth, will serve to convince us, that it is both unwise and dangerous to deny the federal government an unconfined authority, as to all those objects which are intrusted to its management. It will indeed deserve the most vigilant and careful attention of the people, to see that it be modeled in such a manner as to admit of its being safely vested with the requisite powers. If any plan which has been, or may be, offered to our consideration, should not, upon a dispassionate inspection, be found to answer this description, it ought to be rejected. A government, the constitution of which renders it unfit to be trusted with all the powers which a free people OUGHT TO DELEGATE TO ANY GOVERNMENT, would be an unsafe and improper depositary of the NATIONAL INTERESTS. Wherever THESE can with propriety be confided, the coincident powers may safely accompany them. This is the true result of all just reasoning upon the subject. And the adversaries of the plan promulgated by the convention ought to have confined themselves to showing, that the internal structure of the proposed government was such as to render it unworthy of the confidence of the people. They ought not to have wandered into inflammatory declamations and unmeaning cavils about the extent of the powers. The POWERS are not too extensive for the OBJECTS of federal administration, or, in other words, for the management of our NATIONAL INTERESTS; nor can any satisfactory argument be framed to show that they are chargeable with such an excess. If it be true, as has been insinuated by some of the writers on the other side, that the difficulty arises from the nature of the thing, and that the extent of the country will not permit us to form a government in which such ample powers can safely be reposed, it would prove that we ought to contract our views, and resort to the expedient of separate confederacies, which will move within more practicable spheres. For the absurdity must continually stare us in the face of confiding to a government the direction of the most essential national interests, without daring to trust it to the authorities which are indispensible to their proper and efficient management. Let us not attempt to reconcile contradictions, but firmly embrace a rational alternative.

I trust, however, that the impracticability of one general system cannot be shown. I am greatly mistaken, if any thing of weight has yet been advanced of this tendency; and I flatter myself, that the observations which have been made in the course of these papers have served to place the reverse of that position in as clear a light as any matter still in the womb of time and experience can be susceptible of. This, at all events, must be evident, that the very difficulty itself, drawn from the extent of the country, is the strongest argument in favor of an energetic government; for any other can certainly never preserve the Union of so large an empire. If we embrace the tenets of those who oppose the adoption of the proposed Constitution, as the standard of our political creed, we cannot fail to verify the gloomy doctrines which predict the impracticability of a national system pervading entire limits of the present Confederacy.

PUBLIUS.

Federalist No. 25

The Powers Necessary to the Common Defense Further Considered

From the New York Packet.

Friday, December 21, 1787.

HAMILTON

To the People of the State of New York:

IT MAY perhaps be urged that the objects enumerated in the preceding number ought to be provided for by the State governments, under the direction of the Union. But this would be, in reality, an inversion of the primary principle of our political association, as it would in practice transfer the care of the common defense from the federal head to the individual members: a project oppressive to some States, dangerous to all, and baneful to the Confederacy.

The territories of Britain, Spain, and of the Indian nations in our neighborhood do not border on particular States, but encircle the Union from Maine to Georgia. The danger, though in different degrees, is therefore common. And the means of guarding against it ought, in like manner, to be the objects of common councils and of a common treasury. It happens that some States, from local situation, are more directly exposed. New York is of this class. Upon the plan of separate provisions, New York would have to sustain the whole weight of the establishments requisite to her immediate safety, and to the mediate or ultimate protection of her neighbors. This would neither be equitable as it respected New York nor safe as it respected the other States. Various inconveniences would attend such a system. The States, to whose lot it might fall to support the necessary establishments, would be as little able as willing, for a considerable time to come, to bear the burden of competent provisions. The security of all would thus be subjected to the parsimony, improvidence, or inability of a part. If the resources of such part becoming more abundant and extensive, its provisions should be proportionally enlarged, the other States would quickly take the alarm at seeing the whole military force of the Union in the hands of two or three of its members, and those probably amongst the most powerful. They would each choose to have some counterpoise, and pretenses could easily be contrived. In this situation, military establishments, nourished by mutual jealousy, would be apt to swell beyond their natural or proper size; and being at the separate disposal of the members, they would be engines for the abridgment or demolition of the national authority.

Reasons have been already given to induce a supposition that the State governments will too naturally be prone to a rivalship with that of the Union, the foundation of which will be the love of power; and that in any contest between the federal head and one of its members the people will be most apt to unite with their local government. If, in addition to this immense advantage, the ambition of the members should be stimulated by the separate and independent possession of military forces, it would afford too strong a temptation and too great a facility to them to make enterprises upon, and finally to subvert, the constitutional authority of the Union. On the other hand, the liberty of the people would be less safe in this state of things than in that which left the national forces in the hands of the national government. As far as an army may be considered as a dangerous weapon of power, it had better be in those hands of which the people are most likely to be jealous than in those of which they are least likely to be jealous. For it is a truth, which the experience of ages has attested, that the people are always most in danger when the means of injuring their rights are in the possession of those of whom they entertain the least suspicion.

The framers of the existing Confederation, fully aware of the danger to the Union from the separate possession of military forces by the States, have, in express terms, prohibited them from having either ships or troops, unless with the consent of Congress. The truth is, that the existence of a federal government and military establishments under State authority are not less at variance with each other than a due supply of the federal treasury and the system of quotas and requisitions.

There are other lights besides those already taken notice of, in which the impropriety of restraints on the discretion of the national legislature will be equally manifest. The design of the objection, which has been mentioned, is to preclude standing armies in time of peace, though we have never been informed how far it is designed the prohibition should extend; whether to raising armies as well as to KEEPING THEM UP in a season of tranquillity or not. If it be confined to the latter it will have no precise signification, and it will be ineffectual for the purpose intended. When armies are once raised what shall be denominated "keeping them up," contrary to the sense of the Constitution? What time shall be requisite to ascertain the violation? Shall it be a week, a month, a year? Or shall we say they may be continued as long as the danger which occasioned their being raised continues? This would be to admit that they might be kept up IN TIME OF PEACE, against threatening or impending danger, which would be at once to deviate from the literal meaning of the prohibition, and to introduce an extensive latitude of construction. Who shall judge of the continuance of the danger? This must undoubtedly be submitted to the national government, and the matter would then be brought to this issue, that the national government, to provide against apprehended danger, might in the first instance raise troops, and might afterwards keep them on foot as long as they supposed the peace or safety of the community was in any degree of jeopardy. It is easy to perceive that a discretion so latitudinary as this would afford ample room for eluding the force of the provision.

The supposed utility of a provision of this kind can only be founded on the supposed probability, or at least possibility, of a combination between the executive and the legislative, in some scheme of usurpation. Should this at any time happen, how easy would it be to fabricate pretenses of approaching danger! Indian hostilities, instigated by Spain or Britain, would always be at hand. Provocations to produce the desired appearances might even be given to some foreign power, and appeased again by timely concessions. If we can reasonably presume such a combination to have been formed, and that the enterprise is warranted by a sufficient prospect of success, the army, when once raised, from whatever cause, or on whatever pretext, may be applied to the execution of the project.

If, to obviate this consequence, it should be resolved to extend the prohibition to the RAISING of armies in time of peace, the United States would then exhibit the most extraordinary spectacle which the world has yet seen, that of a nation incapacitated by its Constitution to prepare for defense, before it was actually invaded. As the ceremony of a formal denunciation of war has of late fallen into disuse, the presence of an enemy within our territories must be waited for, as the legal warrant to the government to begin its levies of men for the protection of the State. We must receive the blow, before we could even prepare to return it. All that kind of policy by which nations anticipate distant danger, and meet the gathering storm, must be abstained from, as contrary to the genuine maxims of a free government. We must expose our property and liberty to the mercy of foreign invaders, and invite them by our weakness to seize the naked and defenseless prey, because we are afraid that rulers, created by our choice, dependent on our will, might endanger that liberty, by an abuse of the means necessary to its preservation.

Here I expect we shall be told that the militia of the country is its natural bulwark, and would be at all times equal to the national defense. This doctrine, in substance, had like to have lost us our independence. It cost millions to the United States that might have been saved. The facts which, from our own experience, forbid a reliance of this kind, are too recent to permit us to be the dupes of such a suggestion. The steady operations of war against a regular and disciplined army can only be successfully conducted by a force of the same kind. Considerations of economy, not less than of stability and vigor, confirm this position. The American militia, in the course of the late war, have, by their valor on numerous occasions, erected eternal monuments to their fame; but the bravest of them feel and know that the liberty of their country could not have been established by their efforts alone, however great and valuable they were. War, like most other things, is a science to be acquired and perfected by diligence, by perserverance, by time, and by practice.

All violent policy, as it is contrary to the natural and experienced course of human affairs, defeats itself. Pennsylvania, at this instant, affords an example of the truth of this remark. The Bill of Rights of that State declares that standing armies are dangerous to liberty, and ought not to be kept up in time of peace. Pennsylvania, nevertheless, in a time of profound peace, from the existence of partial disorders in one or two of her counties, has resolved to raise a body of troops; and in all probability will keep them up as long as there is any appearance of danger to the public peace. The conduct of Massachusetts affords a lesson on the same subject, though on different ground. That State (without waiting for the sanction of Congress, as the articles of the Confederation require) was compelled to raise troops to quell a domestic insurrection, and still keeps a corps in pay to prevent a revival of the spirit of revolt. The particular constitution of Massachusetts opposed no obstacle to the measure; but the instance is still of use to instruct us that cases are likely to occur under our government, as well as under those of other nations, which will sometimes render a military force in time of peace essential to the security of the society, and that it is therefore improper in this respect to control the legislative discretion. It also teaches us, in its application to the United States, how little the rights of a feeble government are likely to be respected, even by its own constituents. And it teaches us, in addition to the rest, how unequal parchment provisions are to a struggle with public necessity.

It was a fundamental maxim of the Lacedaemonian commonwealth, that the post of admiral should not be conferred twice on the same person. The Peloponnesian confederates, having suffered a severe defeat at sea from the Athenians, demanded Lysander, who had before served with success in that capacity, to command the combined fleets. The Lacedaemonians, to gratify their allies, and yet preserve the semblance of an adherence to their ancient institutions, had recourse to the flimsy subterfuge of investing Lysander with the real power of admiral, under the nominal title of vice-admiral. This instance is selected from among a multitude that might be cited to confirm the truth already advanced and illustrated by domestic examples; which is, that nations pay little regard to rules and maxims calculated in their very nature to run counter to the necessities of society. Wise politicians will be cautious about fettering the government with restrictions that cannot be observed, because they know that every breach of the fundamental laws, though dictated by necessity, impairs that sacred reverence which ought to be maintained in the breast of rulers towards the constitution of a country, and forms a precedent for other breaches where the same plea of necessity does not exist at all, or is less urgent and palpable.

PUBLIUS.

Federalist No. 26

The Idea of Restraining the Legislative Authority in Regard to the Common Defense Considered

For the Independent Journal.

HAMILTON

To the People of the State of New York:

IT WAS a thing hardly to be expected that in a popular revolution the minds of men should stop at that happy mean which marks the salutary boundary between POWER and PRIVILEGE, and combines the energy of government with the security of private rights. A failure in this delicate and important point is the great source of the inconveniences we experience, and if we are not cautious to avoid a repetition of the error, in our future attempts to rectify and ameliorate our system, we may travel from one chimerical project to another; we may try change after change; but we shall never be likely to make any material change for the better.

The idea of restraining the legislative authority, in the means of providing for the national defense, is one of those refinements which owe their origin to a zeal for liberty more ardent than enlightened. We have seen, however, that it has not had thus far an extensive prevalency; that even in this country, where it made its first appearance, Pennsylvania and North Carolina are the only two States by which it has been in any degree patronized; and that all the others have refused to give it the least countenance; wisely judging that confidence must be placed somewhere; that the necessity of doing it, is implied in the very act of delegating power; and that it is better to hazard the abuse of that confidence than to embarrass the government and endanger the public safety by impolitic restrictions on the legislative authority. The opponents of the proposed Constitution combat, in this respect, the general decision of America; and instead of being taught by experience the propriety of correcting any extremes into which we may have heretofore run, they appear disposed to conduct us into others still more dangerous, and more extravagant. As if the tone of government had been found too high, or too rigid, the doctrines they teach are calculated to induce us to depress or to relax it, by expedients which, upon other occasions, have been condemned or forborne. It may be affirmed without the imputation of invective, that if the principles they inculcate, on various points, could so far obtain as to become the popular creed, they would utterly unfit the people of this country for any species of government whatever. But a danger of this kind is not to be apprehended. The citizens of America have too much discernment to be argued into anarchy. And I am much mistaken, if experience has not wrought a deep and solemn conviction in the public mind, that greater energy of government is essential to the welfare and prosperity of the community.

It may not be amiss in this place concisely to remark the origin and progress of the idea, which aims at the exclusion of military establishments in time of peace. Though in speculative minds it may arise from a contemplation of the nature and tendency of such institutions, fortified by the events that have happened in other ages and countries, yet as a national sentiment, it must be traced to those habits of thinking which we derive from the nation from whom the inhabitants of these States have in general sprung.

In England, for a long time after the Norman Conquest, the authority of the monarch was almost unlimited. Inroads were gradually made upon the prerogative, in favor of liberty, first by the barons, and afterwards by the people, till the greatest part of its most formidable pretensions became extinct. But it was not till the revolution in 1688, which elevated the Prince of Orange to the throne of Great Britain, that English liberty was completely triumphant. As incident to the undefined power of making war, an acknowledged prerogative of the crown, Charles II. had, by his own authority, kept on foot in time of peace a body of 5,000 regular troops. And this number James II. increased to 30,000; who were paid out of his civil list. At the revolution, to abolish the exercise of so dangerous an authority, it became an article of the Bill of Rights then framed, that "the raising or keeping a standing army within the kingdom in time of peace, UNLESS WITH THE CONSENT OF PARLIAMENT, was against law."

In that kingdom, when the pulse of liberty was at its highest pitch, no security against the danger of standing armies was thought requisite, beyond a prohibition of their being raised or kept up by the mere authority of the executive magistrate. The patriots, who effected that memorable revolution, were too temperate, too well-informed, to think of any restraint on the legislative discretion. They were aware that a certain number of troops for guards and garrisons were indispensable; that no precise bounds could be set to the national exigencies; that a power equal to every possible contingency must exist somewhere in the government: and that when they referred the exercise of that power to the judgment of the legislature, they had arrived at the ultimate point of precaution which was reconcilable with the safety of the community.

From the same source, the people of America may be said to have derived an hereditary impression of danger to liberty, from standing armies in time of peace. The circumstances of a revolution quickened the public sensibility on every point connected with the security of popular rights, and in some instances raise the warmth of our zeal beyond the degree which consisted with the due temperature of the body politic. The attempts of two of the States to restrict the authority of the legislature in the article of military establishments, are of the number of these instances. The principles which had taught us to be jealous of the power of an hereditary monarch were by an injudicious excess extended to the representatives of the people in their popular assemblies. Even in some of the States, where this error was not adopted, we find unnecessary declarations that standing armies ought not to be kept up, in time of peace, WITHOUT THE CONSENT OF THE LEGISLATURE. I call them unnecessary, because the reason which had introduced a similar provision into the English Bill of Rights is not applicable to any of the State constitutions. The power of raising armies at all, under those constitutions, can by no construction be deemed to reside anywhere else, than in the legislatures themselves; and it was superfluous, if not absurd, to declare that a matter should not be done without the consent of a body, which alone had the power of doing it. Accordingly, in some of these constitutions, and among others, in that of this State of New York, which has been justly celebrated, both in Europe and America, as one of the best of the forms of government established in this country, there is a total silence upon the subject.

It is remarkable, that even in the two States which seem to have meditated an interdiction of military establishments in time of peace, the mode of expression made use of is rather cautionary than prohibitory. It is not said, that standing armies SHALL NOT BE kept up, but that they OUGHT NOT to be kept up, in time of peace. This ambiguity of terms appears to have been the result of a conflict between jealousy and conviction; between the desire of excluding such establishments at all events, and the persuasion that an absolute exclusion would be unwise and unsafe.

Can it be doubted that such a provision, whenever the situation of public affairs was understood to require a departure from it, would be interpreted by the legislature into a mere admonition, and would be made to yield to the necessities or supposed necessities of the State? Let the fact already mentioned, with respect to Pennsylvania, decide. What then (it may be asked) is the use of such a provision, if it cease to operate the moment there is an inclination to disregard it?

Let us examine whether there be any comparison, in point of efficacy, between the provision alluded to and that which is contained in the new Constitution, for restraining the appropriations of money for military purposes to the period of two years. The former, by aiming at too much, is calculated to effect nothing; the latter, by steering clear of an imprudent extreme, and by being perfectly compatible with a proper provision for the exigencies of the nation, will have a salutary and powerful operation.

The legislature of the United States will be OBLIGED, by this provision, once at least in every two years, to deliberate upon the propriety of keeping a military force on foot; to come to a new resolution on the point; and to declare their sense of the matter, by a formal vote in the face of their constituents. They are not AT LIBERTY to vest in the executive department permanent funds for the support of an army, if they were even incautious enough to be willing to repose in it so improper a confidence. As the spirit of party, in different degrees, must be expected to infect all political bodies, there will be, no doubt, persons in the national legislature willing enough to arraign the measures and criminate the views of the majority. The provision for the support of a military force will always be a favorable topic for declamation. As often as the question comes forward, the public attention will be roused and attracted to the subject, by the party in opposition; and if the majority should be really disposed to exceed the proper limits, the community will be warned of the danger, and will have an opportunity of taking measures to guard against it. Independent of parties in the national legislature itself, as often as the period of discussion arrived, the State legislatures, who will always be not only vigilant but suspicious and jealous guardians of the rights of the citizens against encroachments from the federal government, will constantly have their attention awake to the conduct of the national rulers, and will be ready enough, if any thing improper appears, to sound the alarm to the people, and not only to be the VOICE, but, if necessary, the ARM of their discontent.

Schemes to subvert the liberties of a great community REQUIRE TIME to mature them for execution. An army, so large as seriously to menace those liberties, could only be formed by progressive augmentations; which would suppose, not merely a temporary combination between the legislature and executive, but a continued conspiracy for a series of time. Is it probable that such a combination would exist at all? Is it probable that it would be persevered in, and transmitted along through all the successive variations in a representative body, which biennial elections would naturally produce in both houses? Is it presumable, that every man, the instant he took his seat in the national Senate or House of Representatives, would commence a traitor to his constituents and to his country? Can it be supposed that there would not be found one man, discerning enough to detect so atrocious a conspiracy, or bold or honest enough to apprise his constituents of their danger? If such presumptions can fairly be made, there ought at once to be an end of all delegated authority. The people should resolve to recall all the powers they have heretofore parted with out of their own hands, and to divide themselves into as many States as there are counties, in order that they may be able to manage their own concerns in person.

If such suppositions could even be reasonably made, still the concealment of the design, for any duration, would be impracticable. It would be announced, by the very circumstance of augmenting the army to so great an extent in time of profound peace. What colorable reason could be assigned, in a country so situated, for such vast augmentations of the military force? It is impossible that the people could be long deceived; and the destruction of the project, and of the projectors, would quickly follow the discovery.

It has been said that the provision which limits the appropriation of money for the support of an army to the period of two years would be unavailing, because the Executive, when once possessed of a force large enough to awe the people into submission, would find resources in that very force sufficient to enable him to dispense with supplies from the acts of the legislature. But the question again recurs, upon what pretense could he be put in possession of a force of that magnitude in time of peace? If we suppose it to have been created in consequence of some domestic insurrection or foreign war, then it becomes a case not within the principles of the objection; for this is levelled against the power of keeping up troops in time of peace. Few persons will be so visionary as seriously to contend that military forces ought not to be raised to quell a rebellion or resist an invasion; and if the defense of the community under such circumstances should make it necessary to have an army so numerous as to hazard its liberty, this is one of those calamaties for which there is neither preventative nor cure. It cannot be provided against by any possible form of government; it might even result from a simple league offensive and defensive, if it should ever be necessary for the confederates or allies to form an army for common defense.

But it is an evil infinitely less likely to attend us in a united than in a disunited state; nay, it may be safely asserted that it is an evil altogether unlikely to attend us in the latter situation. It is not easy to conceive a possibility that dangers so formidable can assail the whole Union, as to demand a force considerable enough to place our liberties in the least jeopardy, especially if we take into our view the aid to be derived from the militia, which ought always to be counted upon as a valuable and powerful auxiliary. But in a state of disunion (as has been fully shown in another place), the contrary of this supposition would become not only probable, but almost unavoidable.

PUBLIUS.

Federalist No. 27

The Same Subject Continued

(The Idea of Restraining the Legislative Authority in Regard to the Common Defense Considered)

From the New York Packet.

Tuesday, December 25, 1787.

HAMILTON

To the People of the State of New York:

IT HAS been urged, in different shapes, that a Constitution of the kind proposed by the convention cannot operate without the aid of a military force to execute its laws. This, however, like most other things that have been alleged on that side, rests on mere general assertion, unsupported by any precise or intelligible designation of the reasons upon which it is founded. As far as I have been able to divine the latent meaning of the objectors, it seems to originate in a presupposition that the people will be disinclined to the exercise of federal authority in any matter of an internal nature. Waiving any exception that might be taken to the inaccuracy or inexplicitness of the distinction between internal and external, let us inquire what ground there is to presuppose that disinclination in the people. Unless we presume at the same time that the powers of the general government will be worse administered than those of the State government, there seems to be no room for the presumption of ill-will, disaffection, or opposition in the people. I believe it may be laid down as a general rule that their confidence in and obedience to a government will commonly be proportioned to the goodness or badness of its administration. It must be admitted that there are exceptions to this rule; but these exceptions depend so entirely on accidental causes, that they cannot be considered as having any relation to the intrinsic merits or demerits of a constitution. These can only be judged of by general principles and maxims.

Various reasons have been suggested, in the course of these papers, to induce a probability that the general government will be better administered than the particular governments; the principal of which reasons are that the extension of the spheres of election will present a greater option, or latitude of choice, to the people; that through the medium of the State legislatures which are select bodies of men, and which are to appoint the members of the national Senate there is reason to expect that this branch will generally be composed with peculiar care and judgment; that these circumstances promise greater knowledge and more extensive information in the national councils, and that they will be less apt to be tainted by the spirit of faction, and more out of the reach of those occasional ill-humors, or temporary prejudices and propensities, which, in smaller societies, frequently contaminate the public councils, beget injustice and oppression of a part of the community, and engender schemes which, though they gratify a momentary inclination or desire, terminate in general distress, dissatisfaction, and disgust. Several additional reasons of considerable force, to fortify that probability, will occur when we come to survey, with a more critical eye, the interior structure of the edifice which we are invited to erect. It will be sufficient here to remark, that until satisfactory reasons can be assigned to justify an opinion, that the federal government is likely to be administered in such a manner as to render it odious or contemptible to the people, there can be no reasonable foundation for the supposition that the laws of the Union will meet with any greater obstruction from them, or will stand in need of any other methods to enforce their execution, than the laws of the particular members.

The hope of impunity is a strong incitement to sedition; the dread of punishment, a proportionably strong discouragement to it. Will not the government of the Union, which, if possessed of a due degree of power, can call to its aid the collective resources of the whole Confederacy, be more likely to repress the FORMER sentiment and to inspire the LATTER, than that of a single State, which can only command the resources within itself? A turbulent faction in a State may easily suppose itself able to contend with the friends to the government in that State; but it can hardly be so infatuated as to imagine itself a match for the combined efforts of the Union. If this reflection be just, there is less danger of resistance from irregular combinations of individuals to the authority of the Confederacy than to that of a single member.

I will, in this place, hazard an observation, which will not be the less just because to some it may appear new; which is, that the more the operations of the national authority are intermingled in the ordinary exercise of government, the more the citizens are accustomed to meet with it in the common occurrences of their political life, the more it is familiarized to their sight and to their feelings, the further it enters into those objects which touch the most sensible chords and put in motion the most active springs of the human heart, the greater will be the probability that it will conciliate the respect and attachment of the community. Man is very much a creature of habit. A thing that rarely strikes his senses will generally have but little influence upon his mind. A government continually at a distance and out of sight can hardly be expected to interest the sensations of the people. The inference is, that the authority of the Union, and the affections of the citizens towards it, will be strengthened, rather than weakened, by its extension to what are called matters of internal concern; and will have less occasion to recur to force, in proportion to the familiarity and comprehensiveness of its agency. The more it circulates through those channels and currents in which the passions of mankind naturally flow, the less will it require the aid of the violent and perilous expedients of compulsion.

One thing, at all events, must be evident, that a government like the one proposed would bid much fairer to avoid the necessity of using force, than that species of league contend for by most of its opponents; the authority of which should only operate upon the States in their political or collective capacities. It has been shown that in such a Confederacy there can be no sanction for the laws but force; that frequent delinquencies in the members are the natural offspring of the very frame of the government; and that as often as these happen, they can only be redressed, if at all, by war and violence.

The plan reported by the convention, by extending the authority of the federal head to the individual citizens of the several States, will enable the government to employ the ordinary magistracy of each, in the execution of its laws. It is easy to perceive that this will tend to destroy, in the common apprehension, all distinction between the sources from which they might proceed; and will give the federal government the same advantage for securing a due obedience to its authority which is enjoyed by the government of each State, in addition to the influence on public opinion which will result from the important consideration of its having power to call to its assistance and support the resources of the whole Union. It merits particular attention in this place, that the laws of the Confederacy, as to the

ENUMERATED and LEGITIMATE objects of its jurisdiction, will become the SUPREME LAW of the land; to the observance of which all officers, legislative, executive, and judicial, in each State, will be bound by the sanctity of an oath. Thus the legislatures, courts, and magistrates, of the respective members, will be incorporated into the operations of the national government AS FAR AS ITS JUST AND CONSTITUTIONAL AUTHORITY EXTENDS; and will be rendered auxiliary to the enforcement of its laws. [1] Any man who will pursue, by his own reflections, the consequences of this situation, will perceive that there is good ground to calculate upon a regular and peaceable execution of the laws of the Union, if its powers are administered with a common share of prudence. If we will arbitrarily suppose the contrary, we may deduce any inferences we please from the supposition; for it is certainly possible, by an injudicious exercise of the authorities of the best government that ever was, or ever can be instituted, to provoke and precipitate the people into the wildest excesses. But though the adversaries of the proposed Constitution should presume that the national rulers would be insensible to the motives of public good, or to the obligations of duty, I would still ask them how the interests of ambition, or the views of encroachment, can be promoted by such a conduct?

PUBLIUS.

[1] The sophistry which has been employed to show that this will tend to the destruction of the State governments, will, in its will, in its proper place, be fully detected.

Federalist No. 28

The Same Subject Continued
(The Idea of Restraining the Legislative Authority in Regard to the Common Defense Considered)

For the Independent Journal.

HAMILTON

To the People of the State of New York:

THAT there may happen cases in which the national government may be necessitated to resort to force, cannot be denied. Our own experience has corroborated the lessons taught by the examples of other nations; that emergencies of this sort will sometimes arise in all societies, however constituted; that seditions and insurrections are, unhappily, maladies as inseparable from the body politic as tumors and eruptions from the natural body; that the idea of governing at all times by the simple force of law (which we have been told is the only admissible principle of republican government), has no place but in the reveries of those political doctors whose sagacity disdains the admonitions of experimental instruction.

Should such emergencies at any time happen under the national government, there could be no remedy but force. The means to be employed must be proportioned to the extent of the mischief. If it should be a slight commotion in a small part of a State, the militia of the residue would be adequate to its suppression; and the national presumption is that they would be ready to do their duty. An insurrection, whatever may be its immediate cause, eventually endangers all government. Regard to the public peace, if not to the rights of the Union, would engage the citizens to whom the contagion had not communicated itself to oppose the insurgents; and if the general government should be found in practice conducive to the prosperity and felicity of the people, it were irrational to believe that they would be disinclined to its support.

If, on the contrary, the insurrection should pervade a whole State, or a principal part of it, the employment of a different kind of force might become unavoidable. It appears that Massachusetts found it necessary to raise troops for repressing the disorders within that State; that Pennsylvania, from the mere apprehension of commotions among a part of her citizens, has thought proper to have recourse to the same measure. Suppose the State of New York had been inclined to re-establish her lost jurisdiction over the inhabitants of Vermont, could she have hoped for success in such an enterprise from the efforts of the militia alone? Would she not have been compelled to raise and to maintain a more regular force for the execution of her design? If it must then be admitted that the necessity of recurring to a force different from the militia, in cases of this extraordinary nature, is applicable to the State governments themselves, why should the possibility, that the national government might be under a like necessity, in similar extremities, be made an objection to its existence? Is it not surprising that men who declare an attachment to the Union in the abstract, should urge as an objection to the proposed Constitution what applies with tenfold weight to the plan for which they contend; and what, as far as it has any foundation in truth, is an inevitable consequence of civil society upon an enlarged scale? Who would not prefer that possibility to the unceasing agitations and frequent revolutions which are the continual scourges of petty republics?

Let us pursue this examination in another light. Suppose, in lieu of one general system, two, or three, or even four Confederacies were to be formed, would not the same difficulty oppose itself to the operations of either of these Confederacies? Would not each of them be exposed to the same casualties; and when these happened, be obliged to have recourse to the same expedients for upholding its authority which are objected to in a government for all the States? Would the militia, in this supposition, be more ready or more able to support the federal authority than in the case of a general union? All candid and intelligent men must, upon due consideration, acknowledge that the principle of the objection is equally applicable to either of the two cases; and that whether we have one government for all the States, or different governments for different parcels of them, or even if there should be an entire separation of the States, there might sometimes be a necessity to make use of a force constituted differently from the militia, to preserve the peace of the community and to maintain the just authority of the laws against those violent invasions of them which amount to insurrections and rebellions.

Independent of all other reasonings upon the subject, it is a full answer to those who require a more peremptory provision against military establishments in time of peace, to say that the whole power of the proposed government is to be in the hands of the representatives of the people. This is the essential, and, after all, only efficacious security for the rights and privileges of the people, which is attainable in civil society. [1]

If the representatives of the people betray their constituents, there is then no resource left but in the exertion of that original right of self-defense which is paramount to all positive forms of government, and which against the usurpations of the national rulers, may be exerted with infinitely better prospect of success than against those of the rulers of an individual state. In a single state, if the persons intrusted with supreme power become usurpers, the different parcels, subdivisions, or districts of which it consists, having no distinct government in each, can take no regular measures for defense. The citizens must rush tumultuously to arms, without concert, without system, without resource; except in their courage and despair. The usurpers, clothed with the forms of legal authority, can too often crush the opposition in embryo. The smaller the extent of the territory, the more difficult will it be for the people to form a regular or systematic plan of opposition, and the more easy will it be to defeat their early efforts. Intelligence can be more speedily obtained of their preparations and movements, and the military force in the possession of the usurpers can be more rapidly directed against the part where the opposition has begun. In this situation there must be a peculiar coincidence of circumstances to insure success to the popular resistance.

The obstacles to usurpation and the facilities of resistance increase with the increased extent of the state, provided the citizens understand their rights and are disposed to defend them. The natural strength of the people in a large community, in proportion to the artificial strength of the government, is greater than in a small, and of course more competent to a struggle with the attempts of the government to establish a tyranny. But in a confederacy the people, without exaggeration, may be said to be entirely the masters of their own fate. Power being almost always the rival of power, the general government will at all times stand ready to check the usurpations of the state governments, and these will have the same disposition towards the general government. The people, by throwing themselves into either scale, will infallibly make it preponderate. If their rights are invaded by either, they can make use of the other as the instrument of redress. How wise will it be in them by cherishing the union to preserve to themselves an advantage which can never be too highly prized!

It may safely be received as an axiom in our political system, that the State governments will, in all possible contingencies, afford complete security against invasions of the public liberty by the national authority. Projects of usurpation cannot be masked under pretenses so likely to escape the penetration of select bodies of men, as of the people at large. The legislatures will have better means of information. They can discover the danger at a distance; and possessing all the organs of civil power, and the confidence of the people, they can at once adopt a regular plan of opposition, in which they can combine all the resources of the community. They can readily communicate with each other in the different States, and unite their common forces for the protection of their common liberty.

The great extent of the country is a further security. We have already experienced its utility against the attacks of a foreign power. And it would have precisely the same effect against the enterprises of ambitious rulers in the national councils. If the federal army should be able to quell the resistance of one State, the distant States would have it in their power to make head with fresh forces. The advantages obtained in one place must be abandoned to subdue the opposition in others; and the moment the part which had been reduced to submission was left to itself, its efforts would be renewed, and its resistance revive.

We should recollect that the extent of the military force must, at all events, be regulated by the resources of the country. For a long time to come, it will not be possible to maintain a large army; and as the means of doing this increase, the population and natural strength of the community will proportionably increase. When will the time arrive that the federal government can raise and maintain an army capable of erecting a despotism over the great body of the people of an immense empire, who are in a situation, through the medium of their State governments, to take measures for their own defense, with all the celerity, regularity, and system of independent nations? The apprehension may be considered as a disease, for which there can be found no cure in the resources of argument and reasoning.

PUBLIUS.

[1] Its full efficacy will be examined hereafter.

Federalist No. 30

Concerning the General Power of Taxation

From the New York Packet.

Friday, December 28, 1787.

HAMILTON

To the People of the State of New York:

IT HAS been already observed that the federal government ought to possess the power of providing for the support of the national forces; in which proposition was intended to be included the expense of raising troops, of building and equipping fleets, and all other expenses in any wise connected with military arrangements and operations. But these are not the only objects to which the jurisdiction of the Union, in respect to revenue, must necessarily be empowered to extend. It must embrace a provision for the support of the national civil list; for the payment of the national debts contracted, or that may be contracted; and, in general, for all those matters which will call for disbursements out of the national treasury. The conclusion is, that there must be interwoven, in the frame of the government, a general power of taxation, in one shape or another.

Money is, with propriety, considered as the vital principle of the body politic; as that which sustains its life and motion, and enables it to perform its most essential functions. A complete power, therefore, to procure a regular and adequate supply of it, as far as the resources of the community will permit, may be regarded as an indispensable ingredient in every constitution. From a deficiency in this particular, one of two evils must ensue; either the people must be subjected to continual plunder, as a substitute for a more eligible mode of supplying the public wants, or the government must sink into a fatal atrophy, and, in a short course of time, perish.

In the Ottoman or Turkish empire, the sovereign, though in other respects absolute master of the lives and fortunes of his subjects, has no right to impose a new tax. The consequence is that he permits the bashaws or governors of provinces to pillage the people without mercy; and, in turn, squeezes out of them the sums of which he stands in need, to satisfy his own exigencies and those of the state. In America, from a like cause, the government of the Union has gradually dwindled into a state of decay, approaching nearly to annihilation. Who can doubt, that the happiness of the people in both countries would be promoted by competent authorities in the proper hands, to provide the revenues which the necessities of the public might require?

The present Confederation, feeble as it is intended to repose in the United States, an unlimited power of providing for the pecuniary wants of the Union. But proceeding upon an erroneous principle, it has been done in such a manner as entirely to have frustrated the intention. Congress, by the articles which compose that compact (as has already been stated), are authorized to ascertain and call for any sums of money necessary, in their judgment, to the service of the United States; and their requisitions, if conformable to the rule of apportionment, are in every constitutional sense obligatory upon the States. These have no right to question the propriety of the demand; no discretion beyond that of devising the ways and means of furnishing the sums demanded. But though this be strictly and truly the case; though the assumption of such a right would be an infringement of the articles of Union; though it may seldom or never have been avowedly claimed, yet in practice it has been constantly exercised, and would continue to be so, as long as the revenues of the Confederacy should remain dependent on the intermediate agency of its members. What the consequences of this system have been, is within the knowledge of every man the least conversant in our public affairs, and has been amply unfolded in different parts of these inquiries. It is this which has chiefly contributed to reduce us to a situation, which affords ample cause both of mortification to ourselves, and of triumph to our enemies.

What remedy can there be for this situation, but in a change of the system which has produced it in a change of the fallacious and delusive system of quotas and requisitions? What substitute can there be imagined for this ignis fatuus in finance, but that of permitting the national government to raise its own revenues by the ordinary methods of taxation authorized in every well-ordered constitution of civil government? Ingenious men may declaim with plausibility on any subject; but no human ingenuity can point out any other expedient to rescue us from the inconveniences and embarrassments naturally resulting from defective supplies of the public treasury.

The more intelligent adversaries of the new Constitution admit the force of this reasoning; but they qualify their admission by a distinction between what they call INTERNAL and EXTERNAL taxation. The former they would reserve to the State governments; the latter, which they explain into commercial imposts, or rather duties on imported articles, they declare themselves willing to concede to the federal head. This distinction, however, would violate the maxim of good sense and sound policy, which dictates that every POWER ought to be in proportion to its OBJECT; and would still leave the general government in a kind of tutelage to the State governments, inconsistent with every idea of vigor or efficiency. Who can pretend that commercial imposts are, or would be, alone equal to the present and future exigencies of the Union? Taking into the account the existing debt, foreign and domestic, upon any plan of extinguishment which a man moderately impressed with the importance of public justice and public credit could approve, in addition to the establishments which all parties will acknowledge to be necessary, we could not reasonably flatter ourselves, that this resource alone, upon the most improved scale, would even suffice for its present necessities. Its future necessities admit not of calculation or limitation; and upon the principle, more than once adverted to, the power of making provision for them as they arise ought to be equally unconfined. I believe it may be regarded as a position warranted by the history of mankind, that, IN THE USUAL PROGRESS OF THINGS, THE NECESSITIES OF A NATION, IN EVERY STAGE OF ITS EXISTENCE, WILL BE FOUND AT LEAST EQUAL TO ITS RESOURCES.

To say that deficiencies may be provided for by requisitions upon the States, is on the one hand to acknowledge that this system cannot be depended upon, and on the other hand to depend upon it for every thing beyond a certain limit. Those who have carefully attended to its vices and deformities as they have been exhibited by experience or delineated in the course of these papers, must feel invincible repugnancy to trusting the national interests in any degree to its operation. Its inevitable tendency, whenever it is brought into activity, must be to enfeeble the Union, and sow the seeds of discord and contention between the federal head and its members, and between the members themselves. Can it be expected that the deficiencies would be better supplied in this mode than the total wants of the Union have heretofore been supplied in the same mode? It ought to be recollected that if less will be required from the States, they will have proportionably less means to answer the demand. If the opinions of those who contend for the distinction which has been mentioned were to be received as evidence of truth, one would be led to conclude that there was some known point in the economy of national affairs at which it would be safe to stop and to say: Thus far the ends of public happiness will be promoted by supplying the wants of government, and all beyond this is unworthy of our care or anxiety. How is it possible that a government half supplied and always necessitous, can fulfill the purposes of its institution, can provide for the security, advance the prosperity, or support the reputation of the commonwealth? How can it ever possess either energy or stability, dignity or credit, confidence at home or respectability abroad? How can its administration be any thing else than a succession of expedients temporizing, impotent, disgraceful? How will it be able to avoid a frequent sacrifice of its engagements to immediate necessity? How can it undertake or execute any liberal or enlarged plans of public good?

Let us attend to what would be the effects of this situation in the very first war in which we should happen to be engaged. We will presume, for argument's sake, that the revenue arising from the impost duties answers the purposes of a provision for the public debt and of a peace establishment for the Union. Thus circumstanced, a war breaks out. What would be the probable conduct of the government in such an emergency? Taught by experience that proper dependence could not be placed on the success of requisitions, unable by its own authority to lay hold of fresh resources, and urged by considerations of national danger, would it not be driven to the expedient of diverting the funds already appropriated from their proper objects to the defense of the State? It is not easy to see how a step of this kind could be avoided; and if it should be taken, it is evident that it would prove the destruction of public credit at the very moment that it was becoming essential to the public safety. To imagine that at such a crisis credit might be dispensed with, would be the extreme of infatuation. In the modern system of war, nations the most wealthy are obliged to have recourse to large loans. A country so little opulent as ours must feel this necessity in a much stronger degree. But who would lend to a government that prefaced its overtures for borrowing by an act which demonstrated that no reliance could be placed on the steadiness of its measures for paying? The loans it might be able to procure would be as limited in their extent as burdensome in their conditions. They would be made upon the same principles that usurers commonly lend to bankrupt and fraudulent debtors, with a sparing hand and at enormous premiums.

It may perhaps be imagined that, from the scantiness of the resources of the country, the necessity of diverting the established funds in the case supposed would exist, though the national government should possess an unrestrained power of taxation. But two considerations will serve to quiet all apprehension on this head: one is, that we are sure the resources of the community, in their full extent, will be brought into activity for the benefit of the Union; the other is, that whatever deficiencies there may be, can without difficulty be supplied by loans.

The power of creating new funds upon new objects of taxation, by its own authority, would enable the national government to borrow as far as its necessities might require. Foreigners, as well as the citizens of America, could then reasonably repose confidence in its engagements; but to depend upon a government that must itself depend upon thirteen other governments for the means of fulfilling its contracts, when once its situation is clearly understood, would require a degree of credulity not often to be met with in the pecuniary transactions of mankind, and little reconcilable with the usual sharp-sightedness of avarice.

Reflections of this kind may have trifling weight with men who hope to see realized in America the halcyon scenes of the poetic or fabulous age; but to those who believe we are likely to experience a common portion of the vicissitudes and calamities which have fallen to the lot of other nations, they must appear entitled to serious attention. Such men must behold the actual situation of their country with painful solicitude, and deprecate the evils which ambition or revenge might, with too much facility, inflict upon it.

PUBLIUS.

Federalist No. 31

The Same Subject Continued
(Concerning the General Power of Taxation)
From the New York Packet.
Tuesday, January 1, 1788.
HAMILTON

To the People of the State of New York:

IN DISQUISITIONS of every kind, there are certain primary truths, or first principles, upon which all subsequent reasonings must depend. These contain an internal evidence which, antecedent to all reflection or combination, commands the assent of the mind. Where it produces not this effect, it must proceed either from some defect or disorder in the organs of perception, or from the influence of some strong interest, or passion, or prejudice. Of this nature are the maxims in geometry, that "the whole is greater than its part; things equal to the same are equal to one another; two straight lines cannot enclose a space; and all right angles are equal to each other." Of the same nature are these other maxims in ethics and politics, that there cannot be an effect without a cause; that the means ought to be proportioned to the end; that every power ought to be commensurate with its object; that there ought to be no limitation of a power destined to effect a purpose which is itself incapable of limitation. And there are other truths in the two latter sciences which, if they cannot pretend to rank in the class of axioms, are yet such direct inferences from them, and so obvious in themselves, and so agreeable to the natural and unsophisticated dictates of common-sense, that they challenge the assent of a sound and unbiased mind, with a degree of force and conviction almost equally irresistible.

The objects of geometrical inquiry are so entirely abstracted from those pursuits which stir up and put in motion the unruly passions of the human heart, that mankind, without difficulty, adopt not only the more simple theorems of the science, but even those abstruse paradoxes which, however they may appear susceptible of demonstration, are at variance with the natural conceptions which the mind, without the aid of philosophy, would be led to entertain upon the subject. The INFINITE DIVISIBILITY of matter, or, in other words, the INFINITE divisibility of a FINITE thing, extending even to the minutest atom, is a point agreed among geometricians, though not less incomprehensible to common-sense than any of those mysteries in religion, against which the batteries of infidelity have been so industriously leveled.

But in the sciences of morals and politics, men are found far less tractable. To a certain degree, it is right and useful that this should be the case. Caution and investigation are a necessary armor against error and imposition. But this untractableness may be carried too far, and may degenerate into obstinacy, perverseness, or disingenuity. Though it cannot be pretended that the principles of moral and political knowledge have, in general, the same degree of certainty with those of the mathematics, yet they have much better claims in this respect than, to judge from the conduct of men in particular situations, we should be disposed to allow them. The obscurity is much oftener in the passions and prejudices of the reasoner than in the subject. Men, upon too many occasions, do not give their own understandings fair play; but, yielding to some untoward bias, they entangle themselves in words and confound themselves in subtleties.

How else could it happen (if we admit the objectors to be sincere in their opposition), that positions so clear as those which manifest the necessity of a general power of taxation in the government of the Union, should have to encounter any adversaries among men of discernment? Though these positions have been elsewhere fully stated, they will perhaps not be improperly recapitulated in this place, as introductory to an examination of what may have been offered by way of objection to them. They are in substance as follows:

A government ought to contain in itself every power requisite to the full accomplishment of the objects committed to its care, and to the complete execution of the trusts for which it is responsible, free from every other control but a regard to the public good and to the sense of the people.

As the duties of superintending the national defense and of securing the public peace against foreign or domestic violence involve a provision for casualties and dangers to which no possible limits can be assigned, the power of making that provision ought to know no other bounds than the exigencies of the nation and the resources of the community.

As revenue is the essential engine by which the means of answering the national exigencies must be procured, the power of procuring that article in its full extent must necessarily be comprehended in that of providing for those exigencies.

As theory and practice conspire to prove that the power of procuring revenue is unavailing when exercised over the States in their collective capacities, the federal government must of necessity be invested with an unqualified power of taxation in the ordinary modes.

Did not experience evince the contrary, it would be natural to conclude that the propriety of a general power of taxation in the national government might safely be permitted to rest on the evidence of these propositions, unassisted by any additional arguments or illustrations. But we find, in fact, that the antagonists of the proposed Constitution, so far from acquiescing in their justness or truth, seem to make their principal and most zealous effort against this part of the plan. It may therefore be satisfactory to analyze the arguments with which they combat it.

Those of them which have been most labored with that view, seem in substance to amount to this: "It is not true, because the exigencies of the Union may not be susceptible of limitation, that its power of laying taxes ought to be unconfined. Revenue is as requisite to the purposes of the local administrations as to those of the Union; and the former are at least of equal importance with the latter to the happiness of the people. It is, therefore, as necessary that the State governments should be able to command the means of supplying their wants, as that the national government should possess the like faculty in respect to the wants of the Union. But an indefinite power of taxation in the LATTER might, and probably would in time, deprive the FORMER of the means of providing for their own necessities; and would subject them entirely to the mercy of the national legislature. As the laws of the Union are to become the supreme law of the land, as it is to have power to pass all laws that may be NECESSARY for carrying into execution the authorities with which it is proposed to vest it, the national government might at any time abolish the taxes imposed for State objects upon the pretense of an interference with its own. It might allege a necessity of doing this in order to give efficacy to the national revenues. And thus all the resources of taxation might by degrees become the subjects of federal monopoly, to the entire exclusion and destruction of the State governments."

This mode of reasoning appears sometimes to turn upon the supposition of usurpation in the national government; at other times it seems to be designed only as a deduction from the constitutional operation of its intended powers. It is only in the latter light that it can be admitted to have any pretensions to fairness. The moment we launch into conjectures about the usurpations of the federal government, we get into an unfathomable abyss, and fairly put ourselves out of the reach of all reasoning. Imagination may range at pleasure till it gets bewildered amidst the labyrinths of an enchanted castle, and knows not on which side to turn to extricate itself from the perplexities into which it has so rashly adventured. Whatever may be the limits or modifications of the powers of the Union, it is easy to imagine an endless train of possible dangers; and by indulging an excess of jealousy and timidity, we may bring ourselves to a state of absolute scepticism and irresolution. I repeat here what I have observed in substance in another place, that all observations founded upon the danger of usurpation ought to be referred to the composition and structure of the government, not to the nature or extent of its powers. The State governments, by their original constitutions, are invested with complete sovereignty. In what does our security consist against usurpation from that quarter? Doubtless in the manner of their formation, and in a due dependence of those who are to administer them upon the people. If the proposed construction of the federal government be found, upon an impartial examination of it, to be such as to afford, to a proper extent, the same species of security, all apprehensions on the score of usurpation ought to be discarded.

It should not be forgotten that a disposition in the State governments to encroach upon the rights of the Union is quite as probable as a disposition in the Union to encroach upon the rights of the State governments. What side would be likely to prevail in such a conflict, must depend on the means which the contending parties could employ toward insuring success. As in republics strength is always on the side of the people, and as there are weighty reasons to induce a belief that the State governments will commonly possess most influence over them, the natural conclusion is that such contests will be most apt to end to the disadvantage of the Union; and that there is greater probability of encroachments by the members upon the federal head, than by the federal head upon the members. But it is evident that all conjectures of this kind must be extremely vague and fallible: and that it is by far the safest course to lay them altogether aside, and to confine our attention wholly to the nature and extent of the powers as they are delineated in the Constitution. Every thing beyond this must be left to the prudence and firmness of the people; who, as they will hold the scales in their own hands, it is to be hoped, will always take care to preserve the constitutional equilibrium between the general and the State governments. Upon this ground, which is evidently the true one, it will not be difficult to obviate the objections which have been made to an indefinite power of taxation in the United States.

PUBLIUS.

Federalist No. 32

The Same Subject Continued
(Concerning the General Power of Taxation)
From the Daily Advertiser.
Thursday, January 3, 1788.
HAMILTON
To the People of the State of New York:

ALTHOUGH I am of opinion that there would be no real danger of the consequences which seem to be apprehended to the State governments from a power in the Union to control them in the levies of money, because I am persuaded that the sense of the people, the extreme hazard of provoking the resentments of the State governments, and a conviction of the utility and necessity of local administrations for local purposes, would be a complete barrier against the oppressive use of such a power; yet I am willing here to allow, in its full extent, the justness of the reasoning which requires that the individual States should possess an independent and uncontrollable authority to raise their own revenues for the supply of their own wants. And making this concession, I affirm that (with the sole exception of duties on imports and exports) they would, under the plan of the convention, retain that authority in the most absolute and unqualified sense; and that an attempt on the part of the national government to abridge them in the exercise of it, would be a violent assumption of power, unwarranted by any article or clause of its Constitution.

An entire consolidation of the States into one complete national sovereignty would imply an entire subordination of the parts; and whatever powers might remain in them, would be altogether dependent on the general will. But as the plan of the convention aims only at a partial union or consolidation, the State governments would clearly retain all the rights of sovereignty which they before had, and which were not, by that act, EXCLUSIVELY delegated to the United States. This exclusive delegation, or rather this alienation, of State sovereignty, would only exist in three cases: where the Constitution in express terms granted an exclusive authority to the Union; where it granted in one instance an authority to the Union, and in another prohibited the States from exercising the like authority; and where it granted an authority to the Union, to which a similar authority in the States would be absolutely and totally CONTRADICTORY and REPUGNANT. I use these terms to distinguish this last case from another which might appear to resemble it, but which would, in fact, be essentially different; I mean where the exercise of a concurrent jurisdiction might be productive of occasional interferences in the POLICY of any branch of administration, but would not imply any direct contradiction or repugnancy in point of constitutional authority. These three cases of exclusive jurisdiction in the federal government may be exemplified by the following instances: The last clause but one in the eighth section of the first article provides expressly that Congress shall exercise "EXCLUSIVE LEGISLATION" over the district to be appropriated as the seat of government. This answers to the first case. The first clause of the same section empowers Congress "TO LAY AND COLLECT TAXES, DUTIES, IMPOSTS AND EXCISES"; and the second clause of the tenth section of the same article declares that, "NO STATE SHALL, without the consent of Congress, LAY ANY IMPOSTS OR DUTIES ON IMPORTS OR EXPORTS, except for the purpose of executing its inspection laws." Hence would result an exclusive power in the Union to lay duties on imports and exports, with the particular exception mentioned; but this power is abridged by another clause, which declares that no tax or duty shall be laid on articles exported from any State; in consequence of which qualification, it now only extends to the DUTIES ON IMPORTS. This answers to the second case. The third will be found in that clause which declares that Congress shall have power "to establish an UNIFORM RULE of naturalization throughout the United States." This must necessarily be exclusive; because if each State had power to prescribe a DISTINCT RULE, there could not be a UNIFORM RULE.

A case which may perhaps be thought to resemble the latter, but which is in fact widely different, affects the question immediately under consideration. I mean the power of imposing taxes on all articles other than exports and imports. This, I contend, is manifestly a concurrent and coequal authority in the United States and in the individual States. There is plainly no expression in the granting clause which makes that power EXCLUSIVE in the Union. There is no independent clause or sentence which prohibits the States from exercising it. So far is this from being the case, that a plain and conclusive argument to the contrary is to be deduced from the restraint laid upon the States in relation to duties on imports and exports. This restriction implies an admission that, if it were not inserted, the States would possess the power it excludes; and it implies a further admission, that as to all other taxes, the authority of the States remains undiminished. In any other view it would be both unnecessary and dangerous; it would be unnecessary, because if the grant to the Union of the power of laying such duties implied the exclusion of the States, or even their subordination in this particular, there could be no need of such a restriction; it would be dangerous, because the introduction of it leads directly to the conclusion which has been mentioned, and which, if the reasoning of the objectors be just, could not have been intended; I mean that the States, in all cases to which the restriction did not apply, would have a concurrent power of taxation with the Union. The restriction in question amounts to what lawyers call a NEGATIVE PREGNANT that is, a NEGATION of one thing, and an AFFIRMANCE of another; a negation of the authority of the States to impose taxes on imports and exports, and an affirmance of their authority to impose them on all other articles. It would be mere sophistry to argue that it was meant to exclude them ABSOLUTELY from the imposition of taxes of the former kind, and to leave them at liberty to lay others SUBJECT TO THE CONTROL of the national legislature. The restraining or prohibitory clause only says, that they shall not, WITHOUT THE CONSENT OF CONGRESS, lay such duties; and if we are to understand this in the sense last mentioned, the Constitution would then be made to introduce a formal provision for the sake of a very absurd conclusion; which is, that the States, WITH THE CONSENT of the national legislature, might tax imports and exports; and that they might tax every other article, UNLESS CONTROLLED by the same body. If this was the intention, why not leave it, in the first instance, to what is alleged to be the natural operation of the original clause, conferring a general power of taxation upon the Union? It is evident that this could not have been the intention, and that it will not bear a construction of the kind.

As to a supposition of repugnancy between the power of taxation in the States and in the Union, it cannot be supported in that sense which would be requisite to work an exclusion of the States. It is, indeed, possible that a tax might be laid on a particular article by a State which might render it INEXPEDIENT that thus a further tax should be laid on the same article by the Union; but it would not imply a constitutional inability to impose a further tax. The quantity of the imposition, the expediency or inexpediency of an increase on either side, would be mutually questions of prudence; but there would be involved no direct contradiction of power. The particular policy of the national and of the State systems of finance might now and then not exactly coincide, and might require reciprocal forbearances. It is not, however a mere possibility of inconvenience in the exercise of powers, but an immediate constitutional repugnancy that can by implication alienate and extinguish a pre-existing right of sovereignty.

The necessity of a concurrent jurisdiction in certain cases results from the division of the sovereign power; and the rule that all authorities, of which the States are not explicitly divested in favor of the Union, remain with them in full vigor, is not a theoretical consequence of that division, but is clearly admitted by the whole tenor of the instrument which contains the articles of the proposed Constitution. We there find that, notwithstanding the affirmative grants of general authorities, there has been the most pointed care in those cases where it was deemed improper that the like authorities should reside in the States, to insert negative clauses prohibiting the exercise of them by the States. The tenth section of the first article consists altogether of such provisions. This circumstance is a clear indication of the sense of the convention, and furnishes a rule of interpretation out of the body of the act, which justifies the position I have advanced and refutes every hypothesis to the contrary.

PUBLIUS.

Federalist No. 33

The Same Subject Continued
(Concerning the General Power of Taxation)
From the Daily Advertiser.
January 3, 1788.
HAMILTON
To the People of the State of New York:

THE residue of the argument against the provisions of the Constitution in respect to taxation is ingrafted upon the following clause. The last clause of the eighth section of the first article of the plan under consideration authorizes the national legislature "to make all laws which shall be NECESSARY and PROPER for carrying into execution THE POWERS by that Constitution vested in the government of the United States, or in any department or officer thereof"; and the second clause of the sixth article declares, "that the Constitution and the laws of the United States made IN PURSUANCE THEREOF, and the treaties made by their authority shall be the SUPREME LAW of the land, any thing in the constitution or laws of any State to the contrary notwithstanding."

These two clauses have been the source of much virulent invective and petulant declamation against the proposed Constitution. They have been held up to the people in all the exaggerated colors of misrepresentation as the pernicious engines by which their local governments were to be destroyed and their liberties exterminated; as the hideous monster whose devouring jaws would spare neither sex nor age, nor high nor low, nor sacred nor profane; and yet, strange as it may appear, after all this clamor, to those who may not have happened to contemplate them in the same light, it may be affirmed with perfect confidence that the constitutional operation of the intended government would be precisely the same, if these clauses were entirely obliterated, as if they were repeated in every article. They are only declaratory of a truth which would have resulted by necessary and unavoidable implication from the very act of constituting a federal government, and vesting it with certain specified powers. This is so clear a proposition, that moderation itself can scarcely listen to the railings which have been so copiously vented against this part of the plan, without emotions that disturb its equanimity.

What is a power, but the ability or faculty of doing a thing? What is the ability to do a thing, but the power of employing the MEANS necessary to its execution? What is a LEGISLATIVE power, but a power of making LAWS? What are the MEANS to execute a LEGISLATIVE power but LAWS? What is the power of laying and collecting taxes, but a LEGISLATIVE POWER, or a power of MAKING LAWS, to lay and collect taxes? What are the proper means of executing such a power, but NECESSARY and PROPER laws?

This simple train of inquiry furnishes us at once with a test by which to judge of the true nature of the clause complained of. It conducts us to this palpable truth, that a power to lay and collect taxes must be a power to pass all laws NECESSARY and PROPER for the execution of that power; and what does the unfortunate and culminated provision in question do more than declare the same truth, to wit, that the national legislature, to whom the power of laying and collecting taxes had been previously given, might, in the execution of that power, pass all laws NECESSARY and PROPER to carry it into effect? I have applied these observations thus particularly to the power of taxation, because it is the immediate subject under consideration, and because it is the most important of the authorities proposed to be conferred upon the Union. But the same process will lead to the same result, in relation to all other powers declared in the Constitution. And it is EXPRESSLY to execute these powers that the sweeping clause, as it has been affectedly called, authorizes the national legislature to pass all NECESSARY and PROPER laws. If there is any thing exceptionable, it must be sought for in the specific powers upon which this general declaration is predicated. The declaration itself, though it may be chargeable with tautology or redundancy, is at least perfectly harmless.

But SUSPICION may ask, Why then was it introduced? The answer is, that it could only have been done for greater caution, and to guard against all cavilling refinements in those who might hereafter feel a disposition to curtail and evade the legitimate authorities of the Union. The Convention probably foresaw, what it has been a principal aim of these papers to inculcate, that the danger which most threatens our political welfare is that the State governments will finally sap the foundations of the Union; and might therefore think it necessary, in so cardinal a point, to leave nothing to construction. Whatever may have been the inducement to it, the wisdom of the precaution is evident from the cry which has been raised against it; as that very cry betrays a disposition to question the great and essential truth which it is manifestly the object of that provision to declare.

But it may be again asked, Who is to judge of the NECESSITY and PROPRIETY of the laws to be passed for executing the powers of the Union? I answer, first, that this question arises as well and as fully upon the simple grant of those powers as upon the declaratory clause; and I answer, in the second place, that the national government, like every other, must judge, in the first instance, of the proper exercise of its powers, and its constituents in the last. If the federal government should overpass the just bounds of its authority and make a tyrannical use of its powers, the people, whose creature it is, must appeal to the standard they have formed, and take such measures to redress the injury done to the Constitution as the exigency may suggest and prudence justify. The propriety of a law, in a constitutional light, must always be determined by the nature of the powers upon which it is founded. Suppose, by some forced constructions of its authority (which, indeed, cannot easily be imagined), the Federal legislature should attempt to vary the law of descent in any State, would it not be evident that, in making such an attempt, it had exceeded its jurisdiction, and infringed upon that of the State? Suppose, again, that upon the pretense of an interference with its revenues, it should undertake to abrogate a land tax imposed by the authority of a State; would it not be equally evident that this was an invasion of that concurrent jurisdiction in respect to this species of tax, which its Constitution plainly supposes to exist in the State governments? If there ever should be a doubt on this head, the credit of it will be entirely due to those reasoners who, in the imprudent zeal of their animosity to the plan of the convention, have labored to envelop it in a cloud calculated to obscure the plainest and simplest truths.

But it is said that the laws of the Union are to be the SUPREME LAW of the land. But what inference can be drawn from this, or what would they amount to, if they were not to be supreme? It is evident they would amount to nothing. A LAW, by the very meaning of the term, includes supremacy. It is a rule which those to whom it is prescribed are bound to observe. This results from every political association. If individuals enter into a state of society, the laws of that society must be the supreme regulator of their conduct. If a number of political societies enter into a larger political society, the laws which the latter may enact, pursuant to the powers intrusted to it by its constitution, must necessarily be supreme over those societies, and the individuals of whom they are composed. It would otherwise be a mere treaty, dependent on the good faith of the parties, and not a government, which is only another word for POLITICAL POWER AND SUPREMACY. But it will not follow from this doctrine that acts of the large society which are NOT PURSUANT to its constitutional powers, but which are invasions of the residuary authorities of the smaller societies, will become the supreme law of the land. These will be merely acts of usurpation, and will deserve to be treated as such. Hence we perceive that the clause which declares the supremacy of the laws of the Union, like the one we have just before considered, only declares a truth, which flows immediately and necessarily from the institution of a federal government. It will not, I presume, have escaped observation, that it EXPRESSLY confines this supremacy to laws made PURSUANT TO THE CONSTITUTION; which I mention merely as an instance of caution in the convention; since that limitation would have been to be understood, though it had not been expressed.

Though a law, therefore, laying a tax for the use of the United States would be supreme in its nature, and could not legally be opposed or controlled, yet a law for abrogating or preventing the collection of a tax laid by the authority of the State, (unless upon imports and exports), would not be the supreme law of the land, but a usurpation of power not granted by the Constitution. As far as an improper accumulation of taxes on the same object might tend to render the collection difficult or precarious, this would be a mutual inconvenience, not arising from a superiority or defect of power on either side, but from an injudicious exercise of power by one or the other, in a manner equally disadvantageous to both. It is to be hoped and presumed, however, that mutual interest would dictate a concert in this respect which would avoid any material inconvenience. The inference from the whole is, that the individual States would, under the proposed Constitution, retain an independent and uncontrollable authority to raise revenue to any extent of which they may stand in need, by every kind of taxation, except duties on imports and exports. It will be shown in the next paper that this CONCURRENT JURISDICTION in the article of taxation was the only admissible substitute for an entire subordination, in respect to this branch of power, of the State authority to that of the Union.

PUBLIUS.

Federalist No. 37

Concerning the Difficulties of the Convention in Devising a Proper Form of Government

From the Daily Advertiser.

Friday, January 11, 1788.

MADISON

To the People of the State of New York:

IN REVIEWING the defects of the existing Confederation, and showing that they cannot be supplied by a government of less energy than that before the public, several of the most important principles of the latter fell of course under consideration. But as the ultimate object of these papers is to determine clearly and fully the merits of this Constitution, and the expediency of adopting it, our plan cannot be complete without taking a more critical and thorough survey of the work of the convention, without examining it on all its sides, comparing it in all its parts, and calculating its probable effects.

That this remaining task may be executed under impressions conducive to a just and fair result, some reflections must in this place be indulged, which candor previously suggests.

It is a misfortune, inseparable from human affairs, that public measures are rarely investigated with that spirit of moderation which is essential to a just estimate of their real tendency to advance or obstruct the public good; and that this spirit is more apt to be diminished than promoted, by those occasions which require an unusual exercise of it. To those who have been led by experience to attend to this consideration, it could not appear surprising, that the act of the convention, which recommends so many important changes and innovations, which may be viewed in so many lights and relations, and which touches the springs of so many passions and interests, should find or excite dispositions unfriendly, both on one side and on the other, to a fair discussion and accurate judgment of its merits. In some, it has been too evident from their own publications, that they have scanned the proposed Constitution, not only with a predisposition to censure, but with a predetermination to condemn; as the language held by others betrays an opposite predetermination or bias, which must render their opinions also of little moment in the question. In placing, however, these different characters on a level, with respect to the weight of their opinions, I wish not to insinuate that there may not be a material difference in the purity of their intentions. It is but just to remark in favor of the latter description, that as our situation is universally admitted to be peculiarly critical, and to require indispensably that something should be done for our relief, the predetermined patron of what has been actually done may have taken his bias from the weight of these considerations, as well as from considerations of a sinister nature. The predetermined adversary, on the other hand, can have been governed by no venial motive whatever. The intentions of the first may be upright, as they may on the contrary be culpable. The views of the last cannot be upright, and must be culpable. But the truth is, that these papers are not addressed to persons falling under either of these characters. They solicit the attention of those only, who add to a sincere zeal for the happiness of their country, a temper favorable to a just estimate of the means of promoting it.

Persons of this character will proceed to an examination of the plan submitted by the convention, not only without a disposition to find or to magnify faults; but will see the propriety of reflecting, that a faultless plan was not to be expected. Nor will they barely make allowances for the errors which may be chargeable on the fallibility to which the convention, as a body of men, were liable; but will keep in mind, that they themselves also are but men, and ought not to assume an infallibility in rejudging the fallible opinions of others.

With equal readiness will it be perceived, that besides these inducements to candor, many allowances ought to be made for the difficulties inherent in the very nature of the undertaking referred to the convention.

The novelty of the undertaking immediately strikes us. It has been shown in the course of these papers, that the existing Confederation is founded on principles which are fallacious; that we must consequently change this first foundation, and with it the superstructure resting upon it. It has been shown, that the other confederacies which could be consulted as precedents have been vitiated by the same erroneous principles, and can therefore furnish no other light than that of beacons, which give warning of the course to be shunned, without pointing out that which ought to be pursued. The most that the convention could do in such a situation, was to avoid the errors suggested by the past experience of other countries, as well as of our own; and to provide a convenient mode of rectifying their own errors, as future experiences may unfold them.

Among the difficulties encountered by the convention, a very important one must have lain in combining the requisite stability and energy in government, with the inviolable attention due to liberty and to the republican form. Without substantially accomplishing this part of their undertaking, they would have very imperfectly fulfilled the object of their appointment, or the expectation of the public; yet that it could not be easily accomplished, will be denied by no one who is unwilling to betray his ignorance of the subject. Energy in government is essential to that security against external and internal danger, and to that prompt and salutary execution of the laws which enter into the very definition of good government. Stability in government is essential to national character and to the advantages annexed to it, as well as to that repose and confidence in the minds of the people, which are among the chief blessings of civil society. An irregular and mutable legislation is not more an evil in itself than it is odious to the people; and it may be pronounced with assurance that the people of this country, enlightened as they are with regard to the nature, and interested, as the great body of them are, in the effects of good government, will never be satisfied till some remedy be applied to the vicissitudes and uncertainties which characterize the State administrations. On comparing, however, these valuable ingredients with the vital principles of liberty, we must perceive at once the difficulty of mingling them together in their due proportions. The genius of republican liberty seems to demand on one side, not only that all power should be derived from the people, but that those intrusted with it should be kept in independence on the people, by a short duration of their appointments; and that even during this short period the trust should be placed not in a few, but a number of hands. Stability, on the contrary, requires that the hands in which power is lodged should continue for a length of time the same. A frequent change of men will result from a frequent return of elections; and a frequent change of measures from a frequent change of men: whilst energy in government requires not only a certain duration of power, but the execution of it by a single hand.

How far the convention may have succeeded in this part of their work, will better appear on a more accurate view of it. From the cursory view here taken, it must clearly appear to have been an arduous part.

Not less arduous must have been the task of marking the proper line of partition between the authority of the general and that of the State governments. Every man will be sensible of this difficulty, in proportion as he has been accustomed to contemplate and discriminate objects extensive and complicated in their nature. The faculties of the mind itself have never yet been distinguished and defined, with satisfactory precision, by all the efforts of the most acute and metaphysical philosophers. Sense, perception, judgment, desire, volition, memory, imagination, are found to be separated by such delicate shades and minute gradations that their boundaries have eluded the most subtle investigations, and remain a pregnant source of ingenious disquisition and controversy. The boundaries between the great kingdom of nature, and, still more, between the various provinces, and lesser portions, into which they are subdivided, afford another illustration of the same important truth. The most sagacious and laborious naturalists have never yet succeeded in tracing with certainty the line which separates the district of vegetable life from the neighboring region of unorganized matter, or which marks the termination of the former and the commencement of the animal empire. A still greater obscurity lies in the distinctive characters by which the objects in each of these great departments of nature have been arranged and assorted.

When we pass from the works of nature, in which all the delineations are perfectly accurate, and appear to be otherwise only from the imperfection of the eye which surveys them, to the institutions of man, in which the obscurity arises as well from the object itself as from the organ by which it is contemplated, we must perceive the necessity of moderating still further our expectations and hopes from the efforts of human sagacity. Experience has instructed us that no skill in the science of government has yet been able to discriminate and define, with sufficient certainty, its three great provinces the legislative, executive, and judiciary; or even the privileges and powers of the different legislative branches. Questions daily occur in the course of practice, which prove the obscurity which reins in these subjects, and which puzzle the greatest adepts in political science.

The experience of ages, with the continued and combined labors of the most enlightened legislatures and jurists, has been equally unsuccessful in delineating the several objects and limits of different codes of laws and different tribunals of justice. The precise extent of the common law, and the statute law, the maritime law, the ecclesiastical law, the law of corporations, and other local laws and customs, remains still to be clearly and finally established in Great Britain, where accuracy in such subjects has been more industriously pursued than in any other part of the world. The jurisdiction of her several courts, general and local, of law, of equity, of admiralty, etc., is not less a source of frequent and intricate discussions, sufficiently denoting the indeterminate limits by which they are respectively circumscribed. All new laws, though penned with the greatest technical skill, and passed on the fullest and most mature deliberation, are considered as more or less obscure and equivocal, until their meaning be liquidated and ascertained by a series of particular discussions and adjudications. Besides the obscurity arising from the complexity of objects, and the imperfection of the human faculties, the medium through which the conceptions of men are conveyed to each other adds a fresh embarrassment. The use of words is to express ideas. Perspicuity, therefore, requires not only that the ideas should be distinctly formed, but that they should be expressed by words distinctly and exclusively appropriate to them. But no language is so copious as to supply words and phrases for every complex idea, or so correct as not to include many equivocally denoting different ideas. Hence it must happen that however accurately objects may be discriminated in themselves, and however accurately the discrimination may be considered, the definition of them may be rendered inaccurate by the inaccuracy of the terms in which it is delivered. And this unavoidable inaccuracy must be greater or less, according to the complexity and novelty of the objects defined. When the Almighty himself condescends to address mankind in their own language, his meaning, luminous as it must be, is rendered dim and doubtful by the cloudy medium through which it is communicated.

Here, then, are three sources of vague and incorrect definitions: indistinctness of the object, imperfection of the organ of conception, inadequateness of the vehicle of ideas. Any one of these must produce a certain degree of obscurity. The convention, in delineating the boundary between the federal and State jurisdictions, must have experienced the full effect of them all.

To the difficulties already mentioned may be added the interfering pretensions of the larger and smaller States. We cannot err in supposing that the former would contend for a participation in the government, fully proportioned to their superior wealth and importance; and that the latter would not be less tenacious of the equality at present enjoyed by them. We may well suppose that neither side would entirely yield to the other, and consequently that the struggle could be terminated only by compromise. It is extremely probable, also, that after the ratio of representation had been adjusted, this very compromise must have produced a fresh struggle between the same parties, to give such a turn to the organization of the government, and to the distribution of its powers, as would increase the importance of the branches, in forming which they had respectively obtained the greatest share of influence. There are features in the Constitution which warrant each of these suppositions; and as far as either of them is well founded, it shows that the convention must have been compelled to sacrifice theoretical propriety to the force of extraneous considerations.

Nor could it have been the large and small States only, which would marshal themselves in opposition to each other on various points. Other combinations, resulting from a difference of local position and policy, must have created additional difficulties. As every State may be divided into different districts, and its citizens into different classes, which give birth to contending interests and local jealousies, so the different parts of the United States are distinguished from each other by a variety of circumstances, which produce a like effect on a larger scale. And although this variety of interests, for reasons sufficiently explained in a former paper, may have a salutary influence on the administration of the government when formed, yet every one must be sensible of the contrary influence, which must have been experienced in the task of forming it.

Would it be wonderful if, under the pressure of all these difficulties, the convention should have been forced into some deviations from that artificial structure and regular symmetry which an abstract view of the subject might lead an ingenious theorist to bestow on a Constitution planned in his closet or in his imagination? The real wonder is that so many difficulties should have been surmounted, and surmounted with a unanimity almost as unprecedented as it must have been unexpected. It is impossible for any man of candor to reflect on this circumstance without partaking of the astonishment. It is impossible for the man of pious reflection not to perceive in it a finger of that Almighty hand which has been so frequently and signally extended to our relief in the critical stages of the revolution.

We had occasion, in a former paper, to take notice of the repeated trials which have been unsuccessfully made in the United Netherlands for reforming the baneful and notorious vices of their constitution. The history of almost all the great councils and consultations held among mankind for reconciling their discordant opinions, assuaging their mutual jealousies, and adjusting their respective interests, is a history of factions, contentions, and disappointments, and may be classed among the most dark and degraded pictures which display the infirmities and depravities of the human character. If, in a few scattered instances, a brighter aspect is presented, they serve only as exceptions to admonish us of the general truth; and by their lustre to darken the gloom of the adverse prospect to which they are contrasted. In revolving the causes from which these exceptions result, and applying them to the particular instances before us, we are necessarily led to two important conclusions. The first is, that the convention must have enjoyed, in a very singular degree, an exemption from the pestilential influence of party animosities the disease most incident to deliberative bodies, and most apt to contaminate their proceedings. The second conclusion is that all the deputations composing the convention were satisfactorily accommodated by the final act, or were induced to accede to it by a deep conviction of the necessity of sacrificing private opinions and partial interests to the public good, and by a despair of seeing this necessity diminished by delays or by new experiments.

Federalist No. 39

The Conformity of the Plan to Republican Principles

For the Independent Journal.

MADISON

To the People of the State of New York:

THE last paper having concluded the observations which were meant to introduce a candid survey of the plan of government reported by the convention, we now proceed to the execution of that part of our undertaking.

The first question that offers itself is, whether the general form and aspect of the government be strictly republican. It is evident that no other form would be reconcilable with the genius of the people of America; with the fundamental principles of the Revolution; or with that honorable determination which animates every votary of freedom, to rest all our political experiments on the capacity of mankind for self-government. If the plan of the convention, therefore, be found to depart from the republican character, its advocates must abandon it as no longer defensible.

What, then, are the distinctive characters of the republican form? Were an answer to this question to be sought, not by recurring to principles, but in the application of the term by political writers, to the constitution of different States, no satisfactory one would ever be found. Holland, in which no particle of the supreme authority is derived from the people, has passed almost universally under the denomination of a republic. The same title has been bestowed on Venice, where absolute power over the great body of the people is exercised, in the most absolute manner, by a small body of hereditary nobles. Poland, which is a mixture of aristocracy and of monarchy in their worst forms, has been dignified with the same appellation. The government of England, which has one republican branch only, combined with an hereditary aristocracy and monarchy, has, with equal impropriety, been frequently placed on the list of republics. These examples, which are nearly as dissimilar to each other as to a genuine republic, show the extreme inaccuracy with which the term has been used in political disquisitions.

If we resort for a criterion to the different principles on which different forms of government are established, we may define a republic to be, or at least may bestow that name on, a government which derives all its powers directly or indirectly from the great body of the people, and is administered by persons holding their offices during pleasure, for a limited period, or during good behavior. It is ESSENTIAL to such a government that it be derived from the great body of the society, not from an inconsiderable proportion, or a favored class of it; otherwise a handful of tyrannical nobles, exercising their oppressions by a delegation of their powers, might aspire to the rank of republicans, and claim for their government the honorable title of republic. It is SUFFICIENT for such a government that the persons administering it be appointed, either directly or indirectly, by the people; and that they hold their appointments by either of the tenures just specified; otherwise every government in the United States, as well as every other popular government that has been or can be well organized or well executed, would be degraded from the republican character. According to the constitution of every State in the Union, some or other of the officers of government are appointed indirectly only by the people. According to most of them, the chief magistrate himself is so appointed. And according to one, this mode of appointment is extended to one of the co-ordinate branches of the legislature. According to all the constitutions, also, the tenure of the highest offices is extended to a definite period, and in many instances, both within the legislative and executive departments, to a period of years. According to the provisions of most of the constitutions, again, as well as according to the most respectable and received opinions on the subject, the members of the judiciary department are to retain their offices by the firm tenure of good behavior.

On comparing the Constitution planned by the convention with the standard here fixed, we perceive at once that it is, in the most rigid sense, conformable to it. The House of Representatives, like that of one branch at least of all the State legislatures, is elected immediately by the great body of the people. The Senate, like the present Congress, and the Senate of Maryland, derives its appointment indirectly from the people. The President is indirectly derived from the choice of the people, according to the example in most of the States. Even the judges, with all other officers of the Union, will, as in the several States, be the choice, though a remote choice, of the people themselves, the duration of the appointments is equally conformable to the republican standard, and to the model of State constitutions. The House of Representatives is periodically elective, as in all the States; and for the period of two years, as in the State of South Carolina. The Senate is elective, for the period of six years; which is but one year more than the period of the Senate of Maryland, and but two more than that of the Senates of New York and Virginia. The President is to continue in office for the period of four years; as in New York and Delaware, the chief magistrate is elected for three years, and in South Carolina for two years. In the other States the election is annual. In several of the States, however, no constitutional provision is made for the impeachment of the chief magistrate. And in Delaware and Virginia he is not impeachable till out of office. The President of the United States is impeachable at any time during his continuance in office. The tenure by which the judges are to hold their places, is, as it unquestionably ought to be, that of good behavior. The tenure of the ministerial offices generally, will be a subject of legal regulation, conformably to the reason of the case and the example of the State constitutions.

Could any further proof be required of the republican complexion of this system, the most decisive one might be found in its absolute prohibition of titles of nobility, both under the federal and the State governments; and in its express guaranty of the republican form to each of the latter.

"But it was not sufficient," say the adversaries of the proposed Constitution, "for the convention to adhere to the republican form. They ought, with equal care, to have preserved the FEDERAL form, which regards the Union as a CONFEDERACY of sovereign states; instead of which, they have framed a NATIONAL government, which regards the Union as a CONSOLIDATION of the States." And it is asked by what authority this bold and radical innovation was undertaken? The handle which has been made of this objection requires that it should be examined with some precision.

Without inquiring into the accuracy of the distinction on which the objection is founded, it will be necessary to a just estimate of its force, first, to ascertain the real character of the government in question; secondly, to inquire how far the convention were authorized to propose such a government; and thirdly, how far the duty they owed to their country could supply any defect of regular authority.

First. In order to ascertain the real character of the government, it may be considered in relation to the foundation on which it is to be established; to the sources from which its ordinary powers are to be drawn; to the operation of those powers; to the extent of them; and to the authority by which future changes in the government are to be introduced.

On examining the first relation, it appears, on one hand, that the Constitution is to be founded on the assent and ratification of the people of America, given by deputies elected for the special purpose; but, on the other, that this assent and ratification is to be given by the people, not as individuals composing one entire nation, but as composing the distinct and independent States to which they respectively belong. It is to be the assent and ratification of the several States, derived from the supreme authority in each State, the authority of the people themselves. The act, therefore, establishing the Constitution, will not be a NATIONAL, but a FEDERAL act.

That it will be a federal and not a national act, as these terms are understood by the objectors; the act of the people, as forming so many independent States, not as forming one aggregate nation, is obvious from this single consideration, that it is to result neither from the decision of a MAJORITY of the people of the Union, nor from that of a MAJORITY of the States. It must result from the UNANIMOUS assent of the several States that are parties to it, differing no otherwise from their ordinary assent than in its being expressed, not by the legislative authority, but by that of the people themselves. Were the people regarded in this transaction as forming one nation, the will of the majority of the whole people of the United States would bind the minority, in the same manner as the majority in each State must bind the minority; and the will of the majority must be determined either by a comparison of the individual votes, or by considering the will of the majority of the States as evidence of the will of a majority of the people of the United States. Neither of these rules have been adopted. Each State, in ratifying the Constitution, is considered as a sovereign body, independent of all others, and only to be bound by its own voluntary act. In this relation, then, the new Constitution will, if established, be a FEDERAL, and not a NATIONAL constitution.

The next relation is, to the sources from which the ordinary powers of government are to be derived. The House of Representatives will derive its powers from the people of America; and the people will be represented in the same proportion, and on the same principle, as they are in the legislature of a particular State. So far the government is NATIONAL, not FEDERAL. The Senate, on the other hand, will derive its powers from the States, as political and coequal societies; and these will be represented on the principle of equality in the Senate, as they now are in the existing Congress. So far the government is FEDERAL, not NATIONAL. The executive power will be derived from a very compound source. The immediate election of the President is to be made by the States in their political characters. The votes allotted to them are in a compound ratio, which considers them partly as distinct and coequal societies, partly as unequal members of the same society. The eventual election, again, is to be made by that branch of the legislature which consists of the national representatives; but in this particular act they are to be thrown into the form of individual delegations, from so many distinct and coequal bodies politic. From this aspect of the government it appears to be of a mixed character, presenting at least as many FEDERAL as NATIONAL features.

The difference between a federal and national government, as it relates to the OPERATION OF THE GOVERNMENT, is supposed to consist in this, that in the former the powers operate on the political bodies composing the Confederacy, in their political capacities; in the latter, on the individual citizens composing the nation, in their individual capacities. On trying the Constitution by this criterion, it falls under the NATIONAL, not the FEDERAL character; though perhaps not so completely as has been understood. In several cases, and particularly in the trial of controversies to which States may be parties, they must be viewed and proceeded against in their collective and political capacities only. So far the national countenance of the government on this side seems to be disfigured by a few federal features. But this blemish is perhaps unavoidable in any plan; and the operation of the government on the people, in their individual capacities, in its ordinary and most essential proceedings, may, on the whole, designate it, in this relation, a NATIONAL government.

But if the government be national with regard to the OPERATION of its powers, it changes its aspect again when we contemplate it in relation to the EXTENT of its powers. The idea of a national government involves in it, not only an authority over the individual citizens, but an indefinite supremacy over all persons and things, so far as they are objects of lawful government. Among a people consolidated into one nation, this supremacy is completely vested in the national legislature. Among communities united for particular purposes, it is vested partly in the general and partly in the municipal legislatures. In the former case, all local authorities are subordinate to the supreme; and may be controlled, directed, or abolished by it at pleasure. In the latter, the local or municipal authorities form distinct and independent portions of the supremacy, no more subject, within their respective spheres, to the general authority, than the general authority is subject to them, within its own sphere. In this relation, then, the proposed government cannot be deemed a NATIONAL one; since its jurisdiction extends to certain enumerated objects only, and leaves to the several States a residuary and inviolable sovereignty over all other objects. It is true that in controversies relating to the boundary between the two jurisdictions, the tribunal which is ultimately to decide, is to be established under the general government. But this does not change the principle of the case. The decision is to be impartially made, according to the rules of the Constitution; and all the usual and most effectual precautions are taken to secure this impartiality. Some such tribunal is clearly essential to prevent an appeal to the sword and a dissolution of the compact; and that it ought to be established under the general rather than under the local governments, or, to speak more properly, that it could be safely established under the first alone, is a position not likely to be combated.

If we try the Constitution by its last relation to the authority by which amendments are to be made, we find it neither wholly NATIONAL nor wholly FEDERAL. Were it wholly national, the supreme and ultimate authority would reside in the MAJORITY of the people of the Union; and this authority would be competent at all times, like that of a majority of every national society, to alter or abolish its established government. Were it wholly federal, on the other hand, the concurrence of each State in the Union would be essential to every alteration that would be binding on all. The mode provided by the plan of the convention is not founded on either of these principles. In requiring more than a majority, and principles. In requiring more than a majority, and particularly in computing the proportion by STATES, not by CITIZENS, it departs from the NATIONAL and advances towards the FEDERAL character; in rendering the concurrence of less than the whole number of States sufficient, it loses again the FEDERAL and partakes of the NATIONAL character.

The proposed Constitution, therefore, is, in strictness, neither a national nor a federal Constitution, but a composition of both. In its foundation it is federal, not national; in the sources from which the ordinary powers of the government are drawn, it is partly federal and partly national; in the operation of these powers, it is national, not federal; in the extent of them, again, it is federal, not national; and, finally, in the authoritative mode of introducing amendments, it is neither wholly federal nor wholly national.

PUBLIUS.

Federalist No. 41

General View of the Powers Conferred by the Constitution

For the Independent Journal.

MADISON

To the People of the State of New York:

THE Constitution proposed by the convention may be considered under two general points of view. The FIRST relates to the sum or quantity of power which it vests in the government, including the restraints imposed on the States. The SECOND, to the particular structure of the government, and the distribution of this power among its several branches.

Under the FIRST view of the subject, two important questions arise: 1. Whether any part of the powers transferred to the general government be unnecessary or improper? 2. Whether the entire mass of them be dangerous to the portion of jurisdiction left in the several States?

Is the aggregate power of the general government greater than ought to have been vested in it? This is the FIRST question.

It cannot have escaped those who have attended with candor to the arguments employed against the extensive powers of the government, that the authors of them have very little considered how far these powers were necessary means of attaining a necessary end. They have chosen rather to dwell on the inconveniences which must be unavoidably blended with all political advantages; and on the possible abuses which must be incident to every power or trust, of which a beneficial use can be made. This method of handling the subject cannot impose on the good sense of the people of America. It may display the subtlety of the writer; it may open a boundless field for rhetoric and declamation; it may inflame the passions of the unthinking, and may confirm the prejudices of the misthinking: but cool and candid people will at once reflect, that the purest of human blessings must have a portion of alloy in them; that the choice must always be made, if not of the lesser evil, at least of the GREATER, not the PERFECT, good; and that in every political institution, a power to advance the public happiness involves a discretion which may be misapplied and abused. They will see, therefore, that in all cases where power is to be conferred, the point first to be decided is, whether such a power be necessary to the public good; as the next will be, in case of an affirmative decision, to guard as effectually as possible against a perversion of the power to the public detriment.

That we may form a correct judgment on this subject, it will be proper to review the several powers conferred on the government of the Union; and that this may be the more conveniently done they may be reduced into different classes as they relate to the following different objects: 1. Security against foreign danger; 2. Regulation of the intercourse with foreign nations; 3. Maintenance of harmony and proper intercourse among the States; 4. Certain miscellaneous objects of general utility; 5. Restraint of the States from certain injurious acts; 6. Provisions for giving due efficacy to all these powers.

The powers falling within the FIRST class are those of declaring war and granting letters of marque; of providing armies and fleets; of regulating and calling forth the militia; of levying and borrowing money.

Security against foreign danger is one of the primitive objects of civil society. It is an avowed and essential object of the American Union. The powers requisite for attaining it must be effectually confided to the federal councils.

Is the power of declaring war necessary? No man will answer this question in the negative. It would be superfluous, therefore, to enter into a proof of the affirmative. The existing Confederation establishes this power in the most ample form.

Is the power of raising armies and equipping fleets necessary? This is involved in the foregoing power. It is involved in the power of self-defense.

But was it necessary to give an INDEFINITE POWER of raising TROOPS, as well as providing fleets; and of maintaining both in PEACE, as well as in war?

The answer to these questions has been too far anticipated in another place to admit an extensive discussion of them in this place. The answer indeed seems to be so obvious and conclusive as scarcely to justify such a discussion in any place. With what color of propriety could the force necessary for defense be limited by those who cannot limit the force of offense? If a federal Constitution could chain the ambition or set bounds to the exertions of all other nations, then indeed might it prudently chain the discretion of its own government, and set bounds to the exertions for its own safety.

How could a readiness for war in time of peace be safely prohibited, unless we could prohibit, in like manner, the preparations and establishments of every hostile nation? The means of security can only be regulated by the means and the danger of attack. They will, in fact, be ever determined by these rules, and by no others. It is in vain to oppose constitutional barriers to the impulse of self-preservation. It is worse than in vain; because it plants in the Constitution itself necessary usurpations of power, every precedent of which is a germ of unnecessary and multiplied repetitions. If one nation maintains constantly a disciplined army, ready for the service of ambition or revenge, it obliges the most pacific nations who may be within the reach of its enterprises to take corresponding precautions. The fifteenth century was the unhappy epoch of military establishments in the time of peace. They were introduced by Charles VII. of France. All Europe has followed, or been forced into, the example. Had the example not been followed by other nations, all Europe must long ago have worn the chains of a universal monarch. Were every nation except France now to disband its peace establishments, the same event might follow. The veteran legions of Rome were an overmatch for the undisciplined valor of all other nations and rendered her the mistress of the world.

Not the less true is it, that the liberties of Rome proved the final victim to her military triumphs; and that the liberties of Europe, as far as they ever existed, have, with few exceptions, been the price of her military establishments. A standing force, therefore, is a dangerous, at the same time that it may be a necessary, provision. On the smallest scale it has its inconveniences. On an extensive scale its consequences may be fatal. On any scale it is an object of laudable circumspection and precaution. A wise nation will combine all these considerations; and, whilst it does not rashly preclude itself from any resource which may become essential to its safety, will exert all its prudence in diminishing both the necessity and the danger of resorting to one which may be inauspicious to its liberties.

The clearest marks of this prudence are stamped on the proposed Constitution. The Union itself, which it cements and secures, destroys every pretext for a military establishment which could be dangerous. America united, with a handful of troops, or without a single soldier, exhibits a more forbidding posture to foreign ambition than America disunited, with a hundred thousand veterans ready for combat. It was remarked, on a former occasion, that the want of this pretext had saved the liberties of one nation in Europe. Being rendered by her insular situation and her maritime resources impregnable to the armies of her neighbors, the rulers of Great Britain have never been able, by real or artificial dangers, to cheat the public into an extensive peace establishment. The distance of the United States from the powerful nations of the world gives them the same happy security. A dangerous establishment can never be necessary or plausible, so long as they continue a united people. But let it never, for a moment, be forgotten that they are indebted for this advantage to the Union alone. The moment of its dissolution will be the date of a new order of things. The fears of the weaker, or the ambition of the stronger States, or Confederacies, will set the same example in the New, as Charles VII. did in the Old World. The example will be followed here from the same motives which produced universal imitation there. Instead of deriving from our situation the precious advantage which Great Britain has derived from hers, the face of America will be but a copy of that of the continent of Europe. It will present liberty everywhere crushed between standing armies and perpetual taxes. The fortunes of disunited America will be even more disastrous than those of Europe. The sources of evil in the latter are confined to her own limits. No superior powers of another quarter of the globe intrigue among her rival nations, inflame their mutual animosities, and render them the instruments of foreign ambition, jealousy, and revenge. In America the miseries springing from her internal jealousies, contentions, and wars, would form a part only of her lot. A plentiful addition of evils would have their source in that relation in which Europe stands to this quarter of the earth, and which no other quarter of the earth bears to Europe.

This picture of the consequences of disunion cannot be too highly colored, or too often exhibited. Every man who loves peace, every man who loves his country, every man who loves liberty, ought to have it ever before his eyes, that he may cherish in his heart a due attachment to the Union of America, and be able to set a due value on the means of preserving it.

Next to the effectual establishment of the Union, the best possible precaution against danger from standing armies is a limitation of the term for which revenue may be appropriated to their support. This precaution the Constitution has prudently added. I will not repeat here the observations which I flatter myself have placed this subject in a just and satisfactory light. But it may not be improper to take notice of an argument against this part of the Constitution, which has been drawn from the policy and practice of Great Britain. It is said that the continuance of an army in that kingdom requires an annual vote of the legislature; whereas the American Constitution has lengthened this critical period to two years. This is the form in which the comparison is usually stated to the public: but is it a just form? Is it a fair comparison? Does the British Constitution restrain the parliamentary discretion to one year? Does the American impose on the Congress appropriations for two years? On the contrary, it cannot be unknown to the authors of the fallacy themselves, that the British Constitution fixes no limit whatever to the discretion of the legislature, and that the American ties down the legislature to two years, as the longest admissible term.

Had the argument from the British example been truly stated, it would have stood thus: The term for which supplies may be appropriated to the army establishment, though unlimited by the British Constitution, has nevertheless, in practice, been limited by parliamentary discretion to a single year. Now, if in Great Britain, where the House of Commons is elected for seven years; where so great a proportion of the members are elected by so small a proportion of the people; where the electors are so corrupted by the representatives, and the representatives so corrupted by the Crown, the representative body can possess a power to make appropriations to the army for an indefinite term, without desiring, or without daring, to extend the term beyond a single year, ought not suspicion herself to blush, in pretending that the representatives of the United States, elected FREELY by the WHOLE BODY of the people, every SECOND YEAR, cannot be safely intrusted with the discretion over such appropriations, expressly limited to the short period of TWO YEARS?

A bad cause seldom fails to betray itself. Of this truth, the management of the opposition to the federal government is an unvaried exemplification. But among all the blunders which have been committed, none is more striking than the attempt to enlist on that side the prudent jealousy entertained by the people, of standing armies. The attempt has awakened fully the public attention to that important subject; and has led to investigations which must terminate in a thorough and universal conviction, not only that the constitution has provided the most effectual guards against danger from that quarter, but that nothing short of a Constitution fully adequate to the national defense and the preservation of the Union, can save America from as many standing armies as it may be split into States or Confederacies, and from such a progressive augmentation, of these establishments in each, as will render them as burdensome to the properties and ominous to the liberties of the people, as any establishment that can become necessary, under a united and efficient government, must be tolerable to the former and safe to the latter.

The palpable necessity of the power to provide and maintain a navy has protected that part of the Constitution against a spirit of censure, which has spared few other parts. It must, indeed, be numbered among the greatest blessings of America, that as her Union will be the only source of her maritime strength, so this will be a principal source of her security against danger from abroad. In this respect our situation bears another likeness to the insular advantage of Great Britain. The batteries most capable of repelling foreign enterprises on our safety, are happily such as can never be turned by a perfidious government against our liberties.

The inhabitants of the Atlantic frontier are all of them deeply interested in this provision for naval protection, and if they have hitherto been suffered to sleep quietly in their beds; if their property has remained safe against the predatory spirit of licentious adventurers; if their maritime towns have not yet been compelled to ransom themselves from the terrors of a conflagration, by yielding to the exactions of daring and sudden invaders, these instances of good fortune are not to be ascribed to the capacity of the existing government for the protection of those from whom it claims allegiance, but to causes that are fugitive and fallacious. If we except perhaps Virginia and Maryland, which are peculiarly vulnerable on their eastern frontiers, no part of the Union ought to feel more anxiety on this subject than New York. Her seacoast is extensive. A very important district of the State is an island. The State itself is penetrated by a large navigable river for more than fifty leagues. The great emporium of its commerce, the great reservoir of its wealth, lies every moment at the mercy of events, and may almost be regarded as a hostage for ignominious compliances with the dictates of a foreign enemy, or even with the rapacious demands of pirates and barbarians. Should a war be the result of the precarious situation of European affairs, and all the unruly passions attending it be let loose on the ocean, our escape from insults and depredations, not only on that element, but every part of the other bordering on it, will be truly miraculous. In the present condition of America, the States more immediately exposed to these calamities have nothing to hope from the phantom of a general government which now exists; and if their single resources were equal to the task of fortifying themselves against the danger, the object to be protected would be almost consumed by the means of protecting them.

The power of regulating and calling forth the militia has been already sufficiently vindicated and explained.

The power of levying and borrowing money, being the sinew of that which is to be exerted in the national defense, is properly thrown into the same class with it. This power, also, has been examined already with much attention, and has, I trust, been clearly shown to be necessary, both in the extent and form given to it by the Constitution. I will address one additional reflection only to those who contend that the power ought to have been restrained to external taxation by which they mean, taxes on articles imported from other countries. It cannot be doubted that this will always be a valuable source of revenue; that for a considerable time it must be a principal source; that at this moment it is an essential one. But we may form very mistaken ideas on this subject, if we do not call to mind in our calculations, that the extent of revenue drawn from foreign commerce must vary with the variations, both in the extent and the kind of imports; and that these variations do not correspond with the progress of population, which must be the general measure of the public wants. As long as agriculture continues the sole field of labor, the importation of manufactures must increase as the consumers multiply. As soon as domestic manufactures are begun by the hands not called for by agriculture, the imported manufactures will decrease as the numbers of people increase. In a more remote stage, the imports may consist in a considerable part of raw materials, which will be wrought into articles for exportation, and will, therefore, require rather the encouragement of bounties, than to be loaded with discouraging duties. A system of government, meant for duration, ought to contemplate these revolutions, and be able to accommodate itself to them.

Some, who have not denied the necessity of the power of taxation, have grounded a very fierce attack against the Constitution, on the language in which it is defined. It has been urged and echoed, that the power "to lay and collect taxes, duties, imposts, and excises, to pay the debts, and provide for the common defense and general welfare of the United States," amounts to an unlimited commission to exercise every power which may be alleged to be necessary for the common defense or general welfare. No stronger proof could be given of the distress under which these writers labor for objections, than their stooping to such a misconstruction.

Had no other enumeration or definition of the powers of the Congress been found in the Constitution, than the general expressions just cited, the authors of the objection might have had some color for it; though it would have been difficult to find a reason for so awkward a form of describing an authority to legislate in all possible cases. A power to destroy the freedom of the press, the trial by jury, or even to regulate the course of descents, or the forms of conveyances, must be very singularly expressed by the terms "to raise money for the general welfare."

But what color can the objection have, when a specification of the objects alluded to by these general terms immediately follows, and is not even separated by a longer pause than a semicolon? If the different parts of the same instrument ought to be so expounded, as to give meaning to every part which will bear it, shall one part of the same sentence be excluded altogether from a share in the meaning; and shall the more doubtful and indefinite terms be retained in their full extent, and the clear and precise expressions be denied any signification whatsoever? For what purpose could the enumeration of particular powers be inserted, if these and all others were meant to be included in the preceding general power? Nothing is more natural nor common than first to use a general phrase, and then to explain and qualify it by a recital of particulars. But the idea of an enumeration of particulars which neither explain nor qualify the general meaning, and can have no other effect than to confound and mislead, is an absurdity, which, as we are reduced to the dilemma of charging either on the authors of the objection or on the authors of the Constitution, we must take the liberty of supposing, had not its origin with the latter.

The objection here is the more extraordinary, as it appears that the language used by the convention is a copy from the articles of Confederation. The objects of the Union among the States, as described in article third, are "their common defense, security of their liberties, and mutual and general welfare." The terms of article eighth are still more identical: "All charges of war and all other expenses that shall be incurred for the common defense or general welfare, and allowed by the United States in Congress, shall be defrayed out of a common treasury," etc. A similar language again occurs in article ninth. Construe either of these articles by the rules which would justify the construction put on the new Constitution, and they vest in the existing Congress a power to legislate in all cases whatsoever. But what would have been thought of that assembly, if, attaching themselves to these general expressions, and disregarding the specifications which ascertain and limit their import, they had exercised an unlimited power of providing for the common defense and general welfare? I appeal to the objectors themselves, whether they would in that case have employed the same reasoning in justification of Congress as they now make use of against the convention. How difficult it is for error to escape its own condemnation!

PUBLIUS.

Federalist No. 43

The Same Subject Continued
(The Powers Conferred
by the Constitution Further Considered)
For the Independent Journal.
MADISON
To the People of the State of New York:

THE FOURTH class comprises the following miscellaneous powers:

1. A power "to promote the progress of science and useful arts, by securing, for a limited time, to authors and inventors, the exclusive right to their respective writings and discoveries. "The utility of this power will scarcely be questioned. The copyright of authors has been solemnly adjudged, in Great Britain, to be a right of common law. The right to useful inventions seems with equal reason to belong to the inventors. The public good fully coincides in both cases with the claims of individuals. The States cannot separately make effectual provisions for either of the cases, and most of them have anticipated the decision of this point, by laws passed at the instance of Congress.

2. "To exercise exclusive legislation, in all cases whatsoever, over such district (not exceeding ten miles square) as may, by cession of particular States and the acceptance of Congress, become the seat of the government of the United States; and to exercise like authority over all places purchased by the consent of the legislatures of the States in which the same shall be, for the erection of forts, magazines, arsenals, dockyards, and other needful buildings.

"The indispensable necessity of complete authority at the seat of government, carries its own evidence with it. It is a power exercised by every legislature of the Union, I might say of the world, by virtue of its general supremacy. Without it, not only the public authority might be insulted and its proceedings interrupted with impunity; but a dependence of the members of the general government on the State comprehending the seat of the government, for protection in the exercise of their duty, might bring on the national councils an imputation of awe or influence, equally dishonorable to the government and dissatisfactory to the other members of the Confederacy.

This consideration has the more weight, as the gradual accumulation of public improvements at the stationary residence of the government would be both too great a public pledge to be left in the hands of a single State, and would create so many obstacles to a removal of the government, as still further to abridge its necessary independence. The extent of this federal district is sufficiently circumscribed to satisfy every jealousy of an opposite nature. And as it is to be appropriated to this use with the consent of the State ceding it; as the State will no doubt provide in the compact for the rights and the consent of the citizens inhabiting it; as the inhabitants will find sufficient inducements of interest to become willing parties to the cession; as they will have had their voice in the election of the government which is to exercise authority over them; as a municipal legislature for local purposes, derived from their own suffrages, will of course be allowed them; and as the authority of the legislature of the State, and of the inhabitants of the ceded part of it, to concur in the cession, will be derived from the whole people of the State in their adoption of the Constitution, every imaginable objection seems to be obviated. The necessity of a like authority over forts, magazines, etc. , established by the general government, is not less evident. The public money expended on such places, and the public property deposited in them, requires that they should be exempt from the authority of the particular State. Nor would it be proper for the places on which the security of the entire Union may depend, to be in any degree dependent on a particular member of it. All objections and scruples are here also obviated, by requiring the concurrence of the States concerned, in every such establishment.

3. "To declare the punishment of treason, but no attainder of treason shall work corruption of blood, or forfeiture, except during the life of the person attained. "As treason may be committed against the United States, the authority of the United States ought to be enabled to punish it. But as new-fangled and artificial treasons have been the great engines by which violent factions, the natural offspring of free government, have usually wreaked their alternate malignity on each other, the convention have, with great judgment, opposed a barrier to this peculiar danger, by inserting a constitutional definition of the crime, fixing the proof necessary for conviction of it, and restraining the Congress, even in punishing it, from extending the consequences

of guilt beyond the person of its author.

4. "To admit new States into the Union; but no new State shall be formed or erected within the jurisdiction of any other State; nor any State be formed by the junction of two or more States, or parts of States, without the consent of the legislatures of the States concerned, as well as of the Congress. "In the articles of Confederation, no provision is found on this important subject. Canada was to be admitted of right, on her joining in the measures of the United States; and the other COLONIES, by which were evidently meant the other British colonies, at the discretion of nine States. The eventual establishment of NEW STATES seems to have been overlooked by the compilers of that instrument. We have seen the inconvenience of this omission, and the assumption of power into which Congress have been led by it. With great propriety, therefore, has the new system supplied the defect. The general precaution, that no new States shall be formed, without the concurrence of the federal authority, and that of the States concerned, is consonant to the principles which ought to govern such transactions. The particular precaution against the erection of new States, by the partition of a State without its consent, quiets the jealousy of the larger States; as that of the smaller is quieted by a like precaution, against a junction of States without their consent.

5. "To dispose of and make all needful rules and regulations respecting the territory or other property belonging to the United States, with a proviso, that nothing in the Constitution shall be so construed as to prejudice any claims of the United States, or of any particular State. "This is a power of very great importance, and required by considerations similar to those which show the propriety of the former. The proviso annexed is proper in itself, and was probably rendered absolutely necessary by jealousies and questions concerning the Western territory sufficiently known to the public.

6. "To guarantee to every State in the Union a republican form of government; to protect each of them against invasion; and on application of the legislature, or of the executive (when the legislature cannot be convened), against domestic violence.

"In a confederacy founded on republican principles, and composed of republican members, the superintending government ought clearly to possess authority to defend the system against aristocratic or monarchial innovations. The more intimate the nature of such a union may be, the greater interest have the members in the political institutions of each other; and the greater right to insist that the forms of government under which the compact was entered into should be SUBSTANTIALLY maintained. But a right implies a remedy; and where else could the remedy be deposited, than where it is deposited by the Constitution? Governments of dissimilar principles and forms have been found less adapted to a federal coalition of any sort, than those of a kindred nature. "As the confederate republic of Germany," says Montesquieu, "consists of free cities and petty states, subject to different princes, experience shows us that it is more imperfect than that of Holland and Switzerland. " "Greece was undone," he adds, "as soon as the king of Macedon obtained a seat among the Amphictyons." In the latter case, no doubt, the disproportionate force, as well as the monarchical form, of the new confederate, had its share of influence on the events. It may possibly be asked, what need there could be of such a precaution, and whether it may not become a pretext for alterations in the State governments, without the concurrence of the States themselves.

These questions admit of ready answers. If the interposition of the general government should not be needed, the provision for such an event will be a harmless superfluity only in the Constitution. But who can say what experiments may be produced by the caprice of particular States, by the ambition of enterprising leaders, or by the intrigues and influence of foreign powers? To the second question it may be answered, that if the general government should interpose by virtue of this constitutional authority, it will be, of course, bound to pursue the authority. But the authority extends no further than to a GUARANTY of a republican form of government, which supposes a pre-existing government of the form which is to be guaranteed. As long, therefore, as the existing republican forms are continued by the States, they are guaranteed by the federal Constitution. Whenever the States may choose to substitute other republican forms, they have a right to do so, and to claim the federal guaranty for the latter. The only restriction imposed on them is, that they shall not exchange republican for antirepublican Constitutions; a restriction which, it is presumed, will hardly be considered as a grievance.

A protection against invasion is due from every society to the parts composing it. The latitude of the expression here used seems to secure each State, not only against foreign hostility, but against ambitious or vindictive enterprises of its more powerful neighbors. The history, both of ancient and modern confederacies, proves that the weaker members of the union ought not to be insensible to the policy of this article. Protection against domestic violence is added with equal propriety. It has been remarked, that even among the Swiss cantons, which, properly speaking, are not under one government, provision is made for this object; and the history of that league informs us that mutual aid is frequently claimed and afforded; and as well by the most democratic, as the other cantons. A recent and well-known event among ourselves has warned us to be prepared for emergencies of a like nature. At first view, it might seem not to square with the republican theory, to suppose, either that a majority have not the right, or that a minority will have the force, to subvert a government; and consequently, that the federal interposition can never be required, but when it would be improper. But theoretic reasoning, in this as in most other cases, must be qualified by the lessons of practice. Why may not illicit combinations, for purposes of violence, be formed as well by a majority of a State, especially a small State as by a majority of a county, or a district of the same State; and if the authority of the State ought, in the latter case, to protect the local magistracy, ought not the federal authority, in the former, to support the State authority? Besides, there are certain parts of the State constitutions which are so interwoven with the federal Constitution, that a violent blow cannot be given to the one without communicating the wound to the other. Insurrections in a State will rarely induce a federal interposition, unless the number concerned in them bear some proportion to the friends of government. It will be much better that the violence in such cases should be repressed by the superintending power, than that the majority should be left to maintain their cause by a bloody and obstinate contest. The existence of a right to interpose, will generally prevent the necessity of exerting it.

Is it true that force and right are necessarily on the same side in republican governments? May not the minor party possess such a superiority of pecuniary resources, of military talents and experience, or of secret succors from foreign powers, as will render it superior also in an appeal to the sword? May not a more compact and advantageous position turn the scale on the same side, against a superior number so situated as to be less capable of a prompt and collected exertion of its strength? Nothing can be more chimerical than to imagine that in a trial of actual force, victory may be calculated by the rules which prevail in a census of the inhabitants, or which determine the event of an election! May it not happen, in fine, that the minority of CITIZENS may become a majority of PERSONS, by the accession of alien residents, of a casual concourse of adventurers, or of those whom the constitution of the State has not admitted to the rights of suffrage? I take no notice of an unhappy species of population abounding in some of the States, who, during the calm of regular government, are sunk below the level of men; but who, in the tempestuous scenes of civil violence, may emerge into the human character, and give a superiority of strength to any party with which they may associate themselves. In cases where it may be doubtful on which side justice lies, what better umpires could be desired by two violent factions, flying to arms, and tearing a State to pieces, than the representatives of confederate States, not heated by the local flame? To the impartiality of judges, they would unite the affection of friends. Happy would it be if such a remedy for its infirmities could be enjoyed by all free governments; if a project equally effectual could be established for the universal peace of mankind! Should it be asked, what is to be the redress for an insurrection pervading all the States, and comprising a superiority of the entire force, though not a constitutional right? the answer must be, that such a case, as it would be without the compass of human remedies, so it is fortunately not within the compass of human probability; and that it is a sufficient recommendation of the federal Constitution, that it diminishes the risk of a calamity for which no possible constitution can provide a cure. Among the advantages of a confederate republic enumerated by Montesquieu, an important one is, "that should a popular insurrection happen in one of the States, the others are able to quell it. Should abuses creep into one part, they are reformed by those that remain sound. "

7. "To consider all debts contracted, and engagements entered into, before the adoption of this Constitution, as being no less valid against the United States, under this Constitution, than under the Confederation. "This can only be considered as a declaratory proposition; and may have been inserted, among other reasons, for the satisfaction of the foreign creditors of the United States, who cannot

be strangers to the pretended doctrine, that a change in the political form of civil society has the magical effect of dissolving its moral obligations. Among the lesser criticisms which have been exercised on the Constitution, it has been remarked that the validity of engagements ought to have been asserted in favor of the United States, as well as against them; and in the spirit which usually characterizes little critics, the omission has been transformed and magnified into a plot against the national rights. The authors of this discovery may be told, what few others need to be informed of, that as engagements are in their nature reciprocal, an assertion of their validity on one side, necessarily involves a validity on the other side; and that as the article is merely declaratory, the establishment of the principle in one case is sufficient for every case. They may be further told, that every constitution must limit its precautions to dangers that are not altogether imaginary; and that no real danger can exist that the government would DARE, with, or even without, this constitutional declaration before it, to remit the debts justly due to the public, on the pretext here condemned.

8. "To provide for amendments to be ratified by three fourths of the States under two exceptions only. "That useful alterations will be suggested by experience, could not but be foreseen. It was requisite, therefore, that a mode for introducing them should be provided. The mode preferred by the convention seems to be stamped with every mark of propriety. It guards equally against that extreme facility, which would render the Constitution too mutable; and that extreme difficulty, which might perpetuate its discovered faults. It, moreover, equally enables the general and the State governments to originate the amendment of errors, as they may be pointed out by the experience on one side, or on the other. The exception in favor of the equality of suffrage in the Senate, was probably meant as a palladium to the residuary sovereignty of the States, implied and secured by that principle of representation in one branch of the legislature; and was probably insisted on by the States particularly attached to that equality. The other exception must have been admitted on the same considerations which produced the privilege defended by it.

9. "The ratification of the conventions of nine States shall be sufficient for the establishment of this Constitution between the States, ratifying the same. "This article speaks for itself. The express author-

ity of the people alone could give due validity to the Constitution. To have required the unanimous ratification of the thirteen States, would have subjected the essential interests of the whole to the caprice or corruption of a single member. It would have marked a want of foresight in the convention, which our own experience would have rendered inexcusable. Two questions of a very delicate nature present themselves on this occasion:

On what principle the Confederation, which stands in the solemn form of a compact among the States, can be superseded without the unanimous consent of the parties to it?

What relation is to subsist between the nine or more States ratifying the Constitution, and the remaining few who do not become parties to it? The first question is answered at once by recurring to the absolute necessity of the case; to the great principle of self-preservation; to the transcendent law of nature and of nature's God, which declares that the safety and happiness of society are the objects at which all political institutions aim, and to which all such institutions must be sacrificed.

PERHAPS, also, an answer may be found without searching beyond the principles of the compact itself. It has been heretofore noted among the defects of the Confederation, that in many of the States it had received no higher sanction than a mere legislative ratification. The principle of reciprocality seems to require that its obligation on the other States should be reduced to the same standard. A compact between independent sovereigns, founded on ordinary acts of legislative authority, can pretend to no higher validity than a league or treaty between the parties. It is an established doctrine on the subject of treaties, that all the articles are mutually conditions of each other; that a breach of any one article is a breach of the whole treaty; and that a breach, committed by either of the parties, absolves the others, and authorizes them, if they please, to pronounce the compact violated and void. Should it unhappily be necessary to appeal to these delicate truths for a justification for dispensing with the consent of particular States to a dissolution of the federal pact, will not the complaining parties find it a difficult task to answer the MULTIPLIED and IMPORTANT infractions with which they may be confronted? The time has been when it was incumbent on us all to veil the ideas which this paragraph exhibits. The scene is now changed, and with it the part which the same motives dictate.

The second question is not less delicate; and the flattering prospect of its being merely hypothetical forbids an overcurious discussion of it. It is one of those cases which must be left to provide for itself. In general, it may be observed, that although no political relation can subsist between the assenting and dissenting States, yet the moral relations will remain uncancelled. The claims of justice, both on one side and on the other, will be in force, and must be fulfilled; the rights of humanity must in all cases be duly and mutually respected; whilst considerations of a common interest, and, above all, the remembrance of the endearing scenes which are past, and the anticipation of a speedy triumph over the obstacles to reunion, will, it is hoped, not urge in vain MODERATION on one side, and PRUDENCE on the other.

PUBLIUS.

Federalist No. 45

The Alleged Danger from the Powers of the Union to the State Governments Considered

For the Independent Journal.

MADISON

To the People of the State of New York:

HAVING shown that no one of the powers transferred to the federal government is unnecessary or improper, the next question to be considered is, whether the whole mass of them will be dangerous to the portion of authority left in the several States. The adversaries to the plan of the convention, instead of considering in the first place what degree of power was absolutely necessary for the purposes of the federal government, have exhausted themselves in a secondary inquiry into the possible consequences of the proposed degree of power to the governments of the particular States. But if the Union, as has been shown, be essential to the security of the people of America against foreign danger; if it be essential to their security against contentions and wars among the different States; if it be essential to guard them against those violent and oppressive factions which embitter the blessings of liberty, and against those military establishments which must gradually poison its very fountain; if, in a word, the Union be essential to the happiness of the people of America, is it not preposterous, to urge as an objection to a government, without which the objects of the Union cannot be attained, that such a government may derogate from the importance of the governments of the individual States? Was, then, the American Revolution effected, was the American Confederacy formed, was the precious blood of thousands spilt, and the hard-earned substance of millions lavished, not that the people of America should enjoy peace, liberty, and safety, but that the government of the individual States, that particular municipal establishments, might enjoy a certain extent of power, and be arrayed with certain dignities and attributes of sovereignty? We have heard of the impious doctrine in the Old World, that the people were made for kings, not kings for the people. Is the same doctrine to be revived in the New, in another shape that the solid happiness of the people is to be sacrificed to the views of political institutions of a different form?

It is too early for politicians to presume on our forgetting that the public good, the real welfare of the great body of the people, is the supreme object to be pursued; and that no form of government whatever has any other value than as it may be fitted for the attainment of this object. Were the plan of the convention adverse to the public happiness, my voice would be, Reject the plan. Were the Union itself inconsistent with the public happiness, it would be, Abolish the Union. In like manner, as far as the sovereignty of the States cannot be reconciled to the happiness of the people, the voice of every good citizen must be, Let the former be sacrificed to the latter. How far the sacrifice is necessary, has been shown. How far the unsacrificed residue will be endangered, is the question before us. Several important considerations have been touched in the course of these papers, which discountenance the supposition that the operation of the federal government will by degrees prove fatal to the State governments. The more I revolve the subject, the more fully I am persuaded that the balance is much more likely to be disturbed by the preponderancy of the last than of the first scale.

We have seen, in all the examples of ancient and modern confederacies, the strongest tendency continually betraying itself in the members, to despoil the general government of its authorities, with a very ineffectual capacity in the latter to defend itself against the encroachments. Although, in most of these examples, the system has been so dissimilar from that under consideration as greatly to weaken any inference concerning the latter from the fate of the former, yet, as the States will retain, under the proposed Constitution, a very extensive portion of active sovereignty, the inference ought not to be wholly disregarded. In the Achaean league it is probable that the federal head had a degree and species of power, which gave it a considerable likeness to the government framed by the convention. The Lycian Confederacy, as far as its principles and form are transmitted, must have borne a still greater analogy to it. Yet history does not inform us that either of them ever degenerated, or tended to degenerate, into one consolidated government. On the contrary, we know that the ruin of one of them proceeded from the incapacity of the federal authority to prevent the dissensions, and finally the disunion, of the subordinate authorities. These cases are the more worthy of our attention, as the external causes by which the component parts were pressed together were much more numerous and powerful than in our case; and consequently less powerful ligaments within would be sufficient to bind the members to the head, and to each other.

In the feudal system, we have seen a similar propensity exemplified. Notwithstanding the want of proper sympathy in every instance between the local sovereigns and the people, and the sympathy in some instances between the general sovereign and the latter, it usually happened that the local sovereigns prevailed in the rivalship for encroachments. Had no external dangers enforced internal harmony and subordination, and particularly, had the local sovereigns possessed the affections of the people, the great kingdoms in Europe would at this time consist of as many independent princes as there were formerly feudatory barons. The State government will have the advantage of the Federal government, whether we compare them in respect to the immediate dependence of the one on the other; to the weight of personal influence which each side will possess; to the powers respectively vested in them; to the predilection and probable support of the people; to the disposition and faculty of resisting and frustrating the measures of each other. The State governments may be regarded as constituent and essential parts of the federal government; whilst the latter is nowise essential to the operation or organization of the former. Without the intervention of the State legislatures, the President of the United States cannot be elected at all. They must in all cases have a great share in his appointment, and will, perhaps, in most cases, of themselves determine it. The Senate will be elected absolutely and exclusively by the State legislatures. Even the House of Representatives, though drawn immediately from the people, will be chosen very much under the influence of that class of men, whose influence over the people obtains for themselves an election into the State legislatures. Thus, each of the principal branches of the federal government will owe its existence more or less to the favor of the State governments, and must consequently feel a dependence, which is much more likely to beget a disposition too obsequious than too overbearing towards them.

On the other side, the component parts of the State governments will in no instance be indebted for their appointment to the direct agency of the federal government, and very little, if at all, to the local influence of its members. The number of individuals employed under the Constitution of the United States will be much smaller than the number employed under the particular States. There will consequently be less of personal influence on the side of the former than of the latter. The members of the legislative, executive, and judiciary departments of thirteen and more States, the justices of peace, officers of militia, ministerial officers of justice, with all the county, corporation, and town officers, for three millions and more of people, intermixed, and having particular acquaintance with every class and circle of people, must exceed, beyond all proportion, both in number and influence, those of every description who will be employed in the administration of the federal system. Compare the members of the three great departments of the thirteen States, excluding from the judiciary department the justices of peace, with the members of the corresponding departments of the single government of the Union; compare the militia officers of three millions of people with the military and marine officers of any establishment which is within the compass of probability, or, I may add, of possibility, and in this view alone, we may pronounce the advantage of the States to be decisive. If the federal government is to have collectors of revenue, the State governments will have theirs also. And as those of the former will be principally on the seacoast, and not very numerous, whilst those of the latter will be spread over the face of the country, and will be very numerous, the advantage in this view also lies on the same side.

It is true, that the Confederacy is to possess, and may exercise, the power of collecting internal as well as external taxes throughout the States; but it is probable that this power will not be resorted to, except for supplemental purposes of revenue; that an option will then be given to the States to supply their quotas by previous collections of their own; and that the eventual collection, under the immediate authority of the Union, will generally be made by the officers, and according to the rules, appointed by the several States. Indeed it is extremely probable, that in other instances, particularly in the organization of the judicial power, the officers of the States will be clothed with the correspondent authority of the Union. Should it happen, however, that separate collectors of internal revenue should be appointed under the federal government, the influence of the whole number would not bear a comparison with that of the multitude of

State officers in the opposite scale. Within every district to which a federal collector would be allotted, there would not be less than thirty or forty, or even more, officers of different descriptions, and many of them persons of character and weight, whose influence would lie on the side of the State. The powers delegated by the proposed Constitution to the federal government are few and defined. Those which are to remain in the State governments are numerous and indefinite. The former will be exercised principally on external objects, as war, peace, negotiation, and foreign commerce; with which last the power of taxation will, for the most part, be connected.

The powers reserved to the several States will extend to all the objects which, in the ordinary course of affairs, concern the lives, liberties, and properties of the people, and the internal order, improvement, and prosperity of the State. The operations of the federal government will be most extensive and important in times of war and danger; those of the State governments, in times of peace and security. As the former periods will probably bear a small proportion to the latter, the State governments will here enjoy another advantage over the federal government. The more adequate, indeed, the federal powers may be rendered to the national defense, the less frequent will be those scenes of danger which might favor their ascendancy over the governments of the particular States. If the new Constitution be examined with accuracy and candor, it will be found that the change which it proposes consists much less in the addition of NEW POWERS to the Union, than in the invigoration of its ORIGINAL POWERS. The regulation of commerce, it is true, is a new power; but that seems to be an addition which few oppose, and from which no apprehensions are entertained. The powers relating to war and peace, armies and fleets, treaties and finance, with the other more considerable powers, are all vested in the existing Congress by the articles of Confederation. The proposed change does not enlarge these powers; it only substitutes a more effectual mode of administering them.

The change relating to taxation may be regarded as the most important; and yet the present Congress have as complete authority to REQUIRE of the States indefinite supplies of money for the common defense and general welfare, as the future Congress will have to require them of individual citizens; and the latter will be no more bound than the States themselves have been, to pay the quotas respectively taxed on them. Had the States complied punctually with the articles of Confederation, or could their compliance have been enforced by as peaceable means as may be used with success towards single persons, our past experience is very far from countenancing an opinion, that the State governments would have lost their constitutional powers, and have gradually undergone an entire consolidation. To maintain that such an event would have ensued, would be to say at once, that the existence of the State governments is incompatible with any system whatever that accomplishes the essential purposes of the Union.

PUBLIUS.

Federalist No. 46

The Influence of the State and Federal Governments Compared

From the New York Packet. Tuesday, January 29, 1788.

MADISON

To the People of the State of New York:

RESUMING the subject of the last paper, I proceed to inquire whether the federal government or the State governments will have the advantage with regard to the predilection and support of the people. Notwithstanding the different modes in which they are appointed, we must consider both of them as substantially dependent on the great body of the citizens of the United States. I assume this position here as it respects the first, reserving the proofs for another place. The federal and State governments are in fact but different agents and trustees of the people, constituted with different powers, and designed for different purposes. The adversaries of the Constitution seem to have lost sight of the people altogether in their reasonings on this subject; and to have viewed these different establishments, not only as mutual rivals and enemies, but as uncontrolled by any common superior in their efforts to usurp the authorities of each other. These gentlemen must here be reminded of their error. They must be told that the ultimate authority, wherever the derivative may be found, resides in the people alone, and that it will not depend merely on the comparative ambition or address of the different governments, whether either, or which of them, will be able to enlarge its sphere of jurisdiction at the expense of the other.

Truth, no less than decency, requires that the event in every case should be supposed to depend on the sentiments and sanction of their common constituents. Many considerations, besides those suggested on a former occasion, seem to place it beyond doubt that the first and most natural attachment of the people will be to the governments of their respective States. Into the administration of these a greater number of individuals will expect to rise. From the gift of these a greater number of offices and emoluments will flow. By the superintending care of these, all the more domestic and personal interests of the people will be regulated and provided for. With the affairs of these, the people will be more familiarly and minutely conversant. And with the members of these, will a greater proportion of the people have the ties of personal acquaintance and friendship, and of family and party attachments; on the side of these, therefore, the popular bias may well be expected most strongly to incline. Experience speaks the same language in this case. The federal administration, though hitherto very defective in comparison with what may be hoped under a better system, had, during the war, and particularly whilst the independent fund of paper emissions was in credit, an activity and importance as great as it can well have in any future circumstances whatever. It was engaged, too, in a course of measures which had for their object the protection of everything that was dear, and the acquisition of everything that could be desirable to the people at large.

It was, nevertheless, invariably found, after the transient enthusiasm for the early Congresses was over, that the attention and attachment of the people were turned anew to their own particular governments; that the federal council was at no time the idol of popular favor; and that opposition to proposed enlargements of its powers and importance was the side usually taken by the men who wished to build their political consequence on the prepossessions of their fellow-citizens. If, therefore, as has been elsewhere remarked, the people should in future become more partial to the federal than to the State governments, the change can only result from such manifest and irresistible proofs of a better administration, as will overcome all their antecedent propensities. And in that case, the people ought not surely to be precluded from giving most of their confidence where they may discover it to be most due; but even in that case the State governments could have little to apprehend, because it is only within a certain sphere that the federal power can, in the nature of things, be advantageously administered. The remaining points on which I propose to compare the federal and State governments, are the disposition and the faculty they may respectively possess, to resist and frustrate the measures of each other. It has been already proved that the members of the federal will be more dependent on the members of the State governments, than the latter will be on the former.

It has appeared also, that the prepossessions of the people, on whom both will depend, will be more on the side of the State governments, than of the federal government. So far as the disposition of each towards the other may be influenced by these causes, the

State governments must clearly have the advantage. But in a distinct and very important point of view, the advantage will lie on the same side. The prepossessions, which the members themselves will carry into the federal government, will generally be favorable to the States; whilst it will rarely happen, that the members of the State governments will carry into the public councils a bias in favor of the general government. A local spirit will infallibly prevail much more in the members of Congress, than a national spirit will prevail in the legislatures of the particular States.

Every one knows that a great proportion of the errors committed by the State legislatures proceeds from the disposition of the members to sacrifice the comprehensive and permanent interest of the State, to the particular and separate views of the counties or districts in which they reside. And if they do not sufficiently enlarge their policy to embrace the collective welfare of their particular State, how can it be imagined that they will make the aggregate prosperity of the Union, and the dignity and respectability of its government, the objects of their affections and consultations? For the same reason that the members of the State legislatures will be unlikely to attach themselves sufficiently to national objects, the members of the federal legislature will be likely to attach themselves too much to local objects. The States will be to the latter what counties and towns are to the former. Measures will too often be decided according to their probable effect, not on the national prosperity and happiness, but on the prejudices, interests, and pursuits of the governments and people of the individual States. What is the spirit that has in general characterized the proceedings of Congress? A perusal of their journals, as well as the candid acknowledgments of such as have had a seat in that assembly, will inform us, that the members have but too frequently displayed the character, rather of partisans of their respective States, than of impartial guardians of a common interest; that where on one occasion improper sacrifices have been made of local considerations, to the aggrandizement of the federal government, the great interests of the nation have suffered on a hundred, from an undue attention to the local prejudices, interests, and views of the particular States.

I mean not by these reflections to insinuate, that the new federal government will not embrace a more enlarged plan of policy than the existing government may have pursued; much less, that its views will be as confined as those of the State legislatures; but only that it will partake sufficiently of the spirit of both, to be disinclined to invade the rights of the individual States, or the preorgatives of their governments. The motives on the part of the State governments, to augment their prerogatives by defalcations from the federal government, will be overruled by no reciprocal predispositions in the members. Were it admitted, however, that the Federal government may feel an equal disposition with the State governments to extend its power beyond the due limits, the latter would still have the advantage in the means of defeating such encroachments. If an act of a particular State, though unfriendly to the national government, be generally popular in that State and should not too grossly violate the oaths of the State officers, it is executed immediately and, of course, by means on the spot and depending on the State alone. The opposition of the federal government, or the interposition of federal officers, would but inflame the zeal of all parties on the side of the State, and the evil could not be prevented or repaired, if at all, without the employment of means which must always be resorted to with reluctance and difficulty.

On the other hand, should an unwarrantable measure of the federal government be unpopular in particular States, which would seldom fail to be the case, or even a warrantable measure be so, which may sometimes be the case, the means of opposition to it are powerful and at hand. The disquietude of the people; their repugnance and, perhaps, refusal to co-operate with the officers of the Union; the frowns of the executive magistracy of the State; the embarrassments created by legislative devices, which would often be added on such occasions, would oppose, in any State, difficulties not to be despised; would form, in a large State, very serious impediments; and where the sentiments of several adjoining States happened to be in unison, would present obstructions which the federal government would hardly be willing to encounter. But ambitious encroachments of the federal government, on the authority of the State governments, would not excite the opposition of a single State, or of a few States only. They would be signals of general alarm. Every government would espouse the common cause. A correspondence would be opened. Plans of resistance would be concerted. One spirit would animate and conduct the whole. The same combinations, in short, would result from an apprehension of the federal, as was produced by the dread of a foreign, yoke; and unless the projected innovations should be voluntarily renounced, the same appeal to a trial of force would be made in the one case as was made in the other. But what degree of madness could ever drive the federal government to such an extremity. In the contest with Great Britain, one part of the empire was employed against the other. The more numerous part invaded the rights of the less numerous part. The attempt was unjust and unwise; but it was not in speculation absolutely chimerical. But what would be the contest in the case we are supposing? Who would be the parties? A few representatives of the people would be opposed to the people themselves; or rather one set of representatives would be contending against thirteen sets of representatives, with the whole body of their common constituents on the side of the latter.

The only refuge left for those who prophesy the downfall of the State governments is the visionary supposition that the federal government may previously accumulate a military force for the projects of ambition. The reasonings contained in these papers must have been employed to little purpose indeed, if it could be necessary now to disprove the reality of this danger. That the people and the States should, for a sufficient period of time, elect an uninterupted succession of men ready to betray both; that the traitors should, throughout this period, uniformly and systematically pursue some fixed plan for the extension of the military establishment; that the governments and the people of the States should silently and patiently behold the gathering storm, and continue to supply the materials, until it should be prepared to burst on their own heads, must appear to every one more like the incoherent dreams of a delirious jealousy, or the misjudged exaggerations of a counterfeit zeal, than like the sober apprehensions of genuine patriotism.

Extravagant as the supposition is, let it however be made. Let a regular army, fully equal to the resources of the country, be formed; and let it be entirely at the devotion of the federal government; still it would not be going too far to say, that the State governments, with the people on their side, would be able to repel the danger. The highest number to which, according to the best computation, a standing army can be carried in any country, does not exceed one hundredth part of the whole number of souls; or one twenty-fifth part of the number able to bear arms. This proportion would not yield, in the United States, an army of more than twenty-five or thirty thousand men. To these would be opposed a militia amounting to near half a million of citizens with arms in their hands, officered by men chosen from among themselves, fighting for their common liberties, and united and conducted by governments possessing their affections and confidence. It may well be doubted, whether a militia thus circumstanced could ever be conquered by such a proportion of regular troops. Those who are best acquainted with the last successful resistance of this country against the British arms, will be most inclined to deny the possibility of it. Besides the advantage of being armed, which the Americans possess over the people of almost every other nation, the existence of subordinate governments, to which the people are attached, and by which the militia officers are appointed, forms a barrier against the enterprises of ambition, more insurmountable than any which a simple government of any form can admit of. Notwithstanding the military establishments in the several kingdoms of Europe, which are carried as far as the public resources will bear, the governments are afraid to trust the people with arms. And it is not certain, that with this aid alone they would not be able to shake off their yokes. But were the people to possess the additional advantages of local governments chosen by themselves, who could collect the national will and direct the national force, and of officers appointed out of the militia, by these governments, and attached both to them and to the militia, it may be affirmed with the greatest assurance, that the throne of every tyranny in Europe would be speedily overturned in spite of the legions which surround it.

Let us not insult the free and gallant citizens of America with the suspicion, that they would be less able to defend the rights of which they would be in actual possession, than the debased subjects of arbitrary power would be to rescue theirs from the hands of their oppressors. Let us rather no longer insult them with the supposition that they can ever reduce themselves to the necessity of making the experiment, by a blind and tame submission to the long train of insidious measures which must precede and produce it. The argument under the present head may be put into a very concise form, which appears altogether conclusive. Either the mode in which the federal government is to be constructed will render it sufficiently dependent on the people, or it will not. On the first supposition, it will be restrained by that dependence from forming schemes obnoxious to their constituents. On the other supposition, it will not possess the confidence of the people, and its schemes of usurpation will be easily defeated by the State governments, who will be supported by the people. On summing up the considerations stated in this and the last paper, they seem to amount to the most convincing evidence, that the powers proposed to be lodged in the federal government are as little formidable to those reserved to the individual States, as they are indispensably necessary to accomplish the purposes of the Union; and that all those alarms which have been sounded, of a meditated and consequential annihilation of the State governments, must, on the most favorable interpretation, be ascribed to the chimerical fears of the authors of them.

PUBLIUS.

Federalist No. 47

The Particular Structure of the New Government and the Distribution of Power among Its Different Parts

From the New York Packet. Friday, February 1, 1788.

MADISON

To the People of the State of New York:

HAVING reviewed the general form of the proposed government and the general mass of power allotted to it, I proceed to examine the particular structure of this government, and the distribution of this mass of power among its constituent parts. One of the principal objections inculcated by the more respectable adversaries to the Constitution, is its supposed violation of the political maxim, that the legislative, executive, and judiciary departments ought to be separate and distinct. In the structure of the federal government, no regard, it is said, seems to have been paid to this essential precaution in favor of liberty. The several departments of power are distributed and blended in such a manner as at once to destroy all symmetry and beauty of form, and to expose some of the essential parts of the edifice to the danger of being crushed by the disproportionate weight of other parts. No political truth is certainly of greater intrinsic value, or is stamped with the authority of more enlightened patrons of liberty, than that on which the objection is founded.

The accumulation of all powers, legislative, executive, and judiciary, in the same hands, whether of one, a few, or many, and whether hereditary, self-appointed, or elective, may justly be pronounced the very definition of tyranny. Were the federal Constitution, therefore, really chargeable with the accumulation of power, or with a mixture of powers, having a dangerous tendency to such an accumulation, no further arguments would be necessary to inspire a universal reprobation of the system. I persuade myself, however, that it will be made apparent to every one, that the charge cannot be supported, and that the maxim on which it relies has been totally misconceived and misapplied. In order to form correct ideas on this important subject, it will be proper to investigate the sense in which the preservation of liberty requires that the three great departments of power should be separate and distinct. The oracle who is always consulted and cited on this subject is the celebrated Montesquieu. If he be not the author of this invaluable precept in the science of politics, he has the merit at least of displaying and recommending it most effectually to the attention of mankind. Let us endeavor, in the first place, to ascertain his meaning on this point. The British Constitution was to Montesquieu what Homer has been to the didactic writers on epic poetry. As the latter have considered the work of the immortal bard as the perfect model from which the principles and rules of the epic art were to be drawn, and by which all similar works were to be judged, so this great political critic appears to have viewed the Constitution of England as the standard, or to use his own expression, as the mirror of political liberty; and to have delivered, in the form of elementary truths, the several characteristic principles of that particular system. That we may be sure, then, not to mistake his meaning in this case, let us recur to the source from which the maxim was drawn.

On the slightest view of the British Constitution, we must perceive that the legislative, executive, and judiciary departments are by no means totally separate and distinct from each other. The executive magistrate forms an integral part of the legislative authority. He alone has the prerogative of making treaties with foreign sovereigns, which, when made, have, under certain limitations, the force of legislative acts. All the members of the judiciary department are appointed by him, can be removed by him on the address of the two Houses of Parliament, and form, when he pleases to consult them, one of his constitutional councils. One branch of the legislative department forms also a great constitutional council to the executive chief, as, on another hand, it is the sole depositary of judicial power in cases of impeachment, and is invested with the supreme appellate jurisdiction in all other cases. The judges, again, are so far connected with the legislative department as often to attend and participate in its deliberations, though not admitted to a legislative vote. From these facts, by which Montesquieu was guided, it may clearly be inferred that, in saying "There can be no liberty where the legislative and executive powers are united in the same person, or body of magistrates," or, "if the power of judging be not separated from the legislative and executive powers," he did not mean that these departments ought to have no PARTIAL AGENCY in, or no CONTROL over, the acts of each other. His meaning, as his own words import, and still more conclusively as illustrated by the example in his eye, can amount to no more than this, that where the WHOLE power of one department is exercised by the same hands which possess the WHOLE power of another department, the fundamental principles of a free constitution are subverted. This would have been the case in the constitution examined by him, if the king, who is the sole executive magistrate, had possessed also the complete legislative power, or the supreme administration of justice; or if the entire legislative body had possessed the supreme judiciary, or the supreme executive authority.

This, however, is not among the vices of that constitution. The magistrate in whom the whole executive power resides cannot of himself make a law, though he can put a negative on every law; nor administer justice in person, though he has the appointment of those who do administer it. The judges can exercise no executive prerogative, though they are shoots from the executive stock; nor any legislative function, though they may be advised with by the legislative councils. The entire legislature can perform no judiciary act, though by the joint act of two of its branches the judges may be removed from their offices, and though one of its branches is possessed of the judicial power in the last resort. The entire legislature, again, can exercise no executive prerogative, though one of its branches constitutes the supreme executive magistracy, and another, on the impeachment of a third, can try and condemn all the subordinate officers in the executive department. The reasons on which Montesquieu grounds his maxim are a further demonstration of his meaning. "When the legislative and executive powers are united in the same person or body," says he, "there can be no liberty, because apprehensions may arise lest THE SAME monarch or senate should ENACT tyrannical laws to EXECUTE them in a tyrannical manner. " Again: "Were the power of judging joined with the legislative, the life and liberty of the subject would be exposed to arbitrary control, for THE JUDGE would then be THE LEGISLATOR. Were it joined to the executive power, THE JUDGE might behave with all the violence of AN OPPRESSOR. " Some of these reasons are more fully explained in other passages; but briefly stated as they are here, they sufficiently establish the meaning which we have put on this celebrated maxim of this celebrated author.

If we look into the constitutions of the several States, we find that, notwithstanding the emphatical and, in some instances, the unqualified terms in which this axiom has been laid down, there is not a single instance in which the several departments of power have been kept absolutely separate and distinct. New Hampshire, whose constitution was the last formed, seems to have been fully aware of the impossibility and inexpediency of avoiding any mixture whatever of these departments, and has qualified the doctrine by declaring "that the legislative, executive, and judiciary powers ought to be kept as separate from, and independent of, each other AS THE NATURE OF A FREE GOVERNMENT WILL ADMIT; OR AS IS CONSISTENT WITH THAT CHAIN OF CONNECTION THAT BINDS THE WHOLE FABRIC OF THE CONSTITUTION IN ONE INDISSOLUBLE BOND OF UNITY AND AMITY. " Her constitution accordingly mixes these departments in several respects. The Senate, which is a branch of the legislative department, is also a judicial tribunal for the trial of impeachments. The President, who is the head of the executive department, is the presiding member also of the Senate; and, besides an equal vote in all cases, has a casting vote in case of a tie. The executive head is himself eventually elective every year by the legislative department, and his council is every year chosen by and from the members of the same department. Several of the officers of state are also appointed by the legislature. And the members of the judiciary department are appointed by the executive department. The constitution of Massachusetts has observed a sufficient though less pointed caution, in expressing this fundamental article of liberty. It declares "that the legislative department shall never exercise the executive and judicial powers, or either of them; the executive shall never exercise the legislative and judicial powers, or either of them; the judicial shall never exercise the legislative and executive powers, or either of them. " This declaration corresponds precisely with the doctrine of Montesquieu, as it has been explained, and is not in a single point violated by the plan of the convention. It goes no farther than to prohibit any one of the entire departments from exercising the powers of another department. In the very Constitution to which it is prefixed, a partial mixture of powers has been admitted. The executive magistrate has a qualified negative on the legislative body, and the Senate, which is a part of the legislature, is a court of impeachment for members both of the executive and judiciary departments. The members of the judiciary department, again, are appointable by the executive department, and removable by the same authority on the address of the two legislative branches. Lastly, a number of the officers of government are annually appointed by the legislative department.

As the appointment to offices, particularly executive offices, is in its nature an executive function, the compilers of the Constitution have, in this last point at least, violated the rule established by themselves. I pass over the constitutions of Rhode Island and Connecticut, because they were formed prior to the Revolution, and even before the principle under examination had become an object of political attention. The constitution of New York contains no declaration on this subject; but appears very clearly to have been framed with an eye to the danger of improperly blending the different departments. It gives, nevertheless, to the executive magistrate, a partial control over the legislative department; and, what is more, gives a like control to the judiciary department; and even blends the executive and judiciary departments in the exercise of this control. In its council of appointment members of the legislative are associated with the executive authority, in the appointment of officers, both executive and judiciary. And its court for the trial of impeachments and correction of errors is to consist of one branch of the legislature and the principal members of the judiciary department.

The constitution of New Jersey has blended the different powers of government more than any of the preceding. The governor, who is the executive magistrate, is appointed by the legislature; is chancellor and ordinary, or surrogate of the State; is a member of the Supreme Court of Appeals, and president, with a casting vote, of one of the legislative branches. The same legislative branch acts again as executive council of the governor, and with him constitutes the Court of Appeals. The members of the judiciary department are appointed by the legislative department and removable by one branch of it, on the impeachment of the other. According to the constitution of Pennsylvania, the president, who is the head of the executive department, is annually elected by a vote in which the legislative department predominates. In conjunction with an executive council, he appoints the members of the judiciary department, and forms a court of impeachment for trial of all officers, judiciary as well as executive. The judges of the Supreme Court and justices of the peace seem also to be removable by the legislature; and the executive power of pardoning in certain cases, to be referred to the same department. The members of the executive council are made EX-OFFICIO justices of peace throughout the State. In Delaware, the chief executive magistrate is annually elected by the legislative department. The speakers of the two legislative branches are vice-presidents in the executive department. The executive chief, with six others, appointed, three by each of the legislative branches constitutes the Supreme Court of Appeals; he is joined with the legislative department in the appointment of the other judges. Throughout the States, it appears that the members of the legislature may at the same time be justices of the peace; in this State, the members of one branch of it are EX-OFFICIO justices of the peace; as are also the members of the executive council. The principal officers of the executive department are appointed by the legislative; and one branch of the latter forms a court of impeachments. All officers may be removed on address of the legislature.

Maryland has adopted the maxim in the most unqualified terms; declaring that the legislative, executive, and judicial powers of government ought to be forever separate and distinct from each other. Her constitution, notwithstanding, makes the executive magistrate appointable by the legislative department; and the members of the judiciary by the executive department. The language of Virginia is still more pointed on this subject. Her constitution declares, "that the legislative, executive, and judiciary departments shall be separate and distinct; so that neither exercise the powers properly belonging to the other; nor shall any person exercise the powers of more than one of them at the same time, except that the justices of county courts shall be eligible to either House of Assembly. " Yet we find not only this express exception, with respect to the members of the inferior courts, but that the chief magistrate, with his executive council, are appointable by the legislature; that two members of the latter are triennially displaced at the pleasure of the legislature; and that all the principal offices, both executive and judiciary, are filled by the same department. The executive prerogative of pardon, also, is in one case vested in the legislative department.

The constitution of North Carolina, which declares "that the legislative, executive, and supreme judicial powers of government ought to be forever separate and distinct from each other," refers, at the same time, to the legislative department, the appointment not only of the executive chief, but all the principal officers within both that and the judiciary department. In South Carolina, the constitution makes the executive magistracy eligible by the legislative department. It gives to the latter, also, the appointment of the members of the judiciary department, including even justices of the peace and sheriffs; and the appointment of officers in the executive department, down to captains in the army and navy of the State. In the constitution of Georgia, where it is declared "that the legislative, executive, and judiciary departments shall be separate and distinct, so that neither exercise the powers properly belonging to the other," we find that the executive department is to be filled by appointments of the legislature; and the executive prerogative of pardon to be finally exercised by the same authority. Even justices of the peace are to be appointed by the legislature. In citing these cases, in which the legislative, executive, and judiciary departments have not been kept totally separate and distinct, I wish not to be regarded as an advocate for the particular organizations of the several State governments. I am fully aware that among the many excellent principles which they exemplify, they carry strong marks of the haste, and still stronger of the inexperience, under which they were framed. It is but too obvious that in some instances the fundamental principle under consideration has been violated by too great a mixture, and even an actual consolidation, of the different powers; and that in no instance has a competent provision been made for maintaining in practice the separation delineated on paper. What I have wished to evince is, that the charge brought against the proposed Constitution, of violating the sacred maxim of free government, is warranted neither by the real meaning annexed to that maxim by its author, nor by the sense in which it has hitherto been understood in America. This interesting subject will be resumed in the ensuing paper.

PUBLIUS.

Federalist No. 48

These Departments Should Not Be So Far Separated as to Have No Constitutional Control Over Each Other

From the New York Packet. Friday, February 1, 1788.

MADISON

To the People of the State of New York:

IT WAS shown in the last paper that the political apothegm there examined does not require that the legislative, executive, and judiciary departments should be wholly unconnected with each other. I shall undertake, in the next place, to show that unless these departments be so far connected and blended as to give to each a constitutional control over the others, the degree of separation which the maxim requires, as essential to a free government, can never in practice be duly maintained. It is agreed on all sides, that the powers properly belonging to one of the departments ought not to be directly and completely administered by either of the other departments. It is equally evident, that none of them ought to possess, directly or indirectly, an overruling influence over the others, in the administration of their respective powers. It will not be denied, that power is of an encroaching nature, and that it ought to be effectually restrained from passing the limits assigned to it. After discriminating, therefore, in theory, the several classes of power, as they may in their nature be legislative, executive, or judiciary, the next and most difficult task is to provide some practical security for each, against the invasion of the others.

What this security ought to be, is the great problem to be solved. Will it be sufficient to mark, with precision, the boundaries of these departments, in the constitution of the government, and to trust to these parchment barriers against the encroaching spirit of power? This is the security which appears to have been principally relied on by the compilers of most of the American constitutions. But experience assures us, that the efficacy of the provision has been greatly overrated; and that some more adequate defense is indispensably necessary for the more feeble, against the more powerful, members of the government. The legislative department is everywhere extending the sphere of its activity, and drawing all power into its impetuous vortex. The founders of our republics have so much merit for the wisdom which they have displayed, that no task can be less pleasing than that of pointing out the errors into which they have fallen. A respect for truth, however, obliges us to remark, that they seem never for a moment to have turned their eyes from the danger to liberty from the overgrown and all-grasping prerogative of an hereditary magistrate, supported and fortified by an hereditary branch of the legislative authority. They seem never to have recollected the danger from legislative usurpations, which, by assembling all power in the same hands, must lead to the same tyranny as is threatened by executive usurpations. In a government where numerous and extensive prerogatives are placed in the hands of an hereditary monarch, the executive department is very justly regarded as the source of danger, and watched with all the jealousy which a zeal for liberty ought to inspire. In a democracy, where a multitude of people exercise in person the legislative functions, and are continually exposed, by their incapacity for regular deliberation and concerted measures, to the ambitious intrigues of their executive magistrates, tyranny may well be apprehended, on some favorable emergency, to start up in the same quarter. But in a representative republic, where the executive magistracy is carefully limited; both in the extent and the duration of its power; and where the legislative power is exercised by an assembly, which is inspired, by a supposed influence over the people, with an intrepid confidence in its own strength; which is sufficiently numerous to feel all the passions which actuate a multitude, yet not so numerous as to be incapable of pursuing the objects of its passions, by means which reason prescribes; it is against the enterprising ambition of this department that the people ought to indulge all their jealousy and exhaust all their precautions. The legislative department derives a superiority in our governments from other circumstances. Its constitutional powers being at once more extensive, and less susceptible of precise limits, it can, with the greater facility, mask, under complicated and indirect measures, the encroachments which it makes on the co-ordinate departments. It is not unfrequently a question of real nicety in legislative bodies, whether the operation of a particular measure will, or will not, extend beyond the legislative sphere.

On the other side, the executive power being restrained within a narrower compass, and being more simple in its nature, and the judiciary being described by landmarks still less uncertain, projects of usurpation by either of these departments would immediately betray and defeat themselves. Nor is this all: as the legislative department alone has access to the pockets of the people, and has in some constitutions full discretion, and in all a prevailing influence, over the pecuniary rewards of those who fill the other departments, a dependence is thus created in the latter, which gives still greater facility to encroachments of the former. I have appealed to our own experience for the truth of what I advance on this subject. Were it necessary to verify this experience by particular proofs, they might be multiplied without end. I might find a witness in every citizen who has shared in, or been attentive to, the course of public administrations. I might collect vouchers in abundance from the records and archives of every State in the Union. But as a more concise, and at the same time equally satisfactory, evidence, I will refer to the example of two States, attested by two unexceptionable authorities.

The first example is that of Virginia, a State which, as we have seen, has expressly declared in its constitution, that the three great departments ought not to be intermixed. The authority in support of it is Mr. Jefferson, who, besides his other advantages for remarking the operation of the government, was himself the chief magistrate of it. In order to convey fully the ideas with which his experience had impressed him on this subject, it will be necessary to quote a passage of some length from his very interesting "Notes on the State of Virginia," p. 195. "All the powers of government, legislative, executive, and judiciary, result to the legislative body. The concentrating these in the same hands, is precisely the definition of despotic government. It will be no alleviation, that these powers will be exercised by a plurality of hands, and not by a single one. One hundred and seventy-three despots would surely be as oppressive as one. Let those who doubt it, turn their eyes on the republic of Venice. As little will it avail us, that they are chosen by ourselves. An ELECTIVE DESPOTISM was not the government we fought for; but one which should not only be founded on free principles, but in which the powers of government should be so divided and balanced among several bodies of magistracy, as that no one could transcend their legal limits, without being effectually checked and restrained by the others. For this reason, that convention which passed the ordinance of government, laid its foundation on this basis, that the legislative, executive, and judiciary departments should be separate and distinct, so that no person should exercise the powers of more than one of them at the same time. BUT NO BARRIER WAS PROVIDED BETWEEN THESE SEVERAL POWERS. The judiciary and the executive members were left dependent on the legislative for their subsistence in office, and some of them for their continuance in it. If, therefore, the legislature assumes executive and judiciary powers, no opposition is likely to be made; nor, if made, can be effectual; because in that case they may put their proceedings into the form of acts of Assembly, which will render them obligatory on the other branches. They have accordingly, IN MANY instances, DECIDED RIGHTS which should have been left to JUDICIARY CONTROVERSY, and THE DIRECTION OF THE EXECUTIVE, DURING THE WHOLE TIME OF THEIR SESSION, IS BECOMING HABITUAL AND FAMILIAR.

''The other State which I shall take for an example is Pennsylvania; and the other authority, the Council of Censors, which assembled in the years 1783 and 1784. A part of the duty of this body, as marked out by the constitution, was "to inquire whether the constitution had been preserved inviolate in every part; and whether the legislative and executive branches of government had performed their duty as guardians of the people, or assumed to themselves, or exercised, other or greater powers than they are entitled to by the constitution. '' In the execution of this trust, the council were necessarily led to a comparison of both the legislative and executive proceedings, with the constitutional powers of these departments; and from the facts enumerated, and to the truth of most of which both sides in the council subscribed, it appears that the constitution had been flagrantly violated by the legislature in a variety of important instances. A great number of laws had been passed, violating, without any apparent necessity, the rule requiring that all bills of a public nature shall be previously printed for the consideration of the people; although this is one of the precautions chiefly relied on by the constitution against improper acts of legislature. The constitutional trial by jury had been violated, and powers assumed which had not been delegated by the constitution. Executive powers had been usurped. The salaries of the judges, which the constitution expressly requires to be fixed, had been occasionally varied; and cases belonging to the judiciary department frequently drawn within legislative cognizance and determination. Those who wish to see the several particulars falling under each of these heads, may consult the journals of the council, which are in print. Some of them, it will be found, may be imputable to peculiar circumstances connected with the war; but the greater part of them may be considered as the spontaneous shoots of an ill-constituted government.

It appears, also, that the executive department had not been innocent of frequent breaches of the constitution. There are three observations, however, which ought to be made on this head: FIRST, a great proportion of the instances were either immediately produced by the necessities of the war, or recommended by Congress or the commander-in-chief; SECONDLY, in most of the other instances, they conformed either to the declared or the known sentiments of the legislative department; THIRDLY, the executive department of Pennsylvania is distinguished from that of the other States by the number of members composing it. In this respect, it has as much affinity to a legislative assembly as to an executive council. And being at once exempt from the restraint of an individual responsibility for the acts of the body, and deriving confidence from mutual example and joint influence, unauthorized measures would, of course, be more freely hazarded, than where the executive department is administered by a single hand, or by a few hands.

The conclusion which I am warranted in drawing from these observations is, that a mere demarcation on parchment of the constitutional limits of the several departments, is not a sufficient guard against those encroachments which lead to a tyrannical concentration of all the powers of government in the same hands.

PUBLIUS.

Federalist No. 51

The Structure of the Government Must Furnish the Proper Checks and Balances Between the Different Departments

From the New York Packet. Friday, February 8, 1788.

HAMILTON OR MADISON

To the People of the State of New York:

TO WHAT expedient, then, shall we finally resort, for maintaining in practice the necessary partition of power among the several departments, as laid down in the Constitution? The only answer that can be given is, that as all these exterior provisions are found to be inadequate, the defect must be supplied, by so contriving the interior structure of the government as that its several constituent parts may, by their mutual relations, be the means of keeping each other in their proper places. Without presuming to undertake a full development of this important idea, I will hazard a few general observations, which may perhaps place it in a clearer light, and enable us to form a more correct judgment of the principles and structure of the government planned by the convention.

In order to lay a due foundation for that separate and distinct exercise of the different powers of government, which to a certain extent is admitted on all hands to be essential to the preservation of liberty, it is evident that each department should have a will of its own; and consequently should be so constituted that the members of each should have as little agency as possible in the appointment of the members of the others. Were this principle rigorously adhered to, it would require that all the appointments for the supreme executive, legislative, and judiciary magistracies should be drawn from the same fountain of authority, the people, through channels having no communication whatever with one another. Perhaps such a plan of constructing the several departments would be less difficult in practice than it may in contemplation appear. Some difficulties, however, and some additional expense would attend the execution of it. Some deviations, therefore, from the principle must be admitted. In the constitution of the judiciary department in particular, it might be inexpedient to insist rigorously on the principle: first, because peculiar qualifications being essential in the members, the primary consideration ought to be to select that mode of choice which best secures these qualifications; secondly, because the permanent tenure by which the appointments are held in that department, must soon destroy all sense of dependence on the authority conferring them.

It is equally evident, that the members of each department should be as little dependent as possible on those of the others, for the emoluments annexed to their offices. Were the executive magistrate, or the judges, not independent of the legislature in this particular, their independence in every other would be merely nominal. But the great security against a gradual concentration of the several powers in the same department, consists in giving to those who administer each department the necessary constitutional means and personal motives to resist encroachments of the others. The provision for defense must in this, as in all other cases, be made commensurate to the danger of attack. Ambition must be made to counteract ambition. The interest of the man must be connected with the constitutional rights of the place. It may be a reflection on human nature, that such devices should be necessary to control the abuses of government. But what is government itself, but the greatest of all reflections on human nature? If men were angels, no government would be necessary. If angels were to govern men, neither external nor internal controls on government would be necessary. In framing a government which is to be administered by men over men, the great difficulty lies in this: you must first enable the government to control the governed; and in the next place oblige it to control itself.

A dependence on the people is, no doubt, the primary control on the government; but experience has taught mankind the necessity of auxiliary precautions. This policy of supplying, by opposite and rival interests, the defect of better motives, might be traced through the whole system of human affairs, private as well as public. We see it particularly displayed in all the subordinate distributions of power, where the constant aim is to divide and arrange the several offices in such a manner as that each may be a check on the other that the private interest of every individual may be a sentinel over the public rights. These inventions of prudence cannot be less requisite in the distribution of the supreme powers of the State. But it is not possible to give to each department an equal power of self-defense. In republican government, the legislative authority necessarily predominates. The remedy for this inconveniency is to divide the legislature into different branches; and to render them, by different modes of election and different principles of action, as little connected with each other as the nature of their common functions and their common dependence on the society will admit. It may even be necessary to guard against dangerous encroachments by still further precautions. As the weight of the legislative authority requires that it should be thus divided, the weakness of the executive may require, on the other hand, that it should be fortified.

An absolute negative on the legislature appears, at first view, to be the natural defense with which the executive magistrate should be armed. But perhaps it would be neither altogether safe nor alone sufficient. On ordinary occasions it might not be exerted with the requisite firmness, and on extraordinary occasions it might be perfidiously abused. May not this defect of an absolute negative be supplied by some qualified connection between this weaker department and the weaker branch of the stronger department, by which the latter may be led to support the constitutional rights of the former, without being too much detached from the rights of its own department? If the principles on which these observations are founded be just, as I persuade myself they are, and they be applied as a criterion to the several State constitutions, and to the federal Constitution it will be found that if the latter does not perfectly correspond with them, the former are infinitely less able to bear such a test.

There are, moreover, two considerations particularly applicable to the federal system of America, which place that system in a very interesting point of view. First. In a single republic, all the power surrendered by the people is submitted to the administration of a single government; and the usurpations are guarded against by a division of the government into distinct and separate departments. In the compound republic of America, the power surrendered by the people is first divided between two distinct governments, and then the portion allotted to each subdivided among distinct and separate departments. Hence a double security arises to the rights of the people. The different governments will control each other, at the same time that each will be controlled by itself. Second. It is of great importance in a republic not only to guard the society against the oppression of its rulers, but to guard one part of the society against the injustice of the other part. Different interests necessarily exist in different classes of citizens. If a majority be united by a common interest, the rights of the minority will be insecure.

There are but two methods of providing against this evil: the one by creating a will in the community independent of the majority that is, of the society itself; the other, by comprehending in the society so many separate descriptions of citizens as will render an unjust combination of a majority of the whole very improbable, if not impracticable. The first method prevails in all governments possessing an hereditary or self-appointed authority. This, at best, is but a precarious security; because a power independent of the society may as well espouse the unjust views of the major, as the rightful interests of the minor party, and may possibly be turned against both parties. The second method will be exemplified in the federal republic of the United States. Whilst all authority in it will be derived from and dependent on the society, the society itself will be broken into so many parts, interests, and classes of citizens, that the rights of individuals, or of the minority, will be in little danger from interested combinations of the majority.

In a free government the security for civil rights must be the same as that for religious rights. It consists in the one case in the multiplicity of interests, and in the other in the multiplicity of sects. The degree of security in both cases will depend on the number of interests and sects; and this may be presumed to depend on the extent of country and number of people comprehended under the same government. This view of the subject must particularly recommend a proper federal system to all the sincere and considerate friends of republican government, since it shows that in exact proportion as the territory of the Union may be formed into more circumscribed Confederacies, or States oppressive combinations of a majority will be facilitated: the best security, under the republican forms, for the rights of every class of citizens, will be diminished: and consequently the stability and independence of some member of the government, the only other security, must be proportionately increased. Justice is the end of government. It is the end of civil society. It ever has been and ever will be pursued until it be obtained, or until liberty be lost in the pursuit. In a society under the forms of which the stronger faction can readily unite and oppress the weaker, anarchy may as truly be said to reign as in a state of nature, where the weaker individual is not secured against the violence of the stronger; and as, in the latter state, even the stronger individuals are prompted, by the uncertainty of their condition, to submit to a government which may protect the weak as well as themselves; so, in the former state, will the more powerful factions or parties be gradually induced, by a like motive, to wish for a government which will protect all parties, the weaker as well as the more powerful.

It can be little doubted that if the State of Rhode Island was separated from the Confederacy and left to itself, the insecurity of rights under the popular form of government within such narrow limits would be displayed by such reiterated oppressions of factious majorities that some power altogether independent of the people would soon be called for by the voice of the very factions whose misrule had proved the necessity of it. In the extended republic of the United States, and among the great variety of interests, parties, and sects which it embraces, a coalition of a majority of the whole society could seldom take place on any other principles than those of justice and the general good; whilst there being thus less danger to a minor from the will of a major party, there must be less pretext, also, to provide for the security of the former, by introducing into the government a will not dependent on the latter, or, in other words, a will independent of the society itself. It is no less certain than it is important, notwithstanding the contrary opinions which have been entertained, that the larger the society, provided it lie within a practical sphere, the more duly capable it will be of self-government. And happily for the REPUBLICAN CAUSE, the practicable sphere may be carried to a very great extent, by a judicious modification and mixture of the FEDERAL PRINCIPLE.

PUBLIUS.

Federalist No. 53

The House of Representatives

From the New York Packet. Tuesday, February 12, 1788.

HAMILTON OR MADISON

To the People of the State of New York:

I SHALL here, perhaps, be reminded of a current observation, "that where annual elections end, tyranny begins. " If it be true, as has often been remarked, that sayings which become proverbial are generally founded in reason, it is not less true, that when once established, they are often applied to cases to which the reason of them does not extend. I need not look for a proof beyond the case before us. What is the reason on which this proverbial observation is founded? No man will subject himself to the ridicule of pretending that any natural connection subsists between the sun or the seasons, and the period within which human virtue can bear the temptations of power. Happily for mankind, liberty is not, in this respect, confined to any single point of time; but lies within extremes, which afford sufficient latitude for all the variations which may be required by the various situations and circumstances of civil society. The election of magistrates might be, if it were found expedient, as in some instances it actually has been, daily, weekly, or monthly, as well as annual; and if circumstances may require a deviation from the rule on one side, why not also on the other side? Turning our attention to the periods established among ourselves, for the election of the most numerous branches of the State legislatures, we find them by no means coinciding any more in this instance, than in the elections of other civil magistrates.

In Connecticut and Rhode Island, the periods are half-yearly. In the other States, South Carolina excepted, they are annual. In South Carolina they are biennial as is proposed in the federal government. Here is a difference, as four to one, between the longest and shortest periods; and yet it would be not easy to show, that Connecticut or Rhode Island is better governed, or enjoys a greater share of rational liberty, than South Carolina; or that either the one or the other of these States is distinguished in these respects, and by these causes, from the States whose elections are different from both. In searching for the grounds of this doctrine, I can discover but one, and that is wholly inapplicable to our case. The important distinction so well understood in America, between a Constitution established by the people and unalterable by the government, and a law established by the government and alterable by the government, seems to have been little understood and less observed in any other country. Wherever the supreme power of legislation has resided, has been supposed to reside also a full power to change the form of the government.

Even in Great Britain, where the principles of political and civil liberty have been most discussed, and where we hear most of the rights of the Constitution, it is maintained that the authority of the Parliament is transcendent and uncontrollable, as well with regard to the Constitution, as the ordinary objects of legislative provision. They have accordingly, in several instances, actually changed, by legislative acts, some of the most fundamental articles of the government. They have in particular, on several occasions, changed the period of election; and, on the last occasion, not only introduced septennial in place of triennial elections, but by the same act, continued themselves in place four years beyond the term for which they were elected by the people. An attention to these dangerous practices has produced a very natural alarm in the votaries of free government, of which frequency of elections is the corner-stone; and has led them to seek for some security to liberty, against the danger to which it is exposed.

Where no Constitution, paramount to the government, either existed or could be obtained, no constitutional security, similar to that established in the United States, was to be attempted. Some other security, therefore, was to be sought for; and what better security would the case admit, than that of selecting and appealing to some simple and familiar portion of time, as a standard for measuring the danger of innovations, for fixing the national sentiment, and for uniting the patriotic exertions? The most simple and familiar portion of time, applicable to the subject was that of a year; and hence the doctrine has been inculcated by a laudable zeal, to erect some barrier against the gradual innovations of an unlimited government, that the advance towards tyranny was to be calculated by the distance of departure from the fixed point of annual elections. But what necessity can there be of applying this expedient to a government limited, as the federal government will be, by the authority of a paramount

Constitution? Or who will pretend that the liberties of the people of America will not be more secure under biennial elections, unalterably fixed by such a Constitution, than those of any other nation would be, where elections were annual, or even more frequent, but subject to alterations by the ordinary power of the government? The second question stated is, whether biennial elections be necessary or useful. The propriety of answering this question in the affirmative will appear from several very obvious considerations.

No man can be a competent legislator who does not add to an upright intention and a sound judgment a certain degree of knowledge of the subjects on which he is to legislate. A part of this knowledge may be acquired by means of information which lie within the compass of men in private as well as public stations. Another part can only be attained, or at least thoroughly attained, by actual experience in the station which requires the use of it. The period of service, ought, therefore, in all such cases, to bear some proportion to the extent of practical knowledge requisite to the due performance of the service. The period of legislative service established in most of the States for the more numerous branch is, as we have seen, one year. The question then may be put into this simple form: does the period of two years bear no greater proportion to the knowledge requisite for federal legislation than one year does to the knowledge requisite for State legislation? The very statement of the question, in this form, suggests the answer that ought to be given to it. In a single State, the requisite knowledge relates to the existing laws which are uniform throughout the State, and with which all the citizens are more or less conversant; and to the general affairs of the State, which lie within a small compass, are not very diversified, and occupy much of the attention and conversation of every class of people.

The great theatre of the United States presents a very different scene. The laws are so far from being uniform, that they vary in every State; whilst the public affairs of the Union are spread throughout a very extensive region, and are extremely diversified by the local affairs connected with them, and can with difficulty be correctly learnt in any other place than in the central councils to which a knowledge of them will be brought by the representatives of every part of the empire. Yet some knowledge of the affairs, and even of the laws, of all the States, ought to be possessed by the members from each of the States. How can foreign trade be properly regulated by uniform laws, without some acquaintance with the commerce, the ports, the usages, and the regulations of the different States? How can the trade between the different States be duly regulated, without some knowledge of their relative situations in these and other respects? How can taxes be judiciously imposed and effectually collected, if they be not accommodated to the different laws and local circumstances relating to these objects in the different States? How can uniform regulations for the militia be duly provided, without a similar knowledge of many internal circumstances by which the States are distinguished from each other? These are the principal objects of federal legislation, and suggest most forcibly the extensive information which the representatives ought to acquire. The other interior objects will require a proportional degree of information with regard to them.

It is true that all these difficulties will, by degrees, be very much diminished. The most laborious task will be the proper inauguration of the government and the primeval formation of a federal code. Improvements on the first draughts will every year become both easier and fewer. Past transactions of the government will be a ready and accurate source of information to new members. The affairs of the Union will become more and more objects of curiosity and conversation among the citizens at large. And the increased intercourse among those of different States will contribute not a little to diffuse a mutual knowledge of their affairs, as this again will contribute to a general assimilation of their manners and laws. But with all these abatements, the business of federal legislation must continue so far to exceed, both in novelty and difficulty, the legislative business of a single State, as to justify the longer period of service assigned to those who are to transact it. A branch of knowledge which belongs to the acquirements of a federal representative, and which has not been mentioned is that of foreign affairs. In regulating our own commerce he ought to be not only acquainted with the treaties between the United States and other nations, but also with the commercial policy and laws of other nations. He ought not to be altogether ignorant of the law of nations; for that, as far as it is a proper object of municipal legislation, is submitted to the federal government.

And although the House of Representatives is not immediately to participate in foreign negotiations and arrangements, yet from the necessary connection between the several branches of public affairs, those particular branches will frequently deserve attention in the ordinary course of legislation, and will sometimes demand particular legislative sanction and co-operation. Some portion of this knowledge may, no doubt, be acquired in a man's closet; but some of it also can only be derived from the public sources of information; and all of it will be acquired to best effect by a practical attention to the subject during the period of actual service in the legislature. There are other considerations, of less importance, perhaps, but which are not unworthy of notice. The distance which many of the representatives will be obliged to travel, and the arrangements rendered necessary by that circumstance, might be much more serious objections with fit men to this service, if limited to a single year, than if extended to two years. No argument can be drawn on this subject, from the case of the delegates to the existing Congress. They are elected annually, it is true; but their re-election is considered by the legislative assemblies almost as a matter of course. The election of the representatives by the people would not be governed by the same principle. A few of the members, as happens in all such assemblies, will possess superior talents; will, by frequent reelections, become members of long standing; will be thoroughly masters of the public business, and perhaps not unwilling to avail themselves of those advantages. The greater the proportion of new members, and the less the information of the bulk of the members the more apt will they be to fall into the snares that may be laid for them. This remark is no less applicable to the relation which will subsist between the House of Representatives and the Senate.

It is an inconvenience mingled with the advantages of our frequent elections even in single States, where they are large, and hold but one legislative session in a year, that spurious elections cannot be investigated and annulled in time for the decision to have its due effect. If a return can be obtained, no matter by what unlawful means, the irregular member, who takes his seat of course, is sure of holding it a sufficient time to answer his purposes. Hence, a very pernicious encouragement is given to the use of unlawful means, for obtaining irregular returns. Were elections for the federal legislature to be annual, this practice might become a very serious abuse, particularly in the more distant States. Each house is, as it necessarily must be, the judge of the elections, qualifications, and returns of its members; and whatever improvements may be suggested by experience, for simplifying and accelerating the process in disputed cases, so great a portion of a year would unavoidably elapse, before an illegitimate member could be dispossessed of his seat, that the prospect of such an event would be little check to unfair and illicit means of obtaining a seat. All these considerations taken together warrant us in affirming, that biennial elections will be as useful to the affairs of the public as we have seen that they will be safe to the liberty of the people.

PUBLIUS

Federalist No. 54

The Apportionment of Members Among the States

From the New York Packet. Tuesday, February 12, 1788.

HAMILTON OR MADISON

To the People of the State of New York:

THE next view which I shall take of the House of Representatives relates to the appointment of its members to the several States which is to be determined by the same rule with that of direct taxes.

It is not contended that the number of people in each State ought not to be the standard for regulating the proportion of those who are to represent the people of each State. The establishment of the same rule for the appointment of taxes, will probably be as little contested; though the rule itself in this case, is by no means founded on the same principle. In the former case, the rule is understood to refer to the personal rights of the people, with which it has a natural and universal connection. In the latter, it has reference to the proportion of wealth, of which it is in no case a precise measure, and in ordinary cases a very unfit one. But notwithstanding the imperfection of the rule as applied to the relative wealth and contributions of the States, it is evidently the least objectionable among the practicable rules, and had too recently obtained the general sanction of America, not to have found a ready preference with the convention.

All this is admitted, it will perhaps be said; but does it follow, from an admission of numbers for the measure of representation, or of slaves combined with free citizens as a ratio of taxation, that slaves ought to be included in the numerical rule of representation? Slaves are considered as property, not as persons. They ought therefore to be comprehended in estimates of taxation which are founded on property, and to be excluded from representation which is regulated by a census of persons. This is the objection, as I understand it, stated in its full force. I shall be equally candid in stating the reasoning which may be offered on the opposite side. "We subscribe to the doctrine," might one of our Southern brethren observe, "that representation relates more immediately to persons, and taxation more immediately to property, and we join in the application of this distinction to the case of our slaves. But we must deny the fact, that slaves are considered merely as property, and in no respect whatever as persons.

The true state of the case is, that they partake of both these qualities: being considered by our laws, in some respects, as persons, and in other respects as property.

In being compelled to labor, not for himself, but for a master; in being vendible by one master to another master; and in being subject at all times to be restrained in his liberty and chastised in his body, by the capricious will of another, the slave may appear to be degraded from the human rank, and classed with those irrational animals which fall under the legal denomination of property. In being protected, on the other hand, in his life and in his limbs, against the violence of all others, even the master of his labor and his liberty; and in being punishable himself for all violence committed against others, the slave is no less evidently regarded by the law as a member of the society, not as a part of the irrational creation; as a moral person, not as a mere article of property.

The federal Constitution, therefore, decides with great propriety on the case of our slaves, when it views them in the mixed character of persons and of property. This is in fact their true character. It is the character bestowed on them by the laws under which they live; and it will not be denied, that these are the proper criterion; because it is only under the pretext that the laws have transformed the negroes into subjects of property, that a place is disputed them in the computation of numbers; and it is admitted, that if the laws were to restore the rights which have been taken away, the negroes could no longer be refused an equal share of representation with the other inhabitants. "This question may be placed in another light. It is agreed on all sides, that numbers are the best scale of wealth and taxation, as they are the only proper scale of representation. Would the convention have been impartial or consistent, if they had rejected the slaves from the list of inhabitants, when the shares of representation were to be calculated, and inserted them on the lists when the tariff of contributions was to be adjusted? Could it be reasonably expected, that the Southern States would concur in a system, which considered their slaves in some degree as men, when burdens were to be imposed, but refused to consider them in the same light, when advantages were to be conferred? Might not some surprise also be expressed, that those who reproach the Southern States with the barbarous policy of considering as property a part of their human brethren, should themselves contend, that the government to which all the States are to be parties, ought to consider this unfortunate race more completely in the unnatural light of property, than the very laws of which they complain? "It may be replied, perhaps, that slaves are not included in the estimate of representatives in any of the States possessing them. They neither vote themselves nor increase the votes of their masters. Upon what principle, then, ought they to be taken into the federal estimate of representation?

In rejecting them altogether, the Constitution would, in this respect, have followed the very laws which have been appealed to as the proper guide. "This objection is repelled by a single observation. It is a fundamental principle of the proposed Constitution, that as the aggregate number of representatives allotted to the several States is to be determined by a federal rule, founded on the aggregate number of inhabitants, so the right of choosing this allotted number in each State is to be exercised by such part of the inhabitants as the State itself may designate. The qualifications on which the right of suffrage depend are not, perhaps, the same in any two States. In some of the States the difference is very material.

In every State, a certain proportion of inhabitants are deprived of this right by the constitution of the State, who will be included in the census by which the federal Constitution apportions the representatives. In this point of view the Southern States might retort the complaint, by insisting that the principle laid down by the convention required that no regard should be had to the policy of particular States towards their own inhabitants; and consequently, that the slaves, as inhabitants, should have been admitted into the census according to their full number, in like manner with other inhabitants, who, by the policy of other States, are not admitted to all the rights of citizens. A rigorous adherence, however, to this principle, is waived by those who would be gainers by it. All that they ask is that equal moderation be shown on the other side. Let the case of the slaves be considered, as it is in truth, a peculiar one. Let the compromising expedient of the Constitution be mutually adopted, which regards them as inhabitants, but as debased by servitude below the equal level of free inhabitants, which regards the SLAVE as divested of two fifths of the MAN. "After all, may not another ground be taken on which this article of the Constitution will admit of a still more ready defense? We have hitherto proceeded on the idea that representation related to persons only, and not at all to property. But is it a just idea? Government is instituted no less for protection of the property, than of the persons, of individuals. The one as well as the other, therefore, may be considered as represented by those who are charged with the government.

Upon this principle it is, that in several of the States, and particularly in the State of New York, one branch of the government is intended more especially to be the guardian of property, and is accordingly elected by that part of the society which is most interested in this object of government. In the federal Constitution, this policy does not prevail. The rights of property are committed into the same hands with the personal rights. Some attention ought, therefore, to be paid to property in the choice of those hands. "For another reason, the votes allowed in the federal legislature to the people of each State, ought to bear some proportion to the comparative wealth of the States. States have not, like individuals, an influence over each other, arising from superior advantages of fortune. If the law allows an opulent citizen but a single vote in the choice of his representative, the respect and consequence which he derives from his fortunate situation very frequently guide the votes of others to the objects of his choice; and through this imperceptible channel the rights of property are conveyed into the public representation. A State possesses no such influence over other States. It is not probable that the richest State in the Confederacy will ever influence the choice of a single representative in any other State. Nor will the representatives of the larger and richer States possess any other advantage in the federal legislature, over the representatives of other States, than what may result from their superior number alone. As far, therefore, as their superior wealth and weight may justly entitle them to any advantage, it ought to be secured to them by a superior share of representation.

The new Constitution is, in this respect, materially different from the existing Confederation, as well as from that of the United Netherlands, and other similar confederacies. In each of the latter, the efficacy of the federal resolutions depends on the subsequent and voluntary resolutions of the states composing the union. Hence the states, though possessing an equal vote in the public councils, have an unequal influence, corresponding with the unequal importance of these subsequent and voluntary resolutions. Under the proposed Constitution, the federal acts will take effect without the necessary intervention of the individual States. They will depend merely on the majority of votes in the federal legislature, and consequently each vote, whether proceeding from a larger or smaller State, or a State more or less wealthy or powerful, will have an equal weight and efficacy: in the same manner as the votes individually given in a State legislature, by the representatives of unequal counties or other districts, have each a precise equality of value and effect; or if there be any difference in the case, it proceeds from the difference in the personal character of the individual representative, rather than from any regard to the extent of the district from which he comes. "Such is the reasoning which an advocate for the Southern interests might employ on this subject; and although it may appear to be a little strained in some points, yet, on the whole, I must confess that it fully reconciles me to the scale of representation which the convention have established. In one respect, the establishment of a common measure for representation and taxation will have a very salutary effect. As the accuracy of the census to be obtained by the Congress will necessarily depend, in a considerable degree on the disposition, if not on the co-operation, of the States, it is of great importance that the States should feel as little bias as possible, to swell or to reduce the amount of their numbers. Were their share of representation alone to be governed by this rule, they would have an interest in exaggerating their inhabitants. Were the rule to decide their share of taxation alone, a contrary temptation would prevail. By extending the rule to both objects, the States will have opposite interests, which will control and balance each other, and produce the requisite impartiality.

PUBLIUS.

Federalist No. 57

The Alleged Tendency of the New Plan to Elevate the Few at the Expense of the Many Considered in Connection with Representation

From the New York Packet. Tuesday, February 19, 1788.

HAMILTON OR MADISON

To the People of the State of New York:

THE THIRD charge against the House of Representatives is, that it will be taken from that class of citizens which will have least sympathy with the mass of the people, and be most likely to aim at an ambitious sacrifice of the many to the aggrandizement of the few. Of all the objections which have been framed against the federal Constitution, this is perhaps the most extraordinary. Whilst the objection itself is levelled against a pretended oligarchy, the principle of it strikes at the very root of republican government. The aim of every political constitution is, or ought to be, first to obtain for rulers men who possess most wisdom to discern, and most virtue to pursue, the common good of the society; and in the next place, to take the most effectual precautions for keeping them virtuous whilst they continue to hold their public trust. The elective mode of obtaining rulers is the characteristic policy of republican government. The means relied on in this form of government for preventing their degeneracy are numerous and various. The most effectual one, is such a limitation of the term of appointments as will maintain a proper responsibility to the people.

Let me now ask what circumstance there is in the constitution of the House of Representatives that violates the principles of republican government, or favors the elevation of the few on the ruins of the many? Let me ask whether every circumstance is not, on the contrary, strictly conformable to these principles, and scrupulously impartial to the rights and pretensions of every class and description of citizens? Who are to be the electors of the federal representatives? Not the rich, more than the poor; not the learned, more than the ignorant; not the haughty heirs of distinguished names, more than the humble sons of obscurity and unpropitious fortune. The electors are to be the great body of the people of the United States. They are to be the same who exercise the right in every State of electing the corresponding branch of the legislature of the State. Who are to be the objects of popular choice? Every citizen whose merit may recommend him to the esteem and confidence of his country. No qualification of wealth, of birth, of religious faith, or of civil profession is permitted to fetter the judgement or disappoint the inclination of the people. If we consider the situation of the men on whom the free suffrages of their fellow-citizens may confer the representative trust, we shall find it involving every security which can be devised or desired for their fidelity to their constituents. In the first place, as they will have been distinguished by the preference of their fellow-citizens, we are to presume that in general they will be somewhat distinguished also by those qualities which entitle them to it, and which promise a sincere and scrupulous regard to the nature of their engagements. In the second place, they will enter into the public service under circumstances which cannot fail to produce a temporary affection at least to their constituents. There is in every breast a sensibility to marks of honor, of favor, of esteem, and of confidence, which, apart from all considerations of interest, is some pledge for grateful and benevolent returns. Ingratitude is a common topic of declamation against human nature; and it must be confessed that instances of it are but too frequent and flagrant, both in public and in private life. But the universal and extreme indignation which it inspires is itself a proof of the energy and prevalence of the contrary sentiment.

In the third place, those ties which bind the representative to his constituents are strengthened by motives of a more selfish nature. His pride and vanity attach him to a form of government which favors his pretensions and gives him a share in its honors and distinctions. Whatever hopes or projects might be entertained by a few aspiring characters, it must generally happen that a great proportion of the men deriving their advancement from their influence with the people, would have more to hope from a preservation of the favor, than from innovations in the government subversive of the authority of the people. All these securities, however, would be found very insufficient without the restraint of frequent elections. Hence, in the fourth place, the House of Representatives is so constituted as to support in the members an habitual recollection of their dependence on the people. Before the sentiments impressed on their minds by the mode of their elevation can be effaced by the exercise of power, they will be compelled to anticipate the moment when their power is to cease, when their exercise of it is to be reviewed, and when they must descend to the level from which they were raised; there forever to remain unless a faithful discharge of their trust shall have established their title to a renewal of it. I will add, as a fifth circumstance in the situation of the House of Representatives, restraining them from oppressive measures, that they can make no law which will not have its full operation on themselves and their friends, as well as on the great mass of the society.

This has always been deemed one of the strongest bonds by which human policy can connect the rulers and the people together. It creates between them that communion of interests and sympathy of sentiments, of which few governments have furnished examples; but without which every government degenerates into tyranny. If it be asked, what is to restrain the House of Representatives from making legal discriminations in favor of themselves and a particular class of the society? I answer: the genius of the whole system; the nature of just and constitutional laws; and above all, the vigilant and manly spirit which actuates the people of America, a spirit which nourishes freedom, and in return is nourished by it. If this spirit shall ever be so far debased as to tolerate a law not obligatory on the legislature, as well as on the people, the people will be prepared to tolerate any thing but liberty. Such will be the relation between the House of Representatives and their constituents. Duty, gratitude, interest, ambition itself, are the chords by which they will be bound to fidelity and sympathy with the great mass of the people.

It is possible that these may all be insufficient to control the caprice and wickedness of man. But are they not all that government will admit, and that human prudence can devise? Are they not the genuine and the characteristic means by which republican government provides for the liberty and happiness of the people? Are they not the identical means on which every State government in the Union relies for the attainment of these important ends? What then are we to understand by the objection which this paper has combated? What are we to say to the men who profess the most flaming zeal for republican government, yet boldly impeach the fundamental principle of it; who pretend to be champions for the right and the capacity of the people to choose their own rulers, yet maintain that they will prefer those only who will immediately and infallibly betray the trust committed to them? Were the objection to be read by one who had not seen the mode prescribed by the Constitution for the choice of representatives, he could suppose nothing less than that some unreasonable qualification of property was annexed to the right of suffrage; or that the right of eligibility was limited to persons of particular families or fortunes; or at least that the mode prescribed by the State constitutions was in some respect or other, very grossly departed from. We have seen how far such a supposition would err, as to the two first points. Nor would it, in fact, be less erroneous as to the last.

The only difference discoverable between the two cases is, that each representative of the United States will be elected by five or six thousand citizens; whilst in the individual States, the election of a representative is left to about as many hundreds. Will it be pretended that this difference is sufficient to justify an attachment to the State governments, and an abhorrence to the federal government? If this be the point on which the objection turns, it deserves to be examined. Is it supported by REASON? This cannot be said, without maintaining that five or six thousand citizens are less capable of choosing a fit representative, or more liable to be corrupted by an unfit one, than five or six hundred. Reason, on the contrary, assures us, that as in so great a number a fit representative would be most likely to be found, so the choice would be less likely to be diverted from him by the intrigues of the ambitious or the ambitious or the bribes of the rich. Is the CONSEQUENCE from this doctrine admissible? If we say that five or six hundred citizens are as many as can jointly exercise their right of suffrage, must we not deprive the people of the immediate choice of their public servants, in every instance where the administration of the government does not require as many of them as will amount to one for that number of citizens? Is the doctrine warranted by FACTS? It was shown in the last paper, that the real representation in the British House of Commons very little exceeds the proportion of one for every thirty thousand inhabitants. Besides a variety of powerful causes not existing here, and which favor in that country the pretensions of rank and wealth, no person is eligible as a representative of a county, unless he possess real estate of the clear value of six hundred pounds sterling per year; nor of a city or borough, unless he possess a like estate of half that annual value.

To this qualification on the part of the county representatives is added another on the part of the county electors, which restrains the right of suffrage to persons having a freehold estate of the annual value of more than twenty pounds sterling, according to the present rate of money. Notwithstanding these unfavorable circumstances, and notwithstanding some very unequal laws in the British code, it cannot be said that the representatives of the nation have elevated the few on the ruins of the many. But we need not resort to foreign experience on this subject. Our own is explicit and decisive. The districts in New Hampshire in which the senators are chosen immediately by the people, are nearly as large as will be necessary for her representatives in the Congress. Those of Massachusetts are larger than will be necessary for that purpose; and those of New York still more so. In the last State the members of Assembly for the cities and counties of New York and Albany are elected by very nearly as many voters as will be entitled to a representative in the Congress, calculating on the number of sixty-five representatives only. It makes no difference that in these senatorial districts and counties a number of representatives are voted for by each elector at the same time. If the same electors at the same time are capable of choosing four or five representatives, they cannot be incapable of choosing one.

Pennsylvania is an additional example. Some of her counties, which elect her State representatives, are almost as large as her districts will be by which her federal representatives will be elected. The city of Philadelphia is supposed to contain between fifty and sixty thousand souls. It will therefore form nearly two districts for the choice of federal representatives. It forms, however, but one county, in which every elector votes for each of its representatives in the State legislature. And what may appear to be still more directly to our purpose, the whole city actually elects a SINGLE MEMBER for the executive council. This is the case in all the other counties of the State. Are not these facts the most satisfactory proofs of the fallacy which has been employed against the branch of the federal government under consideration? Has it appeared on trial that the senators of New Hampshire, Massachusetts, and New York, or the executive council of Pennsylvania, or the members of the Assembly in the two last States, have betrayed any peculiar disposition to sacrifice the many to the few, or are in any respect less worthy of their places than the representatives and magistrates appointed in other States by very small divisions of the people? But there are cases of a stronger complexion than any which I have yet quoted. One branch of the legislature of Connecticut is so constituted that each member of it is elected by the whole State. So is the governor of that State, of Massachusetts, and of this State, and the president of New Hampshire. I leave every man to decide whether the result of any one of these experiments can be said to countenance a suspicion, that a diffusive mode of choosing representatives of the people tends to elevate traitors and to undermine the public liberty.

PUBLIUS.

Federalist No. 59

Concerning the Power of Congress to Regulate the Election of Members

From the New York Packet. Friday, February 22, 1788.

HAMILTON

To the People of the State of New York:

THE natural order of the subject leads us to consider, in this place, that provision of the Constitution which authorizes the national legislature to regulate, in the last resort, the election of its own members. It is in these words: "The TIMES, PLACES, and MANNER of holding elections for senators and representatives shall be prescribed in each State by the legislature thereof; but the Congress may, at any time, by law, make or alter SUCH REGULATIONS, except as to the PLACES of choosing senators. "[1] This provision has not only been declaimed against by those who condemn the Constitution in the gross, but it has been censured by those who have objected with less latitude and greater moderation; and, in one instance it has been thought exceptionable by a gentleman who has declared himself the advocate of every other part of the system. I am greatly mistaken, notwithstanding, if there be any article in the whole plan more completely defensible than this. Its propriety rests upon the evidence of this plain proposition, that EVERY GOVERNMENT OUGHT TO CONTAIN IN ITSELF THE MEANS OF ITS OWN PRESERVATION. Every just reasoner will, at first sight, approve an adherence to this rule, in the work of the convention; and will disapprove every deviation from it which may not appear to have been dictated by the necessity of incorporating into the work some particular ingredient, with which a rigid conformity to the rule was incompatible. Even in this case, though he may acquiesce in the necessity, yet he will not cease to regard and to regret a departure from so fundamental a principle, as a portion of imperfection in the system which may prove the seed of future weakness, and perhaps anarchy.

It will not be alleged, that an election law could have been framed and inserted in the Constitution, which would have been always applicable to every probable change in the situation of the country; and it will therefore not be denied, that a discretionary power over elections ought to exist somewhere. It will, I presume, be as readily conceded, that there were only three ways in which this power could have been reasonably modified and disposed: that it must either have been lodged wholly in the national legislature, or wholly in the State legislatures, or primarily in the latter and ultimately in the former. The last mode has, with reason, been preferred by the convention. They have submitted the regulation of elections for the federal government, in the first instance, to the local administrations; which, in ordinary cases, and when no improper views prevail, may be both more convenient and more satisfactory; but they have reserved to the national authority a right to interpose, whenever extraordinary circumstances might render that interposition necessary to its safety. Nothing can be more evident, than that an exclusive power of regulating elections for the national government, in the hands of the State legislatures, would leave the existence of the Union entirely at their mercy. They could at any moment annihilate it, by neglecting to provide for the choice of persons to administer its affairs. It is to little purpose to say, that a neglect or omission of this kind would not be likely to take place. The constitutional possibility of the thing, without an equivalent for the risk, is an unanswerable objection. Nor has any satisfactory reason been yet assigned for incurring that risk. The extravagant surmises of a distempered jealousy can never be dignified with that character.

If we are in a humor to presume abuses of power, it is as fair to presume them on the part of the State governments as on the part of the general government. And as it is more consonant to the rules of a just theory, to trust the Union with the care of its own existence, than to transfer that care to any other hands, if abuses of power are to be hazarded on the one side or on the other, it is more rational to hazard them where the power would naturally be placed, than where it would unnaturally be placed. Suppose an article had been introduced into the Constitution, empowering the United States to regulate the elections for the particular States, would any man have hesitated to condemn it, both as an unwarrantable transposition of power, and as a premeditated engine for the destruction of the State governments? The violation of principle, in this case, would have required no comment; and, to an unbiased observer, it will not be less apparent in the project of subjecting the existence of the national government, in a similar respect, to the pleasure of the State governments. An impartial view of the matter cannot fail to result in a conviction, that each, as far as possible, ought to depend on itself for its own preservation.

As an objection to this position, it may be remarked that the constitution of the national Senate would involve, in its full extent, the danger which it is suggested might flow from an exclusive power in the State legislatures to regulate the federal elections. It may be alleged, that by declining the appointment of Senators, they might at any time give a fatal blow to the Union; and from this it may be inferred, that as its existence would be thus rendered dependent upon them in so essential a point, there can be no objection to intrusting them with it in the particular case under consideration. The interest of each State, it may be added, to maintain its representation in the national councils, would be a complete security against an abuse of the trust. This argument, though specious, will not, upon examination, be found solid. It is certainly true that the State legislatures, by forbearing the appointment of senators, may destroy the national government. But it will not follow that, because they have a power to do this in one instance, they ought to have it in every other. There are cases in which the pernicious tendency of such a power may be far more decisive, without any motive equally cogent with that which must have regulated the conduct of the convention in respect to the formation of the Senate, to recommend their admission into the system.

So far as that construction may expose the Union to the possibility of injury from the State legislatures, it is an evil; but it is an evil which could not have been avoided without excluding the States, in their political capacities, wholly from a place in the organization of the national government. If this had been done, it would doubtless have been interpreted into an entire dereliction of the federal principle; and would certainly have deprived the State governments of that absolute safeguard which they will enjoy under this provision. But however wise it may have been to have submitted in this instance to an inconvenience, for the attainment of a necessary advantage or a greater good, no inference can be drawn from thence to favor an accumulation of the evil, where no necessity urges, nor any greater good invites. It may be easily discerned also that the national government would run a much greater risk from a power in the State legislatures over the elections of its House of Representatives, than from their power of appointing the members of its Senate. The senators are to be chosen for the period of six years; there is to be a rotation, by which the seats of a third part of them are to be vacated and replenished every two years; and no State is to be entitled to more than two senators; a quorum of the body is to consist of sixteen members.

The joint result of these circumstances would be, that a temporary combination of a few States to intermit the appointment of senators, could neither annul the existence nor impair the activity of the body; and it is not from a general and permanent combination of the States that we can have any thing to fear. The first might proceed from sinister designs in the leading members of a few of the State legislatures; the last would suppose a fixed and rooted disaffection in the great body of the people, which will either never exist at all, or will, in all probability, proceed from an experience of the inaptitude of the general government to the advancement of their happiness in which event no good citizen could desire its continuance. But with regard to the federal House of Representatives, there is intended to be a general election of members once in two years. If the State legislatures were to be invested with an exclusive power of regulating these elections, every period of making them would be a delicate crisis in the national situation, which might issue in a dissolution of the Union, if the leaders of a few of the most important States should have entered into a previous conspiracy to prevent an election. I shall not deny, that there is a degree of weight in the observation, that the interests of each State, to be represented in the federal councils, will be a security against the abuse of a power over its elections in the hands of the State legislatures. But the security will not be considered as complete, by those who attend to the force of an obvious distinction between the interest of the people in the public felicity, and the interest of their local rulers in the power and consequence of their offices.

The people of America may be warmly attached to the government of the Union, at times when the particular rulers of particular States, stimulated by the natural rivalship of power, and by the hopes of personal aggrandizement, and supported by a strong faction in each of those States, may be in a very opposite temper. This diversity of sentiment between a majority of the people, and the individuals who have the greatest credit in their councils, is exemplified in some of the States at the present moment, on the present question. The scheme of separate confederacies, which will always multiply the chances of ambition, will be a never failing bait to all such influential characters in the State administrations as are capable of preferring their own emolument and advancement to the public weal. With so effectual a weapon in their hands as the exclusive power of regulating elections for the national government, a combination of a few such men, in a few of the most considerable States, where the temptation will always be the strongest, might accomplish the destruction of the Union, by seizing the opportunity of some casual dissatisfaction among the people (and which perhaps they may themselves have excited), to discontinue the choice of members for the federal House of Representatives. It ought never to be forgotten, that a firm union of this country, under an efficient government, will probably be an increasing object of jealousy to more than one nation of Europe; and that enterprises to subvert it will sometimes originate in the intrigues of foreign powers, and will seldom fail to be patronized and abetted by some of them. Its preservation, therefore ought in no case that can be avoided, to be committed to the guardianship of any but those whose situation will uniformly beget an immediate interest in the faithful and vigilant performance of the trust.

PUBLIUS.

[1] 1st clause, 4th section, of the 1st article.

Federalist No. 62

The Senate

For the Independent Journal.

HAMILTON OR MADISON

To the People of the State of New York:

HAVING examined the constitution of the House of Representatives, and answered such of the objections against it as seemed to merit notice, I enter next on the examination of the Senate.

The heads into which this member of the government may be considered are:

The qualification of senators;
The appointment of them by the State legislatures;
The equality of representation in the Senate;
The number of senators, and the term for which they are to be elected;
The powers vested in the Senate.

The qualifications proposed for senators, as distinguished from those of representatives, consist in a more advanced age and a longer period of citizenship. A senator must be thirty years of age at least; as a representative must be twenty-five. And the former must have been a citizen nine years; as seven years are required for the latter. The propriety of these distinctions is explained by the nature of the senatorial trust, which, requiring greater extent of information and stability of character, requires at the same time that the senator should have reached a period of life most likely to supply these advantages; and which, participating immediately in transactions with foreign nations, ought to be exercised by none who are not thoroughly weaned from the prepossessions and habits incident to foreign birth and education. The term of nine years appears to be a prudent mediocrity between a total exclusion of adopted citizens, whose merits and talents may claim a share in the public confidence, and an indiscriminate and hasty admission of them, which might create a channel for foreign influence on the national councils.

It is equally unnecessary to dilate on the appointment of senators by the State legislatures. Among the various modes which might have been devised for constituting this branch of the government, that which has been proposed by the convention is probably the most congenial with the public opinion. It is recommended by the double advantage of favoring a select appointment, and of giving to the State governments such an agency in the formation of the federal government as must secure the authority of the former, and may form a convenient link between the two systems.

The equality of representation in the Senate is another point, which, being evidently the result of compromise between the opposite pretensions of the large and the small States, does not call for much discussion. If indeed it be right, that among a people thoroughly incorporated into one nation, every district ought to have a PROPORTIONAL share in the government, and that among independent and sovereign States, bound together by a simple league, the parties, however unequal in size, ought to have an EQUAL share in the common councils, it does not appear to be without some reason that in a compound republic, partaking both of the national and federal character, the government ought to be founded on a mixture of the principles of proportional and equal representation. But it is superfluous to try, by the standard of theory, a part of the Constitution which is allowed on all hands to be the result, not of theory, but "of a spirit of amity, and that mutual deference and concession which the peculiarity of our political situation rendered indispensable." A common government, with powers equal to its objects, is called for by the voice, and still more loudly by the political situation, of America. A government founded on principles more consonant to the wishes of the larger States, is not likely to be obtained from the smaller States. The only option, then, for the former, lies between the proposed government and a government still more objectionable. Under this alternative, the advice of prudence must be to embrace the lesser evil; and, instead of indulging a fruitless anticipation of the possible mischiefs which may ensue, to contemplate rather the advantageous consequences which may qualify the sacrifice.

In this spirit it may be remarked, that the equal vote allowed to each State is at once a constitutional recognition of the portion of sovereignty remaining in the individual States, and an instrument for preserving that residuary sovereignty. So far the equality ought to be no less acceptable to the large than to the small States; since they are not less solicitous to guard, by every possible expedient, against an improper consolidation of the States into one simple republic.

Another advantage accruing from this ingredient in the constitution of the Senate is, the additional impediment it must prove against improper acts of legislation. No law or resolution can now be passed without the concurrence, first, of a majority of the people, and then, of a majority of the States. It must be acknowledged that this complicated check on legislation may in some instances be injurious as well as beneficial; and that the peculiar defense which it involves in favor of the smaller States, would be more rational, if any interests common to them, and distinct from those of the other States, would otherwise be exposed to peculiar danger. But as the larger States will always be able, by their power over the supplies, to defeat unreasonable exertions of this prerogative of the lesser States, and as the faculty and excess of law-making seem to be the diseases to which our governments are most liable, it is not impossible that this part of the Constitution may be more convenient in practice than it appears to many in contemplation.

The number of senators, and the duration of their appointment, come next to be considered. In order to form an accurate judgment on both of these points, it will be proper to inquire into the purposes which are to be answered by a senate; and in order to ascertain these, it will be necessary to review the inconveniences which a republic must suffer from the want of such an institution.

First. It is a misfortune incident to republican government, though in a less degree than to other governments, that those who administer it may forget their obligations to their constituents, and prove unfaithful to their important trust. In this point of view, a senate, as a second branch of the legislative assembly, distinct from, and dividing the power with, a first, must be in all cases a salutary check on the government. It doubles the security to the people, by requiring the concurrence of two distinct bodies in schemes of usurpation or perfidy, where the ambition or corruption of one would otherwise be sufficient. This is a precaution founded on such clear principles, and now so well understood in the United States, that it would be more than superfluous to enlarge on it. I will barely remark, that as the improbability of sinister combinations will be in proportion to the dissimilarity in the genius of the two bodies, it must be politic to distinguish them from each other by every circumstance which will consist with a due harmony in all proper measures, and with the genuine principles of republican government.

Secondly. The necessity of a senate is not less indicated by the propensity of all single and numerous assemblies to yield to the impulse of sudden and violent passions, and to be seduced by factious leaders into intemperate and pernicious resolutions. Examples on this subject might be cited without number; and from proceedings within the United States, as well as from the history of other nations. But a position that will not be contradicted, need not be proved. All that need be remarked is, that a body which is to correct this infirmity ought itself to be free from it, and consequently ought to be less numerous. It ought, moreover, to possess great firmness, and consequently ought to hold its authority by a tenure of considerable duration.

Thirdly. Another defect to be supplied by a senate lies in a want of due acquaintance with the objects and principles of legislation. It is not possible that an assembly of men called for the most part from pursuits of a private nature, continued in appointment for a short time, and led by no permanent motive to devote the intervals of public occupation to a study of the laws, the affairs, and the comprehensive interests of their country, should, if left wholly to themselves, escape a variety of important errors in the exercise of their legislative trust. It may be affirmed, on the best grounds, that no small share of the present embarrassments of America is to be charged on the blunders of our governments; and that these have proceeded from the heads rather than the hearts of most of the authors of them. What indeed are all the repealing, explaining, and amending laws, which fill and disgrace our voluminous codes, but so many monuments of deficient wisdom; so many impeachments exhibited by each succeeding against each preceding session; so many admonitions to the people, of the value of those aids which may be expected from a well-constituted senate?

A good government implies two things: first, fidelity to the object of government, which is the happiness of the people; secondly, a knowledge of the means by which that object can be best attained. Some governments are deficient in both these qualities; most governments are deficient in the first. I scruple not to assert, that in

American governments too little attention has been paid to the last. The federal Constitution avoids this error; and what merits particular notice, it provides for the last in a mode which increases the security for the first.

Fourthly. The mutability in the public councils arising from a rapid succession of new members, however qualified they may be, points out, in the strongest manner, the necessity of some stable institution in the government. Every new election in the States is found to change one half of the representatives. From this change of men must proceed a change of opinions; and from a change of opinions, a change of measures. But a continual change even of good measures is inconsistent with every rule of prudence and every prospect of success. The remark is verified in private life, and becomes more just, as well as more important, in national transactions.

To trace the mischievous effects of a mutable government would fill a volume. I will hint a few only, each of which will be perceived to be a source of innumerable others.

In the first place, it forfeits the respect and confidence of other nations, and all the advantages connected with national character. An individual who is observed to be inconstant to his plans, or perhaps to carry on his affairs without any plan at all, is marked at once, by all prudent people, as a speedy victim to his own unsteadiness and folly. His more friendly neighbors may pity him, but all will decline to connect their fortunes with his; and not a few will seize the opportunity of making their fortunes out of his. One nation is to another what one individual is to another; with this melancholy distinction perhaps, that the former, with fewer of the benevolent emotions than the latter, are under fewer restraints also from taking undue advantage from the indiscretions of each other. Every nation, consequently, whose affairs betray a want of wisdom and stability, may calculate on every loss which can be sustained from the more systematic policy of their wiser neighbors. But the best instruction on this subject is unhappily conveyed to America by the example of her own situation. She finds that she is held in no respect by her friends; that she is the derision of her enemies; and that she is a prey to every nation which has an interest in speculating on her fluctuating councils and embarrassed affairs.

The internal effects of a mutable policy are still more calamitous. It poisons the blessing of liberty itself. It will be of little avail to the people, that the laws are made by men of their own choice, if the laws be so voluminous that they cannot be read, or so incoherent that they cannot be understood; if they be repealed or revised before they are promulgated, or undergo such incessant changes that no man, who knows what the law is to-day, can guess what it will be to-morrow. Law is defined to be a rule of action; but how can that be a rule, which is little known, and less fixed?

Another effect of public instability is the unreasonable advantage it gives to the sagacious, the enterprising, and the moneyed few over the industrious and uniformed mass of the people. Every new regulation concerning commerce or revenue, or in any way affecting the value of the different species of property, presents a new harvest to those who watch the change, and can trace its consequences; a harvest, reared not by themselves, but by the toils and cares of the great body of their fellow-citizens. This is a state of things in which it may be said with some truth that laws are made for the FEW, not for the MANY.

In another point of view, great injury results from an unstable government. The want of confidence in the public councils damps every useful undertaking, the success and profit of which may depend on a continuance of existing arrangements. What prudent merchant will hazard his fortunes in any new branch of commerce when he knows not but that his plans may be rendered unlawful before they can be executed? What farmer or manufacturer will lay himself out for the encouragement given to any particular cultivation or establishment, when he can have no assurance that his preparatory labors and advances will not render him a victim to an inconstant government? In a word, no great improvement or laudable enterprise can go forward which requires the auspices of a steady system of national policy.

But the most deplorable effect of all is that diminution of attachment and reverence which steals into the hearts of the people, towards a political system which betrays so many marks of infirmity, and disappoints so many of their flattering hopes. No government, any more than an individual, will long be respected without being truly respectable; nor be truly respectable, without possessing a certain portion of order and stability.

PUBLIUS.

Federalist No. 63

The Senate Continued

For the Independent Journal.

HAMILTON OR MADISON

To the People of the State of New York:

A FIFTH desideratum, illustrating the utility of a senate, is the want of a due sense of national character. Without a select and stable member of the government, the esteem of foreign powers will not only be forfeited by an unenlightened and variable policy, proceeding from the causes already mentioned, but the national councils will not possess that sensibility to the opinion of the world, which is perhaps not less necessary in order to merit, than it is to obtain, its respect and confidence.

An attention to the judgment of other nations is important to every government for two reasons: the one is, that, independently of the merits of any particular plan or measure, it is desirable, on various accounts, that it should appear to other nations as the offspring of a wise and honorable policy; the second is, that in doubtful cases, particularly where the national councils may be warped by some strong passion or momentary interest, the presumed or known opinion of the impartial world may be the best guide that can be followed. What has not America lost by her want of character with foreign nations; and how many errors and follies would she not have avoided, if the justice and propriety of her measures had, in every instance, been previously tried by the light in which they would probably appear to the unbiased part of mankind?

Yet however requisite a sense of national character may be, it is evident that it can never be sufficiently possessed by a numerous and changeable body. It can only be found in a number so small that a sensible degree of the praise and blame of public measures may be the portion of each individual; or in an assembly so durably invested with public trust, that the pride and consequence of its members may be sensibly incorporated with the reputation and prosperity of the community. The half-yearly representatives of Rhode Island would probably have been little affected in their deliberations on the iniquitous measures of that State, by arguments drawn from the light in which such measures would be viewed by foreign nations, or even by the sister States; whilst it can scarcely be doubted that if the concurrence of a select and stable body had been necessary, a regard to national character alone would have prevented the calamities under which that misguided people is now laboring.

I add, as a SIXTH defect the want, in some important cases, of a due responsibility in the government to the people, arising from that frequency of elections which in other cases produces this responsibility. This remark will, perhaps, appear not only new, but paradoxical. It must nevertheless be acknowledged, when explained, to be as undeniable as it is important.

Responsibility, in order to be reasonable, must be limited to objects within the power of the responsible party, and in order to be effectual, must relate to operations of that power, of which a ready and proper judgment can be formed by the constituents. The objects of government may be divided into two general classes: the one depending on measures which have singly an immediate and sensible operation; the other depending on a succession of well-chosen and well-connected measures, which have a gradual and perhaps unobserved operation. The importance of the latter description to the collective and permanent welfare of every country, needs no explanation. And yet it is evident that an assembly elected for so short a term as to be unable to provide more than one or two links in a chain of measures, on which the general welfare may essentially depend, ought not to be answerable for the final result, any more than a steward or tenant, engaged for one year, could be justly made to answer for places or improvements which could not be accomplished in less than half a dozen years. Nor is it possible for the people to estimate the SHARE of influence which their annual assemblies may respectively have on events resulting from the mixed transactions of several years. It is sufficiently difficult to preserve a personal responsibility in the members of a NUMEROUS body, for such acts of the body as have an immediate, detached, and palpable operation on its constituents.

The proper remedy for this defect must be an additional body in the legislative department, which, having sufficient permanency to provide for such objects as require a continued attention, and a train of measures, may be justly and effectually answerable for the attainment of those objects.

Thus far I have considered the circumstances which point out the necessity of a well-constructed Senate only as they relate to the representatives of the people. To a people as little blinded by prejudice or corrupted by flattery as those whom I address, I shall not scruple to add, that such an institution may be sometimes necessary as a defense to the people against their own temporary errors and delusions. As the cool and deliberate sense of the community ought, in all governments, and actually will, in all free governments, ultimately prevail over the views of its rulers; so there are particular moments in public affairs when the people, stimulated by some irregular passion, or some illicit advantage, or misled by the artful misrepresentations of interested men, may call for measures which they themselves will afterwards be the most ready to lament and condemn. In these critical moments, how salutary will be the interference of some temperate and respectable body of citizens, in order to check the misguided career, and to suspend the blow meditated by the people against themselves, until reason, justice, and truth can regain their authority over the public mind? What bitter anguish would not the people of Athens have often escaped if their government had contained so provident a safeguard against the tyranny of their own passions? Popular liberty might then have escaped the indelible reproach of decreeing to the same citizens the hemlock on one day and statues on the next.

It may be suggested, that a people spread over an extensive region cannot, like the crowded inhabitants of a small district, be subject to the infection of violent passions, or to the danger of combining in pursuit of unjust measures. I am far from denying that this is a distinction of peculiar importance. I have, on the contrary, endeavored in a former paper to show, that it is one of the principal recommendations of a confederated republic. At the same time, this advantage ought not to be considered as superseding the use of auxiliary precautions. It may even be remarked, that the same extended situation, which will exempt the people of America from some of the dangers incident to lesser republics, will expose them to the inconveniency of remaining for a longer time under the influence of those misrepresentations which the combined industry of interested men may succeed in distributing among them.

It adds no small weight to all these considerations, to recollect that history informs us of no long-lived republic which had not a senate.

Sparta, Rome, and Carthage are, in fact, the only states to whom that character can be applied. In each of the two first there was a senate for life. The constitution of the senate in the last is less known. Circumstantial evidence makes it probable that it was not different in this particular from the two others. It is at least certain, that it had some quality or other which rendered it an anchor against popular fluctuations; and that a smaller council, drawn out of the senate, was appointed not only for life, but filled up vacancies itself. These examples, though as unfit for the imitation, as they are repugnant to the genius, of America, are, notwithstanding, when compared with the fugitive and turbulent existence of other ancient republics, very instructive proofs of the necessity of some institution that will blend stability with liberty. I am not unaware of the circumstances which distinguish the American from other popular governments, as well ancient as modern; and which render extreme circumspection necessary, in reasoning from the one case to the other. But after allowing due weight to this consideration, it may still be maintained, that there are many points of similitude which render these examples not unworthy of our attention. Many of the defects, as we have seen, which can only be supplied by a senatorial institution, are common to a numerous assembly frequently elected by the people, and to the people themselves. There are others peculiar to the former, which require the control of such an institution. The people can never wilfully betray their own interests; but they may possibly be betrayed by the representatives of the people; and the danger will be evidently greater where the whole legislative trust is lodged in the hands of one body of men, than where the concurrence of separate and dissimilar bodies is required in every public act.

The difference most relied on, between the American and other republics, consists in the principle of representation; which is the pivot on which the former move, and which is supposed to have been unknown to the latter, or at least to the ancient part of them. The use which has been made of this difference, in reasonings contained in former papers, will have shown that I am disposed neither to deny its existence nor to undervalue its importance. I feel the less restraint, therefore, in observing, that the position concerning the ignorance of the ancient governments on the subject of representation, is by no means precisely true in the latitude commonly given to it. Without entering into a disquisition which here would be misplaced, I will refer to a few known facts, in support of what I advance.

In the most pure democracies of Greece, many of the executive functions were performed, not by the people themselves, but by officers elected by the people, and REPRESENTING the people in their EXECUTIVE capacity.

Prior to the reform of Solon, Athens was governed by nine Archons, annually ELECTED BY THE PEOPLE AT LARGE. The degree of power delegated to them seems to be left in great obscurity. Subsequent to that period, we find an assembly, first of four, and afterwards of six hundred members, annually ELECTED BY THE PEOPLE; and PARTIALLY representing them in their LEGISLATIVE capacity, since they were not only associated with the people in the function of making laws, but had the exclusive right of originating legislative propositions to the people. The senate of Carthage, also, whatever might be its power, or the duration of its appointment, appears to have been ELECTIVE by the suffrages of the people. Similar instances might be traced in most, if not all the popular governments of antiquity.

Lastly, in Sparta we meet with the Ephori, and in Rome with the Tribunes; two bodies, small indeed in numbers, but annually ELECTED BY THE WHOLE BODY OF THE PEOPLE, and considered as the REPRESENTATIVES of the people, almost in their PLENIPOTENTIARY capacity. The Cosmi of Crete were also annually ELECTED BY THE PEOPLE, and have been considered by some authors as an institution analogous to those of Sparta and Rome, with this difference only, that in the election of that representative body the right of suffrage was communicated to a part only of the people.

From these facts, to which many others might be added, it is clear that the principle of representation was neither unknown to the ancients nor wholly overlooked in their political constitutions. The true distinction between these and the American governments, lies IN THE TOTAL EXCLUSION OF THE PEOPLE, IN THEIR COLLECTIVE CAPACITY, from any share in the LATTER, and not in the TOTAL EXCLUSION OF THE REPRESENTATIVES OF THE PEOPLE from the administration of the FORMER. The distinction, however, thus qualified, must be admitted to leave a most advantageous superiority in favor of the United States. But to insure to this advantage its full effect, we must be careful not to separate it from the other advantage, of an extensive territory. For it cannot be believed, that any form of representative government could have succeeded within the narrow limits occupied by the democracies of Greece.

In answer to all these arguments, suggested by reason, illustrated by examples, and enforced by our own experience, the jealous adversary of the Constitution will probably content himself with repeating, that a senate appointed not immediately by the people, and for the term of six years, must gradually acquire a dangerous pre-eminence in the government, and finally transform it into a tyrannical aristocracy.

To this general answer, the general reply ought to be sufficient, that liberty may be endangered by the abuses of liberty as well as by the abuses of power; that there are numerous instances of the former as well as of the latter; and that the former, rather than the latter, are apparently most to be apprehended by the United States. But a more particular reply may be given.

Before such a revolution can be effected, the Senate, it is to be observed, must in the first place corrupt itself; must next corrupt the State legislatures; must then corrupt the House of Representatives; and must finally corrupt the people at large. It is evident that the Senate must be first corrupted before it can attempt an establishment of tyranny. Without corrupting the State legislatures, it cannot prosecute the attempt, because the periodical change of members would otherwise regenerate the whole body. Without exerting the means of corruption with equal success on the House of Representatives, the opposition of that coequal branch of the government would inevitably defeat the attempt; and without corrupting the people themselves, a succession of new representatives would speedily restore all things to their pristine order. Is there any man who can seriously persuade himself that the proposed Senate can, by any possible means within the compass of human address, arrive at the object of a lawless ambition, through all these obstructions?

If reason condemns the suspicion, the same sentence is pronounced by experience. The constitution of Maryland furnishes the most apposite example. The Senate of that State is elected, as the federal Senate will be, indirectly by the people, and for a term less by one year only than the federal Senate. It is distinguished, also, by the remarkable prerogative of filling up its own vacancies within the term of its appointment, and, at the same time, is not under the control of any such rotation as is provided for the federal Senate. There are some other lesser distinctions, which would expose the former to colorable objections, that do not lie against the latter. If the federal Senate, therefore, really contained the danger which has been so loudly proclaimed, some symptoms at least of a like danger ought by this time to have been betrayed by the Senate of Maryland, but no such symptoms have appeared. On the contrary, the jealousies at first entertained by men of the same description with those who view with terror the correspondent part of the federal Constitution, have been gradually extinguished by the progress of the experiment; and the Maryland constitution is daily deriving, from the salutary operation of this part of it, a reputation in which it will probably not be rivalled by that of any State in the Union.

But if any thing could silence the jealousies on this subject, it ought to be the British example. The Senate there instead of being elected for a term of six years, and of being unconfined to particular families or fortunes, is an hereditary assembly of opulent nobles. The House of Representatives, instead of being elected for two years, and by the whole body of the people, is elected for seven years, and, in very great proportion, by a very small proportion of the people. Here, unquestionably, ought to be seen in full display the aristocratic usurpations and tyranny which are at some future period to be exemplified in the United States. Unfortunately, however, for the anti-federal argument, the British history informs us that this hereditary assembly has not been able to defend itself against the continual encroachments of the House of Representatives; and that it no sooner lost the support of the monarch, than it was actually crushed by the weight of the popular branch.

As far as antiquity can instruct us on this subject, its examples support the reasoning which we have employed. In Sparta, the Ephori, the annual representatives of the people, were found an overmatch for the senate for life, continually gained on its authority and finally drew all power into their own hands. The Tribunes of Rome, who were the representatives of the people, prevailed, it is well known, in almost every contest with the senate for life, and in the end gained the most complete triumph over it. The fact is the more remarkable, as unanimity was required in every act of the Tribunes, even after their number was augmented to ten. It proves the irresistible force possessed by that branch of a free government, which has the people on its side. To these examples might be added that of Carthage, whose senate, according to the testimony of Polybius, instead of drawing all power into its vortex, had, at the commencement of the second Punic War, lost almost the whole of its original portion.

Besides the conclusive evidence resulting from this assemblage of facts, that the federal Senate will never be able to transform itself, by gradual usurpations, into an independent and aristocratic body, we are warranted in believing, that if such a revolution should ever happen from causes which the foresight of man cannot guard against, the House of Representatives, with the people on their side, will at all times be able to bring back the Constitution to its primitive form and principles. Against the force of the immediate representatives of the people, nothing will be able to maintain even the constitutional authority of the Senate, but such a display of enlightened policy, and attachment to the public good, as will divide with that branch of the legislature the affections and support of the entire body of the people themselves.

PUBLIUS.

Federalist No. 65

The Powers of the Senate
From the New York Packet.
Friday, March 7, 1788.
HAMILTON
To the People of the State of New York:

THE remaining powers which the plan of the convention allots to the Senate, in a distinct capacity, are comprised in their participation with the executive in the appointment to offices, and in their judicial character as a court for the trial of impeachments. As in the business of appointments the executive will be the principal agent, the provisions relating to it will most properly be discussed in the examination of that department. We will, therefore, conclude this head with a view of the judicial character of the Senate.

A well-constituted court for the trial of impeachments is an object not more to be desired than difficult to be obtained in a government wholly elective. The subjects of its jurisdiction are those offenses which proceed from the misconduct of public men, or, in other words, from the abuse or violation of some public trust. They are of a nature which may with peculiar propriety be denominated POLITICAL, as they relate chiefly to injuries done immediately to the society itself. The prosecution of them, for this reason, will seldom fail to agitate the passions of the whole community, and to divide it into parties more or less friendly or inimical to the accused. In many cases it will connect itself with the pre-existing factions, and will enlist all their animosities, partialities, influence, and interest on one side or on the other; and in such cases there will always be the greatest danger that the decision will be regulated more by the comparative strength of parties, than by the real demonstrations of innocence or guilt.

The delicacy and magnitude of a trust which so deeply concerns the political reputation and existence of every man engaged in the administration of public affairs, speak for themselves. The difficulty of placing it rightly, in a government resting entirely on the basis of periodical elections, will as readily be perceived, when it is considered that the most conspicuous characters in it will, from that circumstance, be too often the leaders or the tools of the most cunning or the most numerous faction, and on this account, can hardly be expected to possess the requisite neutrality towards those whose conduct may be the subject of scrutiny.

The convention, it appears, thought the Senate the most fit depositary of this important trust. Those who can best discern the intrinsic difficulty of the thing, will be least hasty in condemning that opinion, and will be most inclined to allow due weight to the arguments which may be supposed to have produced it.

What, it may be asked, is the true spirit of the institution itself? Is it not designed as a method of NATIONAL INQUEST into the conduct of public men? If this be the design of it, who can so properly be the inquisitors for the nation as the representatives of the nation themselves? It is not disputed that the power of originating the inquiry, or, in other words, of preferring the impeachment, ought to be lodged in the hands of one branch of the legislative body. Will not the reasons which indicate the propriety of this arrangement strongly plead for an admission of the other branch of that body to a share of the inquiry? The model from which the idea of this institution has been borrowed, pointed out that course to the convention. In Great Britain it is the province of the House of Commons to prefer the impeachment, and of the House of Lords to decide upon it. Several of the State constitutions have followed the example. As well the latter, as the former, seem to have regarded the practice of impeachments as a bridle in the hands of the legislative body upon the executive servants of the government. Is not this the true light in which it ought to be regarded?

Where else than in the Senate could have been found a tribunal sufficiently dignified, or sufficiently independent? What other body would be likely to feel CONFIDENCE ENOUGH IN ITS OWN SITUATION, to preserve, unawed and uninfluenced, the necessary impartiality between an INDIVIDUAL accused, and the REPRESENTATIVES OF THE PEOPLE, HIS ACCUSERS?

Could the Supreme Court have been relied upon as answering this description? It is much to be doubted, whether the members of that tribunal would at all times be endowed with so eminent a portion of fortitude, as would be called for in the execution of so difficult a task; and it is still more to be doubted, whether they would possess the degree of credit and authority, which might, on certain occasions, be indispensable towards reconciling the people to a decision that should happen to clash with an accusation brought by their immediate representatives. A deficiency in the first, would be fatal to the accused; in the last, dangerous to the public tranquillity. The hazard in both these respects, could only be avoided, if at all, by rendering that tribunal more numerous than would consist with a reasonable attention to economy. The necessity of a numerous court for the trial of impeachments, is equally dictated by the nature of the proceeding. This can never be tied down by such strict rules, either in the delineation of the offense by the prosecutors, or in the construction of it by the judges, as in common cases serve to limit the discretion of courts in favor of personal security. There will be no jury to stand between the judges who are to pronounce the sentence of the law, and the party who is to receive or suffer it. The awful discretion which a court of impeachments must necessarily have, to doom to honor or to infamy the most confidential and the most distinguished characters of the community, forbids the commitment of the trust to a small number of persons.

These considerations seem alone sufficient to authorize a conclusion, that the Supreme Court would have been an improper substitute for the Senate, as a court of impeachments. There remains a further consideration, which will not a little strengthen this conclusion. It is this: The punishment which may be the consequence of conviction upon impeachment, is not to terminate the chastisement of the offender. After having been sentenced to a prepetual ostracism from the esteem and confidence, and honors and emoluments of his country, he will still be liable to prosecution and punishment in the ordinary course of law. Would it be proper that the persons who had disposed of his fame, and his most valuable rights as a citizen in one trial, should, in another trial, for the same offense, be also the disposers of his life and his fortune? Would there not be the greatest reason to apprehend, that error, in the first sentence, would be the parent of error in the second sentence? That the strong bias of one decision would be apt to overrule the influence of any new lights which might be brought to vary the complexion of another decision? Those who know anything of human nature, will not hesitate to answer these questions in the affirmative; and will be at no loss to perceive, that by making the same persons judges in both cases, those who might happen to be the objects of prosecution would, in a great measure, be deprived of the double security intended them by a double trial. The loss of life and estate would often be virtually included in a sentence which, in its terms, imported nothing more than dismission from a present, and disqualification for a future, office. It may be said, that the intervention of a jury, in the second instance, would obviate the danger. But juries are frequently influenced by the opinions of judges. They are sometimes induced to find special verdicts, which refer the main question to the decision of the court. Who would be willing to stake his life and his estate upon the verdict of a jury acting under the auspices of judges who had predetermined his guilt?

Would it have been an improvement of the plan, to have united the Supreme Court with the Senate, in the formation of the court of impeachments? This union would certainly have been attended with several advantages; but would they not have been overbalanced by the signal disadvantage, already stated, arising from the agency of the same judges in the double prosecution to which the offender would be liable? To a certain extent, the benefits of that union will be obtained from making the chief justice of the Supreme Court the president of the court of impeachments, as is proposed to be done in the plan of the convention; while the inconveniences of an entire incorporation of the former into the latter will be substantially avoided. This was perhaps the prudent mean. I forbear to remark upon the additional pretext for clamor against the judiciary, which so considerable an augmentation of its authority would have afforded.

Would it have been desirable to have composed the court for the trial of impeachments, of persons wholly distinct from the other departments of the government? There are weighty arguments, as well against, as in favor of, such a plan. To some minds it will not appear a trivial objection, that it could tend to increase the complexity of the political machine, and to add a new spring to the government, the utility of which would at best be questionable. But an objection which will not be thought by any unworthy of attention, is this: a court formed upon such a plan, would either be attended with a heavy expense, or might in practice be subject to a variety of casualties and inconveniences. It must either consist of permanent officers, stationary at the seat of government, and of course entitled to fixed and regular stipends, or of certain officers of the State governments to be called upon whenever an impeachment was actually depending. It will not be easy to imagine any third mode materially different, which could rationally be proposed. As the court, for reasons already given, ought to be numerous, the first scheme will be reprobated by every man who can compare the extent of the public wants with the means of supplying them. The second will be espoused with caution by those who will seriously consider the difficulty of collecting men dispersed over the whole Union; the injury to the innocent, from the procrastinated determination of the charges which might be brought against them; the advantage to the guilty, from the opportunities which delay would afford to intrigue and corruption; and in some cases the detriment to the State, from the prolonged inaction of men whose firm and faithful execution of their duty might have exposed them to the persecution of an intemperate or designing majority in the House of Representatives. Though this latter supposition may seem harsh, and might not be likely often to be verified, yet it ought not to be forgotten that the demon of faction will, at certain seasons, extend his sceptre over all numerous bodies of men.

But though one or the other of the substitutes which have been examined, or some other that might be devised, should be thought preferable to the plan in this respect, reported by the convention, it will not follow that the Constitution ought for this reason to be rejected. If mankind were to resolve to agree in no institution of government, until every part of it had been adjusted to the most exact standard of perfection, society would soon become a general scene of anarchy, and the world a desert. Where is the standard of perfection to be found? Who will undertake to unite the discordant opinions of a whole community, in the same judgment of it; and to prevail upon one conceited projector to renounce his INFALLIBLE criterion for the FALLIBLE criterion of his more CONCEITED NEIGHBOR? To answer the purpose of the adversaries of the Constitution, they ought to prove, not merely that particular provisions in it are not the best which might have been imagined, but that the plan upon the whole is bad and pernicious.

PUBLIUS.

Federalist No. 66

Objections to the Power of the Senate To Set as a Court for Impeachments Further Considered

From the New York Packet.
Tuesday, March 11, 1788.
HAMILTON

To the People of the State of New York:

A REVIEW of the principal objections that have appeared against the proposed court for the trial of impeachments, will not improbably eradicate the remains of any unfavorable impressions which may still exist in regard to this matter.

The FIRST of these objections is, that the provision in question confounds legislative and judiciary authorities in the same body, in violation of that important and well-established maxim which requires a separation between the different departments of power. The true meaning of this maxim has been discussed and ascertained in another place, and has been shown to be entirely compatible with a partial intermixture of those departments for special purposes, preserving them, in the main, distinct and unconnected. This partial intermixture is even, in some cases, not only proper but necessary to the mutual defense of the several members of the government against each other. An absolute or qualified negative in the executive upon the acts of the legislative body, is admitted, by the ablest adepts in political science, to be an indispensable barrier against the encroachments of the latter upon the former. And it may, perhaps, with no less reason be contended, that the powers relating to impeachments are, as before intimated, an essential check in the hands of that body upon the encroachments of the executive. The division of them between the two branches of the legislature, assigning to one the right of accusing, to the other the right of judging, avoids the inconvenience of making the same persons both accusers and judges; and guards against the danger of persecution, from the prevalency of a factious spirit in either of those branches. As the concurrence of two thirds of the Senate will be requisite to a condemnation, the security to innocence, from this additional circumstance, will be as complete as itself can desire.

It is curious to observe, with what vehemence this part of the plan is assailed, on the principle here taken notice of, by men who profess to admire, without exception, the constitution of this State; while that constitution makes the Senate, together with the chancellor and judges of the Supreme Court, not only a court of impeachments, but the highest judicatory in the State, in all causes, civil and criminal. The proportion, in point of numbers, of the chancellor and judges to the senators, is so inconsiderable, that the judiciary authority of New York, in the last resort, may, with truth, be said to reside in its Senate. If the plan of the convention be, in this respect, chargeable with a departure from the celebrated maxim which has been so often mentioned, and seems to be so little understood, how much more culpable must be the constitution of New York? [1]

A SECOND objection to the Senate, as a court of impeachments, is, that it contributes to an undue accumulation of power in that body, tending to give to the government a countenance too aristocratic. The Senate, it is observed, is to have concurrent authority with the Executive in the formation of treaties and in the appointment to offices: if, say the objectors, to these prerogatives is added that of deciding in all cases of impeachment, it will give a decided predominancy to senatorial influence. To an objection so little precise in itself, it is not easy to find a very precise answer. Where is the measure or criterion to which we can appeal, for determining what will give the Senate too much, too little, or barely the proper degree of influence? Will it not be more safe, as well as more simple, to dismiss such vague and uncertain calculations, to examine each power by itself, and to decide, on general principles, where it may be deposited with most advantage and least inconvenience?

If we take this course, it will lead to a more intelligible, if not to a more certain result. The disposition of the power of making treaties, which has obtained in the plan of the convention, will, then, if I mistake not, appear to be fully justified by the considerations stated in a former number, and by others which will occur under the next head of our inquiries. The expediency of the junction of the Senate with the Executive, in the power of appointing to offices, will, I trust, be placed in a light not less satisfactory, in the disquisitions under the same head. And I flatter myself the observations in my last paper must have gone no inconsiderable way towards proving that it was not easy, if practicable, to find a more fit receptacle for the power of determining impeachments, than that which has been chosen. If this be truly the case, the hypothetical dread of the too great weight of the Senate ought to be discarded from our reasonings.

But this hypothesis, such as it is, has already been refuted in the remarks applied to the duration in office prescribed for the senators. It was by them shown, as well on the credit of historical examples, as from the reason of the thing, that the most POPULAR branch of every government, partaking of the republican genius, by being generally the favorite of the people, will be as generally a full match, if not an overmatch, for every other member of the Government.

But independent of this most active and operative principle, to secure the equilibrium of the national House of Representatives, the plan of the convention has provided in its favor several important counterpoises to the additional authorities to be conferred upon the Senate. The exclusive privilege of originating money bills will belong to the House of Representatives. The same house will possess the sole right of instituting impeachments: is not this a complete counterbalance to that of determining them? The same house will be the umpire in all elections of the President, which do not unite the suffrages of a majority of the whole number of electors; a case which it cannot be doubted will sometimes, if not frequently, happen. The constant possibility of the thing must be a fruitful source of influence to that body. The more it is contemplated, the more important will appear this ultimate though contingent power, of deciding the competitions of the most illustrious citizens of the Union, for the first office in it. It would not perhaps be rash to predict, that as a mean of influence it will be found to outweigh all the peculiar attributes of the Senate.

A THIRD objection to the Senate as a court of impeachments, is drawn from the agency they are to have in the appointments to office. It is imagined that they would be too indulgent judges of the conduct of men, in whose official creation they had participated. The principle of this objection would condemn a practice, which is to be seen in all the State governments, if not in all the governments with which we are acquainted: I mean that of rendering those who hold offices during pleasure, dependent on the pleasure of those who appoint them. With equal plausibility might it be alleged in this case, that the favoritism of the latter would always be an asylum for the misbehavior of the former. But that practice, in contradiction to this principle, proceeds upon the presumption, that the responsibility of those who appoint, for the fitness and competency of the persons on whom they bestow their choice, and the interest they will have in the respectable and prosperous administration of affairs, will inspire a sufficient disposition to dismiss from a share in it all such who, by their conduct, shall have proved themselves unworthy of the confidence reposed in them. Though facts may not always correspond with this presumption, yet if it be, in the main, just, it must destroy the supposition that the Senate, who will merely sanction the choice of the Executive, should feel a bias, towards the objects of that choice, strong enough to blind them to the evidences of guilt so extraordinary, as to have induced the representatives of the nation to become its accusers.

If any further arguments were necessary to evince the improbability of such a bias, it might be found in the nature of the agency of the Senate in the business of appointments.

It will be the office of the President to NOMINATE, and, with the advice and consent of the Senate, to APPOINT. There will, of course, be no exertion of CHOICE on the part of the Senate. They may defeat one choice of the Executive, and oblige him to make another; but they cannot themselves CHOOSE, they can only ratify or reject the choice of the President. They might even entertain a preference to some other person, at the very moment they were assenting to the one proposed, because there might be no positive ground of opposition to him; and they could not be sure, if they withheld their assent, that the subsequent nomination would fall upon their own favorite, or upon any other person in their estimation more meritorious than the one rejected. Thus it could hardly happen, that the majority of the Senate would feel any other complacency towards the object of an appointment than such as the appearances of merit might inspire, and the proofs of the want of it destroy.

A FOURTH objection to the Senate in the capacity of a court of impeachments, is derived from its union with the Executive in the power of making treaties. This, it has been said, would constitute the senators their own judges, in every case of a corrupt or perfidious execution of that trust. After having combined with the Executive in betraying the interests of the nation in a ruinous treaty, what prospect, it is asked, would there be of their being made to suffer the punishment they would deserve, when they were themselves to decide upon the accusation brought against them for the treachery of which they have been guilty?

This objection has been circulated with more earnestness and with greater show of reason than any other which has appeared against this part of the plan; and yet I am deceived if it does not rest upon an erroneous foundation.

The security essentially intended by the Constitution against corruption and treachery in the formation of treaties, is to be sought for in the numbers and characters of those who are to make them. The JOINT AGENCY of the Chief Magistrate of the Union, and of two thirds of the members of a body selected by the collective wisdom of the legislatures of the several States, is designed to be the pledge for the fidelity of the national councils in this particular. The convention might with propriety have meditated the punishment of the Executive, for a deviation from the instructions of the Senate, or a want of integrity in the conduct of the negotiations committed to him; they might also have had in view the punishment of a few leading individuals in the Senate, who should have prostituted their influence in that body as the mercenary instruments of foreign corruption: but they could not, with more or with equal propriety, have contemplated the impeachment and punishment of two thirds of the Senate, consenting to an improper treaty, than of a majority of that or of the other branch of the national legislature, consenting to a pernicious or unconstitutional law, a principle which, I believe, has never been admitted into any government. How, in fact, could a majority in the House of Representatives impeach themselves? Not better, it is evident, than two thirds of the Senate might try themselves. And yet what reason is there, that a majority of the House of Representatives, sacrificing the interests of the society by an unjust and tyrannical act of legislation, should escape with impunity, more than two thirds of the Senate, sacrificing the same interests in an injurious treaty with a foreign power? The truth is, that in all such cases it is essential to the freedom and to the necessary independence of the deliberations of the body, that the members of it should be exempt from punishment for acts done in a collective capacity; and the security to the society must depend on the care which is taken to confide the trust to proper hands, to make it their interest to execute it with fidelity, and to make it as difficult as possible for them to combine in any interest opposite to that of the public good.

So far as might concern the misbehavior of the Executive in perverting the instructions or contravening the views of the Senate, we need not be apprehensive of the want of a disposition in that body to punish the abuse of their confidence or to vindicate their own authority. We may thus far count upon their pride, if not upon their virtue. And so far even as might concern the corruption of leading members, by whose arts and influence the majority may have been inveigled into measures odious to the community, if the proofs of that corruption should be satisfactory, the usual propensity of human nature will warrant us in concluding that there would be commonly no defect of inclination in the body to divert the public resentment from themselves by a ready sacrifice of the authors of their mismanagement and disgrace.

PUBLIUS.

[1] In that of New Jersey, also, the final judiciary authority is in a branch of the legislature. In New Hampshire, Massachusetts, Pennsylvania, and South Carolina, one branch of the legislature is the court for the trial of impeachments.

Federalist No. 67

The Executive Department

From the New York Packet.

Tuesday, March 11, 1788.

HAMILTON

To the People of the State of New York:

THE constitution of the executive department of the proposed government, claims next our attention.

There is hardly any part of the system which could have been attended with greater difficulty in the arrangement of it than this; and there is, perhaps, none which has been inveighed against with less candor or criticised with less judgment.

Here the writers against the Constitution seem to have taken pains to signalize their talent of misrepresentation. Calculating upon the aversion of the people to monarchy, they have endeavored to enlist all their jealousies and apprehensions in opposition to the intended President of the United States; not merely as the embryo, but as the full-grown progeny, of that detested parent. To establish the pretended affinity, they have not scrupled to draw resources even from the regions of fiction. The authorities of a magistrate, in few instances greater, in some instances less, than those of a governor of New York, have been magnified into more than royal prerogatives. He has been decorated with attributes superior in dignity and splendor to those of a king of Great Britain. He has been shown to us with the diadem sparkling on his brow and the imperial purple flowing in his train. He has been seated on a throne surrounded with minions and mistresses, giving audience to the envoys of foreign potentates, in all the supercilious pomp of majesty. The images of Asiatic despotism and voluptuousness have scarcely been wanting to crown the exaggerated scene. We have been taught to tremble at the terrific visages of murdering janizaries, and to blush at the unveiled mysteries of a future seraglio.

Attempts so extravagant as these to disfigure or, it might rather be said, to metamorphose the object, render it necessary to take an accurate view of its real nature and form: in order as well to ascertain its true aspect and genuine appearance, as to unmask the disingenuity and expose the fallacy of the counterfeit resemblances which have been so insidiously, as well as industriously, propagated.

In the execution of this task, there is no man who would not find it an arduous effort either to behold with moderation, or to treat with seriousness, the devices, not less weak than wicked, which have been contrived to pervert the public opinion in relation to the subject. They so far exceed the usual though unjustifiable licenses of party artifice, that even in a disposition the most candid and tolerant, they must force the sentiments which favor an indulgent construction of the conduct of political adversaries to give place to a voluntary and unreserved indignation. It is impossible not to bestow the imputation of deliberate imposture and deception upon the gross pretense of a similitude between a king of Great Britain and a magistrate of the character marked out for that of the President of the United States. It is still more impossible to withhold that imputation from the rash and barefaced expedients which have been employed to give success to the attempted imposition. In one instance, which I cite as a sample of the general spirit, the temerity has proceeded so far as to ascribe to the President of the United States a power which by the instrument reported is EXPRESSLY allotted to the Executives of the individual States. I mean the power of filling casual vacancies in the Senate.

This bold experiment upon the discernment of his countrymen has been hazarded by a writer who (whatever may be his real merit) has had no inconsiderable share in the applauses of his party [1]; and who, upon this false and unfounded suggestion, has built a series of observations equally false and unfounded. Let him now be confronted with the evidence of the fact, and let him, if he be able, justify or extenuate the shameful outrage he has offered to the dictates of truth and to the rules of fair dealing.

The second clause of the second section of the second article empowers the President of the United States "to nominate, and by and with the advice and consent of the Senate, to appoint ambassadors, other public ministers and consuls, judges of the Supreme Court, and all other OFFICERS of United States whose appointments are NOT in the Constitution OTHERWISE PROVIDED FOR, and WHICH SHALL BE ESTABLISHED BY LAW." Immediately after this clause follows another in these words: "The President shall have power to fill up ?? VACANCIES that may happen DURING THE RECESS OF THE SENATE, by granting commissions which shall EXPIRE AT THE END OF THEIR NEXT SESSION." It is from this last provision that the pretended power of the President to fill vacancies in the Senate has been deduced. A slight attention to the connection of the clauses, and to the obvious meaning of the terms, will satisfy us that the deduction is not even colorable.

The first of these two clauses, it is clear, only provides a mode for appointing such officers, "whose appointments are NOT OTHERWISE PROVIDED FOR in the Constitution, and which SHALL BE ESTABLISHED BY LAW"; of course it cannot extend to the appointments of senators, whose appointments are OTHERWISE PROVIDED FOR in the Constitution [2], and who are ESTABLISHED BY THE CONSTITUTION, and will not require a future establishment by law. This position will hardly be contested.

The last of these two clauses, it is equally clear, cannot be understood to comprehend the power of filling vacancies in the Senate, for the following reasons: First. The relation in which that clause stands to the other, which declares the general mode of appointing officers of the United States, denotes it to be nothing more than a supplement to the other, for the purpose of establishing an auxiliary method of appointment, in cases to which the general method was inadequate. The ordinary power of appointment is confined to the President and Senate JOINTLY, and can therefore only be exercised during the session of the Senate; but as it would have been improper to oblige this body to be continually in session for the appointment of officers and as vacancies might happen IN THEIR RECESS, which it might be necessary for the public service to fill without delay, the succeeding clause is evidently intended to authorize the President, SINGLY, to make temporary appointments "during the recess of the Senate, by granting commissions which shall expire at the end of their next session."

Secondly. If this clause is to be considered as supplementary to the one which precedes, the VACANCIES of which it speaks must be construed to relate to the "officers" described in the preceding one; and this, we have seen, excludes from its description the members of the Senate. Thirdly. The time within which the power is to operate, "during the recess of the Senate," and the duration of the appointments, "to the end of the next session" of that body, conspire to elucidate the sense of the provision, which, if it had been intended to comprehend senators, would naturally have referred the temporary power of filling vacancies to the recess of the State legislatures, who are to make the permanent appointments, and not to the recess of the national Senate, who are to have no concern in those appointments; and would have extended the duration in office of the temporary senators to the next session of the legislature of the State, in whose representation the vacancies had happened, instead of making it to expire at the end of the ensuing session of the national Senate. The circumstances of the body authorized to make the permanent appointments would, of course, have governed the modification of a power which related to the temporary appointments; and as the national Senate is the body, whose situation is alone contemplated in the clause upon which the suggestion under examination has been founded, the vacancies to which it alludes can only be deemed to respect those officers in whose appointment that body has a concurrent agency with the President.

But lastly, the first and second clauses of the third section of the first article, not only obviate all possibility of doubt, but destroy the pretext of misconception. The former provides, that "the Senate of the United States shall be composed of two Senators from each State, chosen BY THE LEGISLATURE THEREOF for six years"; and the latter directs, that, "if vacancies in that body should happen by resignation or otherwise, DURING THE RECESS OF THE LEGISLATURE OF ANY STATE, the Executive THEREOF may make temporary appointments until the NEXT MEETING OF THE LEGISLATURE, which shall then fill such vacancies." Here is an express power given, in clear and unambiguous terms, to the State Executives, to fill casual vacancies in the Senate, by temporary appointments; which not only invalidates the supposition, that the clause before considered could have been intended to confer that power upon the President of the United States, but proves that this supposition, destitute as it is even of the merit of plausibility, must have originated in an intention to deceive the people, too palpable to be obscured by sophistry, too atrocious to be palliated by hypocrisy.

I have taken the pains to select this instance of misrepresentation, and to place it in a clear and strong light, as an unequivocal proof of the unwarrantable arts which are practiced to prevent a fair and impartial judgment of the real merits of the Constitution submitted to the consideration of the people. Nor have I scrupled, in so flagrant a case, to allow myself a severity of animadversion little congenial with the general spirit of these papers. I hesitate not to submit it to the decision of any candid and honest adversary of the proposed government, whether language can furnish epithets of too much asperity, for so shameless and so prostitute an attempt to impose on the citizens of America.

PUBLIUS.

[1] See CATO, No. V.

[2] Article I, section 3, clause I.

Federalist No. 68

The Mode of Electing the President

From the New York Packet.

Friday, March 14, 1788.

HAMILTON

To the People of the State of New York:

THE mode of appointment of the Chief Magistrate of the United States is almost the only part of the system, of any consequence, which has escaped without severe censure, or which has received the slightest mark of approbation from its opponents. The most plausible of these, who has appeared in print, has even deigned to admit that the election of the President is pretty well guarded. [1] I venture somewhat further, and hesitate not to affirm, that if the manner of it be not perfect, it is at least excellent. It unites in an eminent degree all the advantages, the union of which was to be wished for.

It was desirable that the sense of the people should operate in the choice of the person to whom so important a trust was to be confided. This end will be answered by committing the right of making it, not to any preestablished body, but to men chosen by the people for the special purpose, and at the particular conjuncture.

It was equally desirable, that the immediate election should be made by men most capable of analyzing the qualities adapted to the station, and acting under circumstances favorable to deliberation, and to a judicious combination of all the reasons and inducements which were proper to govern their choice. A small number of persons, selected by their fellow-citizens from the general mass, will be most likely to possess the information and discernment requisite to such complicated investigations.

It was also peculiarly desirable to afford as little opportunity as possible to tumult and disorder. This evil was not least to be dreaded in the election of a magistrate, who was to have so important an agency in the administration of the government as the President of the United States. But the precautions which have been so happily concerted in the system under consideration, promise an effectual security against this mischief. The choice of SEVERAL, to form an intermediate body of electors, will be much less apt to convulse the community with any extraordinary or violent movements, than the choice of ONE who was himself to be the final object of the public wishes. And as the electors, chosen in each State, are to assemble and vote in the State in which they are chosen, this detached and divided situation will expose them much less to heats and ferments, which might be communicated from them to the people, than if they were all to be convened at one time, in one place.

Nothing was more to be desired than that every practicable obstacle should be opposed to cabal, intrigue, and corruption. These most deadly adversaries of republican government might naturally have been expected to make their approaches from more than one quarter, but chiefly from the desire in foreign powers to gain an improper ascendant in our councils. How could they better gratify this, than by raising a creature of their own to the chief magistracy of the Union? But the convention have guarded against all danger of this sort, with the most provident and judicious attention. They have not made the appointment of the President to depend on any preexisting bodies of men, who might be tampered with beforehand to prostitute their votes; but they have referred it in the first instance to an immediate act of the people of America, to be exerted in the choice of persons for the temporary and sole purpose of making the appointment. And they have excluded from eligibility to this trust, all those who from situation might be suspected of too great devotion to the President in office. No senator, representative, or other person holding a place of trust or profit under the United States, can be of the numbers of the electors. Thus without corrupting the body of the people, the immediate agents in the election will at least enter upon the task free from any sinister bias. Their transient existence, and their detached situation, already taken notice of, afford a satisfactory prospect of their continuing so, to the conclusion of it. The business of corruption, when it is to embrace so considerable a number of men, requires time as well as means. Nor would it be found easy suddenly to embark them, dispersed as they would be over thirteen States, in any combinations founded upon motives, which though they could not properly be denominated corrupt, might yet be of a nature to mislead them from their duty.

Another and no less important desideratum was, that the Executive should be independent for his continuance in office on all but the people themselves. He might otherwise be tempted to sacrifice his duty to his complaisance for those whose favor was necessary to the duration of his official consequence. This advantage will also be secured, by making his re-election to depend on a special body of representatives, deputed by the society for the single purpose of making the important choice.

All these advantages will happily combine in the plan devised by the convention; which is, that the people of each State shall choose a number of persons as electors, equal to the number of senators and representatives of such State in the national government, who shall assemble within the State, and vote for some fit person as President. Their votes, thus given, are to be transmitted to the seat of the national government, and the person who may happen to have a majority of the whole number of votes will be the President. But as a majority of the votes might not always happen to centre in one man, and as it might be unsafe to permit less than a majority to be conclusive, it is provided that, in such a contingency, the House of Representatives shall select out of the candidates who shall have the five highest number of votes, the man who in their opinion may be best qualified for the office.

The process of election affords a moral certainty, that the office of President will never fall to the lot of any man who is not in an eminent degree endowed with the requisite qualifications. Talents for low intrigue, and the little arts of popularity, may alone suffice to elevate a man to the first honors in a single State; but it will require other talents, and a different kind of merit, to establish him in the esteem and confidence of the whole Union, or of so considerable a portion of it as would be necessary to make him a successful candidate for the distinguished office of President of the United States. It will not be too strong to say, that there will be a constant probability of seeing the station filled by characters pre-eminent for ability and virtue. And this will be thought no inconsiderable recommendation of the Constitution, by those who are able to estimate the share which the executive in every government must necessarily have in its good or ill administration. Though we cannot acquiesce in the political heresy of the poet who says: "For forms of government let fools contest That which is best administered is best," yet we may safely pronounce, that the true test of a good government is its aptitude and tendency to produce a good administration.

The Vice-President is to be chosen in the same manner with the President; with this difference, that the Senate is to do, in respect to the former, what is to be done by the House of Representatives, in respect to the latter.

The appointment of an extraordinary person, as Vice-President, has been objected to as superfluous, if not mischievous. It has been alleged, that it would have been preferable to have authorized the Senate to elect out of their own body an officer answering that description. But two considerations seem to justify the ideas of the convention in this respect. One is, that to secure at all times the possibility of a definite resolution of the body, it is necessary that the President should have only a casting vote. And to take the senator of any State from his seat as senator, to place him in that of President of the Senate, would be to exchange, in regard to the State from which he came, a constant for a contingent vote. The other consideration is, that as the Vice-President may occasionally become a substitute for the President, in the supreme executive magistracy, all the reasons which recommend the mode of election prescribed for the one, apply with great if not with equal force to the manner of appointing the other. It is remarkable that in this, as in most other instances, the objection which is made would lie against the constitution of this State. We have a Lieutenant-Governor, chosen by the people at large, who presides in the Senate, and is the constitutional substitute for the Governor, in casualties similar to those which would authorize the Vice-President to exercise the authorities and discharge the duties of the President.

PUBLIUS.

[1] Vide FEDERAL FARMER.

Federalist No. 70

The Executive Department Further Considered
From the New York Packet.
Tuesday, March 18, 1788.
HAMILTON
To the People of the State of New York:

THERE is an idea, which is not without its advocates, that a vigorous Executive is inconsistent with the genius of republican government. The enlightened well-wishers to this species of government must at least hope that the supposition is destitute of foundation; since they can never admit its truth, without at the same time admitting the condemnation of their own principles. Energy in the Executive is a leading character in the definition of good government. It is essential to the protection of the community against foreign attacks; it is not less essential to the steady administration of the laws; to the protection of property against those irregular and high-handed combinations which sometimes interrupt the ordinary course of justice; to the security of liberty against the enterprises and assaults of ambition, of faction, and of anarchy. Every man the least conversant in Roman story, knows how often that republic was obliged to take refuge in the absolute power of a single man, under the formidable title of Dictator, as well against the intrigues of ambitious individuals who aspired to the tyranny, and the seditions of whole classes of the community whose conduct threatened the existence of all government, as against the invasions of external enemies who menaced the conquest and destruction of Rome.

There can be no need, however, to multiply arguments or examples on this head. A feeble Executive implies a feeble execution of the government. A feeble execution is but another phrase for a bad execution; and a government ill executed, whatever it may be in theory, must be, in practice, a bad government.

Taking it for granted, therefore, that all men of sense will agree in the necessity of an energetic Executive, it will only remain to inquire, what are the ingredients which constitute this energy? How far can they be combined with those other ingredients which constitute safety in the republican sense? And how far does this combination characterize the plan which has been reported by the convention?

The ingredients which constitute energy in the Executive are, first, unity; secondly, duration; thirdly, an adequate provision for its support; fourthly, competent powers.

The ingredients which constitute safety in the republican sense are, first, a due dependence on the people, secondly, a due responsibility.

Those politicians and statesmen who have been the most celebrated for the soundness of their principles and for the justice of their views, have declared in favor of a single Executive and a numerous legislature. They have with great propriety, considered energy as the most necessary qualification of the former, and have regarded this as most applicable to power in a single hand, while they have, with equal propriety, considered the latter as best adapted to deliberation and wisdom, and best calculated to conciliate the confidence of the people and to secure their privileges and interests.

That unity is conducive to energy will not be disputed. Decision, activity, secrecy, and despatch will generally characterize the proceedings of one man in a much more eminent degree than the proceedings of any greater number; and in proportion as the number is increased, these qualities will be diminished.

This unity may be destroyed in two ways: either by vesting the power in two or more magistrates of equal dignity and authority; or by vesting it ostensibly in one man, subject, in whole or in part, to the control and co-operation of others, in the capacity of counsellors to him. Of the first, the two Consuls of Rome may serve as an example; of the last, we shall find examples in the constitutions of several of the States. New York and New Jersey, if I recollect right, are the only States which have intrusted the executive authority wholly to single men. [1] Both these methods of destroying the unity of the Executive have their partisans; but the votaries of an executive council are the most numerous. They are both liable, if not to equal, to similar objections, and may in most lights be examined in conjunction.

The experience of other nations will afford little instruction on this head. As far, however, as it teaches any thing, it teaches us not to be enamoured of plurality in the Executive. We have seen that the Achaeans, on an experiment of two Praetors, were induced to abolish one. The Roman history records many instances of mischiefs to the republic from the dissensions between the Consuls, and between the military Tribunes, who were at times substituted for the Consuls.

But it gives us no specimens of any peculiar advantages derived to the state from the circumstance of the plurality of those magistrates. That the dissensions between them were not more frequent or more fatal, is a matter of astonishment, until we advert to the singular position in which the republic was almost continually placed, and to the prudent policy pointed out by the circumstances of the state, and pursued by the Consuls, of making a division of the government between them. The patricians engaged in a perpetual struggle with the plebeians for the preservation of their ancient authorities and dignities; the Consuls, who were generally chosen out of the former body, were commonly united by the personal interest they had in the defense of the privileges of their order. In addition to this motive of union, after the arms of the republic had considerably expanded the bounds of its empire, it became an established custom with the Consuls to divide the administration between themselves by lot one of them remaining at Rome to govern the city and its environs, the other taking the command in the more distant provinces. This expedient must, no doubt, have had great influence in preventing those collisions and rivalships which might otherwise have embroiled the peace of the republic.

But quitting the dim light of historical research, attaching ourselves purely to the dictates of reason and good sense, we shall discover much greater cause to reject than to approve the idea of plurality in the Executive, under any modification whatever.

Wherever two or more persons are engaged in any common enterprise or pursuit, there is always danger of difference of opinion. If it be a public trust or office, in which they are clothed with equal dignity and authority, there is peculiar danger of personal emulation and even animosity. From either, and especially from all these causes, the most bitter dissensions are apt to spring. Whenever these happen, they lessen the respectability, weaken the authority, and distract the plans and operation of those whom they divide. If they should unfortunately assail the supreme executive magistracy of a country, consisting of a plurality of persons, they might impede or frustrate the most important measures of the government, in the most critical emergencies of the state. And what is still worse, they might split the community into the most violent and irreconcilable factions, adhering differently to the different individuals who composed the magistracy.

Men often oppose a thing, merely because they have had no agency in planning it, or because it may have been planned by those whom they dislike. But if they have been consulted, and have happened to disapprove, opposition then becomes, in their estimation, an indispensable duty of self-love. They seem to think themselves bound in honor, and by all the motives of personal infallibility, to defeat the success of what has been resolved upon contrary to their sentiments. Men of upright, benevolent tempers have too many opportunities of remarking, with horror, to what desperate lengths this disposition is sometimes carried, and how often the great interests of society are sacrificed to the vanity, to the conceit, and to the obstinacy of individuals, who have credit enough to make their passions and their caprices interesting to mankind. Perhaps the question now before the public may, in its consequences, afford melancholy proofs of the effects of this despicable frailty, or rather detestable vice, in the human character.

Upon the principles of a free government, inconveniences from the source just mentioned must necessarily be submitted to in the formation of the legislature; but it is unnecessary, and therefore unwise, to introduce them into the constitution of the Executive. It is here too that they may be most pernicious. In the legislature, promptitude of decision is oftener an evil than a benefit. The differences of opinion, and the jarrings of parties in that department of the government, though they may sometimes obstruct salutary plans, yet often promote deliberation and circumspection, and serve to check excesses in the majority. When a resolution too is once taken, the opposition must be at an end. That resolution is a law, and resistance to it punishable. But no favorable circumstances palliate or atone for the disadvantages of dissension in the executive department. Here, they are pure and unmixed. There is no point at which they cease to operate. They serve to embarrass and weaken the execution of the plan or measure to which they relate, from the first step to the final conclusion of it. They constantly counteract those qualities in the Executive which are the most necessary ingredients in its composition, vigor and expedition, and this without any counterbalancing good. In the conduct of war, in which the energy of the Executive is the bulwark of the national security, every thing would be to be apprehended from its plurality.

It must be confessed that these observations apply with principal weight to the first case supposed that is, to a plurality of magistrates of equal dignity and authority a scheme, the advocates for which are not likely to form a numerous sect; but they apply, though not with equal, yet with considerable weight to the project of a council, whose concurrence is made constitutionally necessary to the operations of the ostensible Executive. An artful cabal in that council would be able to distract and to enervate the whole system of administration. If no such cabal should exist, the mere diversity of views and opinions would alone be sufficient to tincture the exercise of the executive authority with a spirit of habitual feebleness and dilatoriness.

But one of the weightiest objections to a plurality in the Executive, and which lies as much against the last as the first plan, is, that it tends to conceal faults and destroy responsibility. Responsibility is of two kinds to censure and to punishment. The first is the more important of the two, especially in an elective office. Man, in public trust, will much oftener act in such a manner as to render him unworthy of being any longer trusted, than in such a manner as to make him obnoxious to legal punishment. But the multiplication of the Executive adds to the difficulty of detection in either case. It often becomes impossible, amidst mutual accusations, to determine on whom the blame or the punishment of a pernicious measure, or series of pernicious measures, ought really to fall. It is shifted from one to another with so much dexterity, and under such plausible appearances, that the public opinion is left in suspense about the real author. The circumstances which may have led to any national miscarriage or misfortune are sometimes so complicated that, where there are a number of actors who may have had different degrees and kinds of agency, though we may clearly see upon the whole that there has been mismanagement, yet it may be impracticable to pronounce to whose account the evil which may have been incurred is truly chargeable. "I was overruled by my council. The council were so divided in their opinions that it was impossible to obtain any better resolution on the point." These and similar pretexts are constantly at hand, whether true or false. And who is there that will either take the trouble or incur the odium, of a strict scrutiny into the secret springs of the transaction? Should there be found a citizen zealous enough to undertake the unpromising task, if there happen to be collusion between the parties concerned, how easy it is to clothe the circumstances with so much ambiguity, as to render it uncertain what was the precise conduct of any of those parties?

In the single instance in which the governor of this State is coupled with a council that is, in the appointment to offices, we have seen the mischiefs of it in the view now under consideration. Scandalous appointments to important offices have been made. Some cases, indeed, have been so flagrant that ALL PARTIES have agreed in the impropriety of the thing. When inquiry has been made, the blame has been laid by the governor on the members of the council, who, on their part, have charged it upon his nomination; while the people remain altogether at a loss to determine, by whose influence their interests have been committed to hands so unqualified and so manifestly improper. In tenderness to individuals, I forbear to descend to particulars.

It is evident from these considerations, that the plurality of the Executive tends to deprive the people of the two greatest securities they can have for the faithful exercise of any delegated power, first, the restraints of public opinion, which lose their efficacy, as well on account of the division of the censure attendant on bad measures among a number, as on account of the uncertainty on whom it ought to fall; and, secondly, the opportunity of discovering with facility and clearness the misconduct of the persons they trust, in order either to their removal from office or to their actual punishment in cases which admit of it.

In England, the king is a perpetual magistrate; and it is a maxim which has obtained for the sake of the public peace, that he is unaccountable for his administration, and his person sacred. Nothing, therefore, can be wiser in that kingdom, than to annex to the king a constitutional council, who may be responsible to the nation for the advice they give. Without this, there would be no responsibility whatever in the executive department an idea inadmissible in a free government. But even there the king is not bound by the resolutions of his council, though they are answerable for the advice they give. He is the absolute master of his own conduct in the exercise of his office, and may observe or disregard the counsel given to him at his sole discretion.

But in a republic, where every magistrate ought to be personally responsible for his behavior in office the reason which in the British Constitution dictates the propriety of a council, not only ceases to apply, but turns against the institution. In the monarchy of Great Britain, it furnishes a substitute for the prohibited responsibility of the chief magistrate, which serves in some degree as a hostage to the national justice for his good behavior. In the American republic, it would serve to destroy, or would greatly diminish, the intended and necessary responsibility of the Chief Magistrate himself.

The idea of a council to the Executive, which has so generally obtained in the State constitutions, has been derived from that maxim of republican jealousy which considers power as safer in the hands of a number of men than of a single man. If the maxim should be admitted to be applicable to the case, I should contend that the advantage on that side would not counterbalance the numerous disadvantages on the opposite side. But I do not think the rule at all applicable to the executive power. I clearly concur in opinion, in this particular, with a writer whom the celebrated Junius pronounces to be "deep, solid, and ingenious," that "the executive power is more easily confined when it is ONE"; [2] that it is far more safe there should be a single object for the jealousy and watchfulness of the people; and, in a word, that all multiplication of the Executive is rather dangerous than friendly to liberty.

A little consideration will satisfy us, that the species of security sought for in the multiplication of the Executive, is unattainable. Numbers must be so great as to render combination difficult, or they are rather a source of danger than of security. The united credit and influence of several individuals must be more formidable to liberty, than the credit and influence of either of them separately. When power, therefore, is placed in the hands of so small a number of men, as to admit of their interests and views being easily combined in a common enterprise, by an artful leader, it becomes more liable to abuse, and more dangerous when abused, than if it be lodged in the hands of one man; who, from the very circumstance of his being alone, will be more narrowly watched and more readily suspected, and who cannot unite so great a mass of influence as when he is associated with others. The Decemvirs of Rome, whose name denotes their number, [3] were more to be dreaded in their usurpation than any ONE of them would have been. No person would think of proposing an Executive much more numerous than that body; from six to a dozen have been suggested for the number of the council. The extreme of these numbers, is not too great for an easy combination; and from such a combination America would have more to fear, than from the ambition of any single individual. A council to a magistrate, who is himself responsible for what he does, are generally nothing better than a clog upon his good intentions, are often the instruments and accomplices of his bad and are almost always a cloak to his faults.

I forbear to dwell upon the subject of expense; though it be evident that if the council should be numerous enough to answer the principal end aimed at by the institution, the salaries of the members, who must be drawn from their homes to reside at the seat of government, would form an item in the catalogue of public expenditures too serious to be incurred for an object of equivocal utility. I will only add that, prior to the appearance of the Constitution, I rarely met with an intelligent man from any of the States, who did not admit, as the result of experience, that the UNITY of the executive of this State was one of the best of the distinguishing features of our constitution.

PUBLIUS.

[1] New York has no council except for the single purpose of appointing to offices; New Jersey has a council whom the governor may consult. But I think, from the terms of the constitution, their resolutions do not bind him.

[2] De Lolme.

[3] Ten.

Federalist No. 74

The Command of the Military and Naval Forces, and the Pardoning Power of the Executive

From the New York Packet.
Tuesday, March 25, 1788.
HAMILTON
To the People of the State of New York:

THE President of the United States is to be "commander-in-chief of the army and navy of the United States, and of the militia of the several States WHEN CALLED INTO THE ACTUAL SERVICE of the United States." The propriety of this provision is so evident in itself, and it is, at the same time, so consonant to the precedents of the State constitutions in general, that little need be said to explain or enforce it. Even those of them which have, in other respects, coupled the chief magistrate with a council, have for the most part concentrated the military authority in him alone. Of all the cares or concerns of government, the direction of war most peculiarly demands those qualities which distinguish the exercise of power by a single hand. The direction of war implies the direction of the common strength; and the power of directing and employing the common strength, forms a usual and essential part in the definition of the executive authority.

"The President may require the opinion, in writing, of the principal officer in each of the executive departments, upon any subject relating to the duties of their respective officers." This I consider as a mere redundancy in the plan, as the right for which it provides would result of itself from the office.

He is also to be authorized to grant "reprieves and pardons for offenses against the United States, EXCEPT IN CASES OF IMPEACHMENT." Humanity and good policy conspire to dictate, that the benign prerogative of pardoning should be as little as possible fettered or embarrassed. The criminal code of every country partakes so much of necessary severity, that without an easy access to exceptions in favor of unfortunate guilt, justice would wear a countenance too sanguinary and cruel. As the sense of responsibility is always strongest, in proportion as it is undivided, it may be inferred that a single man would be most ready to attend to the force of those motives which might plead for a mitigation of the rigor of the law, and least apt to yield to considerations which were calculated to shelter a fit object of its vengeance. The reflection that the fate of a fellow-creature depended on his sole fiat, would naturally inspire scrupulousness and caution; the dread of being accused of weakness or connivance, would beget equal circumspection, though of a different kind. On the other hand, as men generally derive confidence from their numbers, they might often encourage each other in an act of obduracy, and might be less sensible to the apprehension of suspicion or censure for an injudicious or affected clemency. On these accounts, one man appears to be a more eligible dispenser of the mercy of government, than a body of men.

The expediency of vesting the power of pardoning in the President has, if I mistake not, been only contested in relation to the crime of treason. This, it has been urged, ought to have depended upon the assent of one, or both, of the branches of the legislative body. I shall not deny that there are strong reasons to be assigned for requiring in this particular the concurrence of that body, or of a part of it. As treason is a crime levelled at the immediate being of the society, when the laws have once ascertained the guilt of the offender, there seems a fitness in referring the expediency of an act of mercy towards him to the judgment of the legislature. And this ought the rather to be the case, as the supposition of the connivance of the Chief Magistrate ought not to be entirely excluded. But there are also strong objections to such a plan. It is not to be doubted, that a single man of prudence and good sense is better fitted, in delicate conjunctures, to balance the motives which may plead for and against the remission of the punishment, than any numerous body whatever. It deserves particular attention, that treason will often be connected with seditions which embrace a large proportion of the community; as lately happened in Massachusetts. In every such case, we might expect to see the representation of the people tainted with the same spirit which had given birth to the offense. And when parties were pretty equally matched, the secret sympathy of the friends and favorers of the condemned person, availing itself of the good-nature and weakness of others, might frequently bestow impunity where the terror of an example was necessary.

On the other hand, when the sedition had proceeded from causes which had inflamed the resentments of the major party, they might often be found obstinate and inexorable, when policy demanded a conduct of forbearance and clemency. But the principal argument for reposing the power of pardoning in this case to the Chief Magistrate is this: in seasons of insurrection or rebellion, there are often critical moments, when a well-timed offer of pardon to the insurgents or rebels may restore the tranquillity of the commonwealth; and which, if suffered to pass unimproved, it may never be possible afterwards to recall. The dilatory process of convening the legislature, or one of its branches, for the purpose of obtaining its sanction to the measure, would frequently be the occasion of letting slip the golden opportunity. The loss of a week, a day, an hour, may sometimes be fatal. If it should be observed, that a discretionary power, with a view to such contingencies, might be occasionally conferred upon the President, it may be answered in the first place, that it is questionable, whether, in a limited Constitution, that power could be delegated by law; and in the second place, that it would generally be impolitic beforehand to take any step which might hold out the prospect of impunity. A proceeding of this kind, out of the usual course, would be likely to be construed into an argument of timidity or of weakness, and would have a tendency to embolden guilt.

PUBLIUS.

Federalist No. 78

The Judiciary Department

From McLEAN'S Edition, New York.

HAMILTON

To the People of the State of New York:

WE PROCEED now to an examination of the judiciary department of the proposed government.

In unfolding the defects of the existing Confederation, the utility and necessity of a federal judicature have been clearly pointed out. It is the less necessary to recapitulate the considerations there urged, as the propriety of the institution in the abstract is not disputed; the only questions which have been raised being relative to the manner of constituting it, and to its extent. To these points, therefore, our observations shall be confined.

The manner of constituting it seems to embrace these several objects: 1st. The mode of appointing the judges. 2d. The tenure by which they are to hold their places. 3d. The partition of the judiciary authority between different courts, and their relations to each other.

First. As to the mode of appointing the judges; this is the same with that of appointing the officers of the Union in general, and has been so fully discussed in the two last numbers, that nothing can be said here which would not be useless repetition.

Second. As to the tenure by which the judges are to hold their places; this chiefly concerns their duration in office; the provisions for their support; the precautions for their responsibility.

According to the plan of the convention, all judges who may be appointed by the United States are to hold their offices DURING GOOD BEHAVIOR; which is conformable to the most approved of the State constitutions and among the rest, to that of this State. Its propriety having been drawn into question by the adversaries of that plan, is no light symptom of the rage for objection, which disorders their imaginations and judgments. The standard of good behavior for the continuance in office of the judicial magistracy, is certainly one of the most valuable of the modern improvements in the practice of government. In a monarchy it is an excellent barrier to the despotism of the prince; in a republic it is a no less excellent barrier to the encroachments and oppressions of the representative body.

And it is the best expedient which can be devised in any government, to secure a steady, upright, and impartial administration of the laws.

Whoever attentively considers the different departments of power must perceive, that, in a government in which they are separated from each other, the judiciary, from the nature of its functions, will always be the least dangerous to the political rights of the Constitution; because it will be least in a capacity to annoy or injure them. The Executive not only dispenses the honors, but holds the sword of the community. The legislature not only commands the purse, but prescribes the rules by which the duties and rights of every citizen are to be regulated. The judiciary, on the contrary, has no influence over either the sword or the purse; no direction either of the strength or of the wealth of the society; and can take no active resolution whatever. It may truly be said to have neither FORCE nor WILL, but merely judgment; and must ultimately depend upon the aid of the executive arm even for the efficacy of its judgments.

This simple view of the matter suggests several important consequences. It proves incontestably, that the judiciary is beyond comparison the weakest of the three departments of power [1]; that it can never attack with success either of the other two; and that all possible care is requisite to enable it to defend itself against their attacks. It equally proves, that though individual oppression may now and then proceed from the courts of justice, the general liberty of the people can never be endangered from that quarter; I mean so long as the judiciary remains truly distinct from both the legislature and the Executive. For I agree, that "there is no liberty, if the power of judging be not separated from the legislative and executive powers." [2] And it proves, in the last place, that as liberty can have nothing to fear from the judiciary alone, but would have every thing to fear from its union with either of the other departments; that as all the effects of such a union must ensue from a dependence of the former on the latter, notwithstanding a nominal and apparent separation; that as, from the natural feebleness of the judiciary, it is in continual jeopardy of being overpowered, awed, or influenced by its co-ordinate branches; and that as nothing can contribute so much to its firmness and independence as permanency in office, this quality may therefore be justly regarded as an indispensable ingredient in its constitution, and, in a great measure, as the citadel of the public justice and the public security.

The complete independence of the courts of justice is peculiarly essential in a limited Constitution. By a limited Constitution, I understand one which contains certain specified exceptions to the legislative authority; such, for instance, as that it shall pass no bills of attainder, no ex-post-facto laws, and the like. Limitations of this kind can be preserved in practice no other way than through the medium of courts of justice, whose duty it must be to declare all acts contrary to the manifest tenor of the Constitution void. Without this, all the reservations of particular rights or privileges would amount to nothing.

Some perplexity respecting the rights of the courts to pronounce legislative acts void, because contrary to the Constitution, has arisen from an imagination that the doctrine would imply a superiority of the judiciary to the legislative power. It is urged that the authority which can declare the acts of another void, must necessarily be superior to the one whose acts may be declared void. As this doctrine is of great importance in all the American constitutions, a brief discussion of the ground on which it rests cannot be unacceptable.

There is no position which depends on clearer principles, than that every act of a delegated authority, contrary to the tenor of the commission under which it is exercised, is void. No legislative act, therefore, contrary to the Constitution, can be valid. To deny this, would be to affirm, that the deputy is greater than his principal; that the servant is above his master; that the representatives of the people are superior to the people themselves; that men acting by virtue of powers, may do not only what their powers do not authorize, but what they forbid.

If it be said that the legislative body are themselves the constitutional judges of their own powers, and that the construction they put upon them is conclusive upon the other departments, it may be answered, that this cannot be the natural presumption, where it is not to be collected from any particular provisions in the Constitution. It is not otherwise to be supposed, that the Constitution could intend to enable the representatives of the people to substitute their WILL to that of their constituents. It is far more rational to suppose, that the courts were designed to be an intermediate body between the people and the legislature, in order, among other things, to keep the latter within the limits assigned to their authority. The interpretation of the laws is the proper and peculiar province of the courts. A constitution is, in fact, and must be regarded by the judges, as a fundamental law. It therefore belongs to them to ascertain its meaning, as well as the meaning of any particular act proceeding from the legislative body. If there should happen to be an irreconcilable variance between the two, that which has the superior obligation and validity ought, of course, to be preferred; or, in other words, the Constitution ought to be preferred to the statute, the intention of the people to the intention of their agents.

Nor does this conclusion by any means suppose a superiority of the judicial to the legislative power. It only supposes that the power of the people is superior to both; and that where the will of the legislature, declared in its statutes, stands in opposition to that of the people, declared in the Constitution, the judges ought to be governed by the latter rather than the former. They ought to regulate their decisions by the fundamental laws, rather than by those which are not fundamental.

This exercise of judicial discretion, in determining between two contradictory laws, is exemplified in a familiar instance. It not uncommonly happens, that there are two statutes existing at one time, clashing in whole or in part with each other, and neither of them containing any repealing clause or expression. In such a case, it is the province of the courts to liquidate and fix their meaning and operation. So far as they can, by any fair construction, be reconciled to each other, reason and law conspire to dictate that this should be done; where this is impracticable, it becomes a matter of necessity to give effect to one, in exclusion of the other. The rule which has obtained in the courts for determining their relative validity is, that the last in order of time shall be preferred to the first. But this is a mere rule of construction, not derived from any positive law, but from the nature and reason of the thing. It is a rule not enjoined upon the courts by legislative provision, but adopted by themselves, as consonant to truth and propriety, for the direction of their conduct as interpreters of the law. They thought it reasonable, that between the interfering acts of an EQUAL authority, that which was the last indication of its will should have the preference.

But in regard to the interfering acts of a superior and subordinate authority, of an original and derivative power, the nature and reason of the thing indicate the converse of that rule as proper to be followed. They teach us that the prior act of a superior ought to be preferred to the subsequent act of an inferior and subordinate authority; and that accordingly, whenever a particular statute contravenes the Constitution, it will be the duty of the judicial tribunals to adhere to the latter and disregard the former.

It can be of no weight to say that the courts, on the pretense of a repugnancy, may substitute their own pleasure to the constitutional intentions of the legislature. This might as well happen in the case of two contradictory statutes; or it might as well happen in every adjudication upon any single statute. The courts must declare the sense of the law; and if they should be disposed to exercise WILL instead of JUDGMENT, the consequence would equally be the substitution of their pleasure to that of the legislative body. The observation, if it prove any thing, would prove that there ought to be no judges distinct from that body.

If, then, the courts of justice are to be considered as the bulwarks of a limited Constitution against legislative encroachments, this consideration will afford a strong argument for the permanent tenure of judicial offices, since nothing will contribute so much as this to that independent spirit in the judges which must be essential to the faithful performance of so arduous a duty.

This independence of the judges is equally requisite to guard the Constitution and the rights of individuals from the effects of those ill humors, which the arts of designing men, or the influence of particular conjunctures, sometimes disseminate among the people themselves, and which, though they speedily give place to better information, and more deliberate reflection, have a tendency, in the meantime, to occasion dangerous innovations in the government, and serious oppressions of the minor party in the community. Though I trust the friends of the proposed Constitution will never concur with its enemies, [3] in questioning that fundamental principle of republican government, which admits the right of the people to alter or abolish the established Constitution, whenever they find it inconsistent with their happiness, yet it is not to be inferred from this principle, that the representatives of the people, whenever a momentary inclination happens to lay hold of a majority of their constituents, incompatible with the provisions in the existing Constitution, would, on that account, be justifiable in a violation of those provisions; or that the courts would be under a greater obligation to connive at infractions in this shape, than when they had proceeded wholly from the cabals of the representative body. Until the people have, by some solemn and authoritative act, annulled or changed the established form, it is binding upon themselves collectively, as well as individually; and no presumption, or even knowledge, of their sentiments, can warrant their representatives in a departure from it, prior to such an act. But it is easy to see, that it would require an uncommon portion of fortitude in the judges to do their duty as faithful guardians of the Constitution, where legislative invasions of it had been instigated by the major voice of the community.

But it is not with a view to infractions of the Constitution only, that the independence of the judges may be an essential safeguard against the effects of occasional ill humors in the society. These sometimes extend no farther than to the injury of the private rights of particular classes of citizens, by unjust and partial laws. Here also the firmness of the judicial magistracy is of vast importance in mitigating the severity and confining the operation of such laws. It not only serves to moderate the immediate mischiefs of those which may have been passed, but it operates as a check upon the legislative body in passing them; who, perceiving that obstacles to the success of iniquitous intention are to be expected from the scruples of the courts, are in a manner compelled, by the very motives of the injustice they meditate, to qualify their attempts. This is a circumstance calculated to have more influence upon the character of our governments, than but few may be aware of. The benefits of the integrity and moderation of the judiciary have already been felt in more States than one; and though they may have displeased those whose sinister expectations they may have disappointed, they must have commanded the esteem and applause of all the virtuous and disinterested. Considerate men, of every description, ought to prize whatever will tend to beget or fortify that temper in the courts: as no man can be sure that he may not be to-morrow the victim of a spirit of injustice, by which he may be a gainer to-day. And every man must now feel, that the inevitable tendency of such a spirit is to sap the foundations of public and private confidence, and to introduce in its stead universal distrust and distress.

That inflexible and uniform adherence to the rights of the Constitution, and of individuals, which we perceive to be indispensable in the courts of justice, can certainly not be expected from judges who hold their offices by a temporary commission. Periodical appointments, however regulated, or by whomsoever made, would, in some way or other, be fatal to their necessary independence. If the power of making them was committed either to the Executive or legislature, there would be danger of an improper complaisance to the branch which possessed it; if to both, there would be an unwillingness to hazard the displeasure of either; if to the people, or to persons chosen by them for the special purpose, there would be too great a disposition to consult popularity, to justify a reliance that nothing would be consulted but the Constitution and the laws.

There is yet a further and a weightier reason for the permanency of the judicial offices, which is deducible from the nature of the qualifications they require. It has been frequently remarked, with great propriety, that a voluminous code of laws is one of the inconveniences necessarily connected with the advantages of a free government. To avoid an arbitrary discretion in the courts, it is indispensable that they should be bound down by strict rules and precedents, which serve to define and point out their duty in every particular case that comes before them; and it will readily be conceived from the variety of controversies which grow out of the folly and wickedness of mankind, that the records of those precedents must unavoidably swell to a very considerable bulk, and must demand long and laborious study to acquire a competent knowledge of them. Hence it is, that there can be but few men in the society who will have sufficient skill in the laws to qualify them for the stations of judges. And making the proper deductions for the ordinary depravity of human nature, the number must be still smaller of those who unite the requisite integrity with the requisite knowledge. These considerations apprise us, that the government can have no great option between fit character; and that a temporary duration in office, which would naturally discourage such characters from quitting a lucrative line of practice to accept a seat on the bench, would have a tendency to throw the administration of justice into hands less able, and less well qualified, to conduct it with utility and dignity. In the present circumstances of this country, and in those in which it is likely to be for a long time to come, the disadvantages on this score would be greater than they may at first sight appear; but it must be confessed, that they are far inferior to those which present themselves under the other aspects of the subject.

Upon the whole, there can be no room to doubt that the convention acted wisely in copying from the models of those constitutions which have established GOOD BEHAVIOR as the tenure of their judicial offices, in point of duration; and that so far from being blamable on this account, their plan would have been inexcusably defective, if it had wanted this important feature of good government. The experience of Great Britain affords an illustrious comment on the excellence of the institution.

PUBLIUS.

[1] The celebrated Montesquieu, speaking of them, says: "Of the three powers above mentioned, the judiciary is next to nothing." "Spirit of Laws." vol. i., page 186.

[2] Idem, page 181.

[3] Vide "Protest of the Minority of the Convention of Pennsylvania," Martin's Speech, etc.

Federalist No. 79
The Judiciary Continued
From McLEAN's Edition, New York.

HAMILTON

To the People of the State of New York:

NEXT to permanency in office, nothing can contribute more to the independence of the judges than a fixed provision for their support. The remark made in relation to the President is equally applicable here. In the general course of human nature, A POWER OVER A MAN's SUBSISTENCE AMOUNTS TO A POWER OVER HIS WILL. And we can never hope to see realized in practice, the complete separation of the judicial from the legislative power, in any system which leaves the former dependent for pecuniary resources on the occasional grants of the latter. The enlightened friends to good government in every State, have seen cause to lament the want of precise and explicit precautions in the State constitutions on this head. Some of these indeed have declared that PERMANENT [1] salaries should be established for the judges; but the experiment has in some instances shown that such expressions are not sufficiently definite to preclude legislative evasions. Something still more positive and unequivocal has been evinced to be requisite. The plan of the convention accordingly has provided that the judges of the United States "shall at STATED TIMES receive for their services a compensation which shall not be DIMINISHED during their continuance in office."

This, all circumstances considered, is the most eligible provision that could have been devised. It will readily be understood that the fluctuations in the value of money and in the state of society rendered a fixed rate of compensation in the Constitution inadmissible. What might be extravagant to-day, might in half a century become penurious and inadequate. It was therefore necessary to leave it to the discretion of the legislature to vary its provisions in conformity to the variations in circumstances, yet under such restrictions as to put it out of the power of that body to change the condition of the individual for the worse. A man may then be sure of the ground upon which he stands, and can never be deterred from his duty by the apprehension of being placed in a less eligible situation. The clause which has been quoted combines both advantages. The salaries of judicial officers may from time to time be altered, as occasion shall require, yet so as never to lessen the allowance with which any particular judge comes into office, in respect to him. It will be observed that a difference has been made by the convention between the compensation of the President and of the judges, That of the former can neither be increased nor diminished; that of the latter can only not be diminished. This probably arose from the difference in the duration of the respective offices. As the President is to be elected for no more than four years, it can rarely happen that an adequate salary, fixed at the commencement of that period, will not continue to be such to its end. But with regard to the judges, who, if they behave properly, will be secured in their places for life, it may well happen, especially in the early stages of the government, that a stipend, which would be very sufficient at their first appointment, would become too small in the progress of their service.

This provision for the support of the judges bears every mark of prudence and efficacy; and it may be safely affirmed that, together with the permanent tenure of their offices, it affords a better prospect of their independence than is discoverable in the constitutions of any of the States in regard to their own judges.

The precautions for their responsibility are comprised in the article respecting impeachments. They are liable to be impeached for malconduct by the House of Representatives, and tried by the Senate; and, if convicted, may be dismissed from office, and disqualified for holding any other. This is the only provision on the point which is consistent with the necessary independence of the judicial character, and is the only one which we find in our own Constitution in respect to our own judges.

The want of a provision for removing the judges on account of inability has been a subject of complaint. But all considerate men will be sensible that such a provision would either not be practiced upon or would be more liable to abuse than calculated to answer any good purpose. The mensuration of the faculties of the mind has, I believe, no place in the catalogue of known arts. An attempt to fix the boundary between the regions of ability and inability, would much oftener give scope to personal and party attachments and enmities than advance the interests of justice or the public good. The result, except in the case of insanity, must for the most part be arbitrary; and insanity, without any formal or express provision, may be safely pronounced to be a virtual disqualification.

The constitution of New York, to avoid investigations that must forever be vague and dangerous, has taken a particular age as the criterion of inability. No man can be a judge beyond sixty. I believe there are few at present who do not disapprove of this provision. There is no station, in relation to which it is less proper than to that of a judge. The deliberating and comparing faculties generally preserve their strength much beyond that period in men who survive it; and when, in addition to this circumstance, we consider how few there are who outlive the season of intellectual vigor, and how improbable it is that any considerable portion of the bench, whether more or less numerous, should be in such a situation at the same time, we shall be ready to conclude that limitations of this sort have little to recommend them. In a republic, where fortunes are not affluent, and pensions not expedient, the dismission of men from stations in which they have served their country long and usefully, on which they depend for subsistence, and from which it will be too late to resort to any other occupation for a livelihood, ought to have some better apology to humanity than is to be found in the imaginary danger of a superannuated bench.

PUBLIUS.

[1] Vide "Constitution of Massachusetts," chapter 2, section I, article 13.

Federalist No. 80

The Powers of the Judiciary
From McLEAN's Edition, New York.
HAMILTON
To the People of the State of New York:

To JUDGE with accuracy of the proper extent of the federal judicature, it will be necessary to consider, in the first place, what are its proper objects.

It seems scarcely to admit of controversy, that the judiciary authority of the Union ought to extend to these several descriptions of cases: 1st, to all those which arise out of the laws of the United States, passed in pursuance of their just and constitutional powers of legislation; 2d, to all those which concern the execution of the provisions expressly contained in the articles of Union; 3d, to all those in which the United States are a party; 4th, to all those which involve the PEACE of the CONFEDERACY, whether they relate to the intercourse between the United States and foreign nations, or to that between the States themselves; 5th, to all those which originate on the high seas, and are of admiralty or maritime jurisdiction; and, lastly, to all those in which the State tribunals cannot be supposed to be impartial and unbiased.

The first point depends upon this obvious consideration, that there ought always to be a constitutional method of giving efficacy to constitutional provisions. What, for instance, would avail restrictions on the authority of the State legislatures, without some constitutional mode of enforcing the observance of them? The States, by the plan of the convention, are prohibited from doing a variety of things, some of which are incompatible with the interests of the Union, and others with the principles of good government. The imposition of duties on imported articles, and the emission of paper money, are specimens of each kind. No man of sense will believe, that such prohibitions would be scrupulously regarded, without some effectual power in the government to restrain or correct the infractions of them. This power must either be a direct negative on the State laws, or an authority in the federal courts to overrule such as might be in manifest contravention of the articles of Union. There is no third course that I can imagine. The latter appears to have been thought by the convention preferable to the former, and, I presume, will be most agreeable to the States.

As to the second point, it is impossible, by any argument or comment, to make it clearer than it is in itself. If there are such things as political axioms, the propriety of the judicial power of a government being coextensive with its legislative, may be ranked among the number. The mere necessity of uniformity in the interpretation of the national laws, decides the question. Thirteen independent courts of final jurisdiction over the same causes, arising upon the same laws, is a hydra in government, from which nothing but contradiction and confusion can proceed.

Still less need be said in regard to the third point. Controversies between the nation and its members or citizens, can only be properly referred to the national tribunals. Any other plan would be contrary to reason, to precedent, and to decorum.

The fourth point rests on this plain proposition, that the peace of the WHOLE ought not to be left at the disposal of a PART. The Union will undoubtedly be answerable to foreign powers for the conduct of its members. And the responsibility for an injury ought ever to be accompanied with the faculty of preventing it. As the denial or perversion of justice by the sentences of courts, as well as in any other manner, is with reason classed among the just causes of war, it will follow that the federal judiciary ought to have cognizance of all causes in which the citizens of other countries are concerned. This is not less essential to the preservation of the public faith, than to the security of the public tranquillity. A distinction may perhaps be imagined between cases arising upon treaties and the laws of nations and those which may stand merely on the footing of the municipal law. The former kind may be supposed proper for the federal jurisdiction, the latter for that of the States. But it is at least problematical, whether an unjust sentence against a foreigner, where the subject of controversy was wholly relative to the lex loci, would not, if unredressed, be an aggression upon his sovereign, as well as one which violated the stipulations of a treaty or the general law of nations. And a still greater objection to the distinction would result from the immense difficulty, if not impossibility, of a practical discrimination between the cases of one complexion and those of the other. So great a proportion of the cases in which foreigners are parties, involve national questions, that it is by far most safe and most expedient to refer all those in which they are concerned to the national tribunals.

The power of determining causes between two States, between one State and the citizens of another, and between the citizens of different States, is perhaps not less essential to the peace of the Union than that which has been just examined. History gives us a horrid picture of the dissensions and private wars which distracted and desolated Germany prior to the institution of the Imperial Chamber by Maximilian, towards the close of the fifteenth century; and informs us, at the same time, of the vast influence of that institution in appeasing the disorders and establishing the tranquillity of the empire. This was a court invested with authority to decide finally all differences among the members of the Germanic body.

A method of terminating territorial disputes between the States, under the authority of the federal head, was not unattended to, even in the imperfect system by which they have been hitherto held together. But there are many other sources, besides interfering claims of boundary, from which bickerings and animosities may spring up among the members of the Union. To some of these we have been witnesses in the course of our past experience. It will readily be conjectured that I allude to the fraudulent laws which have been passed in too many of the States. And though the proposed Constitution establishes particular guards against the repetition of those instances which have heretofore made their appearance, yet it is warrantable to apprehend that the spirit which produced them will assume new shapes, that could not be foreseen nor specifically provided against. Whatever practices may have a tendency to disturb the harmony between the States, are proper objects of federal superintendence and control.

It may be esteemed the basis of the Union, that "the citizens of each State shall be entitled to all the privileges and immunities of citizens of the several States." And if it be a just principle that every government OUGHT TO POSSESS THE MEANS OF EXECUTING ITS OWN PROVISIONS BY ITS OWN AUTHORITY, it will follow, that in order to the inviolable maintenance of that equality of privileges and immunities to which the citizens of the Union will be entitled, the national judiciary ought to preside in all cases in which one State or its citizens are opposed to another State or its citizens. To secure the full effect of so fundamental a provision against all evasion and subterfuge, it is necessary that its construction should be committed to that tribunal which, having no local attachments, will be likely to be impartial between the different States and their citizens, and which, owing its official existence to the Union, will never be likely to feel any bias inauspicious to the principles on which it is founded.

The fifth point will demand little animadversion. The most bigoted idolizers of State authority have not thus far shown a disposition to deny the national judiciary the cognizances of maritime causes. These so generally depend on the laws of nations, and so commonly affect the rights of foreigners, that they fall within the considerations which are relative to the public peace. The most important part of them are, by the present Confederation, submitted to federal jurisdiction.

The reasonableness of the agency of the national courts in cases in which the State tribunals cannot be supposed to be impartial, speaks for itself. No man ought certainly to be a judge in his own cause, or in any cause in respect to which he has the least interest or bias. This principle has no inconsiderable weight in designating the federal courts as the proper tribunals for the determination of controversies between different States and their citizens. And it ought to have the same operation in regard to some cases between citizens of the same State. Claims to land under grants of different States, founded upon adverse pretensions of boundary, are of this description. The courts of neither of the granting States could be expected to be unbiased. The laws may have even prejudged the question, and tied the courts down to decisions in favor of the grants of the State to which they belonged. And even where this had not been done, it would be natural that the judges, as men, should feel a strong predilection to the claims of their own government.

Having thus laid down and discussed the principles which ought to regulate the constitution of the federal judiciary, we will proceed to test, by these principles, the particular powers of which, according to the plan of the convention, it is to be composed. It is to comprehend "all cases in law and equity arising under the Constitution, the laws of the United States, and treaties made, or which shall be made, under their authority; to all cases affecting ambassadors, other public ministers, and consuls; to all cases of admiralty and maritime jurisdiction; to controversies to which the United States shall be a party; to controversies between two or more States; between a State and citizens of another State; between citizens of different States; between citizens of the same State claiming lands and grants of different States; and between a State or the citizens thereof and foreign states, citizens, and subjects." This constitutes the entire mass of the judicial authority of the Union. Let us now review it in detail. It is, then, to extend:

First. To all cases in law and equity, ARISING UNDER THE CONSTITUTION and THE LAWS OF THE UNITED STATES. This corresponds with the two first classes of causes, which have been enumerated, as proper for the jurisdiction of the United States. It has been asked, what is meant by "cases arising under the Constitution," in contradiction from those "arising under the laws of the United States"? The difference has been already explained. All the restrictions upon the authority of the State legislatures furnish examples of it. They are not, for instance, to emit paper money; but the interdiction results from the Constitution, and will have no connection with any law of the United States. Should paper money, notwithstanding, be emited, the controversies concerning it would be cases arising under the Constitution and not the laws of the United States, in the ordinary signification of the terms. This may serve as a sample of the whole.

It has also been asked, what need of the word "equity What equitable causes can grow out of the Constitution and laws of the United States? There is hardly a subject of litigation between individuals, which may not involve those ingredients of FRAUD, ACCIDENT, TRUST, or HARDSHIP, which would render the matter an object of equitable rather than of legal jurisdiction, as the distinction is known and established in several of the States. It is the peculiar province, for instance, of a court of equity to relieve against what are called hard bargains: these are contracts in which, though there may have been no direct fraud or deceit, sufficient to invalidate them in a court of law, yet there may have been some undue and unconscionable advantage taken of the necessities or misfortunes of one of the parties, which a court of equity would not tolerate. In such cases, where foreigners were concerned on either side, it would be impossible for the federal judicatories to do justice without an equitable as well as a legal jurisdiction. Agreements to convey lands claimed under the grants of different States, may afford another example of the necessity of an equitable jurisdiction in the federal courts. This reasoning may not be so palpable in those States where the formal and technical distinction between LAW and EQUITY is not maintained, as in this State, where it is exemplified by every day's practice.

The judiciary authority of the Union is to extend:

Second. To treaties made, or which shall be made, under the authority of the United States, and to all cases affecting ambassadors, other public ministers, and consuls. These belong to the fourth class of the enumerated cases, as they have an evident connection with the preservation of the national peace.

Third. To cases of admiralty and maritime jurisdiction. These form, altogether, the fifth of the enumerated classes of causes proper for the cognizance of the national courts.

Fourth. To controversies to which the United States shall be a party. These constitute the third of those classes.

Fifth. To controversies between two or more States; between a State and citizens of another State; between citizens of different States. These belong to the fourth of those classes, and partake, in some measure, of the nature of the last.

Sixth. To cases between the citizens of the same State, CLAIMING LANDS UNDER GRANTS OF DIFFERENT STATES. These fall within the last class, and ARE THE ONLY INSTANCES IN WHICH THE PROPOSED CONSTITUTION DIRECTLY CONTEMPLATES THE COGNIZANCE OF DISPUTES BETWEEN THE CITIZENS OF THE SAME STATE.

Seventh. To cases between a State and the citizens thereof, and foreign States, citizens, or subjects. These have been already explained to belong to the fourth of the enumerated classes, and have been shown to be, in a peculiar manner, the proper subjects of the national judicature.

From this review of the particular powers of the federal judiciary, as marked out in the Constitution, it appears that they are all conformable to the principles which ought to have governed the structure of that department, and which were necessary to the perfection of the system. If some partial inconveniences should appear to be connected with the incorporation of any of them into the plan, it ought to be recollected that the national legislature will have ample authority to make such EXCEPTIONS, and to prescribe such regulations as will be calculated to obviate or remove these inconveniences. The possibility of particular mischiefs can never be viewed, by a well-informed mind, as a solid objection to a general principle, which is calculated to avoid general mischiefs and to obtain general advantages.

PUBLIUS.

Federalist No. 85

Concluding Remarks

From McLEAN's Edition, New York.

HAMILTON

To the People of the State of New York:

ACCORDING to the formal division of the subject of these papers, announced in my first number, there would appear still to remain for discussion two points: "the analogy of the proposed government to your own State constitution," and "the additional security which its adoption will afford to republican government, to liberty, and to property." But these heads have been so fully anticipated and exhausted in the progress of the work, that it would now scarcely be possible to do any thing more than repeat, in a more dilated form, what has been heretofore said, which the advanced stage of the question, and the time already spent upon it, conspire to forbid.

It is remarkable, that the resemblance of the plan of the convention to the act which organizes the government of this State holds, not less with regard to many of the supposed defects, than to the real excellences of the former. Among the pretended defects are the re-eligibility of the Executive, the want of a council, the omission of a formal bill of rights, the omission of a provision respecting the liberty of the press. These and several others which have been noted in the course of our inquiries are as much chargeable on the existing constitution of this State, as on the one proposed for the Union; and a man must have slender pretensions to consistency, who can rail at the latter for imperfections which he finds no difficulty in excusing in the former. Nor indeed can there be a better proof of the insincerity and affectation of some of the zealous adversaries of the plan of the convention among us, who profess to be the devoted admirers of the government under which they live, than the fury with which they have attacked that plan, for matters in regard to which our own constitution is equally or perhaps more vulnerable.

The additional securities to republican government, to liberty and to property, to be derived from the adoption of the plan under consideration, consist chiefly in the restraints which the preservation of the Union will impose on local factions and insurrections, and on the ambition of powerful individuals in single States, who may acquire credit and influence enough, from leaders and favorites, to become the despots of the people; in the diminution of the opportunities to foreign intrigue, which the dissolution of the Confederacy would invite and facilitate; in the prevention of extensive military establishments, which could not fail to grow out of wars between the States in a disunited situation; in the express guaranty of a republican form of government to each; in the absolute and universal exclusion of titles of nobility; and in the precautions against the repetition of those practices on the part of the State governments which have undermined the foundations of property and credit, have planted mutual distrust in the breasts of all classes of citizens, and have occasioned an almost universal prostration of morals.

Thus have I, fellow-citizens, executed the task I had assigned to myself; with what success, your conduct must determine. I trust at least you will admit that I have not failed in the assurance I gave you respecting the spirit with which my endeavors should be conducted. I have addressed myself purely to your judgments, and have studiously avoided those asperities which are too apt to disgrace political disputants of all parties, and which have been not a little provoked by the language and conduct of the opponents of the Constitution. The charge of a conspiracy against the liberties of the people, which has been indiscriminately brought against the advocates of the plan, has something in it too wanton and too malignant, not to excite the indignation of every man who feels in his own bosom a refutation of the calumny. The perpetual changes which have been rung upon the wealthy, the well-born, and the great, have been such as to inspire the disgust of all sensible men. And the unwarrantable concealments and misrepresentations which have been in various ways practiced to keep the truth from the public eye, have been of a nature to demand the reprobation of all honest men. It is not impossible that these circumstances may have occasionally betrayed me into intemperances of expression which I did not intend; it is certain that I have frequently felt a struggle between sensibility and moderation; and if the former has in some instances prevailed, it must be my excuse that it has been neither often nor much.

Let us now pause and ask ourselves whether, in the course of these papers, the proposed Constitution has not been satisfactorily vindicated from the aspersions thrown upon it; and whether it has not been shown to be worthy of the public approbation, and necessary to the public safety and prosperity. Every man is bound to answer these questions to himself, according to the best of his conscience and understanding, and to act agreeably to the genuine and sober dictates of his judgment. This is a duty from which nothing can give him a dispensation. 'Tis one that he is called upon, nay, constrained by all the obligations that form the bands of society, to discharge sincerely and honestly. No partial motive, no particular interest, no pride of opinion, no temporary passion or prejudice, will justify to himself, to his country, or to his posterity, an improper election of the part he is to act. Let him beware of an obstinate adherence to party; let him reflect that the object upon which he is to decide is not a particular interest of the community, but the very existence of the nation; and let him remember that a majority of America has already given its sanction to the plan which he is to approve or reject.

I shall not dissemble that I feel an entire confidence in the arguments which recommend the proposed system to your adoption, and that I am unable to discern any real force in those by which it has been opposed. I am persuaded that it is the best which our political situation, habits, and opinions will admit, and superior to any the revolution has produced.

Concessions on the part of the friends of the plan, that it has not a claim to absolute perfection, have afforded matter of no small triumph to its enemies. "Why," say they, "should we adopt an imperfect thing? Why not amend it and make it perfect before it is irrevocably established?" This may be plausible enough, but it is only plausible. In the first place I remark, that the extent of these concessions has been greatly exaggerated. They have been stated as amounting to an admission that the plan is radically defective, and that without material alterations the rights and the interests of the community cannot be safely confided to it. This, as far as I have understood the meaning of those who make the concessions, is an entire perversion of their sense. No advocate of the measure can be found, who will not declare as his sentiment, that the system, though it may not be perfect in every part, is, upon the whole, a good one; is the best that the present views and circumstances of the country will permit; and is such an one as promises every species of security which a reasonable people can desire.

I answer in the next place, that I should esteem it the extreme of imprudence to prolong the precarious state of our national affairs, and to expose the Union to the jeopardy of successive experiments, in the chimerical pursuit of a perfect plan. I never expect to see a perfect work from imperfect man. The result of the deliberations of all collective bodies must necessarily be a compound, as well of the errors and prejudices, as of the good sense and wisdom, of the individuals of whom they are composed. The compacts which are to embrace thirteen distinct States in a common bond of amity and union, must as necessarily be a compromise of as many dissimilar interests and inclinations. How can perfection spring from such materials?

The reasons assigned in an excellent little pamphlet lately published in this city,[1] are unanswerable to show the utter improbability of assembling a new convention, under circumstances in any degree so favorable to a happy issue, as those in which the late convention met, deliberated, and concluded. I will not repeat the arguments there used, as I presume the production itself has had an extensive circulation. It is certainly well worthy the perusal of every friend to his country. There is, however, one point of light in which the subject of amendments still remains to be considered, and in which it has not yet been exhibited to public view. I cannot resolve to conclude without first taking a survey of it in this aspect.

It appears to me susceptible of absolute demonstration, that it will be far more easy to obtain subsequent than previous amendments to the Constitution. The moment an alteration is made in the present plan, it becomes, to the purpose of adoption, a new one, and must undergo a new decision of each State. To its complete establishment throughout the Union, it will therefore require the concurrence of thirteen States. If, on the contrary, the Constitution proposed should once be ratified by all the States as it stands, alterations in it may at any time be effected by nine States. Here, then, the chances are as thirteen to nine [2] in favor of subsequent amendment, rather than of the original adoption of an entire system.

This is not all. Every Constitution for the United States must inevitably consist of a great variety of particulars, in which thirteen independent States are to be accommodated in their interests or opinions of interest. We may of course expect to see, in any body of men charged with its original formation, very different combinations of the parts upon different points. Many of those who form a majority on one question, may become the minority on a second, and an association dissimilar to either may constitute the majority on a third. Hence the necessity of moulding and arranging all the particulars which are to compose the whole, in such a manner as to satisfy all the parties to the compact; and hence, also, an immense multiplication of difficulties and casualties in obtaining the collective assent to a final act. The degree of that multiplication must evidently be in a ratio to the number of particulars and the number of parties.

But every amendment to the Constitution, if once established, would be a single proposition, and might be brought forward singly. There would then be no necessity for management or compromise, in relation to any other point no giving nor taking. The will of the requisite number would at once bring the matter to a decisive issue. And consequently, whenever nine, or rather ten States, were united in the desire of a particular amendment, that amendment must infallibly take place. There can, therefore, be no comparison between the facility of affecting an amendment, and that of establishing in the first instance a complete Constitution.

In opposition to the probability of subsequent amendments, it has been urged that the persons delegated to the administration of the national government will always be disinclined to yield up any portion of the authority of which they were once possessed. For my own part I acknowledge a thorough conviction that any amendments which may, upon mature consideration, be thought useful, will be applicable to the organization of the government, not to the mass of its powers; and on this account alone, I think there is no weight in the observation just stated. I also think there is little weight in it on another account. The intrinsic difficulty of governing thirteen States at any rate, independent of calculations upon an ordinary degree of public spirit and integrity, will, in my opinion constantly impose on the national rulers the necessity of a spirit of accommodation to the reasonable expectations of their constituents. But there is yet a further consideration, which proves beyond the possibility of a doubt, that the observation is futile. It is this that the national rulers, whenever nine States concur, will have no option upon the subject. By the fifth article of the plan, the Congress will be obliged "on the application of the legislatures of two thirds of the States, which at present amount to nine, to call a convention for proposing amendments, which shall be valid, to all intents and purposes, as part of the Constitution, when ratified by the legislatures of three fourths of the States, or by conventions in three fourths thereof." The words of this article are peremptory. The Congress "shall call a convention." Nothing in this particular is left to the discretion of that body. And of consequence, all the declamation about the disinclination to a change vanishes in air. Nor however difficult it may be supposed to unite two thirds or three fourths of the State legislatures, in amendments which may affect local interests, can there be any room to apprehend any such difficulty in a union on points which are merely relative to the general liberty or security of the people. We may safely rely on the disposition of the State legislatures to erect barriers against the encroachments of the national authority.

If the foregoing argument is a fallacy, certain it is that I am myself deceived by it, for it is, in my conception, one of those rare instances in which a political truth can be brought to the test of a mathematical demonstration. Those who see the matter in the same light with me, however zealous they may be for amendments, must agree in the propriety of a previous adoption, as the most direct road to their own object.

The zeal for attempts to amend, prior to the establishment of the Constitution, must abate in every man who is ready to accede to the truth of the following observations of a writer equally solid and ingenious: "To balance a large state or society, whether monarchical or republican, on general laws, is a work of so great difficulty, that no human genius, however comprehensive, is able, by the mere dint of reason and reflection, to effect it. The judgments of many must unite in the work; experience must guide their labor; time must bring it to perfection, and the feeling of inconveniences must correct the mistakes which they INEVITABLY fall into in their first trials and experiments."[3] These judicious reflections contain a lesson of moderation to all the sincere lovers of the Union, and ought to put them upon their guard against hazarding anarchy, civil war, a perpetual alienation of the States from each other, and perhaps the military despotism of a victorious demagogue, in the pursuit of what they are not likely to obtain, but from time and experience. It may be in me a defect of political fortitude, but I acknowledge that I cannot entertain an equal tranquillity with those who affect to treat the dangers of a longer continuance in our present situation as imaginary. A nation, without a national government, is, in my view, an awful spectacle. The establishment of a Constitution, in time of profound peace, by the voluntary consent of a whole people, is a prodigy, to the completion of which I look forward with trembling anxiety. I can reconcile it to no rules of prudence to let go the hold we now have, in so arduous an enterprise, upon seven out of the thirteen States, and after having passed over so considerable a part of the ground, to recommence the course. I dread the more the consequences of new attempts, because I know that powerful individuals, in this and in other States, are enemies to a general national government in every possible shape.

PUBLIUS.

[1] Entitled "An Address to the People of the State of New York."

[2] It may rather be said TEN, for though two thirds may set on foot the measure, three fourths must ratify.

[3] Hume's "Essays," vol. i., page 128: "The Rise of Arts and Sciences."

The Northwest Ordinance

An Ordinance for the government of the Territory of the United States northwest of the River Ohio.

Section 1. Be it ordained by the United States in Congress assembled, That the said territory, for the purposes of temporary government, be one district, subject, however, to be divided into two districts, as future circumstances may, in the opinion of Congress, make it expedient.

Sec 2. Be it ordained by the authority aforesaid, That the estates, both of resident and nonresident proprietors in the said territory, dying intestate, shall descent to, and be distributed among their children, and the descendants of a deceased child, in equal parts; the descendants of a deceased child or grandchild to take the share of their deceased parent in equal parts among them: And where there shall be no children or descendants, then in equal parts to the next of kin in equal degree; and among the children of a deceased brother or sister of the intestate shall have, in equal parts among them, their deceased parents' share; and there shall in no case be a distinction between kindred of the whole and half blood; saving, in all cases, to the widow of the intestate her third part of the real estate for life, and one third part of the personal estate; and this law relative to descents and dower, shall remain in full force until altered by the legislature of the district. And until the governor and judges shall adopt laws as hereinafter mentioned, estates in the said territory may be devised or bequeathed by wills in writing, signed and sealed by him or her in whom the estate may be (being of full age), and attested by three witnesses; and real estates may be conveyed by lease and release, or bargain and sale, signed, sealed and delivered by the person being of full age, in whom the estate may be, and attested by two witnesses, provided such wills be duly proved, and such conveyances be acknowledged, or the execution thereof duly proved, and be recorded within one year after proper magistrates, courts, and registers shall be appointed for that purpose; and personal property may be transferred by delivery; saving, however to the French and

Canadian inhabitants, and other settlers of the Kaskaskies, St. Vincents and the neighboring villages who have heretofore professed themselves citizens of Virginia, their laws and customs now in force among them, relative to the descent and conveyance, of property.

Sec. 3. Be it ordained by the authority aforesaid, That there shall be appointed from time to time by Congress, a governor, whose commission shall continue in force for the term of three years, unless sooner revoked by Congress; he shall reside in the district, and have a freehold estate therein in 1,000 acres of land, while in the exercise of his office.

Sec. 4. There shall be appointed from time to time by Congress, a secretary, whose commission shall continue in force for four years unless sooner revoked; he shall reside in the district, and have a freehold estate therein in 500 acres of land, while in the exercise of his office. It shall be his duty to keep and preserve the acts and laws passed by the legislature, and the public records of the district, and the proceedings of the governor in his executive department, and transmit authentic copies of such acts and proceedings, every six months, to the Secretary of Congress: There shall also be appointed a court to consist of three judges, any two of whom to form a court, who shall have a common law jurisdiction, and reside in the district, and have each therein a freehold estate in 500 acres of land while in the exercise of their offices; and their commissions shall continue in force during good behavior.

Sec. 5. The governor and judges, or a majority of them, shall adopt and publish in the district such laws of the original States, criminal and civil, as may be necessary and best suited to the circumstances of the district, and report them to Congress from time to time: which laws shall be in force in the district until the organization of the General Assembly therein, unless disapproved of by Congress; but afterwards the Legislature shall have authority to alter them as they shall think fit.

Sec. 6. The governor, for the time being, shall be commander in chief of the militia, appoint and commission all officers in the same below the rank of general officers; all general officers shall be appointed and commissioned by Congress.

Sec. 7. Previous to the organization of the general assembly, the governor shall appoint such magistrates and other civil officers in each county or township, as he shall find necessary for the preservation of the peace and good order in the same: After the general assembly shall be organized, the powers and duties of the magistrates and other civil officers shall be regulated and defined by the said assembly; but all magistrates and other civil officers not herein otherwise directed, shall during the continuance of this temporary government, be appointed by the governor.

Sec. 8. For the prevention of crimes and injuries, the laws to be adopted or made shall have force in all parts of the district, and for the execution of process, criminal and civil, the governor shall make proper divisions thereof; and he shall proceed from time to time as circumstances may require, to lay out the parts of the district in which the Indian titles shall have been extinguished, into counties and townships, subject, however, to such alterations as may thereafter be made by the legislature.

Sec. 9. So soon as there shall be five thousand free male inhabitants of full age in the district, upon giving proof thereof to the governor, they shall receive authority, with time and place, to elect a representative from their counties or townships to represent them in the general assembly: Provided, That, for every five hundred free male inhabitants, there shall be one representative, and so on progressively with the number of free male inhabitants shall the right of representation increase, until the number of representatives shall amount to twenty five; after which, the number and proportion of representatives shall be regulated by the legislature: Provided, That no person be eligible or qualified to act as a representative unless he shall have been a citizen of one of the United States three years, and be a resident in the district, or unless he shall have resided in the district three years; and, in either case, shall likewise hold in his own right, in fee simple, two hundred acres of land within the same; Provided, also, That a freehold in fifty acres of land in the district, having been a citizen of one of the states, and being resident in the district, or the like freehold and two years residence in the district, shall be necessary to qualify a man as an elector of a representative.

Sec. 10. The representatives thus elected, shall serve for the term of two years; and, in case of the death of a representative, or removal from office, the governor shall issue a writ to the county or township for which he was a member, to elect another in his stead, to serve for the residue of the term.

Sec. 11. The general assembly or legislature shall consist of the governor, legislative council, and a house of representatives. The Legislative Council shall consist of five members, to continue in office five years, unless sooner removed by Congress; any three of whom to be a quorum: and the members of the Council shall be nominated and appointed in the following manner, to wit: As soon as representatives shall be elected, the Governor shall appoint a time and place for them to meet together; and, when met, they shall nominate ten persons, residents in the district, and each possessed of a freehold in five hundred acres of land, and return their names to Congress; five of whom Congress shall appoint and commission to serve as aforesaid; and, whenever a vacancy shall happen in the council, by death or removal from office, the house of representatives shall nominate two persons, qualified as aforesaid, for each vacancy, and return their names to Congress; one of whom congress shall appoint and commission for the residue of the term. And every five years, four months at least before the expiration of the time of service of the members of council, the said house shall nominate ten persons, qualified as aforesaid, and return their names to Congress; five of whom Congress shall appoint and commission to serve as members of the council five years, unless sooner removed. And the governor, legislative council, and house of representatives, shall have authority to make laws in all cases, for the good government of the district, not repugnant to the principles and articles in this ordinance established and declared. And all bills, having passed by a majority in the house, and by a majority in the council, shall be referred to the governor for his assent; but no bill, or legislative act whatever, shall be of any force without his assent. The governor shall have power to convene, prorogue, and dissolve the general assembly, when, in his opinion, it shall be expedient.

Sec. 12. The governor, judges, legislative council, secretary, and such other officers as Congress shall appoint in the district, shall take an oath or affirmation of fidelity and of office; the governor before the president of congress, and all other officers before the Governor. As soon as a legislature shall be formed in the district, the council and house assembled in one room, shall have authority, by joint ballot, to elect a delegate to Congress, who shall have a seat in Congress, with a right of debating but not voting during this temporary government.

Sec. 13. And, for extending the fundamental principles of civil and religious liberty, which form the basis whereon these republics, their laws and constitutions are erected; to fix and establish those principles as the basis of all laws, constitutions, and governments, which forever hereafter shall be formed in the said territory: to provide also for the establishment of States, and permanent government therein, and for their admission to a share in the federal councils on an equal footing with the original States, at as early periods as may be consistent with the general interest:

Sec. 14. It is hereby ordained and declared by the authority aforesaid, That the following articles shall be considered as articles of compact between the original States and the people and States in the said territory and forever remain unalterable, unless by common consent, to wit:

Art. 1. No person, demeaning himself in a peaceable and orderly manner, shall ever be molested on account of his mode of worship or religious sentiments, in the said territory.

Art. 2. The inhabitants of the said territory shall always be entitled to the benefits of the writ of habeas corpus, and of the trial by jury; of a proportionate representation of the people in the legislature; and of judicial proceedings according to the course of the common law. All persons shall be bailable, unless for capital offenses, where the proof shall be evident or the presumption great. All fines shall be moderate; and no cruel or unusual punishments shall be inflicted. No man shall be deprived of his liberty or property, but by the judgment of his peers or the law of the land; and, should the public exigencies make it necessary, for the common preservation, to take any person's property, or to demand his particular services, full compensation shall be made for the same. And, in the just preservation of rights and property, it is understood and declared, that no law ought ever to be made, or have force in the said territory, that shall, in any manner whatever, interfere with or affect private contracts or engagements, bona fide, and without fraud, previously formed.

Art. 3. Religion, morality, and knowledge, being necessary to good government and the happiness of mankind, schools and the means of education shall forever be encouraged. The utmost good faith shall always be observed towards the Indians; their lands and property shall never be taken from them without their consent; and, in their property, rights, and liberty, they shall never be invaded or disturbed, unless in just and lawful wars authorized by Congress; but laws founded in justice and humanity, shall from time to time be made for preventing wrongs being done to them, and for preserving peace and friendship with them.

Art. 4. The said territory, and the States which may be formed therein, shall forever remain a part of this Confederacy of the United States of America, subject to the Articles of Confederation, and to such alterations therein as shall be constitutionally made; and to all the acts and ordinances of the United States in Congress assembled, conformable thereto. The inhabitants and settlers in the said territory shall be subject to pay a part of the federal debts contracted or to be contracted, and a proportional part of the expenses of government, to be apportioned on them by Congress according to the same common rule and measure by which apportionments thereof shall be made on the other States; and the taxes for paying their proportion shall be laid and levied by the authority and direction of the legislatures of the district or districts, or new States, as in the original States, within the time agreed upon by the United States in Congress assembled. The legislatures of those districts or new States, shall never interfere with the primary disposal of the soil by the United States in Congress assembled, nor with any regulations Congress may find necessary for securing the title in such soil to the bona fide purchasers. No tax shall be imposed on lands the property of the United States; and, in no case, shall nonresident proprietors be taxed higher than residents. The navigable waters leading into the Mississippi and St. Lawrence, and the carrying places between the same, shall be common highways and forever free, as well to the inhabitants of the said territory as to the citizens of the United States, and those of any other States that may be admitted into the confederacy, without any tax, impost, or duty therefor.

Art. 5. There shall be formed in the said territory, not less than three nor more than five States; and the boundaries of the States, as soon as Virginia shall alter her act of cession, and consent to the same, shall become fixed and established as follows, to wit: The western State in the said territory, shall be bounded by the Mississippi, the Ohio, and Wabash Rivers; a direct line drawn from the Wabash and Post Vincents, due North, to the territorial line between the United States and

Canada; and, by the said territorial line, to the Lake of the Woods and Mississippi. The middle State shall be bounded by the said direct line, the Wabash from Post Vincents to the Ohio, by the Ohio, by a direct line, drawn due north from the mouth of the Great Miami, to the said territorial line, and by the said territorial line. The eastern State shall be bounded by the last mentioned direct line, the Ohio, Pennsylvania, and the said territorial line: Provided, however, and it is further understood and declared, that the boundaries of these three States shall be subject so far to be altered, that, if Congress shall hereafter find it expedient, they shall have authority to form one or two States in that part of the said territory which lies north of an east and west line drawn through the southerly bend or extreme of Lake Michigan. And, whenever any of the said States shall have sixty thousand free inhabitants therein, such State shall be admitted, by its delegates, into the Congress of the United States, on an equal footing with the original States in all respects whatever, and shall be at liberty to form a permanent constitution and State government: Provided, the constitution and government so to be formed, shall be republican, and in conformity to the principles contained in these articles; and, so far as it can be consistent with the general interest of the confederacy, such admission shall be allowed at an earlier period, and when there may be a less number of free inhabitants in the State than sixty thousand.

Art. 6. There shall be neither slavery nor involuntary servitude in the said territory, otherwise than in the punishment of crimes whereof the party shall have been duly convicted: Provided, always, That any person escaping into the same, from whom labor or service is lawfully claimed in any one of the original States, such fugitive may be lawfully reclaimed and conveyed to the person claiming his or her labor or service as aforesaid.

Be it ordained by the authority aforesaid, That the resolutions of the 23rd of April, 1784, relative to the subject of this ordinance, be, and the same are hereby repealed and declared null and void.

Done by the United States, in Congress assembled, the 13th day of July, in the year of our Lord 1787, and of their sovereignty and independence the twelfth.

Washington's Farewell Address

Friends and Fellow Citizens:

The period for a new election of a citizen to administer the executive government of the United States being not far distant, and the time actually arrived when your thoughts must be employed in designating the person who is to be clothed with that important trust, it appears to me proper, especially as it may conduce to a more distinct expression of the public voice, that I should now apprise you of the resolution I have formed, to decline being considered among the number of those out of whom a choice is to be made.

I beg you, at the same time, to do me the justice to be assured that this resolution has not been taken without a strict regard to all the considerations appertaining to the relation which binds a dutiful citizen to his country; and that in withdrawing the tender of service, which silence in my situation might imply, I am influenced by no diminution of zeal for your future interest, no deficiency of grateful respect for your past kindness, but am supported by a full conviction that the step is compatible with both.

The acceptance of, and continuance hitherto in, the office to which your suffrages have twice called me have been a uniform sacrifice of inclination to the opinion of duty and to a deference for what appeared to be your desire. I constantly hoped that it would have been much earlier in my power, consistently with motives which I was not at liberty to disregard, to return to that retirement from which I had been reluctantly drawn. The strength of my inclination to do this, previous to the last election, had even led to the preparation of an address to declare it to you; but mature reflection on the then perplexed and critical posture of our affairs with foreign nations, and the unanimous advice of persons entitled to my confidence, impelled me to abandon the idea.

I rejoice that the state of your concerns, external as well as internal, no longer renders the pursuit of inclination incompatible with the sentiment of duty or propriety, and am persuaded, whatever partiality may be retained for my services, that, in the present circumstances of our country, you will not disapprove my determination to retire.

The impressions with which I first undertook the arduous trust were explained on the proper occasion. In the discharge of this trust, I will only say that I have, with good intentions, contributed towards the organization and administration of the government the best exertions of which a very fallible judgment was capable. Not unconscious in the outset of the inferiority of my qualifications, experience in my own eyes, perhaps still more in the eyes of others, has strengthened the motives to diffidence of myself; and every day the increasing weight of years admonishes me more and more that the shade of retirement is as necessary to me as it will be welcome. Satisfied that if any circumstances have given peculiar value to my services, they were temporary, I have the consolation to believe that, while choice and prudence invite me to quit the political scene, patriotism does not forbid it.

In looking forward to the moment which is intended to terminate the career of my public life, my feelings do not permit me to suspend the deep acknowledgment of that debt of gratitude which I owe to my beloved country for the many honors it has conferred upon me; still more for the steadfast confidence with which it has supported me; and for the opportunities I have thence enjoyed of manifesting my inviolable attachment, by services faithful and persevering, though in usefulness unequal to my zeal. If benefits have resulted to our country from these services, let it always be remembered to your praise, and as an instructive example in our annals, that under circumstances in which the passions, agitated in every direction, were liable to mislead, amidst appearances sometimes dubious, vicissitudes of fortune often discouraging, in situations in which not unfrequently want of success has countenanced the spirit of criticism, the constancy of your support was the essential prop of the efforts, and a guarantee of the plans by which they were effected. Profoundly penetrated with this idea, I shall carry it with me to my grave, as a strong incitement to unceasing vows that heaven may continue to you the choicest tokens of its beneficence; that your union and brotherly affection may be perpetual; that the free Constitution, which is the work of your hands, may be sacredly maintained; that its administration in every department may be stamped with wisdom and virtue; that, in fine, the happiness of the people of these States, under the auspices of liberty, may be made complete by so careful a preservation and so prudent a use of this blessing as will acquire to them the glory of recommending it to the applause, the affection, and adoption of every nation which is yet a stranger to it.

Here, perhaps, I ought to stop. But a solicitude for your welfare, which cannot end but with my life, and the apprehension of danger, natural to that solicitude, urge me, on an occasion like the present, to offer to your solemn contemplation, and to recommend to your frequent review, some sentiments which are the result of much reflection, of no inconsiderable observation, and which appear to me all-important to the permanency of your felicity as a people. These will be offered to you with the more freedom, as you can only see in them the disinterested warnings of a parting friend, who can possibly have no personal motive to bias his counsel. Nor can I forget, as an encouragement to it, your indulgent reception of my sentiments on a former and not dissimilar occasion.

Interwoven as is the love of liberty with every ligament of your hearts, no recommendation of mine is necessary to fortify or confirm the attachment.

The unity of government which constitutes you one people is also now dear to you. It is justly so, for it is a main pillar in the edifice of your real independence, the support of your tranquility at home, your peace abroad; of your safety; of your prosperity; of that very liberty which you so highly prize. But as it is easy to foresee that, from different causes and from different quarters, much pains will be taken, many artifices employed to weaken in your minds the conviction of this truth; as this is the point in your political fortress against which the batteries of internal and external enemies will be most constantly and actively (though often covertly and insidiously) directed, it is of infinite moment that you should properly estimate the immense value of your national union to your collective and individual happiness; that you should cherish a cordial, habitual, and immovable attachment to it; accustoming yourselves to think and speak of it as of the palladium of your political safety and prosperity; watching for its preservation with jealous anxiety; discountenancing whatever may suggest even a suspicion that it can in any event be abandoned; and indignantly frowning upon the first dawning of every attempt to alienate any portion of our country from the rest, or to enfeeble the sacred ties which now link together the various parts.

For this you have every inducement of sympathy and interest. Citizens, by birth or choice, of a common country, that country has a right to concentrate your affections. The name of American, which belongs to you in your national capacity, must always exalt the just pride of patriotism more than any appellation derived from local discriminations. With slight shades of difference, you have the same religion, manners, habits, and political principles. You have in a common cause fought and triumphed together; the independence and liberty you possess are the work of joint counsels, and joint efforts of common dangers, sufferings, and successes.

But these considerations, however powerfully they address themselves to your sensibility, are greatly outweighed by those which apply more immediately to your interest. Here every portion of our country finds the most commanding motives for carefully guarding and preserving the union of the whole.

The North, in an unrestrained intercourse with the South, protected by the equal laws of a common government, finds in the productions of the latter great additional resources of maritime and commercial enterprise and precious materials of manufacturing industry. The South, in the same intercourse, benefiting by the agency of the North, sees its agriculture grow and its commerce expand. Turning partly into its own channels the seamen of the North, it finds its particular navigation invigorated; and, while it contributes, in different ways, to nourish and increase the general mass of the national navigation, it looks forward to the protection of a maritime strength, to which itself is unequally adapted. The East, in a like intercourse with the West, already finds, and in the progressive improvement of interior communications by land and water, will more and more find a valuable vent for the commodities which it brings from abroad, or manufactures at home. The West derives from the East supplies requisite to its growth and comfort, and, what is perhaps of still greater consequence, it must of necessity owe the secure enjoyment of indispensable outlets for its own productions to the weight, influence, and the future maritime strength of the Atlantic side of the Union, directed by an indissoluble community of interest as one nation. Any other tenure by which the West can hold this essential advantage, whether derived from its own separate strength, or from an apostate and unnatural connection with any foreign power, must be intrinsically precarious.

While, then, every part of our country thus feels an immediate and particular interest in union, all the parts combined cannot fail to find in the united mass of means and efforts greater strength, greater resource, proportionably greater security from external danger, a less frequent interruption of their peace by foreign nations; and, what is of inestimable value, they must derive from union an exemption from those broils and wars between themselves, which so frequently afflict neighboring countries not tied together by the same governments, which their own rival ships alone would be sufficient to produce, but which opposite foreign alliances, attachments, and intrigues would stimulate and embitter. Hence, likewise, they will avoid the necessity of those overgrown military establishments which, under any form of government, are inauspicious to liberty, and which are to be regarded as particularly hostile to republican liberty. In this sense it is that your union ought to be considered as a main prop of your liberty, and that the love of the one ought to endear to you the preservation of the other.

These considerations speak a persuasive language to every reflecting and virtuous mind, and exhibit the continuance of the Union as a primary object of patriotic desire. Is there a doubt whether a common government can embrace so large a sphere? Let experience solve it. To listen to mere speculation in such a case were criminal. We are authorized to hope that a proper organization of the whole with the auxiliary agency of governments for the respective subdivisions, will afford a happy issue to the experiment. It is well worth a fair and full experiment. With such powerful and obvious motives to union, affecting all parts of our country, while experience shall not have demonstrated its impracticability, there will always be reason to distrust the patriotism of those who in any quarter may endeavor to weaken its bands.

In contemplating the causes which may disturb our Union, it occurs as matter of serious concern that any ground should have been furnished for characterizing parties by geographical discriminations, Northern and Southern, Atlantic and Western; whence designing men may endeavor to excite a belief that there is a real difference of local interests and views. One of the expedients of party to acquire influence within particular districts is to misrepresent the opinions and aims of other districts. You cannot shield yourselves too much against the jealousies and heartburnings which spring from these misrepresentations; they tend to render alien to each other those who ought to be bound together by fraternal affection. The inhabitants of our Western country have lately had a useful lesson on this head; they have seen, in the negotiation by the Executive, and in the unanimous ratification by the Senate, of the treaty with Spain, and in the universal satisfaction at that event, throughout the United States, a decisive proof how unfounded were the suspicions propagated among them of a policy in the General Government and in the Atlantic States unfriendly to their interests in regard to the Mississippi; they have been witnesses to the formation of two treaties, that with Great Britain, and that with Spain, which secure to them everything they could desire, in respect to our foreign relations, towards confirming their prosperity. Will it not be their wisdom to rely for the preservation of these advantages on the Union by which they were procured ? Will they not henceforth be deaf to those advisers, if such there are, who would sever them from their brethren and connect them with aliens?

To the efficacy and permanency of your Union, a government for the whole is indispensable. No alliance, however strict, between the parts can be an adequate substitute; they must inevitably experience the infractions and interruptions which all alliances in all times have experienced. Sensible of this momentous truth, you have improved upon your first essay, by the adoption of a constitution of government better calculated than your former for an intimate union, and for the efficacious management of your common concerns. This government, the offspring of our own choice, uninfluenced and unawed, adopted upon full investigation and mature deliberation, completely free in its principles, in the distribution of its powers, uniting security with energy, and containing within itself a provision for its own amendment, has a just claim to your confidence and your support. Respect for its authority, compliance with its laws, acquiescence in its measures, are duties enjoined by the fundamental maxims of true liberty. The basis of our political systems is the right of the people to make and to alter their constitutions of government. But the Constitution which at any time exists, till changed by an explicit and authentic act of the whole people, is sacredly obligatory upon all. The very idea of the power and the right of the people to establish government presupposes the duty of every individual to obey the established government.

All obstructions to the execution of the laws, all combinations and associations, under whatever plausible character, with the real design to direct, control, counteract, or awe the regular deliberation and action of the constituted authorities, are destructive of this fundamental principle, and of fatal tendency. They serve to organize faction, to give it an artificial and extraordinary force; to put, in the place of the delegated will of the nation the will of a party, often a small but artful and enterprising minority of the community; and, according to the alternate triumphs of different parties, to make the public administration the mirror of the ill-concerted and incongruous projects of faction, rather than the organ of consistent and wholesome plans digested by common counsels and modified by mutual interests.

However combinations or associations of the above description may now and then answer popular ends, they are likely, in the course of time and things, to become potent engines, by which cunning, ambitious, and unprincipled men will be enabled to subvert the power of the people and to usurp for themselves the reins of government, destroying afterwards the very engines which have lifted them to unjust dominion.

Towards the preservation of your government, and the permanency of your present happy state, it is requisite, not only that you steadily discountenance irregular oppositions to its acknowledged authority, but also that you resist with care the spirit of innovation upon its principles, however specious the pretexts. One method of assault may be to effect, in the forms of the Constitution, alterations which will impair the energy of the system, and thus to undermine what cannot be directly overthrown. In all the changes to which you may be invited, remember that time and habit are at least as necessary to fix the true character of governments as of other human institutions; that experience is the surest standard by which to test the real tendency of the existing constitution of a country; that facility in changes, upon the credit of mere hypothesis and opinion, exposes to perpetual change, from the endless variety of hypothesis and opinion; and remember, especially, that for the efficient management of your common interests, in a country so extensive as ours, a government of as much vigor as is consistent with the perfect security of liberty is indispensable. Liberty itself will find in such a government, with powers properly distributed and adjusted, its surest guardian. It is, indeed, little else than a name, where the government is too feeble to withstand the enterprises of faction, to confine each member of the society within the limits prescribed by the laws, and to maintain all in the secure and tranquil enjoyment of the rights of person and property.

I have already intimated to you the danger of parties in the State, with particular reference to the founding of them on geographical discriminations. Let me now take a more comprehensive view, and warn you in the most solemn manner against the baneful effects of the spirit of party generally.

This spirit, unfortunately, is inseparable from our nature, having its root in the strongest passions of the human mind. It exists under different shapes in all governments, more or less stifled, controlled, or repressed; but, in those of the popular form, it is seen in its greatest rankness, and is truly their worst enemy.

The alternate domination of one faction over another, sharpened by the spirit of revenge, natural to party dissension, which in different ages and countries has perpetrated the most horrid enormities, is itself a frightful despotism. But this leads at length to a more formal and permanent despotism. The disorders and miseries which result gradually incline the minds of men to seek security and repose in the absolute power of an individual; and sooner or later the chief of some prevailing faction, more able or more fortunate than his competitors, turns this disposition to the purposes of his own elevation, on the ruins of public liberty.

Without looking forward to an extremity of this kind (which nevertheless ought not to be entirely out of sight), the common and continual mischiefs of the spirit of party are sufficient to make it the interest and duty of a wise people to discourage and restrain it.

It serves always to distract the public councils and enfeeble the public administration. It agitates the community with ill-founded jealousies and false alarms, kindles the animosity of one part against another, foments occasionally riot and insurrection. It opens the door to foreign influence and corruption, which finds a facilitated access to the government itself through the channels of party passions. Thus the policy and the will of one country are subjected to the policy and will of another.

There is an opinion that parties in free countries are useful checks upon the administration of the government and serve to keep alive the spirit of liberty. This within certain limits is probably true; and in governments of a monarchical cast, patriotism may look with indulgence, if not with favor, upon the spirit of party. But in those of the popular character, in governments purely elective, it is a spirit not to be encouraged. From their natural tendency, it is certain there will always be enough of that spirit for every salutary purpose. And there being constant danger of excess, the effort ought to be by force of public opinion, to mitigate and assuage it. A fire not to be quenched, it demands a uniform vigilance to prevent its bursting into a flame, lest, instead of warming, it should consume.

It is important, likewise, that the habits of thinking in a free country should inspire caution in those entrusted with its administration, to confine themselves within their respective constitutional spheres, avoiding in the exercise of the powers of one department to encroach upon another. The spirit of encroachment tends to consolidate the powers of all the departments in one, and thus to create, whatever the form of government, a real despotism. A just estimate of that love of power, and proneness to abuse it, which predominates in the human heart, is sufficient to satisfy us of the truth of this position. The necessity of reciprocal checks in the exercise of political power, by dividing and distributing it into different depositaries, and constituting each the guardian of the public weal against invasions by the others, has been evinced by experiments ancient and modern; some of them in our country and under our own eyes. To preserve them must be as necessary as to institute them. If, in the opinion of the people, the distribution or modification of the constitutional powers be in any particular wrong, let it be corrected by an amendment in the way which the Constitution designates. But let there be no change by usurpation; for though this, in one instance, may be the instrument of good, it is the customary weapon by which free governments are destroyed. The precedent must always greatly overbalance in permanent evil any partial or transient benefit, which the use can at any time yield.

Of all the dispositions and habits which lead to political prosperity, religion and morality are indispensable supports. In vain would that man claim the tribute of patriotism, who should labor to subvert these great pillars of human happiness, these firmest props of the duties of men and citizens. The mere politician, equally with the pious man, ought to respect and to cherish them. A volume could not trace all their connections with private and public felicity. Let it simply be asked: Where is the security for property, for reputation, for life, if the sense of religious obligation desert the oaths which are the instruments of investigation in courts of justice ? And let us with caution indulge the supposition that morality can be maintained without religion. Whatever may be conceded to the influence of refined education on minds of peculiar structure, reason and experience both forbid us to expect that national morality can prevail in exclusion of religious principle.

It is substantially true that virtue or morality is a necessary spring of popular government. The rule, indeed, extends with more or less force to every species of free government. Who that is a sincere friend to it can look with indifference upon attempts to shake the foundation of the fabric?

Promote then, as an object of primary importance, institutions for the general diffusion of knowledge. In proportion as the structure of a government gives force to public opinion, it is essential that public opinion should be enlightened.

As a very important source of strength and security, cherish public credit. One method of preserving it is to use it as sparingly as possible, avoiding occasions of expense by cultivating peace, but remembering also that timely disbursements to prepare for danger frequently prevent much greater disbursements to repel it, avoiding likewise the accumulation of debt, not only by shunning occasions of expense, but by vigorous exertion in time of peace to discharge the debts which unavoidable wars may have occasioned, not ungenerously throwing upon posterity the burden which we ourselves ought to bear. The execution of these maxims belongs to your representatives, but it is necessary that public opinion should co-operate. To facilitate to them the performance of their duty, it is essential that you should practically bear in mind that towards the payment of debts there must be revenue; that to have revenue there must be taxes; that no taxes can be devised which are not more or less inconvenient and unpleasant; that the intrinsic embarrassment, inseparable from the selection of the proper objects (which is always a choice of difficulties), ought to be a decisive motive for a candid construction of the conduct of the government in making it, and for a spirit of acquiescence in the measures for obtaining revenue, which the public exigencies may at any time dictate.

Observe good faith and justice towards all nations; cultivate peace and harmony with all. Religion and morality enjoin this conduct; and can it be, that good policy does not equally enjoin it? It will be worthy of a free, enlightened, and at no distant period, a great nation, to give to mankind the magnanimous and too novel example of a people always guided by an exalted justice and benevolence. Who can doubt that, in the course of time and things, the fruits of such a plan would richly repay any temporary advantages which might be lost by a steady adherence to it ? Can it be that Providence has not connected the permanent felicity of a nation with its virtue ? The experiment, at least, is recommended by every sentiment which ennobles human nature. Alas! is it rendered impossible by its vices?

In the execution of such a plan, nothing is more essential than that permanent, inveterate antipathies against particular nations, and passionate attachments for others, should be excluded; and that, in place of them, just and amicable feelings towards all should be cultivated. The nation which indulges towards another a habitual hatred or a habitual fondness is in some degree a slave. It is a slave to its animosity or to its affection, either of which is sufficient to lead it astray from its duty and its interest. Antipathy in one nation against another disposes each more readily to offer insult and injury, to lay hold of slight causes of umbrage, and to be haughty and intractable, when accidental or trifling occasions of dispute occur. Hence, frequent collisions, obstinate, envenomed, and bloody contests. The nation, prompted by ill-will and resentment, sometimes impels to war the government, contrary to the best calculations of policy. The government sometimes participates in the national propensity, and adopts through passion what reason would reject; at other times it makes the animosity of the nation subservient to projects of hostility instigated by pride, ambition, and other sinister and pernicious motives. The peace often, sometimes perhaps the liberty, of nations, has been the victim.

So likewise, a passionate attachment of one nation for another produces a variety of evils. Sympathy for the favorite nation, facilitating the illusion of an imaginary common interest in cases where no real common interest exists, and infusing into one the enmities of the other, betrays the former into a participation in the quarrels and wars of the latter without adequate inducement or justification. It leads also to concessions to the favorite nation of privileges denied to others which is apt doubly to injure the nation making the concessions; by unnecessarily parting with what ought to have been retained, and by exciting jealousy, ill-will, and a disposition to retaliate, in the parties from whom equal privileges are withheld. And it gives to ambitious, corrupted, or deluded citizens (who devote themselves to the favorite nation), facility to betray or sacrifice the interests of their own country, without odium, sometimes even with popularity; gilding, with the appearances of a virtuous sense of obligation, a commendable deference for public opinion, or a laudable zeal for public good, the base or foolish compliances of ambition, corruption, or infatuation.

As avenues to foreign influence in innumerable ways, such attachments are particularly alarming to the truly enlightened and independent patriot. How many opportunities do they afford to tamper with domestic factions, to practice the arts of seduction, to mislead public opinion, to influence or awe the public councils? Such an attachment of a small or weak towards a great and powerful nation dooms the former to be the satellite of the latter.

Against the insidious wiles of foreign influence (I conjure you to believe me, fellow-citizens) the jealousy of a free people ought to be constantly awake, since history and experience prove that foreign influence is one of the most baneful foes of republican government. But that jealousy to be useful must be impartial; else it becomes the instrument of the very influence to be avoided, instead of a defense against it. Excessive partiality for one foreign nation and excessive dislike of another cause those whom they actuate to see danger only on one side, and serve to veil and even second the arts of influence on the other. Real patriots who may resist the intrigues of the favorite are liable to become suspected and odious, while its tools and dupes usurp the applause and confidence of the people, to surrender their interests.

The great rule of conduct for us in regard to foreign nations is in extending our commercial relations, to have with them as little political connection as possible. So far as we have already formed engagements, let them be fulfilled with perfect good faith. Here let us stop. Europe has a set of primary interests which to us have none; or a very remote relation. Hence she must be engaged in frequent controversies, the causes of which are essentially foreign to our concerns. Hence, therefore, it must be unwise in us to implicate ourselves by artificial ties in the ordinary vicissitudes of her politics, or the ordinary combinations and collisions of her friendships or enmities.

Our detached and distant situation invites and enables us to pursue a different course. If we remain one people under an efficient government. the period is not far off when we may defy material injury from external annoyance; when we may take such an attitude as will cause the neutrality we may at any time resolve upon to be scrupulously respected; when belligerent nations, under the impossibility of making acquisitions upon us, will not lightly hazard the giving us provocation; when we may choose peace or war, as our interest, guided by justice, shall counsel.

Why forego the advantages of so peculiar a situation? Why quit our own to stand upon foreign ground? Why, by interweaving our destiny with that of any part of Europe, entangle our peace and prosperity in the toils of European ambition, rivalship, interest, humor or caprice?

It is our true policy to steer clear of permanent alliances with any portion of the foreign world; so far, I mean, as we are now at liberty to do it; for let me not be understood as capable of patronizing infidelity to existing engagements. I hold the maxim no less applicable to public than to private affairs, that honesty is always the best policy. I repeat it, therefore, let those engagements be observed in their genuine sense. But, in my opinion, it is unnecessary and would be unwise to extend them.

Taking care always to keep ourselves by suitable establishments on a respectable defensive posture, we may safely trust to temporary alliances for extraordinary emergencies.

Harmony, liberal intercourse with all nations, are recommended by policy, humanity, and interest. But even our commercial policy should hold an equal and impartial hand; neither seeking nor granting exclusive favors or preferences; consulting the natural course of things; diffusing and diversifying by gentle means the streams of commerce, but forcing nothing; establishing (with powers so disposed, in order to give trade a stable course, to define the rights of our merchants, and to enable the government to support them) conventional rules of intercourse, the best that present circumstances and mutual opinion will permit, but temporary, and liable to be from time to time abandoned or varied, as experience and circumstances shall dictate; constantly keeping in view that it is folly in one nation to look for disinterested favors from another; that it must pay with a portion of its independence for whatever it may accept under that character; that, by such acceptance, it may place itself in the condition of having given equivalents for nominal favors, and yet of being reproached with ingratitude for not giving more. There can be no greater error than to expect or calculate upon real favors from nation to nation. It is an illusion, which experience must cure, which a just pride ought to discard.

In offering to you, my countrymen, these counsels of an old and affectionate friend, I dare not hope they will make the strong and lasting impression I could wish; that they will control the usual current of the passions, or prevent our nation from running the course which has hitherto marked the destiny of nations. But, if I may even flatter myself that they may be productive of some partial benefit, some occasional good; that they may now and then recur to moderate the fury of party spirit, to warn against the mischiefs of foreign intrigue, to guard against the impostures of pretended patriotism; this hope will be a full recompense for the solicitude for your welfare, by which they have been dictated.

How far in the discharge of my official duties I have been guided by the principles which have been delineated, the public records and other evidences of my conduct must witness to you and to the world. To myself, the assurance of my own conscience is, that I have at least believed myself to be guided by them.

In relation to the still subsisting war in Europe, my proclamation of the twenty-second of April, 1793, is the index of my plan. Sanctioned by your approving voice, and by that of your representatives in both houses of Congress, the spirit of that measure has continually governed me, uninfluenced by any attempts to deter or divert me from it.

After deliberate examination, with the aid of the best lights I could obtain, I was well satisfied that our country, under all the circumstances of the case, had a right to take, and was bound in duty and interest to take, a neutral position. Having taken it, I determined, as far as should depend upon me, to maintain it, with moderation, perseverance, and firmness.

The considerations which respect the right to hold this conduct, it is not necessary on this occasion to detail. I will only observe that, according to my understanding of the matter, that right, so far from being denied by any of the belligerent powers, has been virtually admitted by all.

The duty of holding a neutral conduct may be inferred, without anything more, from the obligation which justice and humanity impose on every nation, in cases in which it is free to act, to maintain inviolate the relations of peace and amity towards other nations.

The inducements of interest for observing that conduct will best be referred to your own reflections and experience. With me a predominant motive has been to endeavor to gain time to our country to settle and mature its yet recent institutions, and to progress without interruption to that degree of strength and consistency which is necessary to give it, humanly speaking, the command of its own fortunes.

Though, in reviewing the incidents of my administration, I am unconscious of intentional error, I am nevertheless too sensible of my defects not to think it probable that I may have committed many errors. Whatever they may be, I fervently beseech the Almighty to avert or mitigate the evils to which they may tend. I shall also carry with me the hope that my country will never cease to view them with indulgence; and that, after forty five years of my life dedicated to its service with an upright zeal, the faults of incompetent abilities will be consigned to oblivion, as myself must soon be to the mansions of rest.

Relying on its kindness in this as in other things, and actuated by that fervent love towards it, which is so natural to a man who views in it the native soil of himself and his progenitors for several generations, I anticipate with pleasing expectation that retreat in which I promise myself to realize, without alloy, the sweet enjoyment of partaking, in the midst of my fellow-citizens, the benign influence of good laws under a free government, the ever-favorite object of my heart, and the happy reward, as I trust, of our mutual cares, labors, and dangers.

United States
19th September, 1796
Geo. Washington

Marbury v. Madison (1803)

Chief Justice Marshall delivered the opinion of the Court.

At the last term on the affidavits then read and filed with the clerk, a rule was granted in this case, requiring the Secretary of State to show cause why a mandamus should not issue, directing him to deliver to William Marbury his commission as a justice of the peace for the county of Washington, in the district of Columbia.

No cause has been shown, and the present motion is for a mandamus. The peculiar delicacy of this case, the novelty of some of its circumstances, and the real difficulty attending the points which occur in it, require a complete exposition of the principles on which the opinion to be given by the court is founded. . . .

In the order in which the court has viewed this subject, the following questions have been considered and decided:

1st. Has the applicant a right to the commission he demands?

2d. If he has a right, and that right has been violated, do the laws of his country afford him a remedy?

3d. If they do afford him a remedy, is it a mandamus issuing from this court?

The first object of inquiry is — 1st. Has the applicant a right to the commission he demands? . . .

It [is] decidedly the opinion of the court, that when a commission has been signed by the president, the appointment is made; and that the commission is complete, when the seal of the United States has been affixed to it by the secretary of state. . . .

To withhold his commission, therefore, is an act deemed by the court not warranted by law, but violative of a vested legal right.

This brings us to the second inquiry; which is 2dly. If he has a right, and that right has been violated, do the laws of his country afford him a remedy?

The very essence of civil liberty certainly consists in the right of every individual to claim the protection of the laws, whenever he receives an injury. One of the first duties of government is to afford that protection. [The] government of the United States has been emphatically termed a government of laws, and not of men. It will certainly cease to deserve this high appellation, if the laws furnish no remedy for the violation of a vested legal right. . . .

By the constitution of the United States, the President is invested with certain important political powers, in the exercise of which he is to use his own discretion, and is accountable only to his country in his political character, and to his own conscience. To aid him in the performance of these duties, he is authorized to appoint certain officers, who act by his authority and in conformity with his orders.

In such cases, their acts are his acts; and whatever opinion may be entertained of the manner in which executive discretion may be used, still there exists, and can exist, no power to control that discretion. The subjects are political. They respect the nation, not individual rights, and being entrusted to the executive, the decision of the executive is conclusive. . . .

But when the legislature proceeds to impose on that officer other duties; when he is directed peremptorily to perform certain acts; when the rights of individuals are dependent on the performance of those acts; he is so far the officer of the law; is amenable to the laws for his conduct; and cannot at his discretion sport away the vested rights of others.

The conclusion from this reasoning is, that where the heads of departments are the political or confidential agents of the executive, merely to execute the will of the President, or rather to act in cases in which the executive possesses a constitutional or legal discretion, nothing can be more perfectly clear than that their acts are only politically examinable. But where a specific duty is assigned by law, and individual rights depend upon the performance of that duty, it seems equally clear, that the individual who considers himself injured, has a right to resort to the laws of his country for a remedy. . . .

It is, then, the opinion of the Court [that Marbury has a] right to the commission; a refusal to deliver which is a plain violation of that right, for which the laws of his country afford him a remedy.

It remains to be enquired whether,

3dly. He is entitled to the remedy for which he applies. This depends on — 1st. The nature of the writ applied for, and,

2dly. The power of this court.

1st. The nature of the writ. . . .

This, then, is a plain case for a mandamus, either to deliver the commission, or a copy of it from the record; and it only remains to be enquired,

Whether it can issue from this court.

The act to establish the judicial courts of the United States authorizes the Supreme Court "to issue writs of mandamus in cases warranted by the principles and usages of law, to any courts appointed, or persons holding office, under the authority of the United States."

The Secretary of State, being a person holding an office under the authority of the United States, is precisely within the letter of the description; and if this court is not authorized to issue a writ of mandamus to such an officer, it must be because the law is unconstitutional, and therefore incapable of conferring the authority, and assigning the duties which its words purport to confer and assign.

The constitution vests the whole judicial power of the United States in one Supreme Court, and such inferior courts as congress shall, from time to time, ordain and establish. This power is expressly extended to all cases arising under the laws of the United States; and, consequently, in some form, may be exercised over the present case; because the right claimed is given by a law of the United States.

In the distribution of this power it is declared that "the Supreme Court shall have original jurisdiction in all cases affecting ambassadors, other public ministers and consuls, and those in which a state shall be a party. In all other cases, the Supreme Court shall have appellate jurisdiction."

It has been insisted, at the bar, that as the original grant of jurisdiction, to the supreme and inferior courts, is general, and the clause, assigning original jurisdiction to the Supreme Court, contains no negative or restrictive words, the power remains to the legislature, to assign original jurisdiction to that court in other cases than those specified in the article which has been recited; provided those cases belong to the judicial power of the United States.

If it had been intended to leave it in the discretion of the legislature to apportion the judicial power between the supreme and inferior courts according to the will of that body, it would certainly have been useless to have proceeded further than to have defined the judicial power, and the tribunals in which it should be vested. The subsequent part of the section is mere surplusage, is entirely without meaning, if such is to be the construction. If congress remains at liberty to give this court appellate jurisdiction, where the constitution has declared their jurisdiction shall be original; and original jurisdiction where the constitution has declared it shall be appellate; the distribution of jurisdiction, made in the constitution, is form without substance.

Affirmative words are often, in their operation, negative of other objects than those affirmed; and in this case, a negative or exclusive sense must be given to them or they have no operation at all.

It cannot be presumed that any clause in the constitution is intended to be without effect; and, therefore, such a construction is inadmissible, unless the words require it.

If the solicitude of the convention, respecting our peace with foreign powers, induced a provision that the supreme court should take original jurisdiction in cases which might be supposed to affect them; yet the clause would have proceeded no further than to provide for such cases, if no further restriction on the powers of congress had been intended. That they should have appellate jurisdiction in all other cases, with such exceptions as congress might make, is no restriction; unless the words be deemed exclusive of original jurisdiction.

When an instrument organizing fundamentally a judicial system, divides it into one supreme, and so many inferior courts as the legislature may ordain and establish; then enumerates its powers, and proceeds so far to distribute them, as to define the jurisdiction of the supreme court by declaring the cases in which it shall take original jurisdiction, and that in others it shall take appellate jurisdiction; the plain import of the words seems to be, that in one class of cases its jurisdiction is original, and not appellate; in the other it is appellate, and not original. If any other construction would render the clause inoperative, that is an additional reason for rejecting such other construction, and for adhering to their obvious meaning.

To enable this court, then, to issue a mandamus, it must be shown to be an exercise of appellate jurisdiction, or to be necessary to enable them to exercise appellate jurisdiction.

It has been stated at the bar that the appellate jurisdiction may be exercised in a variety of forms, and that if it be the will of the legislature that a mandamus should be used for that purpose, that will must be obeyed. This is true, yet the jurisdiction must be appellate, not original.

It is the essential criterion of appellate jurisdiction, that it revises and corrects the proceedings in a cause already instituted, and does not create that cause. Although, therefore, a mandamus may be directed to courts, yet to issue such a writ to an officer for the delivery of a paper, is in effect the same as to sustain an original action for that paper, and, therefore, seems not to belong to appellate, but to original jurisdiction. Neither is it necessary in such a case as this, to enable the court to exercise its appellate jurisdiction.

The authority, therefore, given to the Supreme Court, by the act establishing the judicial courts of the United States, to issue writs of mandamus to public officers, appears not to be warranted by the constitution; and it becomes necessary to enquire whether a jurisdiction, so conferred, can be exercised.

The question, whether an act, repugnant to the constitution, can become the law of the land, is a question deeply interesting to the United States; but happily, not of an intricacy proportioned to its interest. It seems only necessary to recognize certain principles, supposed to have been long and well established, to decide it.

That the people have an original right to establish, for their future government, such principles as, in their opinion, shall most conduce to their own happiness, is the basis on which the whole American fabric has been erected. The exercise of this original right is a very great exertion; nor can it, nor ought it, to be frequently repeated. The principles, therefore, so established, are deemed fundamental. And as the authority from which they proceed is supreme, and can seldom act, they are designed to be permanent.

This original and supreme will organizes the government, and assigns to different departments their respective powers. It may either stop here, or establish certain limits not to be transcended by those departments.

The government of the United States is of the latter description. The powers of the legislature are defined and limited; and that those limits may not be mistaken, or forgotten, the constitution is written.

To what purpose are powers limited, and to what purpose is that limitation committed to writing, if these limits may, at any time, be passed by those intended to be restrained? The distinction between a government with limited and unlimited powers is abolished, if those limits do not confine the persons on whom they are imposed, and if acts prohibited and acts allowed, are of equal obligation. It is a proposition too plain to be contested, that the constitution controls any legislative act repugnant to it; or, that the legislature may alter the constitution by an ordinary act.

Between these alternatives there is no middle ground. The constitution is either a superior, paramount law, unchangeable by ordinary means, or it is on a level with ordinary legislative acts, and, like other acts, is alterable when the legislature shall please to alter it.

If the former part of the alternative be true, then a legislative act contrary to the constitution is not law: if the latter part be true, then written constitutions are absurd attempts, on the part of the people, to limit a power in its own nature illimitable.

Certainly all those who have framed written constitutions contemplate them as forming the fundamental and paramount law of the nation, and consequently, the theory of every such government must be, that an act of the legislature, repugnant to the constitution, is void.

This theory is essentially attached to a written constitution, and is, consequently, to be considered, by this court, as one of the fundamental principles of our society. It is not therefore to be lost sight of in the further consideration of this subject.

If an act of the legislature, repugnant to the constitution, is void, does it, notwithstanding its invalidity, bind the courts, and oblige them to give it effect? Or, in other words, though it be not law, does it constitute a rule as operative as if it was a law? This would be to overthrow in fact what was established in theory; and would seem, at first view, an absurdity too gross to be insisted on. It shall, however, receive a more attentive consideration.

It is emphatically the province and duty of the judicial department to say what the law is. Those who apply the rule to particular cases, must of necessity expound and interpret that rule. If two laws conflict with each other, the courts must decide on the operation of each.

So if a law be in opposition to the constitution; if both the law and the constitution apply to a particular case, so that the court must either decide that case conformably to the law, disregarding the constitution; or conformably to the constitution, disregarding the law; the court must determine which of these conflicting rules governs the case. This is of the very essence of judicial duty.

If, then, the courts are to regard the constitution, and the constitution is superior to any ordinary act of the legislature, the constitution, and not such ordinary act, must govern the case to which they both apply.

Those then who controvert the principle that the constitution is to be considered, in court, as a paramount law, are reduced to the necessity of maintaining that the courts must close their eyes on the constitution, and see only the law.

This doctrine would subvert the very foundation of all written constitutions. It would declare that an act which, according to the principles and theory of our government, is entirely void, is yet, in practice, completely obligatory. It would declare that if the legislature shall do what is expressly forbidden, such act, notwithstanding the express prohibition, is in reality effectual. It would be giving to the legislature a practical and real omnipotence, with the same breath which professes to restrict their powers within narrow limits. It is prescribing limits, and declaring that those limits may be passed at pleasure.

That it thus reduces to nothing what we have deemed the greatest improvement on political institutions — a written constitution — would of itself be sufficient, in America, where written constitutions have been viewed with so much reverence, for rejecting the construction. But the peculiar expressions of the constitution of the United States furnish additional arguments in favour of its rejection.

The judicial power of the United States is extended to all cases arising under the constitution.

Could it be the intention of those who gave this power, to say that in using it the constitution should not be looked into? That a case arising under the constitution should be decided without examining the instrument under which it arises?

This is too extravagant to be maintained.

In some cases, then, the constitution must be looked into by the judges. And if they can open it at all, what part of it are they forbidden to read or to obey?

There are many other parts of the constitution which serve to illustrate this subject.

It is declared that "no tax or duty shall be laid on articles exported from any state." Suppose a duty on the export of cotton, of tobacco, or of flour; and a suit instituted to recover it. Ought judgment to be rendered in such a case? Ought the judges to close their eyes on the constitution, and only see the law?

The constitution declares that "no bill of attainder or ex post facto law shall be passed." If, however, such a bill should be passed, and a person should be prosecuted under it; must the court condemn to death those victims whom the constitution endeavors to preserve?

"No person," says the constitution, "shall be convicted of treason unless on the testimony of two witnesses to the same overt act, or on confession in open court."

Here the language of the constitution is addressed especially to the courts. It prescribes, directly for them, a rule of evidence not to be departed from. If the legislature should change that rule, and declare one witness, or a confession out of court, sufficient for conviction, must the constitutional principle yield to the legislative act?

From these, and many other selections which might be made, it is apparent, that the framers of the constitution contemplated that instrument as a rule for the government of courts, as well as of the legislature. Why otherwise does it direct the judges to take an oath to support it? This oath certainly applies, in an especial manner, to their conduct in their official character. How immoral to impose it on them, if they were to be used as the instruments, and the knowing instruments, for violating what they swear to support!

The oath of office, too, imposed by the legislature, is completely demonstrative of the legislative opinion on this subject. It is in these words: "I do solemnly swear that I will administer justice without respect to persons, and do equal right to the poor and to the rich; and that I will faithfully and impartially discharge all the duties incumbent on me as ______, according to the best of my abilities and understanding, agreeably to the constitution, and laws of the United States." Why does a Judge swear to discharge his duties agreeably the constitution of the United States, if that constitution forms no rule for his government? If it is closed upon him, and cannot be inspected by him?

If such be the real state of things, this is worse than solemn mockery. To prescribe, or to take this oath, becomes equally a crime.

It is also not entirely unworthy of observation that in declaring what shall be the supreme law of the land, the constitution itself is first mentioned; and not the laws of the United States generally, but those only which shall be made in pursuance of the constitution, have that rank.

Thus, the particular phraseology of the constitution of the United States confirms and strengthens the principle, supposed to be essential to all written constitutions, that a law repugnant to the constitution is void; and that courts, as well as other departments, are bound by that instrument.

The rule must be discharged.

The Missouri Compromise

An Act to authorize the people of the Missouri territory to form a constitution and state government, and for the admission of such state into the Union on an equal footing with the original states, and to prohibit slavery in certain territories.

Be it enacted by the Senate and House of Representatives of the United States of America, in Congress assembled, That the inhabitants of that portion of the Missouri territory included within the boundaries herein after designated, be, and they are hereby, authorized to form for themselves a constitution and state government, and to assume such name as they shall deem proper; and the said state, when formed, shall be admitted into the Union, upon an equal footing with the original states, in all respects whatsoever.

SEC. 2. And be it further enacted, That the said state shall consist of all the territory included within the following boundaries, to wit: Beginning in the middle of the Mississippi river, on the parallel of thirty-six degrees of north latitude; thence west, along that parallel of latitude, to the St. Francois river; thence up, and following the course of that river, in the middle of the main channel thereof, to the parallel of latitude of thirty-six degrees and thirty minutes; thence west, along the same, to a point where the said parallel is intersected by a meridian line passing through the middle of the mouth of the Kansas river, where the same empties into the Missouri river, thence, from the point aforesaid north, along the said meridian line, to the intersection of the parallel of latitude which passes through the rapids of the river Des Moines, making the said line to correspond with the Indian boundary line; thence east, from the point of intersection last aforesaid, along the said parallel of latitude, to the middle of the channel of the main fork of the said river Des Moines ; thence down arid along the middle of the main channel of the said river Des Moines, to the mouth of the same, where it empties into the Mississippi river; thence, due east, to the middle of the main channel of the Mississippi river; thence down, and following the course of the Mississippi river, in the middle of the main channel thereof, to the place of beginning: Provided, The said state shall ratify the boundaries aforesaid. And provided also, That the said state shall have concurrent jurisdiction on the river Mississippi, and every other river bordering on the said state so far as the said rivers shall form a common boundary to the said state; and any other state or states, now or hereafter to be formed and bounded by the same, such rivers to be common to both; and that the river Mississippi, and the navigable rivers and waters leading into the same, shall be common highways, and for ever free, as well to the inhabitants of the said state as to other citizens of the United States, without any tax, duty impost, or toll, therefor, imposed by the said state.

SEC. 3. And be it further enacted, That all free white male citizens of the United States, who shall have arrived at the age of twenty-one years, and have resided in said territory: three months previous to the day of election, and all other persons qualified to vote for representatives to the general assembly of the said territory, shall be qualified to be elected and they are hereby qualified and authorized to vote, and choose representatives to form a convention, who shall be apportioned amongst the several counties as follows :

From the county of Howard, five representatives. From the county of Cooper, three representatives. From the county of Montgomery, two representatives. From the county of Pike, one representative. From the county of Lincoln, one representative. From the county of St. Charles, three representatives. From the county of Franklin, one representative. From the county of St. Louis, eight representatives. From the county of Jefferson, one representative. From the county of Washington, three representatives. From the county of St. Genevieve, four representatives. From the county of Madison, one representative. From the county of Cape Girardeau, five representatives. From the county of New Madrid, two representatives. From the county of Wayne, and that portion of the county of Lawrence which falls within the boundaries herein designated, one representative.

And the election for the representatives aforesaid shall be holden on the first Monday, and two succeeding days of May next, throughout the several counties aforesaid in the said territory, and shall be, in every respect, held and conducted in the same manner, and under the same regulations as is prescribed by the laws of the said territory regulating elections therein for members of the general assembly, except that the returns of the election in that portion of Lawrence county included in the boundaries aforesaid, shall be made to the county of Wayne, as is provided in other cases under the laws of said territory.

SEC. 4. And be it further enacted, That the members of the convention thus duly elected, shall be, and they are hereby authorized to meet at the seat of government of said territory on the second Monday of the month of June next; and the said convention, when so assembled, shall have power and authority to adjourn to any other place in the said territory, which to them shall seem best for the convenient transaction of their business; and which convention, when so met, shall first determine by a majority of the whole number elected, whether it be, or be not, expedient at that time to form a constitution and state government for the people within the said territory, as included within the boundaries above designated; and if it be deemed expedient, the convention shall be, and hereby is, authorized to form a constitution and state government; or, if it be deemed more expedient, the said convention shall provide by ordinance for electing representatives to form a constitution or frame of government; which said representatives shall be chosen in such manner, and in such proportion as they shall designate; and shall meet at such time and place as shall be prescribed by the said ordinance; and shall then form for the people of said territory, within the boundaries aforesaid, a constitution and state government: Provided, That the same, whenever formed, shall be republican, and not repugnant to the constitution of the United States; and that the legislature of said state shall never interfere with the primary disposal of the soil by the United States, nor with any regulations Congress may find necessary for securing the title in such soil to the bona fide purchasers ; and that no tax shall be imposed on lands the property of the United States ; and in no case shall non-resident proprietors be taxed higher than residents.

SEC. 5. And be it further enacted, That until the next general census shall be taken, the said state shall be entitled to one representative in the House of Representatives of the United States.

SEC. 6. And be it further enacted, That the following propositions be, and the same are hereby, offered to the convention of the said territory of Missouri, when formed, for their free acceptance or rejection, which, if accepted by the convention, shall be obligatory upon the United States:

First. That section numbered sixteen in every township, and when such section has been sold, or otherwise disposed of, other lands equivalent thereto, and as contiguous as may be, shall be granted to the state for the use of the inhabitants of such township, for the use of schools.

Second. That all salt springs, not exceeding twelve in number, with six sections of land adjoining to each, shall be granted to the said state for the use of said state, the same to be selected by the legislature of the said state, on or before the first day of January, in the year one thousand eight hundred and twenty-five ; and the same, when so selected, to be used under such terms, conditions, and regulations, as the legislature of said state shall direct: Provided, That no salt spring, the right whereof now is, or hereafter shall be, confirmed or adjudged to any individual or individuals, shall, by this section, be granted to the said state: And provided also, That the legislature shall never sell or lease the same, at anyone time, for a longer period than ten years, without the consent of Congress.

Third. That five per cent. of the net proceeds of the sale of lands lying within the said territory or state, and which shall be sold by Congress, from and after the first day of January next, after deducting all expenses incident to the same, shall be reserved for making public roads and canals, of which three fifths shall be applied to those objects within the state, under the direction of the legislature thereof; and the other two fifths in defraying, under the direction of Congress, the expenses to be incurred in making of a road or roads, canal or canals, leading to the said state.

Fourth. That four entire sections of land be, and the same are hereby, granted to the said state, for the purpose of fixing their seat of government thereon; which said sections shall, under the direction of the legislature of said state, be located, as near as may be, in one body, at any time, in such townships and ranges as the legislature aforesaid may select, on any of the public lands of the United States: Provided, That such locations shall be made prior to the public sale of the lands of the United States surrounding such location.

Fifth. That thirty-six sections, or one entire township, which shall be designated by the President of the United States, together with the other lands heretofore reserved for that purpose, shall be reserved for the use of a seminary of learning, and vested in the legislature of said state, to be appropriated solely to the use of such seminary by the said legislature: Provided, That the five foregoing propositions herein offered, are on the condition that the convention of the said state shall provide, by an ordinance, irrevocable without the consent or the United States, that every and each tract of land sold by the United States, from and after the first day of January next, shall remain exempt from any tax laid by order or under the authority of the state, whether for state, county, or township, or any other purpose whatever, for the term of five years from and after the day of sale; And further, That the bounty lands granted, or hereafter to be granted, for military services during the late war, shall, while they continue to be held by the patentees, or their heirs remain exempt as aforesaid from taxation for the term of three year; from and after the date of the patents respectively.

SEC. 7. And be it further enacted, That in case a constitution and state government shall be formed for the people of the said territory of Missouri, the said convention or representatives, as soon thereafter as may be, shall cause a true and attested copy of such constitution or frame of state government, as shall be formed or provided, to be transmitted to Congress.

SEC. 8. And be it further enacted. That in all that territory ceded by France to the United States, under the name of Louisiana, which lies north of thirty-six degrees and thirty minutes north latitude, not included within the limits of the state, contemplated by this act, slavery and involuntary servitude, otherwise than in the punishment of crimes, whereof the parties shall have been duly convicted, shall be, and is hereby, forever prohibited: Provided always, That any person escaping into the same, from whom labour or service is lawfully claimed, in any state or territory of the United States, such fugitive may be lawfully reclaimed and conveyed to the person claiming his or her labour or service as aforesaid.

APPROVED, March 6, 1820.

A Plea for Captain John Brown by Henry David Thoreau

[Read to the citizens of Concord, Mass., Sunday Evening, October 30, 1859.]

I trust that you will pardon me for being here. I do not wish to force my thoughts upon you, but I feel forced myself. Little as I know of Captain Brown, I would fain do my part to correct the tone and the statements of the newspapers, and of my countrymen generally, respecting his character and actions. It costs us nothing to be just. We can at least express our sympathy with, and admiration of, him and his companions, and that is what I now propose to do.

First, as to his history. I will endeavor to omit, as much as possible, what you have already read. I need not describe his person to you, for probably most of you have seen and will not soon forget him. I am told that his grandfather, John Brown, was an officer in the Revolution; that he himself was born in Connecticut about the beginning of this century, but early went with his father to Ohio. I heard him say that his father was a contractor who furnished beef to the army there, in the war of 1812; that he accompanied him to the camp, and assisted him in that employment, seeing a good deal of military life, — more, perhaps, than if he had been a soldier; for he was often present at the councils of the officers. Especially, he learned by experience how armies are supplied and maintained in the field, — a work which, he observed, requires at least as much experience and skill as to lead them in battle. He said that few persons had any conception of the cost, even the pecuniary cost, of firing a single bullet in war. He saw enough, at any rate, to disgust him with a military life; indeed, to excite in his a great abhorrence of it; so much so, that though he was tempted by the offer of some petty office in the army, when he was about eighteen, he not only declined that, but he also refused to train when warned, and was fined for it. He then resolved that he would never have anything to do with any war, unless it were a war for liberty.

When the troubles in Kansas began, he sent several of his sons thither to strengthen the party of the Free State men, fitting them out with such weapons as he had; telling them that if the troubles should increase, and there should be need of his, he would follow, to assist them with his hand and counsel. This, as you all know, he soon after did; and it was through his agency, far more than any other's, that Kansas was made free.

For a part of his life he was a surveyor, and at one time he was engaged in wool-growing, and he went to Europe as an agent about that business. There, as everywhere, he had his eyes about him, and made many original observations. He said, for instance, that he saw why the soil of England was so rich, and that of Germany (I think it was) so poor, and he thought of writing to some of the crowned heads about it. It was because in England the peasantry live on the soil which they cultivate, but in Germany they are gathered into villages, at night. It is a pity that he did not make a book of his observations.

I should say that he was an old-fashioned man in respect for the Constitution, and his faith in the permanence of this Union. Slavery he deemed to be wholly opposed to these, and he was its determined foe.

He was by descent and birth a New England farmer, a man of great common-sense, deliberate and practical as that class is, and tenfold more so. He was like the best of those who stood at Concord Bridge once, on Lexington Common, and on Bunker Hill, only he was firmer and higher principled than any that I have chanced to hear of as there. It was no abolition lecturer that converted him. Ethan Allen and Stark, with whom he may in some respects be compared, were rangers in a lower and less important field. They could bravely face their country's foes, but he had the courage to face his country herself, when she was in the wrong. A Western writer says, to account for his escape from so many perils, that he was concealed under a "rural exterior"; as if, in that prairie land, a hero should, by good rights, wear a citizen's dress only.

He did not go to the college called Harvard, good old Alma Mater as she is. He was not fed on the pap that is there furnished. As he phrased it, "I know no more of grammar than one of your calves."

But he went to the great university of the West, where he sedulously pursued the study of Liberty, for which he had early betrayed a fondness, and having taken many degrees, he finally commenced the public practice of Humanity in Kansas, as you all know. Such were his humanities and not any study of grammar. He would have left a Greek accent slanting the wrong way, and righted up a falling man.

He was one of that class of whom we hear a great deal, but, for the most part, see nothing at all, — the Puritans. It would be in vain to kill him. He died lately in the time of Cromwell, but he reappeared here. Why should he not? Some of the Puritan stock are said to have come over and settled in New England. They were a class that did something else than celebrate their forefathers' day, and eat parched corn in remembrance of that time. They were neither Democrats nor Republicans, but men of simple habits, straightforward, prayerful; not thinking much of rulers who did not fear God, not making many compromises, nor seeking after available candidates.

"In his camp," as one has recently written, and as I have myself heard him state, "he permitted no profanity; no man of loose morals was suffered to remain there, unless, indeed, as a prisoner of war. 'I would rather,' said he, 'have the small-pox, yellow-fever, and cholera, all together in my camp, than a man without principle.... It is a mistake, sir, that our people make, when they think that bullies are the best fighters, or that they are the fit men to oppose these Southerners. Give me men of good principles, — God-fearing men, — men who respect themselves, and with a dozen of them I will oppose any hundred such men as these Buford ruffians.'" He said that if one offered himself to be a soldier under him, who was forward to tell what he could or would do, if he could only get sight of the enemy, he had but little confidence in him.

He was never able to find more than a score or so of recruits whom he would accept, and only about a dozen, among them his sons, in whom he had perfect faith. When he was here, some years ago, he showed to a few a little manuscript book, — his "orderly book" I think he called it, — containing the names of his company in Kansas, and the rules by which they bound themselves; and he stated that several of them had already sealed the contract with their blood. When some one remarked that, with the addition of a chaplain, it would have been a perfect Cromwellian troop, he observed that he would have been glad to add a chaplain to the list, if he could have found one who could fill that office worthily. It is easy enough to find one for the United States army. I believe that he had prayers in his camp morning and evening, nevertheless.

He was a man of Spartan habits, and at sixty was scrupulous about his diet at your table, excusing himself by saying that he must eat sparingly and fare hard, as became a soldier, or one who was fitting himself for difficult enterprises, a life of exposure.

A man of rare common-sense and directness of speech, as of action; a transcendentalist above all, a man of ideas and principles, — that was what distinguished him. Not yielding to a whim or transient impulse, but carrying out the purpose of a life. I noticed that he did not overstate anything, but spoke within bounds. I remember, particularly, how, in his speech here, he referred to what his family had suffered in Kansas, without ever giving the least vent to his pent-up fire. It was a volcano with an ordinary chimney-flue. Also referring to the deeds of certain Border Ruffians, he said, rapidly paring away his speech, like an experienced soldier, keeping a reserve of force and meaning, "They had a perfect right to be hung." He was not in the least a rhetorician, was not talking to Buncombe or his constituents anywhere, had no need to invent anything but to tell the simple truth, and communicate his own resolution; therefore he appeared incomparably strong, and eloquence in Congress and elsewhere seemed to me at a discount. It was like the speeches of Cromwell compared with those of an ordinary king.

As for his tact and prudence, I will merely say, that at a time when scarcely a man from the Free States was able to reach Kansas by any direct route, at least without having his arms taken from him, he, carrying what imperfect guns and other weapons he could collect, openly and slowly drove an ox-cart through Missouri, apparently in the capacity of a surveyor, with his surveying compass exposed in it, and so passed unsuspected, and had ample opportunity to learn the designs of the enemy. For some time after his arrival he still followed the same profession. When, for instance, he saw a knot of the ruffians on the prairie, discussing, of course, the single topic which then occupied their minds, he would, perhaps, take his compass and one of his sons, and proceed to run an imaginary line right through the very spot on which that conclave had assembled, and when he came up to them, he would naturally pause and have some talk with them, learning their news, and, at last, all their plans perfectly; and having thus completed his real survey he would resume his imaginary one, and run on his line till he was out of sight.

When I expressed surprise that he could live in Kansas at all, with a price set upon his head, and so large a number, including the authorities, exasperated against him, he accounted for it by saying, "It is perfectly well understood that I will not be taken." Much of the time for some years he has had to skulk in swamps, suffering from poverty and from sickness, which was the consequence of exposure, befriended only by Indians and a few whites. But though it might be known that he was lurking in a particular swamp, his foes commonly did not care to go in after him. He could even come out into a town where there were more Border Ruffians than Free State men, and transact some business, without delaying long, and yet not be molested; for, said he, "No little handful of men were willing to undertake it, and a large body could not be got together in season."

As for his recent failure, we do not know the facts about it. It was evidently far from being a wild and desperate attempt. His enemy, Mr. Vallandigham, is compelled to say, that "it was among the best planned executed conspiracies that ever failed."

Not to mention his other successes, was it a failure, or did it show a want of good management, to deliver from bondage a dozen human beings, and walk off with them by broad daylight, for weeks if not months, at a leisurely pace, through one State after another, for half the length of the North, conspicuous to all parties, with a price set upon his head, going into a court-room on his way and telling what he had done, thus convincing Missouri that it was not profitable to try to hold slaves in his neighborhood? — and this, not because the government menials were lenient, but because they were afraid of him.

Yet he did not attribute his success, foolishly, to "his star," or to any magic. He said, truly, that the reason why such greatly superior numbers quailed before him was, as one of his prisoners confessed, because they lacked a cause, — a kind of armor which he and his party never lacked. When the time came, few men were found willing to lay down their lives in defence of what they knew to be wrong; they did not like that this should be their last act in this world.

But to make haste to his last act, and its effects.

The newspapers seem to ignore, or perhaps are really ignorant of the fact, that there are at least as many as two or three individuals to a town throughout the North who think much as the present speaker does about him and his enterprise. I do not hesitate to say that they are an important and growing party. We aspire to be something more than stupid and timid chattels, pretending to read history and our Bibles, but desecrating every house and every day we breathe in. Perhaps anxious politicians may prove that only seventeen white men and five negroes were concerned in the late enterprise; but their very anxiety to prove this might suggest to themselves that all is not told. Why do they still dodge the truth? They are so anxious because of a dim consciousness of the fact, which they do not distinctly face, that at least a million of the free inhabitants of the United States would have rejoiced if it had succeeded. They at most only criticise the tactics. Though we wear no crape, the thought of that man's position and probable fate is spoiling many a man's day here at the North for other thinking. If any one who has seen him here can pursue successfully any other train of thought, I do not know what he is made of. If there is any such who gets his usual allowance of sleep, I will warrant him to fatten easily under any circumstances which do not touch his body or purse. I put a piece of paper and a pencil under my pillow, and when I could not sleep, I wrote in the dark.

On the whole, my respect for my fellow-men, except as one may outweigh a million, is not being increased these days. I have noticed the cold-blooded way in which newspaper writers and men generally speak of this event, as if an ordinary malefactor, though one of unusual "pluck," — as the Governor of Virginia is reported to have said, using the language of the cock-pit, "the gamest man he ever saw," — had been caught, and were about to be hung. He was not dreaming of his foes when the governor thought he looked so brave. It turns what sweetness I have to gall, to hear, or hear of, the remarks of some of my neighbors. When we heard at first that he was dead, one of my townsmen observed that "he died as the fool dieth"; which, pardon me, for an instant suggested a likeness in him dying to my neighbor living. Others, craven-hearted, said disparagingly, that "he threw his life away," because he resisted the government. Which way have they thrown their lives, pray? — such as would praise a man for attacking singly an ordinary band of thieves or murderers. I hear another ask, Yankee-like, "What will he gain by it?" as if he expected to fill his pockets by this enterprise. Such a one has no idea of gain but in this worldly sense. If it does not lead to a "surprise" party, if he does not get a new pair of boots, or a vote of thanks, it must be a failure. "But he won't gain anything by it." Well, no, I don't suppose he could get four-and-sixpence a day for being hung, take the year round; but then he stands a chance to save a considerable part of his soul, — and such a soul! — when you do not. No doubt you can get more in your market for a quart of milk than for a quart of blood, but that is not the market that heroes carry their blood to.

Such do not know that like the seed is the fruit, and that, in the moral world, when good seed is planted, good fruit is inevitable, and does not depend on our watering and cultivating; that when you plant, or bury, a hero in his field, a crop of heroes is sure to spring up. This is a seed of such force and vitality, that it does not ask our leave to germinate.

The momentary charge at Balaclava, in obedience to a blundering command, proving what a perfect machine the soldier is, has, properly enough, been celebrated by a poet laureate; but the steady, and for the most part successful, charge of this man, for some years, against the legions of Slavery, in obedience to an infinitely higher command, is as much more memorable than that, as an intelligent and conscientious man is superior to a machine. Do you think that that will go unsung?

"Served him right," —"A dangerous man," —"He is undoubtedly insane." So they proceed to live their sane, and wise, and altogether admirable lives, reading their Plutarch a little, but chiefly pausing at that feat of Putnam, who was let down into a wolf's den; and in this wise they nourish themselves for brave and patriotic deeds some time or other. The Tract Society could afford to print that story of Putnam. You might open the district schools with the reading of it, for there is nothing about Slavery or the Church in it; unless it occurs to the reader that some pastors are wolves in sheep's clothing. "The American Board of Commissioners for Foreign Missions" even, might dare to protest against that wolf. I have heard of boards, and of American boards, but it chances that I never heard of this particular lumber till lately. And yet I hear of Northern men, and women, and children, by families, buying a "life membership" in such societies as these. A life-membership in the grave! You can get buried cheaper than that.

Our foes are in our midst and all about us. There is hardly a house but is divided against itself, for our foe is the all but universal woodenness of both head and heart, the want of vitality in man, which is the effect of our vice; and hence are begotten fear, superstition, bigotry, persecution, and slavery of all kinds. We are mere figureheads upon a hulk, with livers in the place of hearts. The curse is the worship of idols, which at length changes the worshipper into a stone image himself; and the New-Englander is just as much an idolater as the Hindoo. This man was an exception, for he did not set up even a political graven image between him and his God.

A church that can never have done with excommunicating Christ while it exists! Away with your broad and flat churches, and your narrow and tall churches! Take a step forward, and invent a new style of out-houses. Invent a salt that will save you, and defend our nostrils.

The modern Christian is a man who has consented to say all the prayers in the liturgy, provided you will let him go straight to bed and sleep quietly afterward. All his prayers begin with "Now I lay me down to sleep," and he is forever looking forward to the time when he shall go to his "long rest." He has consented to perform certain old-established charities, too, after a fashion, but he does not wish to hear of any new-fangled ones; he doesn't wish to have any supplementary articles added to the contract, to fit it to the present time. He shows the whites of his eyes on the Sabbath, and the blacks all the rest of the week. The evil is not merely a stagnation of blood, but a stagnation of spirit. Many, no doubt, are well disposed, but sluggish by constitution and by habit, and they cannot conceive of a man who is actuated by higher motives than they are. Accordingly they pronounce this man insane, for they know that they could never act as he does, as long as they are themselves.

We dream of foreign countries, of other times and races of men, placing them at a distance in history or space; but let some significant event like the present occur in our midst, and we discover, often, this distance and this strangeness between us and our nearest neighbors. They are our Austrias, and Chinas, and South Sea Islands.

Our crowded society becomes well spaced all at once, clean and handsome to the eye, — a city of magnificent distances. We discover why it was that we never got beyond compliments and surfaces with them before; we become aware of as many versts between us and them as there are between a wandering Tartar and a Chinese town. The thoughtful man becomes a hermit in the thoroughfares of the market-place. Impassable seas suddenly find their level between us, or dumb steppes stretch themselves out there. It is the difference of constitution, of intelligence, and faith, and not streams and mountains, that make the true and impassable boundaries between individuals and between states. None but the like-minded can come plenipotentiary to our court.

I read all the newspapers I could get within a week after this event, and I do not remember in them a single expression of sympathy for these men. I have since seen one noble statement, in a Boston paper, not editorial. Some voluminous sheets decided not to print the full report of Brown's words to the exclusion of other matter. It was as if a publisher should reject the manuscript of the New Testament, and print Wilson's last speech. The same journal which contained this pregnant news, was chiefly filled, in parallel columns, with the reports of the political conventions that were being held. But the descent to them was too steep. They should have been spared this contrast, — been printed in an extra, at least. To turn from the voices and deeds of earnest men to the cackling of political conventions! Office-seekers and speech-makers, who do not so much as lay an honest egg, but wear their breasts bare upon an egg of chalk! Their great game is the game of straws, or rather that universal aboriginal game of the platter, at which the Indians cried hub, bub! Exclude the reports of religious and political conventions, and publish the words of a living man.

But I object not so much to what they have omitted, as to what they have inserted. Even the Liberator called it "a misguided, wild, and apparently insane — effort." As for the herd of newspapers and magazines, I do not chance to know an editor in the country who will deliberately print anything which he knows will ultimately and permanently reduce the number of his subscribers. They do not believe that it would be expedient. How then can they print truth? If we do not say pleasant things, they argue, nobody will attend to us. And so they do like some travelling auctioneers, who sing an obscene song, in order to draw a crowd around them. Republican editors, obliged to get their sentences ready for the morning edition, and accustomed to look at everything by the twilight of politics, express no admiration, nor true sorrow even, but call these men "deluded fanatics," — "mistaken men," — "insane," or "crazed." It suggests what a sane set of editors we are blessed with, not "mistaken men"; who know very well on which side their bread is buttered, at least.

A man does a brave and humane deed, and at once, on all sides, we hear people and parties declaring, "I didn't do it, nor countenance him to do it, in any conceivable way. It can't be fairly inferred from my past career." I, for one, am not interested to hear you define your position. I don't know that I ever was, or ever shall be. I think it is mere egotism, or impertinent at this time. Ye needn't take so much pains to wash your skirts of him. No intelligent man will ever be convinced that he was any creature of yours. He went and came, as he himself informs us, "under the auspices of John Brown and nobody else." The Republican party does not perceive how many his failure will make to vote more correctly than they would have them. They have counted the votes of Pennsylvania & Co., but they have not correctly counted Captain Brown's vote. He has taken the wind out of their sails, — the little wind they had, — and they may as well lie to and repair.

What though he did not belong to your clique! Though you may not approve of his method or his principles, recognize his magnanimity. Would you not like to claim kindredship with him in that, though in no other thing he is like, or likely, to you? Do you think that you would lose your reputation so? What you lost at the spile, you would gain at the bung.

If they do not mean all this, then they do not speak the truth, and say what they mean. They are simply at their old tricks still.

"It was always conceded to him," says one who calls him crazy, "that he was a conscientious man, very modest in his demeanor, apparently inoffensive, until the subject of Slavery was introduced, when he would exhibit a feeling of indignation unparalleled."

The slave-ship is on her way, crowded with its dying victims; new cargoes are being added in mid-ocean a small crew of slaveholders, countenanced by a large body of passengers, is smothering four millions under the hatches, and yet the politician asserts that the only proper way by which deliverance is to be obtained, is by "the quiet diffusion of the sentiments of humanity," without any "outbreak." As if the sentiments of humanity were ever found unaccompanied by its deeds, and you could disperse them, all finished to order, the pure article, as easily as water with a watering-pot, and so lay the dust. What is that that I hear cast overboard? The bodies of the dead that have found deliverance. That is the way we are "diffusing" humanity, and its sentiments with it.

Prominent and influential editors, accustomed to deal with politicians, men of an infinitely lower grade, say, in their ignorance, that he acted "on the principle of revenge." They do not know the man. They must enlarge themselves to conceive of him. I have no doubt that the time will come when they will begin to see him as he was. They have got to conceive of a man of faith and of religious principle, and not a politician or an Indian; of a man who did not wait till he was personally interfered with or thwarted in some harmless business before he gave his life to the cause of the oppressed.

If Walker may be considered the representative of the South, I wish I could say that Brown was the representative of the North. He was a superior man. He did not value his bodily life in comparison with ideal things. He did not recognize unjust human laws, but resisted them as he was bid. For once we are lifted out of the trivialness and dust of politics into the region of truth and manhood. No man in America has ever stood up so persistently and effectively for the dignity of human nature, knowing himself for a man, and the equal of any and all governments. In that sense he was the most American of us all. He needed no babbling lawyer, making false issues, to defend him. He was more than a match for all the judges that American voters, or office-holders of whatever grade, can create. He could not have been tried by a jury of his peers, because his peers did not exist. When a man stands up serenely against the condemnation and vengeance of mankind, rising above them literally by a whole body, — even though he were of late the vilest murderer, who has settled that matter with himself, — the spectacle is a sublime one, — didn't ye know it, ye Liberators, ye Tribunes, ye Republicans? — and we become criminal in comparison. Do yourselves the honor to recognize him. He needs none of your respect.

As for the Democratic journals, they are not human enough to affect me at all. I do not feel indignation at anything they may say.

I am aware that I anticipate a little, — that he was still, at the last accounts, alive in the hands of his foes; but that being the case, I have all along found myself thinking and speaking of him as physically dead.

I do not believe in erecting statues to those who still live in our hearts, whose bones have not yet crumbled in the earth around us, but I would rather see the statue of Captain Brown in the Massachusetts State-House yard, than that of any other man whom I know. I rejoice that I live in this age, that I am his contemporary.

What a contrast, when we turn to that political party which is so anxiously shuffling him and his plot out of its way, and looking around for some available slave holder, perhaps, to be its candidate, at least for one who will execute the Fugitive Slave Law, and all those other unjust laws which he took up arms to annul!

Insane! A father and six sons, and one son-in-law, and several more men besides, — as many at least as twelve disciples, — all struck with insanity at once; while the same tyrant holds with a firmer gripe than ever his four millions of slaves, and a thousand sane editors, his abettors, are saving their country and their bacon! Just as insane were his efforts in Kansas. Ask the tyrant who is his most dangerous foe, the sane man or the insane? Do the thousands who know him best, who have rejoiced at his deeds in Kansas, and have afforded him material aid there, think him insane? Such a use of this word is a mere trope with most who persist in using it, and I have no doubt that many of the rest have already in silence retracted their words.

Read his admirable answers to Mason and others. How they are dwarfed and defeated by the contrast! On the one side, half-brutish, half-timid questioning; on the other, truth, clear as lightning, crashing into their obscene temples. They are made to stand with Pilate, and Gesler, and the Inquisition. How ineffectual their speech and action! and what a void their silence! They are but helpless tools in this great work. It was no human power that gathered them about this preacher.

What have Massachusetts and the North sent a few sane representatives to Congress for, of late years? — to declare with effect what kind of sentiments? All their speeches put together and boiled down,

— and probably they themselves will confess it, — do not match for manly directness and force, and for simple truth, the few casual remarks of crazy John Brown, on the floor of the Harper's Ferry engine-house, — that man whom you are about to hang, to send to the other world, though not to represent you there. No, he was not our representative in any sense. He was too fair a specimen of a man to represent the like of us. Who, then, were his constituents? If you read his words understandingly you will find out. In his case there is no idle eloquence, no made, nor maiden speech, no compliments to the oppressor. Truth is his inspirer, and earnestness the polisher of his sentences. He could afford to lose his Sharpe's rifles, while he retained his faculty of speech, — a Sharpe's rifle of infinitely surer and longer range.

And the New York Herald reports the conversation verbatim! It does not know of what undying words it is made the vehicle.

I have no respect for the penetration of any man who can read the report of that conversation, and still call the principal in it insane. It has the ring of a saner sanity than an ordinary discipline and habits of life, than an ordinary organization, secure. Take any sentence of it, — "Any questions that I can honorably answer, I will; not otherwise. So far as I am myself concerned, I have told everything truthfully. I value my word, sir." The few who talk about his vindictive spirit, while they really admire his heroism, have no test by which to detect a noble man, no amalgam to combine with his pure gold. They mix their own dross with it.

It is a relief to turn from these slanders to the testimony of his more truthful, but frightened jailers and hangmen. Governor Wise speaks far more justly and appreciatingly of him than any Northern editor, or politician, or public personage, that I chance to have heard from. I know that you can afford to hear him again on this subject. He says: "They are themselves mistaken who take him to be madman.... He is cool, collected, and indomitable, and it is but just to him to say, that he was humane to his prisoners.... And he inspired me with great trust in his integrity as a man of truth. He is a fanatic, vain and garrulous," (I leave that part to Mr. Wise,) "but firm, truthful, and intelligent. His men, too, who survive, are like him.... Colonel Washington says that he was the coolest and firmest man he ever saw in defying danger and death. With one son dead by his side, and another shot through, he felt the pulse of his dying son with one hand, and held his rifle with the other, and commanded his men with the utmost composure, encouraging them to be firm, and to sell their lives as dear as they could. Of the three white prisoners, Brown, Stephens, and Coppic, it was hard to say which was most firm."

Almost the first Northern men whom the slaveholder has learned to respect!

The testimony of Mr. Vallandigham, though less valuable, is of the same purport, that "it is vain to underrate either the man or his conspiracy.... He is the farthest possible removed from the ordinary ruffian, fanatic, or madman."

"All is quiet at Harper's Ferry," say the journals. What is the character of that calm which follows when the law and the slaveholder prevail? I regard this event as a touchstone designed to bring out, with glaring distinctness, the character of this government. We needed to be thus assisted to see it by the light of history. It needed to see itself. When a government puts forth its strength on the side of injustice, as ours to maintain slavery and kill the liberators of the slave, it reveals itself a merely brute force, or worse, a demoniacal force. It is the head of the Plug-Uglies. It is more manifest than ever that tyranny rules. I see this government to be effectually allied with France and Austria in oppressing mankind. There sits a tyrant holding fettered four millions of slaves; here comes their heroic liberator. This most hypocritical and diabolical government looks up from its seat on the gasping four millions, and inquires with an assumption of innocence: "What do you assault me for? Am I not an honest man? Cease agitation on this subject, or I will make a slave of you, too, or else hang you."

We talk about a representative government; but what a monster of a government is that where the noblest faculties of the mind, and the whole heart, are not represented. A semi-human tiger or ox, stalking over the earth, with its heart taken out and the top of its brain shot away. Heroes have fought well on their stumps when their legs were shot off, but I never heard of any good done by such a government as that.

The only government that I recognize, — and it matters not how few are at the head of it, or how small its army, — is that power that establishes justice in the land, never that which establishes injustice. What shall we think of a government to which all the truly brave and just men in the land are enemies, standing between it and those whom it oppresses? A government that pretends to be Christian and crucifies a million Christs every day!

Treason! Where does such treason take its rise? I cannot help thinking of you as you deserve, ye governments. Can you dry up the fountains of thought? High treason, when it is resistance to tyranny here below, has its origin in, and is first committed by, the power that makes and forever recreates man. When you have caught and hung all these human rebels, you have accomplished nothing but your own guilt, for you have not struck at the fountain-head. You presume to contend with a foe against whom West Point cadets and rifled cannon point not. Can all the art of the cannon-founder tempt matter to turn against its maker? Is the form in which the founder thinks he casts it more essential than the constitution of it and of himself?

The United States have a coffle of four millions of slaves. They are determined to keep them in this condition; and Massachusetts is one of the confederated overseers to prevent their escape. Such are not all the inhabitants of Massachusetts, but such are they who rule and are obeyed here. It was Massachusetts, as well as Virginia, that put down this insurrection at Harper's Ferry. She sent the marines there, and she will have to pay the penalty of her sin.

Suppose that there is a society in this State that out of its own purse and magnanimity saves all the fugitive slaves that run to us, and protects our colored fellow-citizens, and leaves the other work to the government, so-called. Is not that government fast losing its occupation, and becoming contemptible to mankind? If private men are obliged to perform the offices of government, to protect the weak and dispense justice, then the government becomes only a hired man, or clerk, to perform menial or indifferent services. Of course, that is but the shadow of a government who existence necessitates a Vigilant Committee. What should we think of the Oriental Cadi even, behind whom worked in secret a vigilant committee? But such is the character of our Northern States generally; each has its Vigilant Committee. And, to a certain extent, these crazy governments recognize and accept this relation. They say, virtually, "We'll be glad to work for you on these terms, only don't make a noise about it." And thus the government, its salary being insured, withdraws into the back shop, taking the Constitution with it, and bestows most of its labor on repairing that. When I hear it at work sometimes, as I go by, it reminds me, at best, of those farmers who in winter contrive to turn a penny by following the coopering business. And what kind of spirit is their barrel made to hold? They speculate in stocks, and bore holes in mountains, but they are not competent to lay out even a decent highway. The only free road, the Underground Railroad, is owned and managed by the Vigilant Committee. They have tunnelled under the whole breadth of the land. Such a government is losing its power and respectability as surely as water runs out of a leaky vessel, and is held by one that can contain it.

I hear many condemn these men because they were so few. When were the good and the brave ever in a majority? Would you have had him wait till that time came? — till you and I came over to him? The very fact that he had no rabble or troop of hirelings about him would alone distinguish him from ordinary heroes. His company was small indeed, because few could be found worthy to pass muster. Each one who there laid down his life for the poor and oppressed was a picked man, culled out of many thousands, if not millions; apparently a man of principle, of rare courage, and devoted humanity; ready to sacrifice his life at any moment for so much by laymen as by ministers of the Gospel, not so much by the fighting sects as by the Quakers, and not so much by Quaker men as by Quaker women?

This event advertises me that there is such a fact as death, — the possibility of a man's dying. It seems as if no man had ever died in America before; for in order to die you must first have lived. I don't believe in the hearses, and palls, and funerals that they have had. There was no death in the case, because there had been no life; they merely rotted or sloughed off, pretty much as they had rotted or sloughed along. No temple's veil was rent, only a hole dug somewhere. Let the dead bury their dead. The best of them fairly ran down like a clock. Franklin, — Washington, — they were let off without dying; they were merely missing one day. I hear a good many pretend that they are going to die; or that they have died, for aught that I know. Nonsense! I'll defy them to do it. They haven't got life enough in them. They'll deliquesce like fungi, and keep a hundred eulogists mopping the spot where they left off. Only half a dozen or so have died since the world began. Do you think that you are going to die, sir? No!

there's no hope of you. You haven't got your lesson yet. You've got to stay after school. We make a needless ado about capital punishment, — taking lives, when there is no life to take. Memento mori! We don't understand that sublime sentence which some worthy got sculptured on his gravestone once. We've interpreted it in a grovelling and snivelling sense; we've wholly forgotten how to die.

But be sure you do die nevertheless. Do your work, and finish it. If you know how to begin, you will know when to end.

These men, in teaching us how to die, have at the same time taught us how to live. If this man's acts and words do not create a revival, it will be the severest possible satire on the acts and words that do. It is the best news that America has ever heard. It has already quickened the feeble pulse of the North, and infused more and more generous blood into her veins and heart, than any number of years of what is called commercial and political prosperity could. How many a man who was lately contemplating suicide has now something to live for!

One writer says that Brown's peculiar monomania made him to be "dreaded by the Missourians as a supernatural being." Sure enough, a hero in the midst of us cowards is always so dreaded. He is just that thing. He shows himself superior to nature. He has a spark of divinity in him.

"Unless above himself he can Erect himself, how poor a thing is man!"

Newspaper editors argue also that it is a proof of his insanity that he thought he was appointed to do this work which he did, — that he did not suspect himself for a moment! They talk as if it were impossible that a man could be "divinely appointed" in these days to do any work whatever; as if vows and religion were out of date as connected with any man's daily work; as if the agent to abolish slavery could only be somebody appointed by the President, or by some political party. They talk as if a man's death were a failure, and his continued life, be it of whatever character, were a success.

When I reflect to what a cause this man devoted himself, and how religiously, and then reflect to what cause his judges and all who condemn him so angrily and fluently devote themselves, I see that they are as far apart as the heavens and earth are asunder.

The amount of it is, our "leading men" are a harmless kind of folk, and they know well enough that they were not divinely appointed, but elected by the votes of their party.

Who is it whose safety requires that Captain Brown be hung? Is it indispensable to any Northern man? Is there no resource but to cast this man also to the Minotaur? If you do not wish it, say so distinctly. While these things are being done, beauty stands veiled and music is a screeching lie. Think of him, — of his rare qualities! — such a man as it takes ages to make, and ages to understand; no mock hero, nor the representative of any party. A man such as the sun may not rise upon again in this benighted land. To whose making went the costliest material, the finest adamant; sent to be the redeemer of those in captivity; and the only use to which you can put him is to hang him at the end of a rope! You who pretend to care for Christ crucified, consider what you are about to do to him who offered himself to be the savior of four millions of men.

Any man knows when he is justified, and all the wits in the world cannot enlighten him on that point. The murderer always knows that he is justly punished; but when a government takes the life of a man without the consent of his conscience, it is an audacious government, and is taking a step towards its own dissolution. Is it not possible that an individual may be right and a government wrong? Are laws to be enforced simply because they were made? or declared by any number of men to be good, if they are not good? Is there any necessity for a man's being a tool to perform a deed of which his better nature disapproves? Is it the intention of law-makers that good men shall be hung ever? Are judges to interpret the law according to the letter, and not the spirit? What right have you to enter into a compact with yourself that you will do thus or so, against the light within you? Is it for you to make up your mind, — to form any resolution whatever, — and not accept the convictions that are forced upon you, and which ever pass your understanding? I do not believe in lawyers, in that mode of attacking or defending a man, because you descend to meet the judge on his own ground, and, in cases of the highest importance, it is of no consequence whether a man breaks a human law or not. Let lawyers decide trivial cases. Business men may arrange that among themselves. If they were the interpreters of the everlasting laws which rightfully bind man, that would be another thing. A counterfeiting law-factory, standing half in a slave land and half in free! What kind of laws for free men can you expect from that?

I am here to plead his cause with you. I plead not for his life, but for his character, — his immortal life; and so it becomes your cause wholly, and is not his in the least. Some eighteen hundred years ago Christ was crucified; this morning, perchance, Captain Brown was hung. These are the two ends of a chain which is not without its links. He is not Old Brown any longer; he is an angel of light.

I see now that it was necessary that the bravest and humanest man in all the country should be hung. Perhaps he saw it himself. I almost fear that I may yet hear of his deliverance, doubting if a prolonged life, if any life, can do as much good as his death.

"Misguided"! "Garrulous"! "Insane"! "Vindictive"! So ye write in your easy-chairs, and thus he wounded responds from the floor of the Armory, clear as a cloudless sky, true as the voice of nature is: "No man sent me here; it was my own prompting and that of my Maker. I acknowledge no master in human form."

And in what a sweet and noble strain he proceeds, addressing his captors, who stand over him: "I think, my friends, you are guilty of a great wrong against God and humanity, and it would be perfectly right for any one to interfere with you so far as to free those you willfully and wickedly hold in bondage."

And, referring to his movement: "It is, in my opinion, the greatest service a man can render to God."

"I pity the poor in bondage that have none to help them; that is why I am here; not to gratify any personal animosity, revenge, or vindictive spirit. It is my sympathy with the oppressed and the wronged, that are as good as you, and as precious in the sight of God."

You don't know your testament when you see it.

"I want you to understand that I respect the rights of the poorest and weakest of colored people, oppressed by the slave power, just as much as I do those of the most wealthy and powerful."

"I wish to say, furthermore, that you had better, all you people at the South, prepare yourselves for a settlement of that question, that must come up for settlement sooner than your are prepared for it. The sooner you are prepared the better. You may dispose of me very easily. I am nearly disposed of now; but this question is still to be settled, — this negro question, I mean; the end of that is not yet."

I foresee the time when the painter will paint that scene, no longer going to Rome for a subject; the poet will sing it; the historian record it; and, with the Landing of the Pilgrims and the Declaration of Independence, it will be the ornament of some future national gallery, when at least the present form of slavery shall be no more here. We shall then be at liberty to weep for Captain Brown. Then, and not till then, we will take our revenge.

Abraham Lincoln's Cooper Union Address (February 27, 1860)

Mr. President and fellow citizens of New York: —

The facts with which I shall deal this evening are mainly old and familiar; nor is there anything new in the general use I shall make of them. If there shall be any novelty, it will be in the mode of presenting the facts, and the inferences and observations following that presentation.

In his speech last autumn, at Columbus, Ohio, as reported in "The New-York Times," Senator Douglas said:

"Our fathers, when they framed the Government under which we live, understood this question just as well, and even better, than we do now."

I fully indorse this, and I adopt it as a text for this discourse. I so adopt it because it furnishes a precise and an agreed starting point for a discussion between Republicans and that wing of the Democracy headed by Senator Douglas. It simply leaves the inquiry: "What was the understanding those fathers had of the question mentioned?"

What is the frame of government under which we live?

The answer must be: "The Constitution of the United States." That Constitution consists of the original, framed in 1787, (and under which the present government first went into operation,) and twelve subsequently framed amendments, the first ten of which were framed in 1789.

Who were our fathers that framed the Constitution? I suppose the "thirty-nine" who signed the original instrument may be fairly called our fathers who framed that part of the present Government. It is almost exactly true to say they framed it, and it is altogether true to say they fairly represented the opinion and sentiment of the whole nation at that time. Their names, being familiar to nearly all, and accessible to quite all, need not now be repeated.

I take these "thirty-nine," for the present, as being "our fathers who framed the Government under which we live."

What is the question which, according to the text, those fathers understood "just as well, and even better than we do now?"

It is this: Does the proper division of local from federal authority, or anything in the Constitution, forbid our Federal Government to control as to slavery in our Federal Territories?

Upon this, Senator Douglas holds the affirmative, and Republicans the negative. This affirmation and denial form an issue; and this issue — this question — is precisely what the text declares our fathers understood "better than we."

Let us now inquire whether the "thirty-nine," or any of them, ever acted upon this question; and if they did, how they acted upon it — how they expressed that better understanding?

In 1784, three years before the Constitution — the United States then owning the Northwestern Territory, and no other, the Congress of the Confederation had before them the question of prohibiting slavery in that Territory; and four of the "thirty-nine" who afterward framed the Constitution, were in that Congress, and voted on that question. Of these, Roger Sherman, Thomas Mifflin, and Hugh Williamson voted for the prohibition, thus showing that, in their understanding, no line dividing local from federal authority, nor anything else, properly forbade the Federal Government to control as to slavery in federal territory. The other of the four — James M'Henry — voted against the prohibition, showing that, for some cause, he thought it improper to vote for it.

In 1787, still before the Constitution, but while the Convention was in session framing it, and while the Northwestern Territory still was the only territory owned by the United States, the same question of prohibiting slavery in the territory again came before the Congress of the Confederation; and two more of the "thirty-nine" who afterward signed the Constitution, were in that Congress, and voted on the question. They were William Blount and William Few; and they both voted for the prohibition — thus showing that, in their understanding, no line dividing local from federal authority, nor anything else, properly forbids the Federal Government to control as to slavery in Federal territory. This time the prohibition became a law, being part of what is now well known as the Ordinance of '87.

The question of federal control of slavery in the territories, seems not to have been directly before the Convention which framed the original Constitution; and hence it is not recorded that the "thirty-nine," or any of them, while engaged on that instrument, expressed any opinion on that precise question.

In 1789, by the first Congress which sat under the Constitution, an act was passed to enforce the Ordinance of '87, including the prohibition of slavery in the Northwestern Territory. The bill for this act was reported by one of the "thirty-nine," Thomas Fitzsimmons, then a member of the House of Representatives from Pennsylvania. It went through all its stages without a word of opposition, and finally passed both branches without yeas and nays, which is equivalent to a unanimous passage. In this Congress there were sixteen of the thirty-nine fathers who framed the original Constitution. They were John Langdon, Nicholas Gilman, Wm. S. Johnson, Roger Sherman, Robert Morris, Thos. Fitzsimmons, William Few, Abraham Baldwin, Rufus King, William Paterson, George Clymer, Richard Bassett, George Read, Pierce Butler, Daniel Carroll, James Madison.

This shows that, in their understanding, no line dividing local from federal authority, nor anything in the Constitution, properly forbade Congress to prohibit slavery in the federal territory; else both their fidelity to correct principle, and their oath to support the Constitution, would have constrained them to oppose the prohibition.

Again, George Washington, another of the "thirty-nine," was then President of the United States, and, as such approved and signed the bill; thus completing its validity as a law, and thus showing that, in his understanding, no line dividing local from federal authority, nor anything in the Constitution, forbade the Federal Government, to control as to slavery in federal territory.

No great while after the adoption of the original Constitution, North Carolina ceded to the Federal Government the country now constituting the State of Tennessee; and a few years later Georgia ceded that which now constitutes the States of Mississippi and Alabama. In both deeds of cession it was made a condition by the ceding States that the Federal Government should not prohibit slavery in the ceded territory. Besides this, slavery was then actually in the ceded country. Under these circumstances, Congress, on taking charge of these countries, did not absolutely prohibit slavery within them. But they did interfere with it — take control of it — even there, to a certain extent. In 1798, Congress organized the Territory of Mississippi. In the act of organization, they prohibited the bringing of slaves into the Territory, from any place without the United States, by fine, and giving freedom to slaves so bought. This act passed both branches of Congress without yeas and nays. In that Congress were three of the "thirty-nine" who framed the original Constitution. They were John Langdon, George Read and Abraham Baldwin. They all, probably, voted for it. Certainly they would have placed their opposition to it upon record, if, in their understanding, any line dividing local from federal authority, or anything in the Constitution, properly forbade the Federal Government to control as to slavery in federal territory.

In 1803, the Federal Government purchased the Louisiana country. Our former territorial acquisitions came from certain of our own States; but this Louisiana country was acquired from a foreign nation. In 1804, Congress gave a territorial organization to that part of it which now constitutes the State of Louisiana. New Orleans, lying within that part, was an old and comparatively large city. There were other considerable towns and settlements, and slavery was extensively and thoroughly intermingled with the people. Congress did not, in the Territorial Act, prohibit slavery; but they did interfere with it — take control of it — in a more marked and extensive way than they did in the case of Mississippi. The substance of the provision therein made, in relation to slaves, was:

First. That no slave should be imported into the territory from foreign parts.

Second. That no slave should be carried into it who had been imported into the United States since the first day of May, 1798.

Third. That no slave should be carried into it, except by the owner, and for his own use as a settler; the penalty in all the cases being a fine upon the violator of the law, and freedom to the slave.

This act also was passed without yeas and nays. In the Congress which passed it, there were two of the "thirty-nine." They were Abraham Baldwin and Jonathan Dayton. As stated in the case of Mississippi, it is probable they both voted for it. They would not have allowed it to pass without recording their opposition to it, if, in their understanding, it violated either the line properly dividing local from federal authority, or any provision of the Constitution.

In 1819-20, came and passed the Missouri question. Many votes were taken, by yeas and nays, in both branches of Congress, upon the various phases of the general question. Two of the "thirty-nine" — Rufus King and Charles Pinckney — were members of that Congress. Mr. King steadily voted for slavery prohibition and against all compromises, while Mr. Pinckney as steadily voted against slavery prohibition and against all compromises. By this, Mr. King showed that, in his understanding, no line dividing local from federal authority, nor anything in the Constitution, was violated by Congress prohibiting slavery in federal territory; while Mr. Pinckney, by his votes, showed that, in his understanding, there was some sufficient reason for opposing such prohibition in that case.

The cases I have mentioned are the only acts of the "thirty-nine," or of any of them, upon the direct issue, which I have been able to discover.

To enumerate the persons who thus acted, as being four in 1784, two in 1787, seventeen in 1789, three in 1798, two in 1804, and two in 1819-20 — there would be thirty of them. But this would be counting John Langdon, Roger Sherman, William Few, Rufus King, and George Read each twice, and Abraham Baldwin, three times. The true number of those of the "thirty-nine" whom I have shown to have acted upon the question, which, by the text, they understood better than we, is twenty-three, leaving sixteen not shown to have acted upon it in any way.

Here, then, we have twenty-three out of our thirty-nine fathers "who framed the government under which we live," who have, upon their official responsibility and their corporal oaths, acted upon the very question which the text affirms they "understood just as well, and even better than we do now;" and twenty-one of them — a clear majority of the whole "thirty-nine" — so acting upon it as to make them guilty of gross political impropriety and willful perjury, if, in their understanding, any proper division between local and federal authority, or anything in the Constitution they had made themselves, and sworn to support, forbade the Federal Government to control as to slavery in the federal territories. Thus the twenty-one acted; and, as actions speak louder than words, so actions, under such responsibility, speak still louder.

Two of the twenty-three voted against Congressional prohibition of slavery in the federal territories, in the instances in which they acted upon the question. But for what reasons they so voted is not known. They may have done so because they thought a proper division of local from federal authority, or some provision or principle of the Constitution, stood in the way; or they may, without any such question, have voted against the prohibition, on what appeared to them to be sufficient grounds of expediency. No one who has sworn to support the Constitution can conscientiously vote for what he understands to be an unconstitutional measure, however expedient he may think it; but one may and ought to vote against a measure which he deems constitutional, if, at the same time, he deems it inexpedient. It, therefore, would be unsafe to set down even the two who voted against the prohibition, as having done so because, in their understanding, any proper division of local from federal authority, or anything in the Constitution, forbade the Federal Government to control as to slavery in federal territory.

The remaining sixteen of the "thirty-nine," so far as I have discovered, have left no record of their understanding upon the direct question of federal control of slavery in the federal territories. But there is much reason to believe that their understanding upon that question would not have appeared different from that of their twenty-three compeers, had it been manifested at all.

For the purpose of adhering rigidly to the text, I have purposely omitted whatever understanding may have been manifested by any person, however distinguished, other than the thirty-nine fathers who framed the original Constitution; and, for the same reason, I have also omitted whatever understanding may have been manifested by any of the "thirty-nine" even, on any other phase of the general question of slavery. If we should look into their acts and declarations on those other phases, as the foreign slave trade, and the morality and policy of slavery generally, it would appear to us that on the direct question of federal control of slavery in federal territories, the sixteen, if they had acted at all, would probably have acted just as the twenty-three did. Among that sixteen were several of the most noted anti-slavery men of those times — as Dr. Franklin, Alexander Hamilton and Gouverneur Morris — while there was not one now known to have been otherwise, unless it may be John Rutledge, of South Carolina.

The sum of the whole is, that of our thirty-nine fathers who framed the original Constitution, twenty-one — a clear majority of the whole — certainly understood that no proper division of local from federal authority, nor any part of the Constitution, forbade the Federal Government to control slavery in the federal territories; while all the rest probably had the same understanding. Such, unquestionably, was the understanding of our fathers who framed the original Constitution; and the text affirms that they understood the question "better than we."

But, so far, I have been considering the understanding of the question manifested by the framers of the original Constitution. In and by the original instrument, a mode was provided for amending it; and, as I have already stated, the present frame of "the Government under which we live" consists of that original, and twelve amendatory articles framed and adopted since. Those who now insist that federal control of slavery in federal territories violates the Constitution, point us to the provisions which they suppose it thus violates; and, as I understand, that all fix upon provisions in these amendatory articles, and not in the original instrument. The Supreme Court, in the Dred Scott case, plant themselves upon the fifth amendment, which provides that no person shall be deprived of "life, liberty or property without due process of law;" while Senator Douglas and his peculiar adherents plant themselves upon the tenth amendment, providing that "the powers not delegated to the United States by the Constitution" "are reserved to the States respectively, or to the people."

Now, it so happens that these amendments were framed by the first Congress which sat under the Constitution — the identical Congress which passed the act already mentioned, enforcing the prohibition of slavery in the Northwestern Territory. Not only was it the same Congress, but they were the identical, same individual men who, at the same session, and at the same time within the session, had under consideration, and in progress toward maturity, these Constitutional amendments, and this act prohibiting slavery in all the territory the nation then owned. The Constitutional amendments were introduced before, and passed after the act enforcing the Ordinance of '87; so that, during the whole pendency of the act to enforce the Ordinance, the Constitutional amendments were also pending.

The seventy-six members of that Congress, including sixteen of the framers of the original Constitution, as before stated, were preeminently our fathers who framed that part of "the Government under which we live," which is now claimed as forbidding the Federal Government to control slavery in the federal territories.

Is it not a little presumptuous in any one at this day to affirm that the two things which that Congress deliberately framed, and carried to maturity at the same time, are absolutely inconsistent with each other? And does not such affirmation become impudently absurd when coupled with the other affirmation from the same mouth, that those who did the two things, alleged to be inconsistent, understood whether they really were inconsistent better than we — better than he who affirms that they are inconsistent?

It is surely safe to assume that the thirty-nine framers of the original Constitution, and the seventy-six members of the Congress which framed the amendments thereto, taken together, do certainly include those who may be fairly called "our fathers who framed the Government under which we live." And so assuming, I defy any man to show that any one of them ever, in his whole life, declared that, in his understanding, any proper division of local from federal authority, or any part of the Constitution, forbade the Federal Government to control as to slavery in the federal territories. I go a step further. I defy any one to show that any living man in the whole world ever did, prior to the beginning of the present century, (and I might almost say prior to the beginning of the last half of the present century,) declare that, in his understanding, any proper division of local from federal authority, or any part of the Constitution, forbade the Federal Government to control as to slavery in the federal territories. To those who now so declare, I give, not only "our fathers who framed the Government under which we live," but with them all other living men within the century in which it was framed, among whom to search, and they shall not be able to find the evidence of a single man agreeing with them.

Now, and here, let me guard a little against being misunderstood. I do not mean to say we are bound to follow implicitly in whatever our fathers did. To do so, would be to discard all the lights of current experience — to reject all progress — all improvement. What I do say is, that if we would supplant the opinions and policy of our fathers in any case, we should do so upon evidence so conclusive, and argument so clear, that even their great authority, fairly considered and weighed, cannot stand; and most surely not in a case whereof we ourselves declare they understood the question better than we.

If any man at this day sincerely believes that a proper division of local from federal authority, or any part of the Constitution, forbids the Federal Government to control as to slavery in the federal territories, he is right to say so, and to enforce his position by all truthful evidence and fair argument which he can. But he has no right to mislead others, who have less access to history, and less leisure to study it, into the false belief that "our fathers who framed the Government under which we live" were of the same opinion — thus substituting falsehood and deception for truthful evidence and fair argument. If any man at this day sincerely believes "our fathers who framed the Government under which we live," used and applied principles, in other cases, which ought to have led them to understand that a proper division of local from federal authority or some part of the Constitution, forbids the Federal Government to control as to slavery in the federal territories, he is right to say so. But he should, at the same time, brave the responsibility of declaring that, in his opinion, he understands their principles better than they did themselves; and especially should he not shirk that responsibility by asserting that they "understood the question just as well, and even better, than we do now."

But enough! Let all who believe that "our fathers, who framed the Government under which we live, understood this question just as well, and even better, than we do now," speak as they spoke, and act as they acted upon it. This is all Republicans ask — all Republicans desire — in relation to slavery. As those fathers marked it, so let it be again marked, as an evil not to be extended, but to be tolerated and protected only because of and so far as its actual presence among us makes that toleration and protection a necessity. Let all the guarantees those fathers gave it, be, not grudgingly, but fully and fairly, maintained. For this Republicans contend, and with this, so far as I know or believe, they will be content.

And now, if they would listen — as I suppose they will not — I would address a few words to the Southern people.

I would say to them: — You consider yourselves a reasonable and a just people; and I consider that in the general qualities of reason and justice you are not inferior to any other people. Still, when you speak of us Republicans, you do so only to denounce us a reptiles, or, at the best, as no better than outlaws. You will grant a hearing to pirates or murderers, but nothing like it to "Black Republicans." In all your contentions with one another, each of you deems an unconditional condemnation of "Black Republicanism" as the first thing to be attended to. Indeed, such condemnation of us seems to be an indispensable prerequisite — license, so to speak — among you to be admitted or permitted to speak at all. Now, can you, or not, be prevailed upon to pause and to consider whether this is quite just to us, or even to yourselves? Bring forward your charges and specifications, and then be patient long enough to hear us deny or justify.

You say we are sectional. We deny it. That makes an issue; and the burden of proof is upon you. You produce your proof; and what is it? Why, that our party has no existence in your section — gets no votes in your section. The fact is substantially true; but does it prove the issue? If it does, then in case we should, without change of principle, begin to get votes in your section, we should thereby cease to be sectional. You cannot escape this conclusion; and yet, are you willing to abide by it? If you are, you will probably soon find that we have ceased to be sectional, for we shall get votes in your section this very year. You will then begin to discover, as the truth plainly is, that your proof does not touch the issue. The fact that we get no votes in your section, is a fact of your making, and not of ours. And if there be fault in that fact, that fault is primarily yours, and remains until you show that we repel you by some wrong principle or practice. If we do repel you by any wrong principle or practice, the fault is ours; but this brings you to where you ought to have started — to a discussion of the right or wrong of our principle. If our principle, put in practice, would wrong your section for the benefit of ours, or for any other object, then our principle, and we with it, are sectional, and are justly opposed and denounced as such. Meet us, then, on the question of whether our principle, put in practice, would wrong your section; and so meet it as if it were possible that something may be said on our side. Do you accept the challenge? No! Then you really believe that the principle which "our fathers who framed the Government under which we live" thought so clearly right as to adopt it, and indorse it again and again, upon their official oaths, is in fact so clearly wrong as to demand your condemnation without a moment's consideration.

Some of you delight to flaunt in our faces the warning against sectional parties given by Washington in his Farewell Address. Less than eight years before Washington gave that warning, he had, as President of the United States, approved and signed an act of Congress, enforcing the prohibition of slavery in the Northwestern Territory, which act embodied the policy of the Government upon that subject up to and at the very moment he penned that warning; and about one year after he penned it, he wrote LaFayette that he considered that prohibition a wise measure, expressing in the same connection his hope that we should at some time have a confederacy of free States.

Bearing this in mind, and seeing that sectionalism has since arisen upon this same subject, is that warning a weapon in your hands against us, or in our hands against you? Could Washington himself speak, would he cast the blame of that sectionalism upon us, who sustain his policy, or upon you who repudiate it? We respect that warning of Washington, and we commend it to you, together with his example pointing to the right application of it.

But you say you are conservative — eminently conservative — while we are revolutionary, destructive, or something of the sort. What is conservatism? Is it not adherence to the old and tried, against the new and untried? We stick to, contend for, the identical old policy on the point in controversy which was adopted by "our fathers who framed the Government under which we live;" while you with one accord reject, and scout, and spit upon that old policy, and insist upon substituting something new. True, you disagree among yourselves as to what that substitute shall be. You are divided on new propositions and plans, but you are unanimous in rejecting and denouncing the old policy of the fathers. Some of you are for reviving the foreign slave trade; some for a Congressional Slave-Code for the Territories; some for Congress forbidding the Territories to prohibit Slavery within their limits; some for maintaining Slavery in the Territories through the judiciary; some for the "gur-reat pur-rinciple" that "if one man would enslave another, no third man should object," fantastically called "Popular Sovereignty;" but never a man among you is in favor of federal prohibition of slavery in federal territories, according to the practice of "our fathers who framed the Government under which we live." Not one of all your various plans can show a precedent or an advocate in the century within which our Government originated. Consider, then, whether your claim of conservatism for yourselves, and your charge or destructiveness against us, are based on the most clear and stable foundations.

Again, you say we have made the slavery question more prominent than it formerly was. We deny it. We admit that it is more prominent, but we deny that we made it so. It was not we, but you, who discarded the old policy of the fathers. We resisted, and still resist, your innovation; and thence comes the greater prominence of the question. Would you have that question reduced to its former proportions? Go back to that old policy. What has been will be again, under the same conditions. If you would have the peace of the old times, readopt the precepts and policy of the old times.

You charge that we stir up insurrections among your slaves. We deny it; and what is your proof? Harper's Ferry! John Brown!! John Brown was no Republican; and you have failed to implicate a single Republican in his Harper's Ferry enterprise. If any member of our party is guilty in that matter, you know it or you do not know it. If you do know it, you are inexcusable for not designating the man and proving the fact. If you do not know it, you are inexcusable for asserting it, and especially for persisting in the assertion after you have tried and failed to make the proof. You need to be told that persisting in a charge which one does not know to be true, is simply malicious slander.

Some of you admit that no Republican designedly aided or encouraged the Harper's Ferry affair, but still insist that our doctrines and declarations necessarily lead to such results. We do not believe it. We know we hold to no doctrine, and make no declaration, which were not held to and made by "our fathers who framed the Government under which we live." You never dealt fairly by us in relation to this affair. When it occurred, some important State elections were near at hand, and you were in evident glee with the belief that, by charging the blame upon us, you could get an advantage of us in those elections. The elections came, and your expectations were not quite fulfilled. Every Republican man knew that, as to himself at least, your charge was a slander, and he was not much inclined by it to cast his vote in your favor. Republican doctrines and declarations are accompanied with a continual protest against any interference whatever with your slaves, or with you about your slaves. Surely, this does not encourage them to revolt. True, we do, in common with "our fathers, who framed the Government under which we live," declare our belief that slavery is wrong; but the slaves do not hear us declare even this. For anything we say or do, the slaves would scarcely know there is a Republican party. I believe they would not, in fact, generally know it but for your misrepresentations of us, in their hearing. In your political contests among yourselves, each faction charges the other with sympathy with Black Republicanism; and then, to give point to the charge, defines Black Republicanism to simply be insurrection, blood and thunder among the slaves.

Slave insurrections are no more common now than they were before the Republican party was organized. What induced the Southampton insurrection, twenty-eight years ago, in which, at least three times as many lives were lost as at Harper's Ferry? You can scarcely stretch your very elastic fancy to the conclusion that Southampton was "got up by Black Republicanism." In the present state of things in the United States, I do not think a general, or even a very extensive slave insurrection is possible. The indispensable concert of action cannot be attained. The slaves have no means of rapid communication; nor can incendiary freemen, black or white, supply it. The explosive materials are everywhere in parcels; but there neither are, nor can be supplied, the indispensable connecting trains.

Much is said by Southern people about the affection of slaves for their masters and mistresses; and a part of it, at least, is true. A plot for an uprising could scarcely be devised and communicated to twenty individuals before some one of them, to save the life of a favorite master or mistress, would divulge it. This is the rule; and the slave revolution in Hayti was not an exception to it, but a case occurring under peculiar circumstances. The gunpowder plot of British history, though not connected with slaves, was more in point. In that case, only about twenty were admitted to the secret; and yet one of them, in his anxiety to save a friend, betrayed the plot to that friend, and, by consequence, averted the calamity. Occasional poisonings from the kitchen, and open or stealthy assassinations in the field, and local revolts extending to a score or so, will continue to occur as the natural results of slavery; but no general insurrection of slaves, as

I think, can happen in this country for a long time. Whoever much fears, or much hopes for such an event, will be alike disappointed.

In the language of Mr. Jefferson, uttered many years ago, "It is still in our power to direct the process of emancipation, and deportation, peaceably, and in such slow degrees, as that the evil will wear off insensibly; and their places be, pari passu, filled up by free white laborers. If, on the contrary, it is left to force itself on, human nature must shudder at the prospect held up."

Mr. Jefferson did not mean to say, nor do I, that the power of emancipation is in the Federal Government. He spoke of Virginia; and, as to the power of emancipation, I speak of the slaveholding States only. The Federal Government, however, as we insist, has the power of restraining the extension of the institution — the power to insure that a slave insurrection shall never occur on any American soil which is now free from slavery.

John Brown's effort was peculiar. It was not a slave insurrection. It was an attempt by white men to get up a revolt among slaves, in which the slaves refused to participate. In fact, it was so absurd that the slaves, with all their ignorance, saw plainly enough it could not succeed. That affair, in its philosophy, corresponds with the many attempts, related in history, at the assassination of kings and emperors. An enthusiast broods over the oppression of a people till he fancies himself commissioned by Heaven to liberate them. He ventures the attempt, which ends in little else than his own execution. Orsini's attempt on Louis Napoleon, and John Brown's attempt at Harper's Ferry were, in their philosophy, precisely the same. The eagerness to cast blame on old England in the one case, and on New England in the other, does not disprove the sameness of the two things.

And how much would it avail you, if you could, by the use of John Brown, Helper's Book, and the like, break up the Republican organization? Human action can be modified to some extent, but human nature cannot be changed. There is a judgment and a feeling against slavery in this nation, which cast at least a million and a half of votes. You cannot destroy that judgment and feeling — that sentiment — by breaking up the political organization which rallies around it. You can scarcely scatter and disperse an army which has been formed into order in the face of your heaviest fire; but if you could, how much would you gain by forcing the sentiment which created it out of the peaceful channel of the ballot-box, into some other channel? What would that other channel probably be? Would the number of John Browns be lessened or enlarged by the operation?

But you will break up the Union rather than submit to a denial of your Constitutional rights.

That has a somewhat reckless sound; but it would be palliated, if not fully justified, were we proposing, by the mere force of numbers, to deprive you of some right, plainly written down in the Constitution. But we are proposing no such thing.

When you make these declarations, you have a specific and well-understood allusion to an assumed Constitutional right of yours, to take slaves into the federal territories, and to hold them there as property. But no such right is specifically written in the Constitution. That instrument is literally silent about any such right. We, on the contrary, deny that such a right has any existence in the Constitution, even by implication.

Your purpose, then, plainly stated, is that you will destroy the Government, unless you be allowed to construe and enforce the Constitution as you please, on all points in dispute between you and us. You will rule or ruin in all events.

This, plainly stated, is your language. Perhaps you will say the Supreme Court has decided the disputed Constitutional question in your favor. Not quite so. But waiving the lawyer's distinction between dictum and decision, the Court have decided the question for you in a sort of way. The Court have substantially said, it is your Constitutional right to take slaves into the federal territories, and to hold them there as property. When I say the decision was made in a sort of way, I mean it was made in a divided Court, by a bare majority of the Judges, and they not quite agreeing with one another in the reasons for making it; that it is so made as that its avowed supporters disagree with one another about its meaning, and that it was mainly based upon a mistaken statement of fact — the statement in the opinion that "the right of property in a slave is distinctly and expressly affirmed in the Constitution."

An inspection of the Constitution will show that the right of property in a slave is not "distinctly and expressly affirmed" in it. Bear in mind, the Judges do not pledge their judicial opinion that such right is impliedly affirmed in the Constitution; but they pledge their veracity that it is "distinctly and expressly" affirmed there — "distinctly," that is, not mingled with anything else — "expressly," that is, in words meaning just that, without the aid of any inference, and susceptible of no other meaning.

If they had only pledged their judicial opinion that such right is affirmed in the instrument by implication, it would be open to others to show that neither the word "slave" nor "slavery" is to be found in the Constitution, nor the word "property" even, in any connection with language alluding to the things slave, or slavery; and that wherever in that instrument the slave is alluded to, he is called a "person;" — and wherever his master's legal right in relation to him is alluded to, it is spoken of as "service or labor which may be due," — as a debt payable in service or labor. Also, it would be open to show, by contemporaneous history, that this mode of alluding to slaves and slavery, instead of speaking of them, was employed on purpose to exclude from the Constitution the idea that there could be property in man.

To show all this, is easy and certain.

When this obvious mistake of the Judges shall be brought to their notice, is it not reasonable to expect that they will withdraw the mistaken statement, and reconsider the conclusion based upon it?

And then it is to be remembered that "our fathers, who framed the Government under which we live" — the men who made the Constitution — decided this same Constitutional question in our favor, long ago — decided it without division among themselves, when making the decision; without division among themselves about the meaning of it after it was made, and, so far as any evidence is left, without basing it upon any mistaken statement of facts.

Under all these circumstances, do you really feel yourselves justified to break up this Government unless such a court decision as yours is, shall be at once submitted to as a conclusive and final rule of political action? But you will not abide the election of a Republican president! In that supposed event, you say, you will destroy the Union; and then, you say, the great crime of having destroyed it will be upon us! That is cool. A highwayman holds a pistol to my ear, and mutters through his teeth, "Stand and deliver, or I shall kill you, and then you will be a murderer!"

To be sure, what the robber demanded of me — my money — was

my own; and I had a clear right to keep it; but it was no more my own than my vote is my own; and the threat of death to me, to extort my money, and the threat of destruction to the Union, to extort my vote, can scarcely be distinguished in principle.

A few words now to Republicans. It is exceedingly desirable that all parts of this great Confederacy shall be at peace, and in harmony, one with another. Let us Republicans do our part to have it so. Even though much provoked, let us do nothing through passion and ill temper. Even though the southern people will not so much as listen to us, let us calmly consider their demands, and yield to them if, in our deliberate view of our duty, we possibly can. Judging by all they say and do, and by the subject and nature of their controversy with us, let us determine, if we can, what will satisfy them.

Will they be satisfied if the Territories be unconditionally surrendered to them? We know they will not. In all their present complaints against us, the Territories are scarcely mentioned. Invasions and insurrections are the rage now. Will it satisfy them, if, in the future, we have nothing to do with invasions and insurrections? We know it will not. We so know, because we know we never had anything to do with invasions and insurrections; and yet this total abstaining does not exempt us from the charge and the denunciation.

The question recurs, what will satisfy them? Simply this: We must not only let them alone, but we must somehow, convince them that we do let them alone. This, we know by experience, is no easy task. We have been so trying to convince them from the very beginning of our organization, but with no success. In all our platforms and speeches we have constantly protested our purpose to let them alone; but this has had no tendency to convince them. Alike unavailing to convince them, is the fact that they have never detected a man of us in any attempt to disturb them.

These natural, and apparently adequate means all failing, what will convince them? This, and this only: cease to call slavery wrong, and join them in calling it right. And this must be done thoroughly — done in acts as well as in words. Silence will not be tolerated — we must place ourselves avowedly with them. Senator Douglas' new sedition law must be enacted and enforced, suppressing all declarations that slavery is wrong, whether made in politics, in presses, in pulpits, or in private. We must arrest and return their fugitive slaves with greedy pleasure. We must pull down our Free State constitutions. The whole atmosphere must be disinfected from all taint of opposition to slavery, before they will cease to believe that all their troubles proceed from us.

I am quite aware they do not state their case precisely in this way. Most of them would probably say to us, "Let us alone, do nothing to us, and say what you please about slavery." But we do let them alone — have never disturbed them — so that, after all, it is what we say, which dissatisfies them. They will continue to accuse us of doing, until we cease saying.

I am also aware they have not, as yet, in terms, demanded the overthrow of our Free-State Constitutions. Yet those Constitutions declare the wrong of slavery, with more solemn emphasis, than do all other sayings against it; and when all these other sayings shall have been silenced, the overthrow of these Constitutions will be demanded, and nothing be left to resist the demand. It is nothing to the contrary, that they do not demand the whole of this just now. Demanding what they do, and for the reason they do, they can voluntarily stop nowhere short of this consummation. Holding, as they do, that slavery is morally right, and socially elevating, they cannot cease to demand a full national recognition of it, as a legal right, and a social blessing.

Nor can we justifiably withhold this, on any ground save our conviction that slavery is wrong. If slavery is right, all words, acts, laws, and constitutions against it, are themselves wrong, and should be silenced, and swept away. If it is right, we cannot justly object to its nationality — its universality; if it is wrong, they cannot justly insist upon its extension — its enlargement. All they ask, we could readily grant, if we thought slavery right; all we ask, they could as readily grant, if they thought it wrong. Their thinking it right, and our thinking it wrong, is the precise fact upon which depends the whole controversy. Thinking it right, as they do, they are not to blame for desiring its full recognition, as being right; but, thinking it wrong, as we do, can we yield to them? Can we cast our votes with their view, and against our own? In view of our moral, social, and political responsibilities, can we do this?

Wrong as we think slavery is, we can yet afford to let it alone where it is, because that much is due to the necessity arising from its actual presence in the nation; but can we, while our votes will prevent it, allow it to spread into the National Territories, and to overrun us here in these Free States? If our sense of duty forbids this, then let us stand by our duty, fearlessly and effectively. Let us be diverted by none of those sophistical contrivances wherewith we are so industriously plied and belabored — contrivances such as groping for some middle ground between the right and the wrong, vain as the search for a man who should be neither a living man nor a dead man — such as a policy of "don't care" on a question about which all true men do care — such as Union appeals beseeching true Union men to yield to Disunionists, reversing the divine rule, and calling, not the sinners, but the righteous to repentance — such as invocations to Washington, imploring men to unsay what Washington said, and undo what Washington did.

Neither let us be slandered from our duty by false accusations against us, nor frightened from it by menaces of destruction to the Government nor of dungeons to ourselves. LET US HAVE FAITH THAT RIGHT MAKES MIGHT, AND IN THAT FAITH, LET US, TO THE END, DARE TO DO OUR DUTY AS WE UNDERSTAND IT.

Emancipation Proclamation

By the President of the United States of America:

A Proclamation.

Whereas, on the twenty-second day of September, in the year of our Lord one thousand eight hundred and sixty two, a proclamation was issued by the President of the United States, containing, among other things, the following, to wit:

"That on the first day of January, in the year of our Lord one thousand eight hundred and sixty-three, all persons held as slaves within any State or designated part of a State, the people whereof shall then be in rebellion against the United States, shall be then, thenceforward, and forever free; and the Executive Government of the United States, including the military and naval authority thereof, will recognize and maintain the freedom of such persons, and will do no act or acts to repress such persons, or any of them, in any efforts they may make for their actual freedom.

"That the Executive will, on the first day of January aforesaid, by proclamation, designate the States and parts of States, if any, in which the people thereof, respectively, shall then be in rebellion against the United States; and the fact that any State, or the people thereof, shall on that day be, in good faith, represented in the Congress of the United States by members chosen thereto at elections wherein a majority of the qualified voters of such State shall have participated, shall, in the absence of strong countervailing testimony, be deemed conclusive evidence that such State, and the people thereof, are not then in rebellion against the United States."

Now, therefore I, Abraham Lincoln, President of the United States, by virtue of the power in me vested as Commander-in-Chief, of the Army and Navy of the United States in time of actual armed rebellion against the authority and government of the United States, and as a fit and necessary war measure for suppressing said rebellion, do, on this first day of January, in the year of our Lord one thousand eight hundred and sixty three, and in accordance with my purpose so to do publicly proclaimed for the full period of one hundred days, from the day first above mentioned, order and designate as the States and parts of States wherein the people thereof respectively, are this day in rebellion against the United States, the following, to wit:

Arkansas, Texas, Louisiana, (except the Parishes of St. Bernard, Plaquemines, Jefferson, St. Johns, St. Charles, St. James Ascension, Assumption, Terrebonne, Lafourche, St. Mary, St. Martin, and Orleans, including the City of New Orleans) Mississippi, Alabama, Florida, Georgia, South-Carolina, North-Carolina, and Virginia, (except the fortyeight counties designated as West Virginia, and also the counties of Berkley, Accomac, Northampton, Elizabeth-City, York, Princess Ann, and Norfolk, including the cities of Norfolk and Portsmouth[)], and which excepted parts, are for the present, left precisely as if this proclamation were not issued.

And by virtue of the power, and for the purpose aforesaid, I do order and declare that all persons held as slaves within said designated States, and parts of States, are, and henceforward shall be free; and that the Executive government of the United States, including the military and naval authorities thereof, will recognize and maintain the freedom of said persons.

And I hereby enjoin upon the people so declared to be free to abstain from all violence, unless in necessary self-defence; and I recommend to them that, in all cases when allowed, they labor faithfully for reasonable wages.

And I further declare and make known, that such persons of suitable condition, will be received into the armed service of the United States to garrison forts, positions, stations, and other places, and to man vessels of all sorts in said service.

And upon this act, sincerely believed to be an act of justice, warranted by the Constitution, upon military necessity, I invoke the considerate judgment of mankind, and the gracious favor of Almighty God.

In witness whereof, I have hereunto set my hand and caused the seal of the United States to be affixed.

Done at the City of Washington, this first day of January, in the year of our Lord one thousand eight hundred and sixty three, and of the Independence of the United States of America the eighty-seventh.

By the President: ABRAHAM LINCOLN

WILLIAM H. SEWARD, Secretary of State.

The Gettysburg Address (November 19, 1863)

Four score and seven years ago our fathers brought forth on this continent, a new nation, conceived in Liberty, and dedicated to the proposition that all men are created equal.

Now we are engaged in a great civil war, testing whether that nation, or any nation so conceived and so dedicated, can long endure. We are met on a great battle-field of that war. We have come to dedicate a portion of that field, as a final resting place for those who here gave their lives that that nation might live. It is altogether fitting and proper that we should do this.

But, in a larger sense, we can not dedicate — we can not consecrate — we can not hallow — this ground. The brave men, living and dead, who struggled here, have consecrated it, far above our poor power to add or detract. The world will little note, nor long remember what we say here, but it can never forget what they did here. It is for us the living, rather, to be dedicated here to the unfinished work which they who fought here have thus far so nobly advanced. It is rather for us to be here dedicated to the great task remaining before us — that from these honored dead we take increased devotion to that cause for which they gave the last full measure of devotion — that we here highly resolve that these dead shall not have died in vain — that this nation, under God, shall have a new birth of freedom — and that government of the people, by the people, for the people, shall not perish from the earth.

Lincoln's Second Inaugural Address (March 4, 1865)

At this second appearing to take the oath of the presidential office, there is less occasion for an extended address than there was at the first. Then a statement, somewhat in detail, of a course to be pursued, seemed fitting and proper. Now, at the expiration of four years, during which public declarations have been constantly called forth on every point and phase of the great contest which still absorbs the attention, and engrosses the energies of the nation, little that is new could be presented. The progress of our arms, upon which all else chiefly depends, is as well known to the public as to myself; and it is, I trust, reasonably satisfactory and encouraging to all. With high hope for the future, no prediction in regard to it is ventured.

On the occasion corresponding to this four years ago, all thoughts were anxiously directed to an impending civil war. All dreaded it — all sought to avert it. While the inaugeral [sic] address was being delivered from this place, devoted altogether to saving the Union without war, insurgent agents were in the city seeking to destroy it without war— seeking to dissole [sic] the Union, and divide effects, by negotiation. Both parties deprecated war; but one of them would make war rather than let the nation survive; and the other would accept war rather than let it perish. And the war came.

One eighth of the whole population were colored slaves, not distributed generally over the Union, but localized in the Southern part of it. These slaves constituted a peculiar and powerful interest. All knew that this interest was, somehow, the cause of the war. To strengthen, perpetuate, and extend this interest was the object for which the insurgents would rend the Union, even by war; while the government claimed no right to do more than to restrict the territorial enlargement of it. Neither party expected for the war, the magnitude, or the duration, which it has already attained. Neither anticipated that the cause of the conflict might cease with, or even before, the conflict itself should cease. Each looked for an easier triumph, and a result less fundamental and astounding. Both read the same Bible, and pray to the same God; and each invokes His aid against the other. It may seem strange that any men should dare to ask a just God's assistance in wringing their bread from the sweat of other men's faces; but let us judge not that we be not judged. The prayers of both could not be answered; that of neither has been answered fully. The Almighty has his own purposes. "Woe unto the world because of offences! for it must needs be that offences come; but woe to that man by whom the offence cometh!" If we shall suppose that American Slavery is one of those offences which, in the providence of God, must needs come, but which, having continued through His appointed time, He now wills to remove, and that He gives to both North and South, this terrible war, as the woe due to those by whom the offence came, shall we discern therein any departure from those divine attributes which the believers in a Living God always ascribe to Him? Fondly do we hope — fervently do we pray — that this mighty scourge of war may speedily pass away. Yet, if God wills that it continue, until all the wealth piled by the bond-man's two hundred and fifty years of unrequited toil shall be sunk, and until every drop of blood drawn with the lash, shall be paid by another drawn with the sword, as was said three thousand years ago, so still it must be said "the judgments of the Lord, are true and righteous altogether"

With malice toward none; with charity for all; with firmness in the right, as God gives us to see the right, let us strive on to finish the work we are in; to bind up the nation's wounds; to care for him who shall have borne the battle, and for his widow, and his orphan — to do all which may achieve and cherish a just and lasting peace, among ourselves, and with all nations.

Plessy v. Ferguson,

U.S. Supreme Court
163 U.S. 537
PLESSY
v.
FERGUSON.
No. 210.
May 18, 1896.

This was a petition for writs of prohibition and certiorari originally filed in the supreme court of the state by Plessy, the plaintiff in error, against the Hon. John H. Ferguson, judge of the criminal district court for the parish of Orleans, and setting forth, in substance, the following facts:

That petitioner was a citizen of the United States and a resident of the state of Louisiana, of mixed descent, in the proportion of seven-e ghths Caucasian and one-eighth African blood; that the mixture of colored blood was not discernible in him, and that he was entitled to every recognition, right, privilege, and immunity secured to the citizens of the United States of the white race by its constitution and laws; that on June 7, 1892, he engaged and paid for a first-class passage on the East Louisiana Railway, from New Orleans to Covington, in the same state, and thereupon entered a passenger train, and took possession of a vacant seat in a coach where passengers of the white race were accommodated; that such railroad company was incorporated by the laws of Louisiana as a common carrier, and was not authorized to distinguish between citizens according to their race, but, notwithstanding this, petitioner was required by the conductor, under penalty of ejection from said train and imprisonment, to vacate said coach, and occupy another seat, in a coach assigned by said company for persons not of the white race, and for no other reason than that petitioner was of the colored race; that, upon petitioner's refusal to comply with such order, he was, with the aid of a police officer, forcibly ejected from said coach, and hurried off to, and imprisoned in, the parish jail of New Orleans, and there held to answer a charge made by such officer to the effect that he was guilty of having criminally violated an act of the general assembly of the state, approved July 10, 1890, in such case made and provided.

The petitioner was subsequently brought before the recorder of the city for preliminary examination, and committed for trial to the criminal district court for the parish of Orleans, where an information was filed against him in the matter above set forth, for a violation of the above act, which act the petitioner affirmed to be null and void, because in conflict with the constitution of the United States; that petitioner interposed a plea to such information, based upon the unconstitutionality of the act of the general assembly, to which the district attorney, on behalf of the state, filed a demurrer; that, upon issue being joined upon such demurrer and plea, the court sustained the demurrer, overruled the plea, and ordered petitioner to plead over to the facts set forth in the information, and that, unless the judge of the said court be enjoined by a writ of prohibition from further proceeding in such case, the court will proceed to fine and sentence petitioner to imprisonment, and thus deprive him of his constitutional rights set forth in his said plea, notwithstanding the unconstitutionality of the act under which he was being prosecuted; that no appeal lay from such sentence, and petitioner was without relief or remedy except by writs of prohibition and certiorari. Copies of the information and other proceedings in the criminal district court were annexed to the petition as an exhibit.

Upon the filing of this petition, an order was issued upon the respondent to show cause why a writ of prohibition should not issue, and be made perpetual, and a further order that the record of the proceedings had in the criminal cause be certified and transmitted to the supreme court.

To this order the respondent made answer, transmitting a certified copy of the proceedings, asserting the constitutionality of the law, and averring that, instead of pleading or admitting that he belonged to the colored race, the said Plessy declined and refused, either by pleading or otherwise, to admit that he was in any sense or in any proportion a colored man.

The case coming on for hearing before the supreme court, that court was of opinion that the law under which the prosecution was had was constitutional and denied the relief prayed for by the petitioner (Ex parte Plessy, 45 La. Ann. 80, 11 South. 948); whereupon petitioner prayed for a writ of error from this court, which was allowed by the chief justice of the supreme court of Louisiana.

Mr. Justice Harlan dissenting.

A. W. Tourgee and S. F. Phillips, for plaintiff in error.

Alex. Porter Morse, for defendant in error.

Mr. Justice BROWN, after stating the facts in the foregoing language, delivered the opinion of the court.

This case turns upon the constitutionality of an act of the general assembly of the state of Louisiana, passed in 1890, providing for separate railway carriages for the white and colored races. Acts 1890, No. 111, p. 152.

The first section of the statute enacts 'that all railway companies carrying passengers in their coaches in this state, shall provide equal but separate accommodations for the white, and colored races, by providing two or more passenger coaches for each passenger train, or by dividing the passenger coaches by a partition so as to secure separate accommodations: provided, that this section shall not be construed to apply to street railroads. No person or persons shall be permitted to occupy seats in coaches, other than the ones assigned to them, on account of the race they belong to.'

By the second section it was enacted 'that the officers of such passenger trains shall have power and are hereby required to assign each passenger to the coach or compartment used for the race to which such passenger belongs; any passenger insisting on going into a coach or compartment to which by race he does not belong, shall be liable to a fine of twenty-five dollars, or in lieu thereof to imprisonment for a period of not more than twenty days in the parish prison, and any officer of any railroad insisting on assigning a passenger to a coach or compartment other than the one set aside for the race to which said passenger belongs, shall be liable to a fine of twenty-five dollars, or in lieu thereof to imprisonment for a period of not more than twenty days in the parish prison; and should any passenger refuse to occupy the coach or compartment to which he or she is assigned by the officer of such railway, said officer shall have power to refuse to carry such passenger on his train, and for such refusal neither he nor the railway company which he represents shall be liable for damages in any of the courts of this state.'

The third section provides penalties for the refusal or neglect of the officers, directors, conductors, and employees of railway companies to comply with the act, with a proviso that 'nothing in this act shall be construed as applying to nurses attending children of the other race.' The fourth section is immaterial.

The information filed in the criminal district court charged, in substance, that Plessy, being a passenger between two stations within the state of Louisiana, was assigned by officers of the company to the coach used for the race to which he belonged, but he insisted upon going into a coach used by the race to which he did not belong. Neither in the information nor plea was his particular race or color averred.

The petition for the writ of prohibition averred that petitioner was seven-eights Caucasian and one-eighth African blood; that the mixture of colored blood was not discernible in him; and that he was entitled to every right, privilege, and immunity secured to citizens of the United States of the white race; and that, upon such theory, he took possession of a vacant seat in a coach where passengers of the white race were accommodated, and was ordered by the conductor to vacate said coach, and take a seat in another, assigned to persons of the colored race, and, having refused to comply with such demand, he was forcibly ejected, with the aid of a police officer, and imprisoned in the parish jail to answer a charge of having violated the above act.

The constitutionality of this act is attacked upon the ground that it conflicts both with the thirteenth amendment of the constitution, abolishing slavery, and the fourteenth amendment, which prohibits certain restrictive legislation on the part of the states.

1. That it does not conflict with the thirteenth amendment, which abolished slavery and involuntary servitude, except a punishment for crime, is too clear for argument. Slavery implies involuntary servitude, — a state of bondage; the ownership of mankind as a chattel, or, at least, the control of the labor and services of one man for the benefit of another, and the absence of a legal right to the disposal of his

own person, property, and services. This amendment was said in the Slaughter-House Cases, 16 Wall. 36, to have been intended primarily to abolish slavery, as it had been previously known in this country, and that it equally forbade Mexican peonage or the Chinese coolie trade, when they amounted to slavery or involuntary servitude, and that the use of the word 'servitude' was intended to prohibit the use of all forms of involuntary slavery, of whatever class or name. It was intimated, however, in that case, that this amendment was regarded by the statesmen of that day as insufficient to protect the colored race from certain laws which had been enacted in the Southern states, imposing upon the colored race onerous disabilities and burdens, and curtailing their rights in the pursuit of life, liberty, and property to such an extent that their freedom was of little value; and that the fourteenth amendment was devised to meet this exigency.

So, too, in the Civil Rights Cases, 109 U.S. 3, 3 Sup. Ct. 18, it was said that the act of a mere individual, the owner of an inn, a public conveyance or place of amusement, refusing accommodations to colored people, cannot be justly regarded as imposing any badge of slavery or servitude upon the applicant, but only as involving an ordinary civil injury, properly cognizable by the laws of the state, and presumably subject to redress by those laws until the contrary appears. 'It would be running the slavery question into the ground,' said Mr. Justice Bradley, 'to make it apply to every act of discrimination which a person may see fit to make as to the guests he will entertain, or as to the people he will take into his coach or cab or car, or admit to his concert or theater, or deal with in other matters of intercourse or business.'

A statute which implies merely a legal distinction between the white and colored races-a distinction which is founded in the color of the two races, and which must always exist so long as white men are distinguished from the other race by color-has no tendency to destroy the legal equality of the two races, or re-establish a state of involuntary servitude. Indeed, we do not understand that the thirteenth amendment is strenuously relied upon by the plaintiff in error in this connection.

2. By the fourteenth amendment, all persons born or naturalized in the United States, and subject to the jurisdiction thereof, are made citizens of the United States and of the state wherein they reside; and

the states are forbidden from making or enforcing any law which shall abridge the privileges or immunities of citizens of the United States, or shall deprive any person of life, liberty, or property without due process of law, or deny to any person within their jurisdiction the equal protection of the laws.

The proper construction of this amendment was first called to the attention of this court in the Slaughter-House Cases, 16 Wall. 36, which involved, however, not a question of race, but one of exclusive privileges. The case did not call for any expression of opinion as to the exact rights it was intended to secure to the colored race, but it was said generally that its main purpose was to establish the citizenship of the negro, to give definitions of citizenship of the United States and of the states, and to protect from the hostile legislation of the states the privileges and immunities of citizens of the United States, as distinguished from those of citizens of the states. The object of the amendment was undoubtedly to enforce the absolute equality of the two races before the law, but, in the nature of things, it could not have been intended to abolish distinctions based upon color, or to enforce social, as distinguish d from political, equality, or a commingling of the two races upon terms unsatisfactory to either. Laws permitting, and even requiring, their separation, in places where they are liable to be brought into contact, do not necessarily imply the inferiority of either race to the other, and have been generally, if not universally, recognized as within the competency of the state legislatures in the exercise of their police power. The most common instance of this is connected with the establishment of separate schools for white and colored children, which have been held to be a valid exercise of the legislative power even by courts of states where the political rights of the colored race have been longest and most earnestly enforced.

One of the earliest of these cases is that of Roberts v. City of Boston, 5 Cush. 198, in which the supreme judicial court of Massachusetts held that the general school committee of Boston had power to make provision for the instruction of colored children in separate schools established exclusively for them, and to prohibit their attendance upon the other schools. 'The great principle,' said Chief Justice Shaw, 'advanced by the learned and eloquent advocate for the plaintiff [Mr. Charles Sumner], is that, by the constitution and laws of Massachusetts, all persons, without distinction of age or sex, birth or color, origin or condition, are equal before the law. ... But, when this great principle comes to be applied to the actual and various conditions of persons in society, it will not warrant the assertion that men and women are legally clothed with the same civil and political powers, and that children and adults are legally to have the same functions and be subject to the same treatment; but only that the rights of all, as they are settled and regulated by law, are equally entitled to the paternal consideration and protection of the law for their maintenance and security.' It was held that the powers of the committee extended to the establishment of separate schools for children of different ages, sexes and colors, and that they might also establish special schools for poor and neglected children, who have become too old to attend the primary school, and yet have not acquired the rudiments of learning, to enable them to enter the ordinary schools. Similar laws have been enacted by congress under its general power of legislation over the District of Columbia (sections 281- 283, 310, 319, Rev. St. D. C.), as well as by the legislatures of many of the states, and have been generally, if not uniformly, sustained by the courts. State v. McCann, 21 Ohio St. 210; Lehew v. Brummell (Mo. Sup.) 15 S. W. 765; Ward v. Flood, 48 Cal. 36; Bertonneau v. Directors of City Schools, 3 Woods, 177, Fed. Cas. No. 1,361; People v. Gallagher, 93 N. Y. 438; Cory v. Carter, 48 Ind. 337; Dawson v. Lee, 83 Ky. 49.

Laws forbidding the intermarriage of the two races may be said in a technical sense to interfere with the freedom of contract, and yet have been universally recognized as within the police power of the state. State v. Gibson, 36 Ind. 389.

The distinction between laws interfering with the political equality of the negro and those requiring the separation of the two races in schools, theaters, and railway carriages has been frequently drawn by this court. Thus, in Strauder v. West Virginia, 100 U.S. 303, it was held that a law of West Virginia limiting to white male persons 21 years of age, and citizens of the state, the right to sit upon juries, was a discrimination which implied a legal inferiority in civil society, which lessened the security of the right of the colored race, and was a step towards reducing them to a condition of servility. Indeed, the right of a colored man that, in the selection of jurors to pass upon his life, liberty, and property, there shall be no exclusion of his race, and no discrimination against them because of color, has been asserted in a number of cases. Virginia v. Rivers, 100 U.S. 313 ; Neal v. Delaware, 103 U.S. 370 ; ush v. Com., 107 U.S. 110 , 1 Sup. Ct. 625; Gibson v. Mississippi, 162 U.S. 565 , 16 Sup. Ct. 904. So, where the laws of a particular locality or the charter of a particular railway corporation has provided that no person shall be excluded from the cars on account of color, we have held that this meant that persons of color should travel in the same car as white ones, and that the enactment was not satisfied by the company providing cars assigned exclusively to people of color, though they were as good as those which they assigned exclusively to white persons. Railroad Co. v. Brown, 17 Wall. 445.

Upon the other hand, where a statute of Louisiana required those engaged in the transportation of passengers among the states to give to all persons traveling within that state, upon vessels employed in that business, equal rights and privileges in all parts of the vessel, without distinction on account of race or color, and subjected to an action for damages the owner of such a vessel who excluded colored passengers on account of their color from the cabin set aside by him for the use of whites, it was held to be, so far as it applied to interstate commerce, unconstitutional and void. Hall v. De Cuir, 95 U.S. 485 . The court in this case, however, expressly disclaimed that it had anything whatever to do with the statute as a regulation of internal commerce, or affecting anything else than commerce among the states.

In the Civil Rights Cases, 109 U.S. 3 , 3 Sup. Ct. 18, it was held that an act of congress entitling all persons within the jurisdiction of the United States to the full and equal enjoyment of the accommodations, advantages, facilities, and privileges of inns, public conveyances, on land or water, theaters, and other places of public amusement, and made applicable to citizens of every race and color, regardless of any previous condition of servitude, was unconstitutional and void, upon the ground that the fourteenth amendment was prohibitory upon the states only, and the legislation authorized to be adopted by congress for enforcing it was not direct legislation on matters respecting which the states were prohibited from making or enforcing certain laws, or doing certain acts, but was corrective legislation, such as might be necessary or proper for counter-acting and redressing the effect of such laws or acts. In delivering the opinion of the court, Mr. Justice Bradley observed that the fourteenth amendment 'does not invest congress with power to legislate upon subjects that are within the domain of state legislation, but to provide modes of relief against state legislation or state action of the kind referred to. It does not authorize congress to create a code of municipal law for the regulation of private rights, but to provide modes of redress against the operation of state laws, and the action of state officers, executive or judicial, when these are subversive of the fundamental rights specified in the amendment. Positive rights and privileges are undoubtedly secured by the fourteenth amendment; but they are secured by way of prohibition against state laws and state proceedings affecting those rights and privileges, and by power given to congress to legislate for the purpose of carrying such prohibition into effect; and such legislation must necessarily be predicated upon such supposed state laws or state proceedings, and be directed to the correction of their operation and effect.'

Much nearer, and, indeed, almost directly in point, is the case of the Louisville, N. O. & T. Ry. Co. v. State, 133 U.S. 587 , 10 Sup. Ct. 348, wherein the railway company was indicted for a violation of a statute of Mississippi, enacting that all railroads carrying passengers should provide equal, but separate, accommodations for the white and colored races, by providing two or more passenger cars for each passenger train, or by dividing the passenger cars by a partition, so as to secure separate accommodations. The case was presented in a different aspe t from the one under consideration, inasmuch as it was an indictment against the railway company for failing to provide the separate accommodations, but the question considered was the constitutionality of the law. In that case, the supreme court of Mississippi (66 Miss. 662, 6 South. 203) had held that the statute applied solely to commerce within the state, and, that being the construction of the state statute by its highest court, was accepted as conclusive. 'If it be a matter,' said the court (page 591, 133 U. S., and page 348, 10 Sup. Ct.), 'respecting commerce wholly within a state, and not interfering with commerce between the states, then, obviously, there is no violation of the commerce clause of the federal constitution. ... No question arises under this section as to the power of the state to separate in different compartments interstate pas- sengers, or affect, in any manner, the privileges and rights of such passengers. All that we can consider is whether the state has the power to require that railroad trains within her limits shall have separate accommodations for the two races. That affecting only commerce within the state is no invasion of the power given to congress by the commerce clause.'

A like course of reasoning applies to the case under consideration, since the supreme court of Louisiana, in the case of State v. Judge, 44 La. Ann. 770, 11 South. 74, held that the statute in question did not apply to interstate passengers, but was confined in its application to passengers traveling exclusively within the borders of the state. The case was decided largely upon the authority of Louisville, N. O. & T. Ry. Co. v. State, 66 Miss. 662, 6 South, 203, and affirmed by this court in 133 U.S. 587 , 10 Sup. Ct. 348. In the present case no question of interference with interstate commerce can possibly arise, since the East Louisiana Railway appears to have been purely a local line, with both its termini within the state of Louisiana. Similar statutes for the separation of the two races upon public conveyances were held to be constitutional in Railroad v. Miles, 55 Pa. St. 209; Day v. Owen 5 Mich. 520; Railway Co. v. Williams, 55 Ill. 185; Railroad Co. v. Wells, 85 Tenn. 613; 4 S. W. 5; Railroad Co. v. Benson, 85 Tenn. 627, 4 S. W. 5; The Sue, 22 Fed. 843; Logwood v. Railroad Co., 23 Fed. 318; McGuinn v. Forbes, 37 Fed. 639; People v. King (N. Y. App.) 18 N. E. 245; Houck v. Railway Co., 38 Fed. 226; Heard v. Railroad Co., 3 Inter St. Commerce Com. R. 111, 1 Inter St. Commerce Com. R. 428.

While we think the enforced separation of the races, as applied to the internal commerce of the state, neither abridges the privileges or immunities of the colored man, deprives him of his property without due process of law, nor denies him the equal protection of the laws, within the meaning of the fourteenth amendment, we are not prepared to say that the conductor, in assigning passengers to the coaches according to their race, does not act at his peril, or that the provision of the second section of the act that denies to the passenger compensa- tion in damages for a refusal to receive him into the coach in which he properly belongs is a valid exercise of the legislative power. Indeed, we understand it to be conceded by the state's attorney that such part of the act as exempts from liability the railway company and its officers is unconstitutional. The power to assign to a particular coach obviously implies the power to determine to which race the passenger belongs, as well as the power to determine who, under the laws of the particular state, is to be deemed a white, and who a colored, person. This question, though indicated in the brief of the plaintiff in error, does not properly arise upon the record in this case, since the only issue made is as to the unconstitutionality of the act, so far as it requires the railway to provide separate accommodations, and the conductor to assign passengers according to their race.

It is claimed by the plaintiff in error that, in an mixed community, the reputation of belonging to the dominant race, in this instance the white race, is 'property,' in the same sense that a right of action or of inheritance is property. Conceding this to be so, for the purposes of this case, we are unable to see how this statute deprives him of, or in any way affects his right to, such property. If he be a white man, and assigned to a colored coach, he may have his action for damages against the company for being deprived of his so-called 'property.' Upon the other hand, if he be a colored man, and be so assigned, he has been deprived of no property, since he is not lawfully entitled to the reputation of being a white man.

In this connection, it is also suggested by the learned counsel for the plaintiff in error that the same argument that will justify the state legislature in requiring railways to provide separate accommodations for the two races will also authorize them to require separate cars to be provided for people whose hair is of a certain color, or who are aliens, or who belong to certain nationalities, or to enact laws requiring colored people to walk upon one side of the street, and white people upon the other, or requiring white men's houses to be painted white, and colored men's black, or their vehicles or business signs to be of different colors, upon the theory that one side of the street is as good as the other, or that a house or vehicle of one color is as good as one of another color. The reply to all this is that every exercise of the police power must be reasonable, and extend only to such laws as are enacted in good faith for the promotion of the public good, and not for the annoyance or oppression of a particular class. Thus, in Yick Wo v. Hopkins, 118 U.S. 356 , 6 Sup. Ct. 1064, it was held by this court that a municipal ordinance of the city of San Francisco, to regulate the carrying on of public laundries within the limits of the municipality, violated the provisions of the constitution of the United States, if it conferred upon the municipal authorities arbitrary power, at their own will, and without regard to discretion, in the legal sense of the term, to give or withhold consent as to persons or places, without regard to the competency of the persons applying or the propriety of the places selected for the carrying on of the business. It was held to be a covert attempt on the part of the municipality to make an arbitrary and unjust discrimination against the Chinese race. While this was the case of a municipal ordinance, a like principle has been held to apply to acts of a state legislature passed in the exercise of the police power. Railroad Co. v. Husen, 95 U.S. 465 ; Louisville & N. R. Co. v. Kentucky, 161 U.S. 677 , 16 Sup. Ct. 714, and cases cited on page 700, 161 U. S., and page 714, 16 Sup. Ct.; Daggett v. Hudson, 43 Ohio St. 548, 3 N. E. 538; Capen v. Foster, 12 Pick. 485; State v. Baker, 38 Wis. 71; Monroe v. Collins, 17 Ohio St. 665; Hulseman v. Rems, 41 Pa. St. 396; Osman v. Riley, 15 Cal. 48.

So far, then, as a conflict with the fourteenth amendment is concerned, the case reduces itself to the question whether the statute of Louisiana is a reasonable regulation, and with respect to this there must necessarily be a large discretion on the part of the legislature. In determining the question of reasonableness, it is at liberty to act with reference to the established usages, customs, and traditions of the people, and with a view to the promotion of their comfort, and the preservation of the public peace and good order. Gauged by this standard, we cannot say that a law which authorizes or even requires the separation of the two races in public conveyances is unreasonable, or more obnoxious to the fourteenth amendment than the acts of congress requiring separate schools for colored children in the District of Columbia, the constitutionality of which does not seem to have been questioned, or the corresponding acts of state legislatures.

We consider the u derlying fallacy of the plaintiff's argument to consist in the assumption that the enforced separation of the two races stamps the colored race with a badge of inferiority. If this be so, it is not by reason of anything found in the act, but solely because the colored race chooses to put that construction upon it. The argument necessarily assumes that if, as has been more than once the case, and is not unlikely to be so again, the colored race should become the dominant power in the state legislature, and should enact a law in precisely similar terms, it would thereby relegate the white race to an inferior position. We imagine that the white race, at least, would not acquiesce in this assumption. The argument also assumes that social prejudices may be overcome by legislation, and that equal rights cannot be secured to the negro except by an enforced commingling of the two races. We cannot accept this proposition. If the two races are to meet upon terms of social equality, it must be the result of natural affinities, a mutual appreciation of each other's merits, and a voluntary consent of individuals. As was said by the court of appeals of New York in People v. Gallagher, 93 N. Y. 438, 448: 'This end can neither be accomplished nor promoted by laws which conflict with the general sentiment of the community upon whom they are designed to operate. When the government, therefore, has secured to each of its citizens equal rights before the law, and equal opportunities for improvement and progress, it has accomplished the end for which it was organized, and performed all of the functions respecting social advantages with which it is endowed.' Legislation is powerless to eradicate racial instincts, or to abolish distinctions based upon physical differences, and the attempt to do so can only result in accentuating the difficulties of the present situation. If the civil and political rights of both races be equal, one cannot be inferior to the other civilly or politically. If one race be inferior to the other socially, the constitution of the United States cannot put them upon the same plane.

It is true that the question of the proportion of colored blood necessary to constitute a colored person, as distinguished from a white person, is one upon which there is a difference of opinion in the different states; some holding that any visible admixture of black blood stamps the person as belonging to the colored race (State v. Chavers, 5 Jones [N. C.] 1); others, that it depends upon the preponderance of blood (Gray v. State, 4 Ohio, 354; Monroe v. Collins, 17 Ohio St. 665); and still others, that the predominance of white blood must only be in the proportion of three-fourths (People v. Dean, 14 Mich. 406; Jones v. Com., 80 Va. 544). But these are questions to be determined under the laws of each state, and are not properly put in issue in this case. Under the allegations of his petition, it may undoubtedly become a question of importance whether, under the laws of Louisiana, the petitioner belongs to the white or colored race.

The judgment of the court below is therefore affirmed.

Mr. Justice BREWER did not hear the argument or participate in the decision of this case.

Mr. Justice HARLAN dissenting.

By the Louisiana statute the validity of which is here involved, all railway companies (other than street-railroad companies) carry passengers in that state are required to have separate but equal accommodations for white and colored persons, 'by providing two or more passenger coaches for each passenger train, or by dividing the passenger coaches by a partition so as to secure separate accommodations.' Under this statute, no colored person is permitted to occupy a seat in a coach assigned to white persons; nor any white person to occupy a seat in a coach assigned to colored persons. The managers of the railroad are not allowed to exercise any discretion in the premises, but are required to assign each passenger to some coach or compartment set apart for the exclusive use of is race. If a passenger insists upon going into a coach or compartment not set apart for persons of his race, he is subject to be fined, or to be imprisoned in the parish jail. Penalties are prescribed for the refusal or neglect of the officers, directors, conductors, and employees of railroad companies to comply with the provisions of the act.

Only 'nurses attending children of the other race' are excepted from the operation of the statute. No exception is made of colored attendants traveling with adults. A white man is not permitted to have his colored servant with him in the same coach, even if his condition of health requires the constant personal assistance of such servant. If a colored maid insists upon riding in the same coach with a white woman whom she has been employed to serve, and who may need her personal attention while traveling, she is subject to be fined or imprisoned for such an exhibition of zeal in the discharge of duty.

While there may be in Louisiana persons of different races who are not citizens of the United States, the words in the act 'white and colored races' necessarily include all citizens of the United States of both races residing in that state. So that we have before us a state enactment that compels, under penalties, the separation of the two races in railroad passenger coaches, and makes it a crime for a citizen of either race to enter a coach that has been assigned to citizens of the other race.

Thus, the state regulates the use of a public highway by citizens of the United States solely upon the basis of race.

However apparent the injustice of such legislation may be, we have only to consider whether it is consistent with the constitution of the United States.

That a railroad is a public highway, and that the corporation which owns or operates it is in the exercise of public functions, is not, at this day, to be disputed. Mr. Justice Nelson, speaking for this court in New Jersey Steam Nav. Co. v. Merchants' Bank, 6 How. 344, 382, said that a common carrier was in the exercise 'of a sort of public office, and has public duties to perform, from which he should not be permitted to exonerate himself without the assent of the parties concerned.' Mr. Justice Strong, delivering the judgment of this court in Olcott v. Supervisors, 16 Wall. 678, 694, said: 'That railroads, though constructed by private corporations, and owned by them, are public highways, has been the doctrine of nearly all the courts ever since such conveniences for passage and transportation have had any existence. Very early the question arose whether a state's right of eminent domain could be exercised by a private corporation created for the purpose of constructing a railroad. Clearly, it could not, unless taking land for such a purpose by such an agency is taking land for public use. The right of eminent domain nowhere justifies taking property for a private use. Yet it is a doctrine universally accepted that a state legislature may authorize a private corporation to take land for the construction of such a road, making compensation to the owner. What else does this doctrine mean if not that building a railroad, though it be built by a private corporation, is an act done for a public use?' So, in Township of Pine Grove v. Talcott, 19 Wall. 666, 676: 'Though the corporation [a railroad company] was private, its work was public, as much so as if it were to be constructed by the state.' So, in Inhabitants of Worcester v. Western R. Corp., 4 Metc. (Mass.) 564: 'The establishment of that great thoroughfare is regarded as a public work, established by public authority, intended for the public use and benefit, the use of which is secured to the whole community, and constitutes, therefore, like a canal, turnpike, or highway, a public easement.' 'It is true that the real and personal property, necessary to the establishment and management of the railroad, is vested in the corporation; but it is in trust for the public.'

In respect of civil rights, common to all citizens, the constitution of the United States does not, I think, permit any public authority to know the race of those entitled to be protected in the enjoyment of such rights. Every true man has pride of race, and under appropriate circumstances, when the rights of others, his equals before the law, are not to be affected, it is his privilege to express such pride and to take such action based upon it as to him seems proper. But I deny that any legislative body or judicial tribunal may have regard to the race of citizens when the civil rights of those citizens are involved. Indeed, such legislation as that here in question is inconsistent not only with that equality of rights which pertains to citizenship, national and state, but with the personal liberty enjoyed by every one within the United States.

The thirteenth amendment does not permit the withholding or the deprivation of any right necessarily inhering in freedom. It not only struck down the institution of slavery as previously existing in the United States, but it prevents the imposition of any burdens or disabilities that constitute badges of slavery or servitude. It decreed universal civil freedom in this country. This court has so adjudged. But, that amendment having been found inadequate to the protection of the rights of those who had been in slavery, it was followed by the fourteenth amendment, which added greatly to the dignity and glory of American citizenship, and to the security of personal liberty, by declaring that 'all persons born or naturalized in the United States, and subject to the jurisdiction thereof, are citizens of the United States and of the state wherein they reside,' and that 'no state shall make or enforce any law which shall abridge the privileges or immunities of citizens of the United States; nor shall any state deprive any person of life, liberty or property without due process of law, nor deny to any person within its jurisdiction the equal protection of the laws.' These two amendments, if enforced according to their true intent and meaning, will protect all the civil rights that pertain to freedom and citizenship. Finally, and to the end that no citizen should be denied, on account of his race, the privilege of participating in the political control of his country, it was declared by the fifteenth amendment that 'the right of citizens of the United States to vote shall not be denied or abridged by the United States or by any state on account of race, color or previous condition of servitude.'

These notable additions to the fundamental law were welcomed by the friends of liberty throughout the world. They removed the race line from our governmental systems. They had, as this court has said, a common purpose, namely, to secure 'to a race recently emancipated, a race that through many generations have been held in slavery, all the civil rights that the superior race enjoy.' They declared, in legal effect, this court has further said, 'that the law in the states shall be the same for the black as for the white; that all persons, whether colored or white, shall stand equal before the laws of the states; and in regard to the colored race, for whose protection the amendment was primarily designed, that no discrimination shall be made against them by law because of their color.' We also said: 'The words of the amendment, it is true, are prohibitory, but they contain a necessary implication of a positive immunity or right, most valuable to the colored race,-the right to exemption from unfriendly legislation against them distinctively as colored; exemption from legal discriminations, implying inferiority in civil society, lessening the security of their enjoyment of the rights which others enjoy; and discriminations which are steps towards reducing them to the condition of a subject race.' It was, consequently, adjudged that a state law that excluded citizens of the colored race from juries, because of their race, however well qualified in other respects to dischar e the duties of jurymen, was repugnant to the fourteenth amendment. Strauder v. West Virginia, 100 U.S. 303, 306 , 307 S.; Virginia v. Rives, Id. 313; Ex parte Virginia, Id. 339; Neal v. Delaware, 103 U.S. 370 , 386; Bush v. Com., 107 U.S. 110, 116 , 1 S. Sup. Ct. 625. At the present term, referring to the previous adjudications, this court declared that 'underlying all of those decisions is the principle that the constitution of the United States, in its present form, forbids, so far as civil and political rights are concerned, discrimination by the general government or the states against any citizen because of his race. All citizens are equal before the law.' Gibson v. State, 162 U.S. 565 , 16 Sup. Ct. 904.

The decisions referred to show the scope of the recent amendments of the constitution. They also show that it is not within the power of a state to prohibit colored citizens, because of their race, from participating as jurors in the administration of justice.

It was said in argument that the statute of Louisiana does not discriminate against either race, but prescribes a rule applicable alike to white and colored citizens. But this argument does not meet the difficulty. Every one knows that the statute in question had its origin in the purpose, not so much to exclude white persons from railroad cars occupied by blacks, as to exclude colored people from coaches occupied by or assigned to white persons. Railroad corporations of Louisiana did not make discrimination among whites in the matter of commodation for travelers. The thing to accomplish was, under the guise of giving equal accommodation for whites and blacks, to compel the latter to keep to themselves while traveling in railroad passenger coaches. No one would be so wanting in candor as to assert the contrary. The fundamental objection, therefore, to the statute, is that it interferes with the personal freedom of citizens. 'Personal liberty,' it has been well said, 'consists in the power of locomotion, of changing situation, or removing one's person to whatsoever places one's own inclination may direct, without imprisonment or restraint, unless by due course of law.' 1 Bl. Comm. *134. If a white man and a black man choose to occupy the same public conveyance on a public highway, it is their right to do so; and no government, proceeding alone on grounds of race, can prevent it without infringing the personal liberty of each.

It is one thing for railroad carriers to furnish, or to be required by law to furnish, equal accommodations for all whom they are under a legal duty to carry. It is quite another thing for government to forbid citizens of the white and black races from traveling in the same public conveyance, and to punish officers of railroad companies for permitting persons of the two races to occupy the same passenger coach. If a state can prescribe, as a rule of civil conduct, that whites and blacks shall not travel as passengers in the same railroad coach, why may it not so regulate the use of the streets of its cities and towns as to compel white citizens to keep on one side of a street, and black citizens to keep on the other? Why may it not, upon like grounds, punish whites and blacks who ride together in street cars or in open vehicles on a public road or street? Why may it not require sheriffs to assign whites to one side of a court room, and blacks to the other? And why may it not also prohibit the commingling of the two races in the galleries of legislative halls or in public assemblages convened for the consideration of the political questions of the day? Further, if this statute of Louisiana is consistent with the personal liberty of citizens, why may not the state require the separation in railroad coaches of native and naturalized citizens of the United States, or of Protestants and Roman Catholics?

The answer given at the argument to these questions was that regulations of the kind they suggest would be unreasonable, and could not, therefore, stand before the la . Is it meant that the determination of questions of legislative power depends upon the inquiry whether the statute whose validity is questioned is, in the judgment of the courts, a reasonable one, taking all the circumstances into consideration? A statute may be unreasonable merely because a sound public policy forbade its enactment. But I do not understand that the courts have anything to do with the policy or expediency of legislation. A statute may be valid, and yet, upon grounds of public policy, may well be characterized as unreasonable. Mr. Sedgwick correctly states the rule when he says that, the legislative intention being clearly ascertained, 'the courts have no other duty to perform than to execute the legislative will, without any regard to their views as to the wisdom or justice of the particular enactment.' Sedg. St. & Const. Law, 324. There is a dangerous tendency in these latter days to enlarge the functions of the courts, by means of judicial interference with the will of the people as expressed by the legislature. Our institutions have the distinguishing characteristic that the three departments of government are co-ordinate and separate. Each much keep within the limits defined by the constitution. And the courts best discharge their duty by executing the will of the law-making power, constitutionally expressed, leaving the results of legislation to be dealt with by the people through their representatives. Statutes must always have a reasonable construction. Sometimes they are to be construed strictly, sometimes literally, in order to carry out the legisla- tive will. But, however construed, the intent of the legislature is to be respected if the particular statute in question is valid, although the courts, looking at the public interests, may conceive the statute to be both unreasonable and impolitic. If the power exists to enact a statute, that ends the matter so far as the courts are concerned. The adjudged cases in which statutes have been held to be void, because unreasonable, are those in which the means employed by the legislature were not at all germane to the end to which the legislature was competent.

The white race deems itself to be the dominant race in this country.

And so it is, in prestige, in achievements, in education, in wealth, and in power. So, I doubt not, it will continue to be for all time, if it remains true to its great heritage, and holds fast to the principles of constitutional liberty. But in view of the constitution, in the eye of the law, there is in this country no superior, dominant, ruling class of citizens. There is no caste here. Our constitution is color-blind, and neither knows nor tolerates classes among citizens. In respect of civil rights, all citizens are equal before the law. The humblest is the peer of the most powerful. The law regards man as man, and takes no account of his surroundings or of his color when his civil rights as guarantied by the spreme law of the land are involved. It is therefore to be regretted that this high tribunal, the final expositor of the fundamental law of the land, has reached the conclusion that it is competent for a state to regulate the enjoyment by citizens of their civil rights solely upon the basis of race.

In my opinion, the judgment this day rendered will, in time, prove to be quite as pernicious as the decision made by this tribunal in the Dred Scott Case.

It was adjudged in that case that the descendants of Africans who were imported into this country, and sold as slaves, were not included nor intended to be included under the word 'citizens' in the constitution, and could not claim any of the rights and privileges which that instrument provided for and secured to citizens of the United States; that, at time of the adoption of the constitution, they were 'considered as a subordinate and inferior class of beings, who had been subjugated by the dominant race, and, whether emancipated or not, yet remained subject to their authority, and had no rights or privileges but such as those who held the power and the government might choose to grant them.' 17 How. 393, 404. The recent amendments of the constitution, it was supposed, had eradicated these principles from our institutions. But it seems that we have yet, in some of the states, a dominant race,-a superior class of citizens,-which assumes to regulate the enjoyment of civil rights, common to all citizens, upon the basis of race. The present decision, it may well be apprehended, will not only stimulate aggressions, more or less brutal and irritating, upon the admitted rights of colored citizens, but will encourage the belief that it is possible, by means of state enactments, to defeat the beneficent purposes which the people of the United States had in view when they adopted the recent amendments of the constitution, by one of which the blacks of this country were made citizens of the United States and of the states in which they respectively reside, and whose privileges and immunities, as citizens, the states are forbidden to abridge. Sixty millions of whites are in no danger from the presence here of eight millions of blacks. The destinies of the two races, in this country, are indissolubly linked together, and the interests of both require that the common government of all shall not permit the seeds of race hate to be planted under the sanction of law. What can more certainly arouse race hate, what more certainly create and perpetuate a feeling of distrust between these races, than state enactments which, in fact, proceed on the ground that colored citizens are so inferior and degraded that they cannot be allowed to sit in public coaches occupied by white citizens? That, as all will admit, is the real meaning of such legislation as was enacted in Louisiana.

The sure guaranty of the peace and security of each race is the clear, distinct, unconditional recognition by our governments, national and state, of every right that inheres in civil freedom, and of the equality before the law of all citizens of the United States, without regard to race. State enactments regulating the enjoyment of civil rights upon the basis of race, and cunningly devised to defeat legitimate results of the war, under the pretense of recognizing equality of rights, can have no other result than to render permanent peace impossible, and to keep alive a conflict of races, the continuance of which must do harm to all concerned. This question is not met by the suggestion that social equality cannot exist between the white and black races in this country. That argument, if it can be properly regarded as one, is scarcely worthy of consideration; for social equality no more exists between two races when traveling in a passenger coach or a public highway than when members of the same races sit by each other in a street car or in the jury box, or stand or sit with each other in a political assembly, or when they use in common the streets of a city or town, or when they are in the same room for the purpose of having their names placed on the registry of voters, or when they approach the ballot box in order to exercise the high privilege of voting.

There is a race so different from our own that we do not permit those belonging to it to become citizens of the United States. Persons belonging to it are, with few exceptions, absolutely excluded from our country. I allude to the Chinese race. But, by the statute in question, a Chinaman can ride in the same passenger coach with white citizens of the United States, while citizens of the black race in Louisiana, many of whom, perhaps, risked their lives for the preservation of the Union, who are entitled, by law, to participate in the political control of the state and nation, who are not excluded, by law or by reason of their race, from public stations of any kind, and who have all the legal rights that belong to white citizens, are yet declared to be criminals, liable to imprisonment, if they ride in a public coach occupied by citizens of the white race. It is scarcely just to say that a colored citizen should not object to occupying a public coach assigned to his own race. He does not object, nor, perhaps, would he object to separate coaches for his race if his rights under the law were recognized. But he does object, and he ought never to cease objecting, that citizens of the white and black races can be adjudged criminals because they sit, or claim the right to sit, in the same public coach on a public highway. The arbitrary separation of citizens, on the basis of race, while they are on a public highway, is a badge of servitude wholly inconsistent with the civil freedom and the equality before the law established by the constitution. It cannot be justified upon any legal grounds.

If evils will result from the commingling of the two races upon public highways established for the benefit of all, they will be infinitely less than those that will surely come from state legislation regulating the enjoyment of civil rights upon the basis of race. We boast of the freedom enjoyed by our people above all other peoples. But it is difficult to reconcile that boast with a state of the law which, practically, puts the brand of servitude and degradation upon a large class of our fellow citizens,-our equals before the law. The thin disguise of 'equal' accommodations for passengers in railroad coaches will not mislead any one, nor atone for the wrong this day done.

The result of the whole matter is that while this court has frequently adjudged, and at the present term has recognized the doctrine, that a state cannot, consistently with the constitution of the United States, prevent white and black citizens, having the required qualifications for jury service, from sitting in the same jury box, it is now solemnly held that a state may prohibit white and black citizens from sitting in the same passenger coach on a public highway, or may require that they be separated by a 'partition' when in the same passenger coach. May it not now be reasonably expected that astute men of the dominant race, who affect to be disturbed at the possibility that the integrity of the white race may be corrupted, or that its supremacy will be imperiled, by contact on public highways with black people, will endeavor to procure statutes requiring white and black jurors to be separated in the jury box by a 'partition,' and that, upon retiring from the court room to consult as to their verdict, such partition, if it be a movable one, shall be taken to their consultation room, and set up in such way as to prevent black jurors from coming too close to their brother jurors of the white race. If the 'partition' used in the court room happens to be stationary, provision could be made for screens with openings through which jurors of the two races could confer as to their verdict without coming into personal contact with each other. I cannot see but that, according to the principles this day announced, such state legislation, although conceived in hostility to, and enacted for the purpose of humiliating, citizens of the United States of a particular race, would be held to be consistent with the constitution.

I do not deem it necessary to review the decisions of state courts to which reference was made in argument. Some, and the most important, of them, are wholly inapplicable, because rendered prior to the adoption of the last amendments of the constitution, when colored people had very few rights which the dominant race felt obliged to respect. Others were made at a time when public opinion, in many localities, was dominated by the institution of slavery; when it would not have been safe to do justice to the black man; and when, so far as the rights of blacks were concerned, race prejudice was, practically, the supreme law of the land. Those decisions cannot be guides in the era introduced by the recent amendments of the supreme law, which established universal civil freedom, gave citizenship to all born or naturalized in the United States, and residing ere, obliterated the race line from our systems of governments, national and state, and placed our free institutions upon the broad and sure foundation of the equality of all men before the law.

I am of opinion that the state of Louisiana is inconsistent with the personal liberty of citizens, white and black, in that state, and hostile to both the spirit and letter of the constitution of the United States. If laws of like character should be enacted in the several states of the Union, the effect would be in the highest degree mischievous. Slavery, as an institution tolerated by law, would, it is true, have disappeared from our country; but there would remain a power in the states, by sinister legislation, to interfere with the full enjoyment of the blessings of freedom, to regulate civil rights, common to all citizens, upon the basis of race, and to place in a condition of legal inferiority a large body of American citizens, now constituting a part of the political community, called the 'People of the United States,' for whom, and by whom through representatives, our government is administered. Such a system is inconsistent with the guaranty given by the constitution to each state of a republican form of government, and may be stricken down by congressional action, or by the courts in the discharge of their solemn duty to maintain the supreme law of the land, anything in the constitution or laws of any state to the contrary notwithstanding.

For the reason stated, I am constrained to withhold my assent from the opinion and judgment of the majority.

Woodrow Wilson's 14 Points (1918)

It will be our wish and purpose that the processes of peace, when they are begun, shall be absolutely open and that they shall involve and permit henceforth no secret understandings of any kind. The day of conquest and aggrandizement is gone by; so is also the day of secret covenants entered into in the interest of particular governments and likely at some unlooked-for moment to upset the peace of the world. It is this happy fact, now clear to the view of every public man whose thoughts do not still linger in an age that is dead and gone, which makes it possible for every nation whose purposes are consistent with justice and the peace of the world to avow nor or at any other time the objects it has in view.

We entered this war because violations of right had occurred which touched us to the quick and made the life of our own people impossible unless they were corrected and the world secure once for all against their recurrence. What we demand in this war, therefore, is nothing peculiar to ourselves. It is that the world be made fit and safe to live in; and particularly that it be made safe for every peace-loving nation which, like our own, wishes to live its own life, determine its own institutions, be assured of justice and fair dealing by the other peoples of the world as against force and selfish aggression. All the peoples of the world are in effect partners in this interest, and for our own part we see very clearly that unless justice be done to others it will not be done to us. The programme of the world's peace, therefore, is our programme; and that programme, the only possible programme, as we see it, is this:

I. Open covenants of peace, openly arrived at, after which there shall be no private international understandings of any kind but diplomacy shall proceed always frankly and in the public view.

II. Absolute freedom of navigation upon the seas, outside territorial waters, alike in peace and in war, except as the seas may be closed in whole or in part by international action for the enforcement of international covenants.

III. The removal, so far as possible, of all economic barriers and the establishment of an equality of trade conditions among all the nations consenting to the peace and associating themselves for its maintenance.

IV. Adequate guarantees given and taken that national armaments will be reduced to the lowest point consistent with domestic safety.

V. A free, open-minded, and absolutely impartial adjustment of all colonial claims, based upon a strict observance of the principle that in determining all such questions of sovereignty the interests of the populations concerned must have equal weight with the equitable claims of the government whose title is to be determined.

VI. The evacuation of all Russian territory and such a settlement of all questions affecting Russia as will secure the best and freest co-operation of the other nations of the world in obtaining for her an unhampered and unembarrassed opportunity for the independent determination of her own political development and national policy and assure her of a sincere welcome into the society of free nations under institutions of her own choosing; and, more than a welcome, assistance also of every kind that she may need and may herself desire. The treatment accorded Russia by her sister nations in the months to come will be the acid test of their good will, of their comprehension of her needs as distinguished from their own interests, and of their intelligent and unselfish sympathy.

VII. Belgium, the whole world will agree, must be evacuated and restored, without any attempt to limit the sovereignty which she enjoys in common with all other free nations. No other single act will serve as this will serve to restore confidence among the nations in the laws which they have themselves set and determined for the government of their relations with one another. Without this healing act the whole structure and validity of international law is forever impaired.

VIII. All French territory should be freed and the invaded portions restored, and the wrong done to France by Prussia in 1871 in the matter of Alsace-Lorraine, which has unsettled the peace of the world for nearly fifty years, should be righted, in order that peace may once more be made secure in the interest of all.

IX. A readjustment of the frontiers of Italy should be effected along clearly recognizable lines of nationality.

X. The peoples of Austria-Hungary, whose place among the nations we wish to see safeguarded and assured, should be accorded the freest opportunity to autonomous development.

XI. Rumania, Serbia, and Montenegro should be evacuated; occupied territories restored; Serbia accorded free and secure access to the sea; and the relations of the several Balkan states to one another determined by friendly counsel along historically established lines of allegiance and nationality; and international guarantees of the political and economic independence and territorial integrity of the several Balkan states should be entered into.

XII. The turkish portion of the present Ottoman Empire should be assured a secure sovereignty, but the other nationalities which are now under Turkish rule should be assured an undoubted security of life and an absolutely unmolested opportunity of autonomous development, and the Dardanelles should be permanently opened as a free passage to the ships and commerce of all nations under international guarantees.

XIII. An independent Polish state should be erected which should include the territories inhabited by indisputably Polish populations, which should be assured a free and secure access to the sea, and whose political and economic independence and territorial integrity should be guaranteed by international covenant.

XIV. A general association of nations must be formed under specific covenants for the purpose of affording mutual guarantees of political independence and territorial integrity to great and small states alike.

In regard to these essential rectifications of wrong and assertions of right we feel ourselves to be intimate partners of all the governments and peoples associated together against the Imperialists. We cannot be separated in interest or divided in purpose. We stand together until the end.

For such arrangements and covenants we are willing to fight and to continue to fight until they are achieved; but only because we wish the right to prevail and desire a just and stable peace such as can be secured only by removing the chief provocations to war, which this programme does remove. We have no jealousy of German greatness, and there is nothing in this programme that impairs it. We grudge her no achievement or distinction of learning or of pacific enterprise such as have made her record very bright and very enviable. We do not wish to injure her or to block in any way her legitimate influence or power. We do not wish to fight her either with arms or with hostile arrangements of trade if she is willing to associate herself with us and the other peace- loving nations of the world in covenants of justice and law and fair dealing. We wish her only to accept a place of equality among the peoples of the world, — the new world in which we now live, — instead of a place of mastery.

First Inaugural Address of Franklin D. Roosevelt

(March 4, 1933)

I am certain that my fellow Americans expect that on my induction into the Presidency I will address them with a candor and a decision which the present situation of our people impel. This is preeminently the time to speak the truth, the whole truth, frankly and boldly. Nor need we shrink from honestly facing conditions in our country today. This great Nation will endure as it has endured, will revive and will prosper. So, first of all, let me assert my firm belief that the only thing we have to fear is fear itself—nameless, unreasoning, unjustified terror which paralyzes needed efforts to convert retreat into advance. In every dark hour of our national life a leadership of frankness and vigor has met with that understanding and support of the people themselves which is essential to victory. I am convinced that you will again give that support to leadership in these critical days.

In such a spirit on my part and on yours we face our common difficulties. They concern, thank God, only material things. Values have shrunken to fantastic levels; taxes have risen; our ability to pay has fallen; government of all kinds is faced by serious curtailment of income; the means of exchange are frozen in the currents of trade; the withered leaves of industrial enterprise lie on every side; farmers find no markets for their produce; the savings of many years in thousands of families are gone.

More important, a host of unemployed citizens face the grim problem of existence, and an equally great number toil with little return. Only a foolish optimist can deny the dark realities of the moment.

Yet our distress comes from no failure of substance. We are stricken by no plague of locusts. Compared with the perils which our forefathers conquered because they believed and were not afraid, we have still much to be thankful for. Nature still offers her bounty and human efforts have multiplied it. Plenty is at our doorstep, but a generous use of it languishes in the very sight of the supply. Primarily this is because the rulers of the exchange of mankind's goods have failed, through their own stubbornness and their own incompetence, have admitted their failure, and abdicated. Practices of the unscrupulous money changers stand indicted in the court of public opinion, rejected by the hearts and minds of men.

True they have tried, but their efforts have been cast in the pattern of an outworn tradition. Faced by failure of credit they have proposed only the lending of more money. Stripped of the lure of profit by which to induce our people to follow their false leadership, they have resorted to exhortations, pleading tearfully for restored confidence. They know only the rules of a generation of self-seekers. They have no vision, and when there is no vision the people perish.

The money changers have fled from their high seats in the temple of our civilization. We may now restore that temple to the ancient truths. The measure of the restoration lies in the extent to which we apply social values more noble than mere monetary profit.

Happiness lies not in the mere possession of money; it lies in the joy of achievement, in the thrill of creative effort. The joy and moral stimulation of work no longer must be forgotten in the mad chase of evanescent profits. These dark days will be worth all they cost us if they teach us that our true destiny is not to be ministered unto but to minister to ourselves and to our fellow men.

Recognition of the falsity of material wealth as the standard of success goes hand in hand with the abandonment of the false belief that public office and high political position are to be valued only by the standards of pride of place and personal profit; and there must be an end to a conduct in banking and in business which too often has given to a sacred trust the likeness of callous and selfish wrongdoing. Small wonder that confidence languishes, for it thrives only on honesty, on honor, on the sacredness of obligations, on faithful protection, on unselfish performance; without them it cannot live.

Restoration calls, however, not for changes in ethics alone. This Nation asks for action, and action now.

Our greatest primary task is to put people to work. This is no unsolvable problem if we face it wisely and courageously. It can be accomplished in part by direct recruiting by the Government itself, treating the task as we would treat the emergency of a war, but at the same time, through this employment, accomplishing greatly needed projects to stimulate and reorganize the use of our natural resources.

Hand in hand with this we must frankly recognize the overbalance of population in our industrial centers and, by engaging on a national scale in a redistribution, endeavor to provide a better use of the land for those best fitted for the land. The task can be helped by definite efforts to raise the values of agricultural products and with this the power to purchase the output of our cities. It can be helped by preventing realistically the tragedy of the growing loss through foreclosure of our small homes and our farms. It can be helped by insistence that the Federal, State, and local governments act forthwith on the demand that their cost be drastically reduced. It can be helped by the unifying of relief activities which today are often scattered, uneconomical, and unequal. It can be helped by national planning for and supervision of all forms of transportation and of communications and other utilities which have a definitely public character. There are many ways in which it can be helped, but it can never be helped merely by talking about it. We must act and act quickly.

Finally, in our progress toward a resumption of work we require two safeguards against a return of the evils of the old order; there must be a strict supervision of all banking and credits and investments; there must be an end to speculation with other people's money, and there must be provision for an adequate but sound currency.

There are the lines of attack. I shall presently urge upon a new Congress in special session detailed measures for their fulfillment, and I shall seek the immediate assistance of the several States.

Through this program of action we address ourselves to putting our own national house in order and making income balance outgo. Our international trade relations, though vastly important, are in point of time and necessity secondary to the establishment of a sound national economy. I favor as a practical policy the putting of first things first. I shall spare no effort to restore world trade by international economic readjustment, but the emergency at home cannot wait on that accomplishment.

The basic thought that guides these specific means of national recovery is not narrowly nationalistic. It is the insistence, as a first consideration, upon the interdependence of the various elements in all parts of the United States—a recognition of the old and permanently important manifestation of the American spirit of the pioneer. It is the way to recovery. It is the immediate way. It is the strongest assurance that the recovery will endure.

In the field of world policy I would dedicate this Nation to the policy of the good neighbor—the neighbor who resolutely respects himself and, because he does so, respects the rights of others—the neighbor who respects his obligations and respects the sanctity of his agreements in and with a world of neighbors.

If I read the temper of our people correctly, we now realize as we have never realized before our interdependence on each other; that we can not merely take but we must give as well; that if we are to go forward, we must move as a trained and loyal army willing to sacrifice for the good of a common discipline, because without such discipline no progress is made, no leadership becomes effective. We are, I know, ready and willing to submit our lives and property to such discipline, because it makes possible a leadership which aims at a larger good. This I propose to offer, pledging that the larger purposes will bind upon us all as a sacred obligation with a unity of duty hitherto evoked only in time of armed strife.

With this pledge taken, I assume unhesitatingly the leadership of this great army of our people dedicated to a disciplined attack upon our common problems.

Action in this image and to this end is feasible under the form of government which we have inherited from our ancestors. Our Constitution is so simple and practical that it is possible always to meet extraordinary needs by changes in emphasis and arrangement without loss of essential form. That is why our constitutional system has proved itself the most superbly enduring political mechanism the modern world has produced. It has met every stress of vast expansion of territory, of foreign wars, of bitter internal strife, of world relations.

It is to be hoped that the normal balance of executive and legislative authority may be wholly adequate to meet the unprecedented task before us. But it may be that an unprecedented demand and need for undelayed action may call for temporary departure from that normal balance of public procedure.

I am prepared under my constitutional duty to recommend the measures that a stricken nation in the midst of a stricken world may require. These measures, or such other measures as the Congress may build out of its experience and wisdom, I shall seek, within my constitutional authority, to bring to speedy adoption.

But in the event that the Congress shall fail to take one of these two courses, and in the event that the national emergency is still critical, I shall not evade the clear course of duty that will then confront me. I shall ask the Congress for the one remaining instrument to meet the crisis—broad Executive power to wage a war against the emergency, as great as the power that would be given to me if we were in fact invaded by a foreign foe.

For the trust reposed in me I will return the courage and the devotion that befit the time. I can do no less.

We face the arduous days that lie before us in the warm courage of the national unity; with the clear consciousness of seeking old and precious moral values; with the clean satisfaction that comes from the stern performance of duty by old and young alike. We aim at the assurance of a rounded and permanent national life.

We do not distrust the future of essential democracy. The people of the United States have not failed. In their need they have registered a mandate that they want direct, vigorous action. They have asked for discipline and direction under leadership. They have made me the present instrument of their wishes. In the spirit of the gift I take it.

In this dedication of a Nation we humbly ask the blessing of God. May He protect each and every one of us. May He guide me in the days to come.

Tennessee Valley Authority Act (1933)

An Act to Improve the Navigability and to Provide for the Flood Control of the Tennessee River: To Provide for Reforestation and the Proper Use of Marginal Lands in the Tennessee Valley; to Provide for the Agricultural and Industrial Development of Said Valley; to Provide for the National Defense by the Creation of a Corporation for the Operation of Government Properties at and Near Muscle Shoals in the State of Alabama, and for Other Purposes May 18, 1933.

Be it enacted by the Senate and House of Representatives of the United States of America in Congress assembled, That for the purpose of maintaining and operating the properties now owned by the United States in the vicinity of Muscle Shoals, Alabama, in the interest of the national defense and for agriculture and industrial development, and to improve navigation in the Tennessee River and to control the destructive flood waters in the Tennessee River and Mississippi River Basins, there is hereby created a body corporate by the name of the "Tennessee Valley Authority" (hereinafter referred to as the "Corporation"). The board of directors first appointed shall be deemed the incorporators and the incorporation shall be held to have been effected from the date of the first meeting of the board. This Act may be cited as the "Tennessee Valley Authority Act of 1933."

Sec. 2. (a) The board of directors of the Corporation (hereinafter referred to as the "board") shall be composed of three members, to be appointed by the President, by and with the advice and consent of the Senate. In appointing the members of the board, the President shall designate the chairman. All other officials, agents, and employees shall be designated and selected by the board.

(b) The terms of office of the members first taking office after the approval of this Act shall expire as designated by the President at the time of nomination, one at the end of the third year, one at the end of the sixth year, and one at the end of the ninth year, after the date of approval of this Act. A successor to a member of the board shall be appointed in the same manner as the original members and shall have a term of office expiring nine years from the date of the expiration of the term for which his predecessor was appointed.

(c) Any member appointed to fill a vacancy in the board occurring prior to the expiration of the term for which his predecessor was appointed shall be appointed for the remainder of such term.

(d) Vacancies in the board so long as there shall be two members in office shall not impair the powers of the board to execute the functions of the Corporation, and two of the members in office shall constitute a quorum for the transaction of the business of the board.

(e) Each of the members of the board shall be a citizen of the United States, and shall receive a salary at the rate of $10,000 a year, to be paid by the Corporation as current expenses. Each member of the board, in addition to his salary, shall be permitted to occupy as his residence one of the dwelling houses owned by the Government in the vicinity of Muscle Shoals, Alabama, the same to be designated by the President of the United States. Members of the board shall be reimbursed by the Corporation for actual expenses (including traveling and subsistence expenses) incurred by them in the performance of the duties vested in the board by this Act. No member of said board shall, during his continuance in office, be engaged in other business, but each member shall devote himself to the work of the Corporation .

(f) No director shall have financial interest in any public-utility corporation engaged in the business of distributing and selling power to the public nor in any corporation engaged in the manufacture, selling, or distribution of fixed nitrogen or fertilizer, or any ingredients thereof, nor shall any member have any interest in any business that may be adversely affected by the success of the Corporation as a producer of concentrated fertilizers or as a producer of electric power.

(g) The board shall direct the exercise of all the powers of the Corporation .

(h) All members of the board shall be persons who profess a belief in the feasibility and wisdom of this Act.

Sec. 3. The Board shall without regard to the provisions of Civil Service laws applicable to officers and employees of the United States, appoint such managers, assistant managers, officers, employees, attorneys, and agents, as are necessary for the transaction of its business, fix their compensation, define their duties, require bonds of such of them as the board may designate, and provide a system of organization to fix responsibility and promote efficiency. Any appointee of the board may be removed in the discretion of the board. No regular officer or employee of the Corporation shall receive a salary in excess of that received by the members of the board.

All contracts to which the Corporation is a party and which require the employment of laborers and mechanics in the construction, alteration, maintenance or repair of buildings, dams, locks, or other projects shall contain a provision that not less than the prevailing rate of wages for work of a similar nature prevailing in the vicinity shall be paid to such laborers or mechanics.

In the event any dispute arises as to what are the prevailing rates of wages, the question shall be referred to the Secretary of Labor for determination, and his decision shall be final. In the determination of such prevailing rate or rates, due regard shall be given to those rates which have been secured through collective agreement by representatives of employers and employees.

Where such work as is described in the two preceding paragraphs is done directly by the Corporation the prevailing rate of wages shall be paid in the same manner as though such work had been let by contract.

Insofar as applicable, the benefits of the Act entitled "An Act to provide compensation for employees of the United States suffering injuries while in the performance of their duties, and for other purposes," approved September 7, 1916, as amended, shall extend to persons given employment under the provisions of this Act.

Sec. 4. Except as otherwise specifically provided in this Act, the Corporation —

(a) Shall have succession in its corporate name.

(b) May sue and be sued in its corporate name.

(c) May adopt and use a corporate seal, which shall be judicially noticed.

(d) May make contracts, as herein authorized.

(e) May adopt, amend, and repeal bylaws.

(f) May purchase or lease and hold such real and personal property as it deems necessary or convenient in the transaction of its business, and may dispose of any such personal property held by it.

The board shall select a treasurer and as many assistant treasurers as it deems proper, which treasurer and assistant treasurers shall give such bonds for the safe-keeping of the securities and moneys of the said Corporation as the board may require: Provided, That any member of said board may be removed from office at any time by a concurrent resolution of the Senate and the House of Representatives.

(g) Shall have such powers as may be necessary or appropriate for the exercise of the powers herein specifically conferred upon the Corporation.

(h) Shall have power in the name of the United States of America to exercise the right of eminent domain, and in the purchase of any real estate or the condemnation of real estate by condemnation proceedings, the title to such real estate shall be taken in the name of the United States of America, and thereupon all such real estate shall be entrusted to the Corporation as the agent of the United States to accomplish the purposes of this Act.

(i) Shall have power to acquire real estate for the construction of dams, reservoirs, transmission lines, power houses, and other structures, and navigation projects at any point along the Tennessee River, or any of its tributaries, and in the event that the owner or owners of such property shall fail and refuse to sell to the Corporation at a price deemed fair and reasonable by the board, then the Corporation may proceed to exercise the right of eminent domain, and to condemn all property that it deems necessary for carrying out the purposes of this Act, and all such condemnation proceedings shall be had pursuant to the provisions and requirements hereinafter specified, with reference to any and all condemnation proceedings.

(i) Shall have power to construct dams, reservoirs, power houses, power structures, transmission lines, navigation projects, and incidental works in the Tennessee River and its tributaries, and to unite the various power installations into one or more systems by transmission lines.

Sec. 5. The board is hereby authorized —

(a) To contract with commercial producers for the production of such fertilizers or fertilizer materials as may be needed in the Government's program of development and introduction in excess of that produced by Government plants. Such contracts may provide either for outright purchase of materials by the board or only for the payment of carrying charges on special materials manufactured at the board's request for its program.

(b) To arrange with farmers and farm organizations for large scale practical use of the new forms of fertilizers under conditions permitting an accurate measure of the economic return they produce.

(c) To cooperate with National, State, district, or county experimental stations or demonstration farms, for the use of new forms of fertilizer or fertilizer practices during the initial or experimental period of their introduction.

(d) The board in order to improve and cheapen the production of fertilizer is authorized to manufacture and sell fixed nitrogen, fertilizer, and fertilizer ingredients at Muscle Shoals by the employment of existing facilities, by modernizing existing plants, or by any other process or processes that in its judgment shall appear wise and profitable for the fixation of atmospheric nitrogen or the cheapening of the production of fertilizer.

(e) Under the authority of this Act the board may make donations or sales of the product of the plant or plants operated by it to be fairly and equitably distributed through the agency of county demonstration agents, agricultural colleges, or otherwise as the board may direct, for experimentation, education, and introduction of the use of such products in cooperation with practical farmers so as to obtain information as to the value, effect, and best methods of their use.

(f) The board is authorized to make alterations, modifications, or improvements in existing plants and facilities, and to construct new plants.

(g) In the event it is not used for the fixation of nitrogen for agricultural purposes or leased, then the board shall maintain in standby condition nitrate plant numbered 2, or its equivalent, for the fixation of atmospheric nitrogen, for the production of explosives in the event of war or a national emergency until the Congress shall by joint resolution release the board from this obligation, and if any part thereof be used by the board for the manufacture or phosphoric acid or potash, the balance of nitrate plant numbered 2 shall be kept in stand-by condition.

(h) To establish, maintain, and operate laboratories and experimental plants, and to undertake experiments for the purpose of enabling the Corporation to furnish nitrogen products for military purposes, and nitrogen and other fertilizer products for agricultural purposes in the most economical manner and at the highest standard of efficiency.

(i) To request the assistance and advice of any officer, agent, or employee of any executive department or of any independent office of the United States, to enable the Corporation the better to carry out its powers successfully, and as far as practicable shall utilize the services of such officers, agents, and employees, and the President shall, if in his opinion, the public interest, service, or economy so require, direct that such assistance, advice, and service be rendered to the Corporation, and any individual that may be by the President directed to render such assistance, advice, and service shall be thereafter subject to the orders, rules, and regulations of the board: Provided, That any invention or discovery made by virtue of and incidental to such service by an employee of the Government of the United States serving under this section, or by any employee of the Corporation, together with any patents which may be granted thereon, shall be the sole and exclusive property of the Corporation, which is hereby authorized to grant licenses thereunder as shall be authorized by the board: Provided further, That the board may pay to such inventor such sum from the income from sale of licenses as it may deem proper.

(j) Upon the requisition of the Secretary of War or the Secretary of the Navy to manufacture for and sell at cost to the United States explosives or their nitrogenous content.

(k) Upon the requisition of the Secretary of War the Corporation shall allot and deliver without charge to the War Department so much power as shall be necessary in the judgment of said Department for use in operation of all locks, lifts, or other facilities in aid of navigation.

(l) To produce, distribute, and sell electric power, as herein particularly specified.

(m) No products of the Corporation shall be sold for use outside of the United States, its Territories and possessions, except to the United States Government for the use of its Army and Navy, or to its allies in case of war.

(n) The President is authorized, within twelve months after the passage of this Act, to lease to any responsible farm organization or to any corporation organized by it nitrate plant number 2 and Waco Quarry, together with the railroad connecting said quarry with nitrate plant number 2, for a term not exceeding fifty years at a rental of not less than $1 per year, but such authority shall be subject to the express condition that the lessee shall use said property during the term of said lease exclusively for the manufacture of fertilizer and fertilizer ingredients to be used only in the manufacture of fertilizer by said lessee and sold for use as fertilizer. The said lessee shall covenant to keep said property in first-class condition, but the lessee shall be authorized to modernize said plant numbered 2 by the installation of such machinery as may be necessary, and is authorized to amortize the cost of said machinery and improvements over the term of said lease or any part thereof. Said lease shall also provide that the board shall sell to the lessee power for the operation of said plant at the same schedule of prices that it charges all other customers for power of the same class and quantity. Said lease shall also provide that if the said lessee does not desire to buy power of the publicly owned plant it shall have the right to purchase power for the operation of said plant of the Alabama Power Company or any other publicly or privately owned corporation engaged in the generation and sale of electrical power, and in such case the lease shall provide further that the said lessee shall have a free right of way to build a transmission line over Government property to said plant paying the actual expenses and damages, if any, incurred by the Corporation on account of such line. Said lease shall also provide that the said lessee shall covenant that during the term of said lease the said lessee shall not enter into any illegal monopoly, combination, or trust with any privately owned corporation engaged in the manufacture, production, and sale of fertilizer with the object or effect of increasing the price of fertilizer to the farmer.

Sec. 6. In the appointment of officials and the selection of employees for said Corporation, and in the promotion of any such employees or officials, no political test or qualification shall be permitted or given consideration, but all such appointments and promotions shall be given and made on the basis of merit and efficiency. Any member of said board who is found by the President of the United States to be guilty of a violation of this section shall be removed from office by the President of the United States, and any appointee of said board who is found by the board to be guilty of a violation of this section shall be removed from office by said board.

Sec. 7. In order to enable the Corporation to exercise the powers and duties vested in it by this Act —

(a) The exclusive use, possession, and control of the United States nitrate plants numbered 1 and 2, including steam plants, located, respectively, at Sheffield, Alabama, and Muscle Shoals, Alabama, together with all real estate and buildings connected therewith, all tools and machinery, equipment, accessories, and materials belonging thereto, and all laboratories and plants used as auxiliaries thereto; the fixed-nitrogen research laboratory, the Waco limestone quarry, in Alabama, and Dam Numbered 2, located at Muscle Shoals, its power house, and all hydroelectric and operating appurtenances (except the locks), and all machinery, lands, and buildings in connection therewith, and all appurtenances thereof, and all other property to be acquired by the Corporation in its own name or in the name of the United States of America, are hereby intrusted to the Corporation for the purposes of the Act.

(b) The President of the United States is authorized to provide for the transfer to the Corporation of the use, possession, and control of such other real or personal property of the United States as he may from time to time deem necessary and proper for the purposes of the Corporation as herein stated.

Sec. 8. (a) The Corporation shall maintain its principal office in the immediate vicinity of Muscle Shoals, Alabama. The Corporation shall be held to be an inhabitant and resident of the northern judicial district of Alabama within the meaning of the laws of the United States relating to the venue of civil suits.

(b) The Corporation shall at all times maintain complete and accurate books of accounts.

(c) Each member of the board, before entering upon the duties of his office, shall subscribe to an oath (or affirmation) to support the Constitution of the United States and to faithfully and impartially perform the duties imposed upon him by this Act.

Sec. 9. (a) The board shall file with the President and with the Congress, in December of each year, a financial statement and a complete report as to the business of the Corporation covering the preceding governmental fiscal] year. This report shall include an itemized statement of the cost of power al each power station, the total number of employees and the names, salaries, and duties of those receiving compensation at the rate of more than $1,500 a year.

(b) The Comptroller General of the United States shall audit the transactions of the Corporation at such times as he shall determine, but not less frequently than once each governmental fiscal year, with personnel of his selection. In such connection he and his representatives shall have free and open access to all papers, books, records, files, accounts, plants, warehouses offices, and all other things, property and places belonging to or under the control of or used or employed by the Corporation, and shall be afforded full facilities for counting all cash and verifying transactions with and balance in depositaries. He shall make report of each such audit in quadruplicate, one copy for the President of the United States, one for the chairman of the board one for public inspection at the principal office of the Corporation, and the other to be retained by him for the uses of the Congress. The expenses for each such audit may be paid from moneys advanced therefor by the Corporation, or from any appropriation or appropriations for the General Accounting Office, and appropriations so used shall be reimbursed promptly by the Corporation as billed by the Comptroller General. All such audit expenses shall be charged to operating expenses of the Corporation. The Comptroller General shall make special report to the President of the United States and to the Congress of any transaction or condition found by him to be in conflict with the powers or duties intrusted to the Corporation by law.

Sec. 10. The board is hereby empowered and authorized to sell the surplus power not used in its operations, and for operation of locks and other works generated by it, to States, counties, municipalities, corporations, partnerships, or individuals, according to the policies hereinafter set forth- and to carry out said authority, the board is authorized to enter into contracts for such sale for a term not exceeding twenty years, and in the sale of such current by the board it shall give preference to States, counties, municipalities, and cooperative organizations of citizens or farmers, not organized or doing business for profit, but primarily for the purpose of supplying electricity to its own citizens or members: Provided, That all contracts made with private companies or individuals for the sale of power, which is to be resold for a profit, shall contain a provision authorizing the board to cancel said contract upon five years' notice in writing, if the board needs said power to supply the demands of States, counties, or municipalities. In order to promote and encourage the fullest possible use of electric light and power on farms within reasonable distance of any of its transmission lines the board in its discretion shall have power to construct transmission lines to farms and small villages that are not otherwise supplied with electricity at reasonable rates, and to make such rules and regulations governing such sale and distribution of such electric power as in its judgment may be just and equitable: Provided further That the board is hereby authorized and directed to make studies, experiments, and determinations to promote the wider and better use of electric power for agricultural and domestic use, or for small or local industries, and it may cooperate with State governments, or their subdivisions or agencies with educational or research institutions, and with cooperatives or other organizations, in the application of electric power to the fuller and better balanced development of the resources of the region.

Sec. 11. It is hereby declared to be the policy of the Government so far as practical to distribute and sell the surplus power generated at Muscle Shoals equitably among the States, counties, and municipalities within transmission distance. This policy is further declared to be that the projects herein provided for shall be considered primarily as for the benefit of the people of the section as a whole and particularly the domestic and rural consumers to whom the power can economically be made available, and accordingly that sale to and use by industry shall be a secondary purpose, to be utilized principally to secure a sufficiently high load factor and revenue returns which will permit domestic and rural use at the lowest possible rates and in such manner as to encourage increased domestic and rural use of electricity. It is further hereby declared to be the policy of the Government to utilize the Muscle Shoals properties so far as may be necessary to improve, increase, and cheapen the production of fertilizer and fertilizer ingredients by carrying out the provisions of this Act.

Sec. 12. In order to place the board upon a fair basis for making such Contracts and for receiving bids for the sale of such power, it is hereby expressly authorized, either from appropriations made by Congress or from funds secured from the sale of such power, or from funds secured by the sale of bonds hereafter provided for, to construct, lease, purchase, or authorize the construction of transmission lines within transmission distance from the place where generated, and to interconnect with other systems. The board is also authorized to lease to any person, persons, or corporation the use of any transmission line owned by the Government and operated by the board, but no such lease shall be made that in any way interferes with the use of such transmission line by the board: Provided, That if any State, county, municipality, or other public or cooperative organization of citizens or farmers, not organized or doing business for profit, but primarily for the purpose of supplying electricity to its own citizens or members, or any two or more of such municipalities or organizations, shall construct or agree to construct and maintain a properly designed and built transmission line to the Government reservation upon which is located a Government generating plant, or to a main transmission line owned by the Government or leased by the board and under the control of the board, the board is hereby authorized and directed to contract with such State, county, municipality, or other organization, or two or more of them, for the sale of electricity for a term not exceeding thirty years; and in such case the board shall give to such State, county, municipality, or other organization ample time to fully comply with any local law now in existence or hereafter enacted providing for the necessary legal authority for such State, county, municipality, or other organization to contract with the board for such power: Provided further, That all contracts entered into between the Corporation and any municipality or other political subdivision or cooperative organization shall provide that the electric power shall be sold and distributed to the ultimate consumer without discrimination as between consumers of the same class, and such contract shall be voidable at the election of the board if a discriminatory rate, rebate, or other special concession is made or given to any consumer or user by the municipality or other political subdivision or cooperative organization: And provided further, That as to any surplus power not so sold as above provided to States, counties, municipalities, or other said organizations, before the board shall sell the same to any person or corporation engaged in the distribution and resale of electricity for profit, it shall require said person or corporation to agree that any resale of such electric power by said person or corporation shall be made to the ultimate consumer of such electric power at prices that shall not exceed a schedule fixed by the board from time to time as reasonable, just, and fair; and in case of any such sale, if an amount is charged the ultimate consumer which is in excess of the price so deemed to be just, reasonable, and fair by the board the contract for such sale between the board and such distributor of electricity shall be voidable at the election of the board: And provided further, That the board is hereby authorized to enter into contracts with other power systems for the mutual exchange of unused excess power upon suitable terms, for the conservation of stored water, and as an emergency or break-down relief.

Sec. 13. Five per centum of the gross proceeds received by the board for the sale of power generated at Dam Numbered 2, or from any other hydropower plant hereafter constructed in the State of Alabama, shall be paid to the State of Alabama; and 5 per centum of the gross proceeds from the sale of power generated at Cove Creek Dam, hereinafter provided for, or any other dam located in the State of Tennessee, shall be paid to the State of Tennessee. Upon the completion of said Cove Creek Dam the board shall ascertain how much additional power is thereby generated at Dam Numbered 2 and at any other dam hereafter constructed by the Government of the United States on the Tennessee River, in the State of Alabama, or in the State of Tennessee, and from the gross proceeds of the sale of such additional power two and a half per centum shall be paid to the State of Alabama and 2 and a half per centum to the State of Tennessee. These percentages shall apply to any other dam that may hereafter be constructed and controlled and operated by the board on the Tennessee River or any of its tributaries, the main purpose of which is to control flood waters and where the development of electric power is incidental to the operation of such flood-control dam. In ascertaining the gross proceeds from the sale of such power upon which a percentage is paid to the States of Alabama and Tennessee, the board shall not take into consideration the proceeds of any power sold or delivered to the Government of the United States, or any department or agency of the Government of the United States used in the operation of any locks on the Tennessee River or for any experimental purpose, or for the manufacture of fertilizer or any of the ingredients thereof, or for any other governmental purpose: Provided, That the percentages to be paid to the States of Alabama and Tennessee, as provided in this section, shall be subject to revision and change by the board, and any new percentages established by the board, when approved by the President, shall remain in effect until and unless again changed by the board with the approval of the President. No change of said percentages shall be made more often than once in five years, and no change shall be made without giving to the States of Alabama and Tennessee an opportunity to be heard.

Sec. 14. The board shall make a thorough investigation as to the present value of Dam Numbered 2, and the steam plants at nitrate plant numbered 1, and nitrate plant numbered 2, and as to the cost of Cove Creek Dam, for the purpose of ascertaining how much of the value or the cost of said properties shall be allocated and charged up to (1) flood control, (2) navigation, (3) fertilizer (4) national defense, and (5) the development of power. The findings thus made by the board, when approved by the President of the United States, shall be final, and such findings shall thereafter be used in all allocation of value for the purpose of keeping the book value of said properties. In a like manner, the cost and book value of any dams, steam plants, or other similar improvements hereafter constructed and turned over to said board for the purpose of control and management shall be ascertained and allocated.

Sec. 15. In the construction of any future dam, steam plant, or other facility, to be used in whole or in part for the generation or transmission of electric power the board is hereby authorized and empowered to issue on the credit of the United States and to sell serial bonds not exceeding $50,000,000 in amount, having a maturity not more than fifty years from the date of issue thereof, and bearing interest not exceeding 3-1/2 per centum per annum. Said bonds shall be issued and sold in amounts and prices approved by the Secretary of the Treasury, but all such bonds as may be so issued and sold shall have equal rank. None of said bonds shall be sold below par, and no fee, commission, or compensation whatever shall be paid to any person, firm, or corporation for handling, negotiating the sale, or selling the said bonds. All of such bonds so issued and sold shall have all the rights and privileges accorded by law to Panama Canal bonds, authorized by section 8 of the Act of June 28, 1902, chapter 1302, as amended by the Act of December 21, 1905 (ch. 3, sec. 1, 34 Stat. 5), as now compiled in section 743 of title 31 of the United States Code. All funds derived from the sale of such bonds shall be paid over to the Corporation.

Sec. 16. The board, whenever the President deems it advisable, is hereby empowered and directed to complete Dam Numbered 2 at Muscle Shoals Alabama, and the steam plant at nitrate plant numbered 2, in the vicinity of Muscle Shoals, by installing in Dam Numbered 2 the additional power units according to the plans and specifications of said dam, and the additional power unit in the steam plant at nitrate plant numbered 2. Sec. 17. The Secretary of War, or the Secretary of the Interior, is hereby authorized to construct, either directly or by contract to the lowest responsible bidder, after due advertisement, a dam in and across Clinch River in the State of Tennessee, which has by long custom become known and designates as the Cove Creek Dam, together with a transmission line from Muscle Shoals, according to the latest and most approved designs, including power house and hydroelectric installations and equipment for the generation of power, in order that the waters of the said Clinch River may be impounded and stored above said dam for the purpose of increasing and regulating the flow of the Clinch River and the Tennessee River below, so that the maximum amount of primary power may be developed at Dam Numbered 2 and at any and all other dams below the said Cove Creek Dam: Provided, however, That the President is hereby authorized by appropriate order to direct the employment by the Secretary of War, or by the Secretary of the Interior, of such engineer or engineers as he may designate, to perform such duties and obligations as he may deem proper, either in the drawing of plans and specifications for said dam, or to perform any other work in the building or construction of the same. The President may, by such order, place the control of the construction of said dam in the hands of such engineer or engineers taken from private life as he may desire: And provided further, That the President is hereby expressly authorized, without regard to the restriction or limitation of any other statute, to select attorneys and assistants for the purpose of making any investigation he may deem proper to ascertain whether, in the control and management of Dam Numbered 2, or any other dam or property owned by the Government in the Tennessee River Basin, or in the authorization of any improvement therein, there has been any undue or unfair advantage given to private persons, partnerships, or corporations, by any officials or employees of the Government, or whether in any such matters the Government has been injured or unjustly deprived of any of its rights.

Sec. 18. In order to enable and empower the Secretary of War, the Secretary of the Interior, or the board to carry out the authority hereby conferred, in the most economical and efficient manner, he or it is hereby authorized and empowered in the exercise of the powers of national defense in aid of navigation, and in the control of the flood waters of the Tennessee and Mississippi Rivers, constituting channels of interstate commerce, to exercise the right of eminent domain for all purposes of this Act, and to condemn all lands, easements, rights of way, and other area necessary in order to obtain a site for said Cove Creek Dam, and the flowage rights for the reservoir of water above said dam, and to negotiate and conclude contracts with States, counties, municipalities, and all State agencies and with railroads, railroad corporations, common carriers, and all public utility commissions and any other person, firm or corporation, for the relocation of railroad tracks, highways, highway bridges, mills, ferries, electric-light plants, and any and all other properties, enterprises, and projects whose removal may be necessary in order to carry out the provisions of this Act. When said Cove Creek Dam, transmission line, and power house shall have been completed, the possession, use, and control thereof shall be intrusted to the Corporation for use and operation in connection with the general Tennessee Valley project, and to promote flood control and navigation in the Tennessee River.

Sec. 19. The Corporation, as an instrumentality and agency of the Government of the United States for the purpose of executing its constitutional powers, shall have access to the Patent Office of the United States for the purpose of studying, ascertaining, and copying all methods, formulae, and scientific information (not including access to pending applications for patents) necessary to enable the Corporation to use and employ the most efficacious and economical process for the production of fixed nitrogen, or any essential ingredient of fertilizer, or any method of improving and cheapening the production of hydroelectric power, and any owner of a patent whose patent rights may have been thus in any way copied, used, infringed, or employed by the exercise of this authority by the Corporation shall have as the exclusive remedy a cause of action against the Corporation to be instituted and prosecuted on the equity side of the appropriate district court of the United States, for the recovery of reasonable compensation for such infringement. The Commissioner of Patents shall furnish to the Corporation, at its request and without payment of fees, copies of documents on file in his office: Provided, That the benefits of this section shall not apply to any art, machine, method of manufacture, or composition of matter, discovered or invented by such employee during the time of his employment or services with the Corporation or with the Government of the United States .

Sec. 20. The Government of the United States hereby reserves the right, in case of war or national emergency declared by Congress, to take possession of all or any part of the property described or referred to in this Act for the purpose of manufacturing explosives or for other war purposes; but, if this right is exercised by the Government, it shall pay the reasonable and fair damages that may be suffered by any party whose contract for the purchase of electric power or fixed nitrogen or fertilizer ingredients is hereby violated, after the amount of the damages has been fixed by the United States Court of Claims in proceedings instituted and conducted for that purpose under rules prescribed by the court.

Sec. 21. (a) All general penal statutes relating to the larceny, embezzlement, conversion, or to the improper handling, retention, use, or disposal of public moneys or property of the United States, shall apply to the moneys and property of the Corporation and to moneys and properties of the United States intrusted to the Corporation.

(b) Any person who, with intent to defraud the Corporation, or to deceive any director, officer, or employee of the Corporation or any officer or employee of the United States (1) makes any false entry in any book of the Corporation, or (2) makes any false report or statement for the Corporation, shall, upon conviction thereof, be fined not more than $10,000 or imprisoned not more than five years, or both.

(c) Any person who shall receive any compensation, rebate, or reward, or shall enter into any conspiracy, collusion, or agreement, express or implied, with intent to defraud the Corporation or wrongfully and unlawfully to defeat its purposes, shall, on conviction thereof, be fined not more than $5,000 or imprisoned not more than five years, or both.

Sec. 22. To aid further the proper use, conservation, and development of the natural resources of the Tennessee River drainage basin and of such adjoining territory as may be related to or materially affected by the development consequent to this Act, and to provide for the general welfare of the citizens of said areas, the President is hereby authorized, by such means or methods as he may deem proper within the limits of appropriations made therefor by Congress, to make such surveys of and general plans for said Tennessee basin and adjoining territory as may be useful to the Congress and to the several States in guiding and controlling the extent, sequence, and nature of development that may be equitably and economically advanced through the expenditure of public funds, or through the guidance or control of public authority, all for the general purpose of fostering an orderly and proper physical, economic, and social development of said areas; and the President is further authorized in making said surveys and plans to cooperate with the States affected thereby, or subdivisions or agencies of such States, or with cooperative or other organizations, and to make such studies, experiments, or demonstrations as may be necessary and suitable to that end.

Sec. 23. The President shall, from time to time, as the work provided for in the preceding section progresses, recommend to Congress such legislation as he deems proper to carry out the general purposes stated in said section, and for the especial purpose of bringing about in said Tennessee drainage basin and adjoining territory in conformity with said general purposes (1) the maximum amount of flood control; (2) the maximum development of said Tennessee River for navigation purposes; (3) the maximum generation of electric power consistent with flood control and navigation; (4) the proper use of marginal lands; (5) the proper method of reforestation of all lands in said drainage basin suitable for reforestation; and (6) the economic and social well-being of the people living in said river basin.

Sec. 24. For the purpose of securing any rights of flowage, or obtaining title to or possession of any property, real or personal, that may be necessary or may become necessary, in the carrying out of any of the provisions of this Act, the President of the United States for a period of three years from the date of the enactment of this Act, is hereby authorized to acquire title in the name of the United States to such rights or such property, and to provide for the payment for same by directing the board to contract to deliver power generated at any of the plants now owned or hereafter owned or constructed by the Government or by said Corporation, such future delivery of power to continue for a period not exceeding thirty years. Likewise, for one year after the enactment of this Act, the President is further authorized to sell or lease any parcel or part of any vacant real estate now owned by the Government in said Tennessee River Basin, to persons, firms, or corporations who shall contract to erect thereon factories or manufacturing establishments, and who shall contract to purchase of said Corporation electric power for the operation of any such factory or manufacturing establishment. No contract shall be made by the President for the sale of any of such real estate as may be necessary for present or future use on the part of the Government for any of the purposes of this Act. Any such contract made by the President of the United States shall be carried out by the board: Provided, That no such contract shall be made that will in any way abridge or take away the preference right to purchase power given in this Act to States, counties, municipalities, or farm organizations: Provided further, That no lease shall be for a term to exceed fifty years: Provided further, That any sale shall be on condition that said land shall be used for industrial purposes only.

Sec. 25. The Corporation may cause proceedings to be instituted for the acquisition by condemnation of any lands, easements, or rights of way which, in the opinion of the Corporation, are necessary to carry out the provisions of this Act. The proceedings shall be instituted in the United States district court for the district in which the land, easement, right of way, or other interest, or any part thereof, is located, and such court shall have full jurisdiction to divest the complete title to the property sought to be acquired out of all persons or claimants and vest the same in the United States in fee simple, and to enter a decree quieting the title thereto in the United States of America.

Upon the filing of a petition for condemnation and for the purpose of ascertaining the value of the property to be acquired, and assessing the compensation to be paid, the court shall appoint three commissioners who shall be disinterested persons and who shall take and subscribe an oath that they do not own any lands, or interest or easement in any lands, which it may be desirable for the United States to acquire in the furtherance of said project and such commissioners shall not be selected from the locality wherein the land sought to be condemned lies. Such commissioners shall receive a per diem of not to exceed $15 for their services, together with an additional amount of $5 per day for subsistence for time actually spent in performing their duties as commissioners.

It shall be the duty of such commissioners to examine into the value of the lands sought to be condemned, to conduct hearings and receive evidence, and generally to take such appropriate steps as may be proper for the determination of the value of the said lands sought to be condemned, and for such purpose the commissioners are authorized to administer oaths and subpoena witnesses, which said witnesses shall receive the same fees as are provided for witnesses in the Federal courts. The said commissioners shall thereupon file a report setting forth their conclusions as to the value of the said property sought to be condemned, making a separate award and valuation in the premises with respect to each separate parcel involved. Upon the filing of such award in court the clerk of said court shall give notice of the filing of such award to the parties to said proceeding, in manner and form as directed by the judge of said court.

Either or both parties may file exceptions to the award of said commissioners within twenty days from the date of the filing of said award in court. Exceptions filed to such award shall be heard before three Federal district judges unless the parties, in writing, in person, or by their attorneys, stipulate that the exceptions may be heard before a lesser number of judges. On such hearing such judges shall pass de novo upon the proceedings had before the commissioners, may view the property, and may take additional evidence. Upon such hearings the said judges shall file their own award, fixing therein the value of the property sought to be condemned, regardless of the award previously made by the said commissioners.

At any time within thirty days from the filing of the decision of the district judges upon the hearing on exceptions to the award made by the commissioners, either party may appeal from such decision of the said judges to the circuit court of appeals, and the said circuit court of appeals shall upon the hearing on said appeal dispose of the same upon the record, without regard to the awards or findings theretofore made by the commissioners or the district judges, and such circuit court of appeals shall thereupon fix the value of the said property sought to be condemned.

Upon acceptance of an award by the owner of any property herein provided to be appropriated, and the payment of the money awarded or upon the failure of either party to file exceptions to the award of the commissioners within the time specified, or upon the award of the commissioners, and the payment of the money by the United States pursuant thereto, or the payment of the money awarded into the registry of the court by the Corporation, the title to said property and the right to the possession thereof shall pass to the United States, and the United States shall be entitled to a writ in the same proceeding to dispossess the former owner of said property, and all lessees, agents, and attorneys of such former owner, and to put the United States, by its corporate creature and agent, the Corporation, into possession of said property.

In the event of any property owned in Whole or in part by minors, or insane persons, or incompetent persons, or estates of deceased persons, then the legal representatives of such minors, insane persons, incompetent persons, or estates shall have power, by and with the consent and approval of the trial judge in whose court said matter is for determination, to consent to or reject the awards of the commissioners herein provided for, and in the event that there be no legal representatives, or that the legal representatives for such minors, insane persons, or incompetent persons shall fail or decline to act, then such trial judge may, upon motion, appoint a guardian ad litem to act for such minors, insane persons, or incompetent persons, and such guardian ad litem shall act to the full extent and to the same purpose and effect as his ward could act, if competent, and such guardian ad litem shall be deemed to have full power and authority to respond, to conduct, or to maintain any proceeding herein provided for affecting his said ward.

Sec. 26. The net proceeds derived by the board from the sale of power and any of the products manufactured by the Corporation, after deducting the cost of operation, maintenance, depreciation, amortization, and an amount deemed by the board as necessary to withhold as operating capital, or devoted by the board to new construction, shall be paid into the Treasury of the United States at the end of each calendar year.

Sec. 27. All appropriations necessary to carry out the provisions of this Act are hereby authorized.

Sec. 28. That all Acts or parts of Acts in conflict herewith are hereby repealed, so far as they affect the operations contemplated by this Act.

Sec. 29. The right to alter, amend, or repeal this Act is hereby expressly declared and reserved, but no such amendment or repeal shall operate to impair the obligation of any contract made by said Corporation under any power conferred in this Act.

Sec. 30. The sections of this Act are hereby declared to be separable, and in the event any one or more sections of this Act be held to be unconstitutional, the same shall not affect the validity of other sections of this Act. Approved, May 18, 1933.

Franklin D. Roosevelt's "Four Freedoms" Speech (January 6, 1941)

Mr. President, Mr. Speaker, members of the 77th Congress:

I address you, the members of this new Congress, at a moment unprecedented in the history of the union. I use the word "unprecedented" because at no previous time has American security been as seriously threatened from without as it is today.

Since the permanent formation of our government under the Constitution in 1789, most of the periods of crisis in our history have related to our domestic affairs. And, fortunately, only one of these — the four-year war between the States — ever threatened our national unity. Today, thank God, 130,000,000 Americans in 48 States have forgotten points of the compass in our national unity.

It is true that prior to 1914 the United States often has been disturbed by events in other continents. We have even engaged in two wars with European nations and in a number of undeclared wars in the West Indies, in the Mediterranean and in the Pacific, for the maintenance of American rights and for the principles of peaceful commerce. But in no case had a serious threat been raised against our national safety or our continued independence.

What I seek to convey is the historic truth that the United States as a nation has at all times maintained opposition — clear, definite opposition — to any attempt to lock us in behind an ancient Chinese wall while the procession of civilization went past. Today, thinking of our children and of their children, we oppose enforced isolation for ourselves or for any other part of the Americas.

That determination of ours, extending over all these years, was proved, for example, in the early days during the quarter century of wars following the French Revolution. While the Napoleonic struggles did threaten interests of the United States because of the French foothold in the West Indies and in Louisiana, and while we engaged in the War of 1812 to vindicate our right to peaceful trade, it is nevertheless clear that neither France nor Great Britain nor any other nation was aiming at domination of the whole world.

And in like fashion, from 1815 to 1914 — ninety-nine years — no single war in Europe or in Asia constituted a real threat against our future or against the future of any other American nation.

Except in the Maximilian interlude in Mexico, no foreign power sought to establish itself in this hemisphere. And the strength of the British fleet in the Atlantic has been a friendly strength; it is still a friendly strength.

Even when the World War broke out in 1914, it seemed to contain only small threat of danger to our own American future. But as time went on, as we remember, the American people began to visualize what the downfall of democratic nations might mean to our own democracy.

We need not overemphasize imperfections in the peace of Versailles. We need not harp on failure of the democracies to deal with problems of world reconstruction. We should remember that the peace of 1919 was far less unjust than the kind of pacification which began even before Munich, and which is being carried on under the new order of tyranny that seeks to spread over every continent today. The American people have unalterably set their faces against that tyranny.

I suppose that every realist knows that the democratic way of life is at this moment being directly assailed in every part of the world — assailed either by arms or by secret spreading of poisonous propaganda by those who seek to destroy unity and promote discord in nations that are still at peace. During 16 long months this assault has blotted out the whole pattern of democratic life in an appalling number of independent nations, great and small. And the assailants are still on the march, threatening other nations, great and small.

Therefore, as your President, performing my constitutional duty to "give to the Congress information of the state of the union," I find it unhappily necessary to report that the future and the safety of our country and of our democracy are overwhelmingly involved in events far beyond our borders.

Armed defense of democratic existence is now being gallantly waged in four continents. If that defense fails, all the population and all the resources of Europe and Asia, and Africa and Austral-Asia will be dominated by conquerors. And let us remember that the total of those populations in those four continents, the total of those populations and their resources greatly exceed the sum total of the population and the resources of the whole of the Western Hemisphere — yes, many times over.

In times like these it is immature — and, incidentally, untrue — for anybody to brag that an unprepared America, single-handed and with one hand tied behind its back, can hold off the whole world.

No realistic American can expect from a dictator's peace international generosity, or return of true independence, or world disarmament, or freedom of expression, or freedom of religion — or even good business. Such a peace would bring no security for us or for our neighbors. Those who would give up essential liberty to purchase a little temporary safety deserve neither liberty nor safety.

As a nation we may take pride in the fact that we are soft-hearted; but we cannot afford to be soft-headed. We must always be wary of those who with sounding brass and a tinkling cymbal preach the "ism" of appeasement. We must especially beware of that small group of selfish men who would clip the wings of the American eagle in order to feather their own nests.

I have recently pointed out how quickly the tempo of modern warfare could bring into our very midst the physical attack which we must eventually expect if the dictator nations win this war.

There is much loose talk of our immunity from immediate and direct invasion from across the seas. Obviously, as long as the British Navy retains its power, no such danger exists. Even if there were no British Navy, it is not probable that any enemy would be stupid enough to attack us by landing troops in the United States from across thousands of miles of ocean, until it had acquired strategic bases from which to operate.

But we learn much from the lessons of the past years in Europe — particularly the lesson of Norway, whose essential seaports were captured by treachery and surprise built up over a series of years. The first phase of the invasion of this hemisphere would not be the landing of regular troops. The necessary strategic points would be occupied by secret agents and by their dupes — and great numbers of them are already here and in Latin America. As long as the aggressor nations maintain the offensive they, not we, will choose the time and the place and the method of their attack.

And that is why the future of all the American Republics is today in serious danger. That is why this annual message to the Congress is unique in our history. That is why every member of the executive branch of the government and every member of the Congress face great responsibility, great accountability. The need of the moment is that our actions and our policy should be devoted primarily — almost exclusively — to meeting this foreign peril. For all our domestic problems are now a part of the great emergency.

Just as our national policy in internal affairs has been based upon a decent respect for the rights and the dignity of all our fellow men within our gates, so our national policy in foreign affairs has been based on a decent respect for the rights and the dignity of all nations, large and small. And the justice of morality must and will win in the end.

Our national policy is this:

First, by an impressive expression of the public will and without regard to partisanship, we are committed to all-inclusive national defense.

Secondly, by an impressive expression of the public will and without regard to partisanship, we are committed to full support of all those resolute people everywhere who are resisting aggression and are thereby keeping war away from our hemisphere. By this support we express our determination that the democratic cause shall prevail, and we strengthen the defense and the security of our own nation.

Third, by an impressive expression of the public will and without regard to partisanship, we are committed to the proposition that principles of morality and considerations for our own security will never permit us to acquiesce in a peace dictated by aggressors and sponsored by appeasers. We know that enduring peace cannot be bought at the cost of other people's freedom.

In the recent national election there was no substantial difference between the two great parties in respect to that national policy. No issue was fought out on this line before the American electorate. And today it is abundantly evident that American citizens everywhere are demanding and supporting speedy and complete action in recognition of obvious danger.

Therefore, the immediate need is a swift and driving increase in our armament production. Leaders of industry and labor have responded to our summons. Goals of speed have been set. In some cases these goals are being reached ahead of time. In some cases we are on schedule; in other cases there are slight but not serious delays. And in some cases — and, I am sorry to say, very important cases — we are all concerned by the slowness of the accomplishment of our plans.

The Army and Navy, however, have made substantial progress during the past year. Actual experience is improving and speeding up our methods of production with every passing day. And today's best is not good enough for tomorrow.

I am not satisfied with the progress thus far made. The men in charge of the program represent the best in training, in ability, and in patriotism. They are not satisfied with the progress thus far made. None of us will be satisfied until the job is done.

No matter whether the original goal was set too high or too low, our objective is quicker and better results.

To give you two illustrations:

We are behind schedule in turning out finished airplanes. We are working day and night to solve the innumerable problems and to catch up.

We are ahead of schedule in building warships, but we are working to get even further ahead of that schedule.

To change a whole nation from a basis of peacetime production of implements of peace to a basis of wartime production of implements of war is no small task. And the greatest difficulty comes at the beginning of the program, when new tools, new plant facilities, new assembly lines, new shipways must first be constructed before the actual material begins to flow steadily and speedily from them.

The Congress of course, must rightly keep itself informed at all times of the progress of the program. However, there is certain information, as the Congress itself will readily recognize, which, in the interests of our own security and those of the nations that we are supporting, must of needs be kept in confidence.

New circumstances are constantly begetting new needs for our safety. I shall ask this Congress for greatly increased new appropriations and authorizations to carry on what we have begun.

I also ask this Congress for authority and for funds sufficient to manufacture additional munitions and war supplies of many kinds, to be turned over to those nations which are now in actual war with aggressor nations. Our most useful and immediate role is to act as an arsenal for them as well as for ourselves. They do not need manpower, but they do need billions of dollars' worth of the weapons of defense.

The time is near when they will not be able to pay for them all in ready cash. We cannot, and we will not, tell them that they must surrender merely because of present inability to pay for the weapons which we know they must have.

I do not recommend that we make them a loan of dollars with which to pay for these weapons — a loan to be repaid in dollars. I recommend that we make it possible for those nations to continue to obtain war materials in the United States, fitting their orders into our own program. And nearly all of their material would, if the time ever came, be useful in our own defense.

Taking counsel of expert military and naval authorities, considering what is best for our own security, we are free to decide how much should be kept here and how much should be sent abroad to our friends who, by their determined and heroic resistance, are giving us time in which to make ready our own defense.

For what we send abroad we shall be repaid, repaid within a reasonable time following the close of hostilities, repaid in similar materials, or at our option in other goods of many kinds which they can produce and which we need.

Let us say to the democracies: "We Americans are vitally concerned in your defense of freedom. We are putting forth our energies, our resources, and our organizing powers to give you the strength to regain and maintain a free world. We shall send you in ever-increasing numbers, ships, planes, tanks, guns. That is our purpose and our pledge."

In fulfillment of this purpose we will not be intimidated by the threats of dictators that they will regard as a breach of international law or as an act of war our aid to the democracies which dare to resist their aggression. Such aid — Such aid is not an act of war, even if a dictator should unilaterally proclaim it so to be.

And when the dictators — if the dictators — are ready to make war upon us, they will not wait for an act of war on our part.

They did not wait for Norway or Belgium or the Netherlands to commit an act of war. Their only interest is in a new one-way international law, which lacks mutuality in its observance and therefore becomes an instrument of oppression. The happiness of future generations of Americans may well depend on how effective and how immediate we can make our aid felt. No one can tell the exact character of the emergency situations that we may be called upon to meet. The nation's hands must not be tied when the nation's life is in danger.

Yes, and we must prepare, all of us prepare, to make the sacrifices that the emergency — almost as serious as war itself — demands. Whatever stands in the way of speed and efficiency in defense, in defense preparations of any kind, must give way to the national need.

A free nation has the right to expect full cooperation from all groups. A free nation has the right to look to the leaders of business, of labor, and of agriculture to take the lead in stimulating effort, not among other groups but within their own group.

The best way of dealing with the few slackers or trouble-makers in our midst is, first, to shame them by patriotic example, and if that fails, to use the sovereignty of government to save government.

As men do not live by bread alone, they do not fight by armaments alone. Those who man our defenses and those behind them who build our defenses must have the stamina and the courage which come from unshakable belief in the manner of life which they are defending. The mighty action that we are calling for cannot be based on a disregard of all the things worth fighting for.

The nation takes great satisfaction and much strength from the things which have been done to make its people conscious of their individual stake in the preservation of democratic life in America. Those things have toughened the fiber of our people, have renewed their faith and strengthened their devotion to the institutions we make ready to protect.

Certainly this is no time for any of us to stop thinking about the social and economic problems which are the root cause of the social revolution which is today a supreme factor in the world. For there is nothing mysterious about the foundations of a healthy and strong democracy.

The basic things expected by our people of their political and economic systems are simple. They are:

Equality of opportunity for youth and for others.

Jobs for those who can work.

Security for those who need it.

The ending of special privilege for the few.

The preservation of civil liberties for all.

The enjoyment — The enjoyment of the fruits of scientific progress in a wider and constantly rising standard of living.

These are the simple, the basic things that must never be lost sight of in the turmoil and unbelievable complexity of our modern world. The inner and abiding strength of our economic and political systems is dependent upon the degree to which they fulfill these expectations.

Many subjects connected with our social economy call for immediate improvement. As examples:

We should bring more citizens under the coverage of old-age pensions and unemployment insurance.

We should widen the opportunities for adequate medical care.

We should plan a better system by which persons deserving or needing gainful employment may obtain it.

I have called for personal sacrifice, and I am assured of the willingness of almost all Americans to respond to that call. A part of the sacrifice means the payment of more money in taxes. In my budget message I will recommend that a greater portion of this great defense program be paid for from taxation than we are paying for today. No person should try, or be allowed to get rich out of the program, and the principle of tax payments in accordance with ability to pay should be constantly before our eyes to guide our legislation.

If the Congress maintains these principles the voters, putting patriotism ahead pocketbooks, will give you their applause.

In the future days, which we seek to make secure, we look forward to a world founded upon four essential human freedoms.

The first is freedom of speech and expression — everywhere in the world.

The second is freedom of every person to worship God in his own way — everywhere in the world.

The third is freedom from want, which, translated into world terms, means economic understandings which will secure to every nation a healthy peacetime life for its inhabitants — everywhere in the world.

The fourth is freedom from fear, which, translated into world terms, means a world-wide reduction of armaments to such a point and in such a thorough fashion that no nation will be in a position to commit an act of physical aggression against any neighbor — anywhere in the world.

That is no vision of a distant millennium. It is a definite basis for a kind of world attainable in our own time and generation. That kind of world is the very antithesis of the so-called "new order" of tyranny which the dictators seek to create with the crash of a bomb.

To that new order we oppose the greater conception — the moral order. A good society is able to face schemes of world domination and foreign revolutions alike without fear.

Since the beginning of our American history we have been engaged in change, in a perpetual, peaceful revolution, a revolution which goes on steadily, quietly, adjusting itself to changing conditions without the concentration camp or the quicklime in the ditch. The world order which we seek is the cooperation of free countries, working together in a friendly, civilized society.

This nation has placed its destiny in the hands and heads and hearts of its millions of free men and women, and its faith in freedom under the guidance of God. Freedom means the supremacy of human rights everywhere. Our support goes to those who struggle to gain those rights and keep them. Our strength is our unity of purpose.

To that high concept there can be no end save victory.

Inaugural Address of John F. Kennedy (January 20, 1961)

Vice President Johnson, Mr. Speaker, Mr. Chief Justice, President Eisenhower, Vice President Nixon, President Truman, Reverend Clergy, fellow citizens:

We observe today not a victory of party but a celebration of freedom — symbolizing an end as well as a beginning — signifying renewal as well as change. For I have sworn before you and Almighty God the same solemn oath our forbears prescribed nearly a century and three-quarters ago.

The world is very different now. For man holds in his mortal hands the power to abolish all forms of human poverty and all forms of human life. And yet the same revolutionary beliefs for which our forebears fought are still at issue around the globe — the belief that the rights of man come not from the generosity of the state but from the hand of God.

We dare not forget today that we are the heirs of that first revolution. Let the word go forth from this time and place, to friend and foe alike, that the torch has been passed to a new generation of Americans — born in this century, tempered by war, disciplined by a hard and bitter peace, proud of our ancient heritage — and unwilling to witness or permit the slow undoing of those human rights to which this nation has always been committed, and to which we are committed today at home and around the world.

Let every nation know, whether it wishes us well or ill, that we shall pay any price, bear any burden, meet any hardship, support any friend, oppose any foe to assure the survival and the success of liberty.

This much we pledge — and more.

To those old allies whose cultural and spiritual origins we share, we pledge the loyalty of faithful friends. United there is little we cannot do in a host of cooperative ventures. Divided there is little we can do — for we dare not meet a powerful challenge at odds and split asunder.

To those new states whom we welcome to the ranks of the free, we pledge our word that one form of colonial control shall not have passed away merely to be replaced by a far more iron tyranny. We shall not always expect to find them supporting our view. But we shall always hope to find them strongly supporting their own freedom — and to remember that, in the past, those who foolishly sought power by riding the back of the tiger ended up inside.

To those people in the huts and villages of half the globe struggling to break the bonds of mass misery, we pledge our best efforts to help them help themselves, for whatever period is required — not because the communists may be doing it, not because we seek their votes, but because it is right. If a free society cannot help the many who are poor, it cannot save the few who are rich.

To our sister republics south of our border, we offer a special pledge — to convert our good words into good deeds — in a new alliance for progress — to assist free men and free governments in casting off the chains of poverty. But this peaceful revolution of hope cannot become the prey of hostile powers. Let all our neighbors know that we shall join with them to oppose aggression or subversion anywhere in the Americas. And let every other power know that this Hemisphere intends to remain the master of its own house.

To that world assembly of sovereign states, the United Nations, our last best hope in an age where the instruments of war have far outpaced the instruments of peace, we renew our pledge of support — to prevent it from becoming merely a forum for invective — to strengthen its shield of the new and the weak — and to enlarge the area in which its writ may run.

Finally, to those nations who would make themselves our adversary, we offer not a pledge but a request: that both sides begin anew the quest for peace, before the dark powers of destruction unleashed by science engulf all humanity in planned or accidental self-destruction.

We dare not tempt them with weakness. For only when our arms are sufficient beyond doubt can we be certain beyond doubt that they will never be employed.

But neither can two great and powerful groups of nations take comfort from our present course — both sides overburdened by the cost of modern weapons, both rightly alarmed by the steady spread of the deadly atom, yet both racing to alter that uncertain balance of terror that stays the hand of mankind's final war.

So let us begin anew — remembering on both sides that civility is not a sign of weakness, and sincerity is always subject to proof. Let us never negotiate out of fear. But let us never fear to negotiate.

Let both sides explore what problems unite us instead of belaboring those problems which divide us.

Let both sides, for the first time, formulate serious and precise proposals for the inspection and control of arms — and bring the absolute power to destroy other nations under the absolute control of all nations.

Let both sides seek to invoke the wonders of science instead of its terrors. Together let us explore the stars, conquer the deserts, eradicate disease, tap the ocean depths and encourage the arts and commerce.

Let both sides unite to heed in all corners of the earth the command of Isaiah — to "undo the heavy burdens . . . (and) let the oppressed go free."

And if a beachhead of cooperation may push back the jungle of suspicion, let both sides join in creating a new endeavor, not a new balance of power, but a new world of law, where the strong are just and the weak secure and the peace preserved.

All this will not be finished in the first one hundred days. Nor will it be finished in the first one thousand days, nor in the life of this Administration, nor even perhaps in our lifetime on this planet. But let us begin.

In your hands, my fellow citizens, more than mine, will rest the final success or failure of our course. Since this country was founded, each generation of Americans has been summoned to give testimony to its national loyalty. The graves of young Americans who answered the call to service surround the globe.

Now the trumpet summons us again — not as a call to bear arms, though arms we need — not as a call to battle, though embattled we are — but a call to bear the burden of a long twilight struggle, year in and year out, "rejoicing in hope, patient in tribulation" — a struggle against the common enemies of man: tyranny, poverty, disease and war itself.

Can we forge against these enemies a grand and global alliance, North and South, East and West, that can assure a more fruitful life for all mankind? Will you join in that historic effort?

In the long history of the world, only a few generations have been granted the role of defending freedom in its hour of maximum danger. I do not shrink from this responsibility — I welcome it. I do not believe that any of us would exchange places with any other people or any other generation. The energy, the faith, the devotion which we bring to this endeavor will light our country and all who serve it — and the glow from that fire can truly light the world.

And so, my fellow Americans: ask not what your country can do for you — ask what you can do for your country.

My fellow citizens of the world: ask not what America will do for you, but what together we can do for the freedom of man.

Finally, whether you are citizens of America or citizens of the world, ask of us here the same high standards of strength and sacrifice which we ask of you. With a good conscience our only sure reward, with history the final judge of our deeds, let us go forth to lead the land we love, asking His blessing and His help, but knowing that here on earth God's work must truly be our own.

Ronald Reagan's "City on a Hill" Speech (January 25, 1974)

There are three men here tonight I am very proud to introduce. It was a year ago this coming February when this country had its spirits lifted as they have never been lifted in many years. This happened when planes began landing on American soil and in the Philippines, bringing back men who had lived with honor for many miserable years in North Vietnam prisons. Three of those men are here tonight, John McCain, Bill Lawrence and Ed Martin. It is an honor to be here tonight. I am proud that you asked me and I feel more than a little humble in the presence of this distinguished company.

There are men here tonight who, through their wisdom, their foresight and their courage, have earned the right to be regarded as prophets of our philosophy. Indeed they are prophets of our times. In years past when others were silent or too blind to the facts, they spoke up forcefully and fearlessly for what they believed to be right. A decade has passed since Barry Goldwater walked a lonely path across this land reminding us that even a land as rich as ours can't go on forever borrowing against the future, leaving a legacy of debt for another generation and causing a runaway inflation to erode the savings and reduce the standard of living. Voices have been raised trying to rekindle in our country all of the great ideas and principles which set this nation apart from all the others that preceded it, but louder and more strident voices utter easily sold cliches.

Cartoonists with acid-tipped pens portray some of the reminders of our heritage and our destiny as old-fashioned. They say that we are trying to retreat into a past that actually never existed. Looking to the past in an effort to keep our country from repeating the errors of history is termed by them as "taking the country back to McKinley." Of course I never found that was so bad — under McKinley we freed Cuba. On the span of history, we are still thought of as a young upstart country celebrating soon only our second century as a nation, and yet we are the oldest continuing republic in the world.

I thought that tonight, rather than talking on the subjects you are discussing, or trying to find something new to say, it might be appropriate to reflect a bit on our heritage.

You can call it mysticism if you want to, but I have always believed that there was some divine plan that placed this great continent between two oceans to be sought out by those who were possessed of an abiding love of freedom and a special kind of courage.

This was true of those who pioneered the great wilderness in the beginning of this country, as it is also true of those later immigrants who were willing to leave the land of their birth and come to a land where even the language was unknown to them. Call it chauvinistic, but our heritage does not set us apart. Some years ago a writer, who happened to be an avid student of history, told me a story about that day in the little hall in Philadelphia where honorable men, hard-pressed by a King who was flouting the very law they were willing to obey, debated whether they should take the fateful step of declaring their independence from that king. I was told by this man that the story could be found in the writings of Jefferson. I confess, I never researched or made an effort to verify it. Perhaps it is only legend. But story, or legend, he described the atmosphere, the strain, the debate, and that as men for the first time faced the consequences of such an irretrievable act, the walls resounded with the dread word of treason and its price — the gallows and the headman's axe. As the day wore on the issue hung in the balance, and then, according to the story, a man rose in the small gallery. He was not a young man and was obviously calling on all the energy he could muster. Citing the grievances that had brought them to this moment he said, "Sign that parchment. They may turn every tree into a gallows, every home into a grave and yet the words of that parchment can never die. For the mechanic in his workshop, they will be words of hope, to the slave in the mines — freedom." And he added, "If my hands were freezing in death, I would sign that parchment with my last ounce of strength. Sign, sign if the next moment the noose is around your neck, sign even if the hall is ringing with the sound of headman's axe, for that parchment will be the textbook of freedom, the bible of the rights of man forever." And then it is said he fell back exhausted. But

56 delegates, swept by his eloquence, signed the Declaration of Independence, a document destined to be as immortal as any work of man can be. And according to the story, when they turned to thank him for his timely oratory, he could not be found nor were there any who knew who he was or how he had come in or gone out through the locked and guarded doors.

Well, as I say, whether story or legend, the signing of the document that day in Independence Hall was miracle enough. Fifty-six men, a little band so unique — we have never seen their like since — pledged their lives, their fortunes and their sacred honor. Sixteen gave their lives, most gave their fortunes and all of them preserved their sacred honor. What manner of men were they? Certainly they were not an unwashed, revolutionary rebel, nor were then adventurers in a heroic mood. Twenty-four were lawyers and jurists, 11 were merchants and tradesmen, nine were farmers. They were men who would achieve security but valued freedom more.

And what price did they pay? John Hart was driven from the side of his desperately ill wife. After more than a year of living almost as an animal in the forest and in caves, he returned to find his wife had died and his children had vanished. He never saw them again, his property was destroyed and he died of a broken heart — but with no regret, only pride in the part he had played that day in Independence Hall. Carter Braxton of Virginia lost all his ships — they were sold to pay his debts. He died in rags. So it was with Ellery, Clymer, Hall, Walton, Gwinnett, Rutledge, Morris, Livingston, and Middleton. Nelson, learning that Cornwallis was using his home for a headquarters, personally begged Washington to fire on him and destroy his home — he died bankrupt. It has never been reported that any of these men ever expressed bitterness or renounced their action as not worth the price. Fifty-six rank-and-file, ordinary citizens had founded a nation that grew from sea to shining sea, five million farms, quiet villages, cities that never sleep — all done without an area re-development plan, urban renewal or a rural legal assistance program.

Now we are a nation of 211 million people with a pedigree that includes blood lines from every corner of the world. We have shed that American-melting-pot blood in every corner of the world, usually in defense of someone's freedom. Those who remained of that remarkable band we call our Founding Fathers tied up some of the loose ends about a dozen years after the Revolution. It had been the first revolution in all man's history that did not just exchange one set of rulers for another. This had been a philosophical revolution. The culmination of men's dreams for 6,000 years were formalized with the Constitution, probably the most unique document ever drawn in the long history of man's relation to man. I know there have been other constitutions, new ones are being drawn today by newly emerging nations. Most of them, even the one of the Soviet Union, contains many of the same guarantees as our own Constitution, and still there is a difference. The difference is so subtle that we often overlook it, but it is so great that it tells the whole story. Those other constitutions say, "Government grants you these rights" and ours says, "You are born with these rights, they are yours by the grace of God, and no government on earth can take them from you."

Lord Acton of England, who once said, "Power corrupts, and absolute power corrupts absolutely," would say of that document, "They had solved with astonishing ease and unduplicated success two problems which had heretofore baffled the capacity of the most enlightened nations. They had contrived a system of federal government which prodigiously increased national power and yet respected local liberties and authorities, and they had founded it on a principle of equality without surrendering the securities of property or freedom." Never in any society has the preeminence of the individual been so firmly established and given such a priority.

In less than twenty years we would go to war because the God-given rights of the American sailors, as defined in the Constitution, were being violated by a foreign power. We served notice then on the world that all of us together would act collectively to safeguard the rights of even the least among us. But still, in an older, cynical world, they were not convinced. The great powers of Europe still had the idea that one day this great continent would be open again to colonizing and they would come over and divide us up.

In the meantime, men who yearned to breathe free were making their way to our shores. Among them was a young refugee from the Austro-Hungarian Empire. He had been a leader in an attempt to free Hungary from Austrian rule. The attempt had failed and he fled to escape execution. In America, this young Hungarian, Koscha by name, became an importer by trade and took out his first citizenship papers. One day, business took him to a Mediterranean port. There was a large Austrian warship under the command of an admiral in the harbor. He had a manservant with him. He had described to this manservant what the flag of his new country looked like. Word was passed to the Austrian warship that this revolutionary was there and in the night he was kidnapped and taken aboard that large ship. This man's servant, desperate, walking up and down the harbor, suddenly spied a flag that resembled the description he had heard. It was a small American war sloop. He went aboard and told Captain Ingraham, of that war sloop, his story. Captain Ingraham went to the American Consul. When the American Consul learned that Koscha had only taken out his first citizenship papers, the consul washed his hands of the incident. Captain Ingraham said, "I am the senior officer in this port and I believe, under my oath of my office, that I owe this man the protection of our flag."

He went aboard the Austrian warship and demanded to see their prisoner, our citizen. The Admiral was amused, but they brought the man on deck. He was in chains and had been badly beaten. Captain Ingraham said, "I can hear him better without those chains," and the chains were removed. He walked over and said to Kocha, "I will ask you one question; consider your answer carefully. Do you ask the protection of the American flag?" Kocha nodded dumbly "Yes," and the Captain said, "You shall have it." He went back and told the frightened consul what he had done. Later in the day three more Austrian ships sailed into harbor. It looked as though the four were getting ready to leave. Captain Ingraham sent a junior officer over to the Austrian flag ship to tell the Admiral that any attempt to leave that harbor with our citizen aboard would be resisted with appropriate force. He said that he would expect a satisfactory answer by four o'clock that afternoon. As the hour neared they looked at each other through the glasses. As it struck four he had them roll the cannons into the ports and had then light the tapers with which they would set off the cannons — one little sloop. Suddenly the lookout tower called out and said, "They are lowering a boat," and they rowed Kocha over to the little American ship.

Captain Ingraham then went below and wrote his letter of resignation to the United States Navy. In it he said, "I did what I thought my oath of office required, but if I have embarrassed my country in any way, I resign." His resignation was refused in the United States Senate with these words: "This battle that was never fought may turn out to be the most important battle in our Nation's history." Incidentally, there is to this day, and I hope there always will be, a USS Ingraham in the United States Navy.

I did not tell that story out of any desire to be narrowly chauvinistic or to glorify aggressive militarism, but it is an example of government meeting its highest responsibility.

In recent years we have been treated to a rash of noble-sounding phrases. Some of them sound good, but they don't hold up under close analysis. Take for instance the slogan so frequently uttered by the young senator from Massachusetts, "The greatest good for the greatest number." Certainly under that slogan, no modern day Captain Ingraham would risk even the smallest craft and crew for a single citizen. Every dictator who ever lived has justified the enslavement of his people on the theory of what was good for the majority.

We are not a warlike people. Nor is our history filled with tales of aggressive adventures and imperialism, which might come as a shock to some of the placard painters in our modern demonstrations. The lesson of Vietnam, I think, should be that never again will young Americans be asked to fight and possibly die for a cause unless that cause is so meaningful that we, as a nation, pledge our full resources to achieve victory as quickly as possible.

I realize that such a pronouncement, of course, would possibly be laying one open to the charge of warmongering — but that would also be ridiculous. My generation has paid a higher price and has fought harder for freedom that any generation that had ever lived. We have known four wars in a single lifetime. All were horrible, all could have been avoided if at a particular moment in time we had made it plain that we subscribed to the words of John Stuart Mill when he said that "war is an ugly thing, but not the ugliest of things."

The decayed and degraded state of moral and patriotic feeling which thinks nothing is worth a war is worse. The man who has nothing which he cares about more than his personal safety is a miserable creature and has no chance of being free unless made and kept so by the exertions of better men than himself.

The widespread disaffection with things military is only a part of the philosophical division in our land today. I must say to you who have recently, or presently are still receiving an education, I am awed by your powers of resistance. I have some knowledge of the attempts that have been made in many classrooms and lecture halls to persuade you that there is little to admire in America. For the second time in this century, capitalism and the free enterprise are under assault. Privately owned business is blamed for spoiling the environment, exploiting the worker and seducing, if not outright raping, the customer. Those who make the charge have the solution, of course — government regulation and control. We may never get around to explaining how citizens who are so gullible that they can be suckered into buying cereal or soap that they don't need and would not be good for them, can at the same time be astute enough to choose representatives in government to which they would entrust the running of their lives.

Not too long ago, a poll was taken on 2,500 college campuses in this country. Thousands and thousands of responses were obtained. Overwhelmingly, 65, 70, and 75 percent of the students found business responsible, as I have said before, for the things that were wrong in this country. That same number said that government was the solution and should take over the management and the control of private business. Eighty percent of the respondents said they wanted government to keep its paws out of their private lives.

We are told every day that the assembly-line worker is becoming a dull-witted robot and that mass production results in standardization. Well, there isn't a socialist country in the world that would not give its copy of Karl Marx for our standardization.

Standardization means production for the masses and the assembly line means more leisure for the worker — freedom from backbreaking and mind-dulling drudgery that man had known for centuries past. Karl Marx did not abolish child labor or free the women from working in the coal mines in England – the steam engine and modern machinery did that. Unfortunately, the disciples of the new order have had a hand in determining too much policy in recent decades. Government has grown in size and power and cost through the New Deal, the Fair Deal, the New Frontier and the Great Society. It costs more for government today than a family pays for food, shelter and clothing combined. Not even the Office of Management and

Budget knows how many boards, commissions, bureaus and agencies there are in the federal government, but the federal registry, listing their regulations, is just a few pages short of being as big as the Encyclopedia Britannica.

During the Great Society we saw the greatest growth of this government. There were eight cabinet departments and 12 independent agencies to administer the federal health program. There were 35 housing programs and 20 transportation projects. Public utilities had to cope with 27 different agencies on just routine business. There were 192 installations and nine departments with 1,000 projects having to do with the field of pollution.

One Congressman found the federal government was spending 4 billion dollars on research in its own laboratories but did not know where they were, how many people were working in them, or what they were doing. One of the research projects was "The Demography of Happiness," and for 249,000 dollars we found that "people who make more money are happier than people who make less, young people are happier than old people, and people who are healthier are happier than people who are sick." For 15 cents they could have bought an Almanac and read the old bromide, "It's better to be rich, young and healthy, than poor, old and sick."

The course that you have chosen is far more in tune with the hopes and aspirations of our people than are those who would sacrifice freedom for some fancied security.

Standing on the tiny deck of the Arabella in 1630 off the Massachusetts coast, John Winthrop said, "We will be as a city upon a hill. The eyes of all people are upon us, so that if we deal falsely with our God in this work we have undertaken and so cause Him to withdraw His present help from us, we shall be made a story and a byword throughout the world." Well, we have not dealt falsely with our God, even if He is temporarily suspended from the classroom.

When I was born my life expectancy was 10 years less than I have already lived – that's a cause of regret for some people in California, I know. Ninety percent of Americans at that time lived beneath what is considered the poverty line today, three-quarters lived in what is considered substandard housing. Today each of those figures is less than 10 percent. We have increased our life expectancy by wiping out, almost totally, diseases that still ravage mankind in other parts of the world. I doubt if the young people here tonight know the names of some of the diseases that were commonplace when we were growing up. We have more doctors per thousand people than any nation in the world. We have more hospitals that any nation in the world.

When I was your age, believe it or not, none of us knew that we even had a racial problem. When I graduated from college and became a radio sport announcer, broadcasting major league baseball, I didn't have a Hank Aaron or a Willie Mays to talk about. The Spaulding Guide said baseball was a game for Caucasian gentlemen. Some of us then began editorializing and campaigning against this. Gradually we campaigned against all those other areas where the constitutional rights of a large segment of our citizenry were being denied. We have not finished the job. We still have a long way to go, but we have made more progress in a few years than we have made in more than a century.

One-third of all the students in the world who are pursuing higher education are doing so in the United States. The percentage of our young Negro community that is going to college is greater than the percentage of whites in any other country in the world.

One-half of all the economic activity in the entire history of man has taken place in this republic. We have distributed our wealth more widely among our people than any society known to man. Americans work less hours for a higher standard of living than any other people. Ninety-five percent of all our families have an adequate daily intake of nutrients — and a part of the five percent that don't are trying to lose weight! Ninety-nine percent have gas or electric refrigeration, 92 percent have televisions, and an equal number have telephones. There are 120 million cars on our streets and highways — and all of them are on the street at once when you are trying to get home at night. But isn't this just proof of our materialism — the very thing that we are charged with? Well, we also have more churches, more libraries, we support voluntarily more symphony orchestras, and opera companies, non-profit theaters, and publish more books than all the other nations of the world put together.

Somehow America has bred a kindliness into our people unmatched anywhere, as has been pointed out in that best-selling record by a Canadian journalist. We are not a sick society. A sick society could not produce the men that set foot on the moon, or who are now circling the earth above us in the Skylab. A sick society bereft of morality and courage did not produce the men who went through those year of torture and captivity in Vietnam. Where did we find such men? They are typical of this land as the Founding Fathers were typical. We found them in our streets, in the offices, the shops and the working places of our country and on the farms.

We cannot escape our destiny, nor should we try to do so. The leadership of the free world was thrust upon us two centuries ago in that little hall of Philadelphia. In the days following World War II, when the economic strength and power of America was all that stood between the world and the return to the dark ages, Pope Pius XII said, "The American people have a great genius for splendid and unselfish actions. Into the hands of America God has placed the destinies of an afflicted mankind."

We are indeed, and we are today, the last best hope of man on earth.

Ronald Reagan's Speech in West Berlin (June 12, 1987)

Chancellor Kohl, Governing Mayor Diepgen, ladies and gentlemen: Twenty-four years ago, President John F. Kennedy visited Berlin, speaking to the people of this city and the world at the City Hall. Well, since then two other presidents have come, each in his turn, to Berlin. And today I, myself, make my second visit to your city.

We come to Berlin, we American presidents, because it's our duty to speak, in this place, of freedom. But I must confess, we're drawn here by other things as well: by the feeling of history in this city, more than 500 years older than our own nation; by the beauty of the Grunewald and the Tiergarten; most of all, by your courage and determination. Perhaps the composer Paul Lincke understood something about American presidents. You see, like so many presidents before me, I come here today because wherever I go, whatever I do: *Ich hab noch einen Koffer in Berlin.*

Our gathering today is being broadcast throughout Western Europe and North America. I understand that it is being seen and heard as well in the East. To those listening throughout Eastern Europe, a special word: Although I cannot be with you, I address my remarks to you just as surely as to those standing here before me. For I join you, as I join your fellow countrymen in the West, in this firm, this unalterable belief: *Es gibt nur ein Berlin.*

Behind me stands a wall that encircles the free sectors of this city, part of a vast system of barriers that divides the entire continent of Europe. From the Baltic, south, those barriers cut across Germany in a gash of barbed wire, concrete, dog runs, and guard towers. Farther south, there may be no visible, no obvious wall. But there remain armed guards and checkpoints all the same — still a restriction on the right to travel, still an instrument to impose upon ordinary men and women the will of a totalitarian state. Yet it is here in Berlin where the wall emerges most clearly; here, cutting across your city, where the news photo and the television screen have imprinted this brutal division of a continent upon the mind of the world. Standing before the Brandenburg Gate, every man is a German, separated from his fellow men. Every man is a Berliner, forced to look upon a scar.

President von Weizsacker has said, "The German question is open as long as the Brandenburg Gate is closed." Today I say: As long as the gate is closed, as long as this scar of a wall is permitted to stand, it is not the German question alone that remains open, but the question of freedom for all mankind. Yet I do not come here to lament. For I find in Berlin a message of hope, even in the shadow of this wall, a message of triumph.

In this season of spring in 1945, the people of Berlin emerged from their air-raid shelters to find devastation. Thousands of miles away, the people of the United States reached out to help. And in 1947 Secretary of State — as you've been told — George Marshall announced the creation of what would become known as the Marshall Plan. Speaking precisely 40 years ago this month, he said: "Our policy is directed not against any country or doctrine, but against hunger, poverty, desperation, and chaos."

In the Reichstag a few moments ago, I saw a display commemorating this 40th anniversary of the Marshall Plan. I was struck by the sign on a burnt-out, gutted structure that was being rebuilt. I understand that Berliners of my own generation can remember seeing signs like it dotted throughout the western sectors of the city. The sign read simply: "The Marshall Plan is helping here to strengthen the free world." A strong, free world in the West, that dream became real. Japan rose from ruin to become an economic giant. Italy, France, Belgium — virtually every nation in Western Europe saw political and economic rebirth; the European Community was founded.

In West Germany and here in Berlin, there took place an economic miracle, the *Wirtschaftswunder*. Adenauer, Erhard, Reuter, and other leaders understood the practical importance of liberty — that just as truth can flourish only when the journalist is given freedom of speech, so prosperity can come about only when the farmer and businessman enjoy economic freedom. The German leaders reduced tariffs, expanded free trade, lowered taxes. From 1950 to 1960 alone, the standard of living in West Germany and Berlin doubled.

Where four decades ago there was rubble, today in West Berlin there is the greatest industrial output of any city in Germany — busy office blocks, fine homes and apartments, proud avenues, and the spreading lawns of parkland. Where a city's culture seemed to have been destroyed, today there are two great universities, orchestras and an opera, countless theaters, and museums. Where there was want, today there's abundance — food, clothing, automobiles — the wonderful goods of the Ku'damm. From devastation, from utter ruin, you Berliners have, in freedom, rebuilt a city that once again ranks as one of the greatest on earth. The Soviets may have had other plans. But my friends, there were a few things the Soviets didn't count on — *Berliner Herz, Berliner Humor, ja, und Berliner Schnauze.*

In the 1950s, Khrushchev predicted: "We will bury you." But in the West today, we see a free world that has achieved a level of prosperity and well-being unprecedented in all human history. In the Communist world, we see failure, technological backwardness, declining standards of health, even want of the most basic kind — too little food. Even today, the Soviet Union still cannot feed itself. After these four decades, then, there stands before the entire world one great and inescapable conclusion: Freedom leads to prosperity. Freedom replaces the ancient hatreds among the nations with comity and peace. Freedom is the victor.

And now the Soviets themselves may, in a limited way, be coming to understand the importance of freedom. We hear much from Moscow about a new policy of reform and openness. Some political prisoners have been released. Certain foreign news broadcasts are no longer being jammed. Some economic enterprises have been permitted to operate with greater freedom from state control.

Are these the beginnings of profound changes in the Soviet state? Or are they token gestures, intended to raise false hopes in the West, or to strengthen the Soviet system without changing it? We welcome change and openness; for we believe that freedom and security go together, that the advance of human liberty can only strengthen the cause of world peace. There is one sign the Soviets can make that would be unmistakable, that would advance dramatically the cause of freedom and peace.

General Secretary Gorbachev, if you seek peace, if you seek prosperity for the Soviet Union and Eastern Europe, if you seek liberalization: Come here to this gate! Mr. Gorbachev, open this gate! Mr. Gorbachev, tear down this wall!

I understand the fear of war and the pain of division that afflict this continent — and I pledge to you my country's efforts to help overcome these burdens. To be sure, we in the West must resist Soviet expansion. So we must maintain defenses of unassailable strength. Yet we seek peace; so we must strive to reduce arms on both sides.

Beginning 10 years ago, the Soviets challenged the Western alliance with a grave new threat, hundreds of new and more deadly SS-20 nuclear missiles, capable of striking every capital in Europe. The Western alliance responded by committing itself to a counter-deployment unless the Soviets agreed to negotiate a better solution; namely, the elimination of such weapons on both sides. For many months, the Soviets refused to bargain in earnestness. As the alliance, in turn, prepared to go forward with its counter-deployment, there were difficult days — days of protests like those during my 1982 visit to this city — and the Soviets later walked away from the table.

But through it all, the alliance held firm. And I invite those who protested then — I invite those who protest today — to mark this fact: Because we remained strong, the Soviets came back to the table. And because we remained strong, today we have within reach the possibility, not merely of limiting the growth of arms, but of eliminating, for the first time, an entire class of nuclear weapons from the face of the earth.

As I speak, NATO ministers are meeting in Iceland to review the progress of our proposals for eliminating these weapons. At the talks in Geneva, we have also proposed deep cuts in strategic offensive weapons. And the Western allies have likewise made far-reaching proposals to reduce the danger of conventional war and to place a total ban on chemical weapons.

While we pursue these arms reductions, I pledge to you that we will maintain the capacity to deter Soviet aggression at any level at which it might occur. And in cooperation with many of our allies, the United States is pursuing the Strategic Defense Initiative — research to base deterrence not on the threat of offensive retaliation, but on defenses that truly defend; on systems, in short, that will not target populations, but shield them. By these means we seek to increase the safety of Europe and all the world. But we must remember a crucial fact: East and West do not mistrust each other because we are armed; we are armed because we mistrust each other. And our differences are not about weapons but about liberty. When President Kennedy spoke at the City Hall those 24 years ago, freedom was encircled, Berlin was under siege. And today, despite all the pressures upon this city, Berlin stands secure in its liberty. And freedom itself is transforming the globe.

In the Philippines, in South and Central America, democracy has been given a rebirth. Throughout the Pacific, free markets are working miracle after miracle of economic growth. In the industrialized nations, a technological revolution is taking place — a revolution marked by rapid, dramatic advances in computers and telecommunications.

In Europe, only one nation and those it controls refuse to join the community of freedom. Yet in this age of redoubled economic growth, of information and innovation, the Soviet Union faces a choice: It must make fundamental changes, or it will become obsolete.

Today thus represents a moment of hope. We in the West stand ready to cooperate with the East to promote true openness, to break down barriers that separate people, to create a safe, freer world. And surely there is no better place than Berlin, the meeting place of East and West, to make a start. Free people of Berlin: Today, as in the past, the United States stands for the strict observance and full implementation of all parts of the Four Power Agreement of 1971. Let us use this occasion, the 750th anniversary of this city, to usher in a new era, to seek a still fuller, richer life for the Berlin of the future. Together, let us maintain and develop the ties between the Federal Republic and the Western sectors of Berlin, which is permitted by the 1971 agreement.

And I invite Mr. Gorbachev: Let us work to bring the Eastern and Western parts of the city closer together, so that all the inhabitants of all Berlin can enjoy the benefits that come with life in one of the great cities of the world.

To open Berlin still further to all Europe, East and West, let us expand the vital air access to this city, finding ways of making commercial air service to Berlin more convenient, more comfortable, and more economical. We look to the day when West Berlin can become one of the chief aviation hubs in all central Europe. With our French and British partners, the United States is prepared to help bring international meetings to Berlin. It would be only fitting for Berlin to serve as the site of United Nations meetings, or world conferences on human rights and arms control or other issues that call for international cooperation.

There is no better way to establish hope for the future than to enlighten young minds, and we would be honored to sponsor summer youth exchanges, cultural events, and other programs for young Berliners from the East. Our French and British friends, I'm certain, will do the same. And it's my hope that an authority can be found in East Berlin to sponsor visits from young people of the Western sectors.

One final proposal, one close to my heart: Sport represents a source of enjoyment and ennoblement, and you may have noted that the Republic of Korea — South Korea — has offered to permit certain events of the 1988 Olympics to take place in the North. International sports competitions of all kinds could take place in both parts of this city. And what better way to demonstrate to the world the openness of this city than to offer in some future year to hold the Olympic games here in Berlin, East and West? In these four decades, as I have said, you Berliners have built a great city. You've done so in spite of threats — the Soviet attempts to impose the East-mark, the blockade. Today the city thrives in spite of the challenges implicit in the very presence of this wall. What keeps you here? Certainly there's a great deal to be said for your fortitude, for your defiant courage. But I believe there's something deeper, something that involves Berlin's whole look and feel and way of life — not mere sentiment. No one could live long in Berlin without being completely disabused of illusions. Something instead, that has seen the difficulties of life in Berlin but chose to accept them, that continues to build this good and proud city in contrast to a surrounding totalitarian presence that refuses to release human energies or aspirations. Something that speaks with a powerful voice of affirmation, that says yes to this city, yes to the future, yes to freedom. In a word, I would submit that what keeps you in Berlin is love — love both profound and abiding.

Perhaps this gets to the root of the matter, to the most fundamental distinction of all between East and West. The totalitarian world produces backwardness because it does such violence to the spirit, thwarting the human impulse to create, to enjoy, to worship. The totalitarian world finds even symbols of love and of worship an affront. Years ago, before the East Germans began rebuilding their churches, they erected a secular structure: the television tower at Alexander Platz. Virtually ever since, the authorities have been working to correct what they view as the tower's one major flaw, treating the glass sphere at the top with paints and chemicals of every kind. Yet even today when the sun strikes that sphere — that sphere that towers over all Berlin — the light makes the sign of the cross. There in Berlin, like the city itself, symbols of love, symbols of worship, cannot be suppressed.

As I looked out a moment ago from the Reichstag, that embodiment of German unity, I noticed words crudely spray-painted upon the wall, perhaps by a young Berliner: "This wall will fall. Beliefs become reality." Yes, across Europe, this wall will fall. For it cannot withstand faith; it cannot withstand truth. The wall cannot withstand freedom.

And I would like, before I close, to say one word. I have read, and I have been questioned since I've been here about certain demonstrations against my coming. And I would like to say just one thing, and to those who demonstrate so. I wonder if they have ever asked themselves that if they should have the kind of government they apparently seek, no one would ever be able to do what they're doing again.

Thank you and God bless you all.

Inaugural Address of Barack Obama

My fellow citizens:

I stand here today humbled by the task before us, grateful for the trust you have bestowed, mindful of the sacrifices borne by our ancestors. I thank President Bush for his service to our nation, as well as the generosity and cooperation he has shown throughout this transition.

Forty-four Americans have now taken the presidential oath. The words have been spoken during rising tides of prosperity and the still waters of peace. Yet, every so often, the oath is taken amidst gathering clouds and raging storms. At these moments, America has carried on not simply because of the skill or vision of those in high office, but because We the People have remained faithful to the ideals of our forebearers, and true to our founding documents. So it has been. So it must be with this generation of Americans.

That we are in the midst of crisis is now well understood. Our nation is at war, against a far-reaching network of violence and hatred. Our economy is badly weakened, a consequence of greed and irresponsibility on the part of some, but also our collective failure to make hard choices and prepare the nation for a new age. Homes have been lost; jobs shed; businesses shuttered. Our health care is too costly; our schools fail too many; and each day brings further evidence that the ways we use energy strengthen our adversaries and threaten our planet.

These are the indicators of crisis, subject to data and statistics. Less measurable but no less profound is a sapping of confidence across our land -- a nagging fear that America's decline is inevitable, and that the next generation must lower its sights.

Today I say to you that the challenges we face are real. They are serious and they are many. They will not be met easily or in a short span of time. But know this, America: They will be met.

On this day, we gather because we have chosen hope over fear, unity of purpose over conflict and discord.

On this day, we come to proclaim an end to the petty grievances and false promises, the recriminations and worn-out dogmas, that for far too long have strangled our politics.

We remain a young nation, but in the words of Scripture, the time has come to set aside childish things. The time has come to reaffirm our enduring spirit; to choose our better history; to carry forward that precious gift, that noble idea, passed on from generation to generation: the God-given promise that all are equal, all are free, and all deserve a chance to pursue their full measure of happiness.

In reaffirming the greatness of our nation, we understand that greatness is never a given. It must be earned. Our journey has never been one of shortcuts or settling for less. It has not been the path for the fainthearted -- for those who prefer leisure over work, or seek only the pleasures of riches and fame. Rather, it has been the risk-takers, the doers, the makers of things -- some celebrated, but more often men and women obscure in their labor -- who have carried us up the long, rugged path toward prosperity and freedom.

For us, they packed up their few worldly possessions and traveled across oceans in search of a new life.

For us, they toiled in sweatshops and settled the West; endured the lash of the whip and plowed the hard earth.

For us, they fought and died, in places like Concord and Gettysburg; Normandy and Khe Sahn.

Time and again, these men and women struggled and sacrificed and worked till their hands were raw so that we might live a better life. They saw America as bigger than the sum of our individual ambitions; greater than all the differences of birth or wealth or faction.

This is the journey we continue today. We remain the most prosperous, powerful nation on Earth. Our workers are no less productive than when this crisis began. Our minds are no less inventive, our goods and services no less needed than they were last week or last month or last year. Our capacity remains undiminished. But our time of standing pat, of protecting narrow interests and putting off unpleasant decisions -- that time has surely passed. Starting today, we must pick ourselves up, dust ourselves off, and begin again the work of remaking America.

For everywhere we look, there is work to be done. The state of the economy calls for action, bold and swift, and we will act -- not only to create new jobs, but to lay a new foundation for growth. We will build the roads and bridges, the electric grids and digital lines that feed our commerce and bind us together. We will restore science to its rightful place, and wield technology's wonders to raise health care's quality and lower its cost. We will harness the sun and the winds and the soil to fuel our cars and run our factories. And we will transform our schools and colleges and universities to meet the demands of a new age. All this we can do. And all this we will do.

Now, there are some who question the scale of our ambitions -- who suggest that our system cannot tolerate too many big plans. Their memories are short. For they have forgotten what this country has already done; what free men and women can achieve when imagination is joined to common purpose, and necessity to courage.

What the cynics fail to understand is that the ground has shifted beneath them -- that the stale political arguments that have consumed us for so long no longer apply. The question we ask today is not whether our government is too big or too small, but whether it works -- whether it helps families find jobs at a decent wage, care they can afford, a retirement that is dignified. Where the answer is yes, we intend to move forward. Where the answer is no, programs will end. And those of us who manage the public's dollars will be held to account -- to spend wisely, reform bad habits, and do our business in the light of day -- because only then can we restore the vital trust between a people and their government.

Nor is the question before us whether the market is a force for good or ill. Its power to generate wealth and expand freedom is unmatched, but this crisis has reminded us that without a watchful eye, the market can spin out of control -- and that a nation cannot prosper long when it favors only the prosperous. The success of our economy has always depended not just on the size of our gross domestic product, but on the reach of our prosperity; on our ability to extend opportunity to every willing heart -- not out of charity, but because it is the surest route to our common good.

As for our common defense, we reject as false the choice between our safety and our ideals. Our Founding Fathers, faced with perils we can scarcely imagine, drafted a charter to assure the rule of law and the rights of man, a charter expanded by the blood of generations. Those ideals still light the world, and we will not give them up for expedience's sake. And so to all other peoples and governments who are watching today, from the grandest capitals to the small village where my father was born: Know that America is a friend of each nation and every man, woman and child who seeks a future of peace and dignity, and that we are ready to lead once more.

Recall that earlier generations faced down fascism and communism not just with missiles and tanks, but with sturdy alliances and enduring convictions. They understood that our power alone cannot protect us, nor does it entitle us to do as we please. Instead, they knew that our power grows through its prudent use; our security emanates from the justness of our cause, the force of our example, the tempering qualities of humility and restraint.

We are the keepers of this legacy. Guided by these principles once more, we can meet those new threats that demand even greater effort -- even greater cooperation and understanding between nations. We will begin to responsibly leave Iraq to its people, and forge a hard-earned peace in Afghanistan. With old friends and former foes, we will work tirelessly to lessen the nuclear threat, and roll back the specter of a warming planet. We will not apologize for our way of life, nor will we waver in its defense, and for those who seek to advance their aims by inducing terror and slaughtering innocents, we say to you now that our spirit is stronger and cannot be broken; you cannot outlast us, and we will defeat you.

For we know that our patchwork heritage is a strength, not a weakness. We are a nation of Christians and Muslims, Jews and Hindus -- and nonbelievers. We are shaped by every language and culture, drawn from every end of this Earth; and because we have tasted the bitter swill of civil war and segregation, and emerged from that dark chapter stronger and more united, we cannot help but believe that the old hatreds shall someday pass; that the lines of tribe shall soon dissolve; that as the world grows smaller, our common humanity shall reveal itself; and that America must play its role in ushering in a new era of peace.

To the Muslim world, we seek a new way forward, based on mutual interest and mutual respect. To those leaders around the globe who seek to sow conflict, or blame their society's ills on the West: Know that your people will judge you on what you can build, not what you destroy. To those who cling to power through corruption and deceit and the silencing of dissent, know that you are on the wrong side of history; but that we will extend a hand if you are willing to unclench your fist.

To the people of poor nations, we pledge to work alongside you to make your farms flourish and let clean waters flow; to nourish starved bodies and feed hungry minds. And to those nations like ours that enjoy relative plenty, we say we can no longer afford indifference to suffering outside our borders; nor can we consume the world's resources without regard to effect. For the world has changed, and we must change with it.

As we consider the road that unfolds before us, we remember with humble gratitude those brave Americans who, at this very hour, patrol far-off deserts and distant mountains. They have something to tell us today, just as the fallen heroes who lie in Arlington whisper through the ages. We honor them not only because they are guardians of our liberty, but because they embody the spirit of service; a willingness to find meaning in something greater than themselves. And yet, at this moment -- a moment that will define a generation -- it is precisely this spirit that must inhabit us all.

For as much as government can do and must do, it is ultimately the faith and determination of the American people upon which this nation relies. It is the kindness to take in a stranger when the levees break, the selflessness of workers who would rather cut their hours than see a friend lose their job which sees us through our darkest hours. It is the firefighter's courage to storm a stairway filled with smoke, but also a parent's willingness to nurture a child, that finally decides our fate.

Our challenges may be new. The instruments with which we meet them may be new. But those values upon which our success depends -- hard work and honesty, courage and fair play, tolerance and curiosity, loyalty and patriotism -- these things are old. These things are true. They have been the quiet force of progress throughout our history. What is demanded then is a return to these truths. What is required of us now is a new era of responsibility -- a recognition, on the part of every American, that we have duties to ourselves, our nation and the world; duties that we do not grudgingly accept but rather seize gladly, firm in the knowledge that there is nothing so satisfying to the spirit, so defining of our character, than giving our all to a difficult task.

This is the price and the promise of citizenship.

This is the source of our confidence -- the knowledge that God calls on us to shape an uncertain destiny.

This is the meaning of our liberty and our creed -- why men and women and children of every race and every faith can join in celebration across this magnificent Mall, and why a man whose father less than 60 years ago might not have been served at a local restaurant can now stand before you to take a most sacred oath.

So let us mark this day with remembrance, of who we are and how far we have traveled. In the year of America's birth, in the coldest of months, a small band of patriots huddled by dying campfires on the shores of an icy river. The capital was abandoned. The enemy was advancing. The snow was stained with blood. At a moment when the outcome of our revolution was most in doubt, the father of our nation ordered these words be read to the people:

"Let it be told to the future world ... that in the depth of winter, when nothing but hope and virtue could survive... that the city and the country, alarmed at one common danger, came forth to meet [it]."

America. In the face of our common dangers, in this winter of our hardship, let us remember these timeless words. With hope and virtue, let us brave once more the icy currents, and endure what storms may come. Let it be said by our children's children that when we were tested, we refused to let this journey end, that we did not turn back, nor did we falter; and with eyes fixed on the horizon and God's grace upon us, we carried forth that great gift of freedom and delivered it safely to future generations.